Issues in
Web-Based Pedagogy

Issues in Web-Based Pedagogy

A Critical Primer

Edited by
Robert A. Cole

The Greenwood Educators' Reference Collection

GREENWOOD PRESS
Westport, Connecticut • London

Library of Congress Cataloging-in-Publication Data

Issues in Web-based pedagogy : a critical primer / edited by Robert A. Cole.
     p. cm.—(The Greenwood educators' reference collection, ISSN 1056–2192)
   Includes bibliographical references and index.
   ISBN 0–313–31226–5 (alk. paper)
   1. Education, Higher—Computer network resources. 2. Internet (Computer network) in
education. 3. Education, Higher—Computer-assisted instruction. I. Cole, Robert A.,
1958– II. Series.
   LB1044.87 .I88 2000
   378.1'73'4—dc21   99–049046

British Library Cataloguing in Publication Data is available.

Library of Congress Catalog Card Number: 99–049046
ISBN: 0–313–31226–5
ISSN: 1056–2192

First published in 2000

Greenwood Press, 88 Post Road West, Westport, CT 06881
An imprint of Greenwood Publishing Group, Inc.
www.greenwood.com

Printed in the United States of America

The paper used in this book complies with the
Permanent Paper Standard issued by the National
Information Standards Organization (Z39.48–1984).

10 9 8 7 6 5 4 3 2

Contents

Introduction

Web-based learning, as many have discovered, allows participants to collapse time and space. Facilitators and students do course work on their own time and at their own place, thus freeing themselves of schedules imposed by others. For some, Web-based pedagogy is also seen as a more egalitarian form of instruction insofar as it allows greater accessibility between the facilitator and the student, and among students. Consequently, learning communities are likely to develop wherein students teach each other rather than endure a passive, "sender/receiver" mode of learning. These two properties—liberty and equality—mirror the tension of the at once egocentric and sociocentric culture of North America and, in part, account for the enthusiasm exhibited by many over Web-based pedagogy.

A further source of ardor over Web-based learning is the promise it holds for widespread delivery, a key ingredient in the move to commodify and market education. In one instance, a recent press release from Western Governors University (WGU) announced its partnership with America Online (AOL) in which the commercial Internet access and content provider would give WGU $250,000 in funds and services. The drive behind such a partnership was made clear by WGU's president, who said, "With AOL's remarkable reach into the homes of millions of learners worldwide, WGU will be able to better fulfill its goal of expanding access to higher education" (*Western Governors University*).

Yet, there are some voices raising questions about the panacea of Web-based pedagogy. On the more cautious side, Web-based learning is, for example, very time consuming. It takes tremendous time resources to build and sustain a Web course. This is equally true for both facilitator and student. Moreover, although it was noted above that Web-based pedagogy is egalitarian, oftentimes there is only the illusion of an egalitarian community. Frequently, there is a distracting undertow to the community dynamic of a Web-based course because, ultimately, the instructor is still charged with making a final evaluation, formalized as an institutionally sanctioned grade.

More subtle in its implications is the fact that Web-based pedagogy privileges the written word. Students must be literate if they are to capitalize on the formal properties of on-line learning. This point may strike one as odd because, recast, it means that students must be able to read if they are to succeed. However, many students are inadequately skilled in the art and science of "close reading." Students are often better versed in a culture of what Walter Ong calls "secondary orality." Elsewhere, I have suggested that students present themselves to us with an admixture of communication skills closer to those of preliterate, pre-Socratic times. Steeped as they are in the technologically mediated world of film, television, radio, and graphics-intensive computer applications, they are adept at "reading" the nonlinearity of those mass media, but less dexterous in the hermeneutics of a book's linear codes (Cole). To the students' disadvantage, in a Web-based course virtually all communication must pass through the portal of the written word. There is no "discussion" of the sort where people exchange ideas in the give-and-take of the moment, modifying their thoughts and beliefs through real-time discourse with others. Lost to Web-based courses is the opportunity to think aloud, to work through, constitute, and articulate new ideas in the transactional moment of dialogic heteroglot with others. For, as Mikhail Bakhtin notes, the social milieu of dialogue provides an opportunity for interaction amid a sociocultural, political matrix in which new and unforeseen possibilities emerge.

Forfeited, too, is the opportunity to participate in what might be termed a "peripatetic reasoning." Unlike the Ancients, the on-line student and teacher cannot stroll side by side, wherein the rhythmic gaits of their bodies might synchronize, and their minds likewise form a oneness. Had Socrates not sauntered upon the roads with the likes of young Phaedrus, there would have been no *Dialogues*.

Teacher and student cannot "walk and talk" because Web-based pedagogy enforces a Cartesian duality that splits the mind from the body (Descartes). On-line, we are literally disembodied as we go about the exercise of teaching and learning. Only the tiring of one's typing and mouse-clicking fingers or the dull ache of sitting for too long brings us to a foregrounding of the incarnate. Ironically, we are only aware in these moments because our bodies threaten to fail us as we pursue the exercise of the mind. The result of promoting the mind over the body is not only to dichotomize the two, but to make more difficult a mode of "learning by doing." The emphasis shifts, instead, to "learning by thinking," thereby further entrenching antiquated notions of rationality as the sole source of knowledge.

These are but a few of the concerns raised by reflecting on emerging teaching technologies. This book's contributors take up nontechnical issues associated with World Wide Web–based pedagogy. Aimed at a variety of disciplines, they bring together diverse perspectives on the Web as a mode of education. The audiences for this book are several. First, administrators at institutes of higher education will discover a range of nontechnical issues they should attend to as their schools or departments move toward, or increase their commitment to, Web-based pedagogy. Second, teachers from all disciplines who presently design and deliver Web-based instruction will find this book useful in enhancing their teaching abilities in that environment. The same holds true for educators considering developing Web-based courses. Finally, this volume provides useful ideas for students of curriculum and instruction, educational and instructional technology, and distance learning, by promoting critical thinking about the changing definitions of "teacher," "student," and "learning."

As its title suggests, this book takes a critical look at Web-based pedagogy. That is, contributors ask: What assumptions should be challenged and which skeptical questions should be addressed by those presently using this technology or those thinking of embracing it? Through discussion of pedagogical philosophy, theory, and/or praxis, authors identify these questions (and in many cases resolve them) in order to raise the readers' critical reflections on the practices and potentials of Web-based pedagogy.

Featuring intellectual access and appeal for all readers, the book's essays appraise the form and content of Web-based instruction, from both qualitative and quantitative grounding. Authors' contributions speak to a mix of pedagogical styles, a range of disciplinary content, and a variety of political and personal issues.

The book has two parts. Part I focuses on philosophical and theoretical considerations of Web-based pedagogy, while Part II focuses on empirical and practical considerations. Topics include social, psychological, and economic implications of Web-based pedagogy; philosophical considerations; questions of intellectual property and content ownership; quality control; and form and design issues drawn from case studies and empirical analyses. It is important to note that while these chapters are categorized as either theoretical or practical, their impulses are not so clean. In other words, throughout Part I, philosophy slides into theory, revealing considerations bound by empirical and practical roots. Likewise, the empirical and practical chapters in Part II reflect tacit knowledge of theoretical and philosophical considerations.

Several general themes work their way through the chapters of this book. First, most contributors believe that Web-based pedagogy may well redefine postsecondary education as it is traditionally understood. Education is more easily packaged and marketed as a product through Internet technologies, the implications of which are that traditional faculty roles in teaching (and research) are at risk. Moreover, current understandings of what it means to be a teacher or a student are undergoing redefinition as a result of new distance-learning technologies.

A second theme emerging from these readings is that Web-based pedagogy can be associated with sound instruction when particular strategies are adopted. However, this form of teaching is least effective when attempts are made to directly translate traditional styles of teaching.

Yet another point many authors highlight is that competing political, social, and economic interests are currently in dialogue to shape the direction on-line education will take in the future. They note that opportunities exist for administrators and faculty to enter this conversation in an effort to circumscribe the terms under which Web-based learning will occur. The chapters in this book are an attempt to provide educators with a language with which to do precisely that.

We have been warned that the technologies that liberate us also threaten to enslave us. Meanwhile, Ong argues that how we think is a function of the medium by which we think and communicate. The contributors to this volume are neither neo-Luddites nor dystopians. Rather, they are concerned pedagogues who are asking critical questions about both the form and content of Web-based teaching and learning.

WORKS CITED

Bakhtin, Mikhail M. *The Dialogic Imagination: Four Essays*. Ed. Michael Holquist. Trans. Carol Emerson and Michael Holquist. Austin: University of Texas Press, 1981.

Cole, Robert A. "Beyond the Textbook: Teaching Communication Concepts Through Computers and Music Videos." *Communication Education* 48 (1999): 327–328.

Descartes, René. "Meditations on First Philosophy." In *Classics of Western Philosophy*. Ed. Steven Cahn. Trans. Elizabeth Haldane and G. R. T. Ross. Indianapolis: Hackett Publishing, 1977. 303–46.

Ong, Walter. *Orality and Literacy*. New York: Routledge, 1982.

Western Governors University. "America Online Joins Western Governors University National Advisory Board." Press release. 14 July 1999. 1 Aug. 1999 <http://www.wgu.edu/wgu/about/release30.html>.

PART I

PHILOSOPHICAL AND THEORETICAL CONSIDERATIONS

Chapter 1

Expectations Exploded

R. Stanton Hales

Years ago, several friends and I went on a weekend retreat in the San Bernardino Mountains of California with a group of eighth graders. They were students at a Southern California elementary school, a school for which at the time we were serving as trustees. One of the purposes of the retreat was for us all to commune with nature. When our first walk in the woods was closely accompanied by mosquitoes and poison oak, we questioned whether nature had quite the same expectations about communing with us. However, the real purpose of the retreat was for the eighth graders to benefit from the adult presence, to enter with us into deeper, more meaningful, more mature discussions about life than eighth graders normally have. Those with eighth graders in their families know what I mean.

We split off into smaller groups to facilitate these interchanges, and I was introduced to my charges. But before the intended conversation could get under way one of the less restrained eighth graders blurted out, "Hey, what is a trustee?"

Fair question, I thought, and then I thought further, What kind of an answer would mean most to an eighth grader? Simplicity, frank simplicity, seemed the wisest approach, so I quickly replied that "trustees are the legal owners of the school." It may have taken a while for this notion to sink into the other students, but not so for my interrogator. He came right back at me, asking, "So, do you make a lot of money on it?"

This time, my answer did not come so quickly. There was no simple answer.

"No" would suggest that I was a bad investor, or that the school was badly managed, or both. "Yes" was a lie, but even if that lie were offered tongue-in-cheek it would confirm his obvious suspicion. So, I took a deep breath and said, in so many words, that things were more complicated than he thought and that schools were unusual sorts of places, because the owners of schools constantly looked for ways to give money to them rather than make money off them. A sharp wave of adolescent incredulity washed over his face, and all he could manage was a stunned "Boy, that's really weird."

Weird or not, this turned out to provoke the best topics of discussion of the weekend, at least in my group: economic motivation, social responsibility, philanthropy, and more. Thirteen is an age of a certain self-centeredness. Watching out for one's self is to be expected. Expecting to spend one's life gathering things for one's own enjoyment was normal, at least in the limited experience of these thirteen-year-olds. Imagine the shock to their system—the explosion of their expectations—when they learned that there are people in the world who work hard to make a million dollars just so that they can give most of it away.

Yet, at the age of thirteen my student friends were not yet hardened cynics. The idealism of the altruistic motive could still touch them, and by the end of the weekend they were not just sympathetic with, but even elevated by, this new perspective on life. They were entranced by the outlook of Andrew Carnegie, whose dictum, a bit oversimplified, was to spend the first third of one's life getting all the education one can, the next third making all the money one can, and the last third giving it all away for worthwhile causes.

These eighth graders' expectations for life were overturned. I feel justified in hoping that when they reached college they would not fall into the popular trap of expecting pay or academic credit for their volunteer work. Once upon a time it was enough to say that one would receive one's reward in heaven. Somehow, that explanation does not suffice now. Nevertheless, it hardly rings as inspirational to say that one will receive one's reward on one's transcript, or as a credit on the next college bill. What my student friends needed, and got, was a new concept of reward.

This mountain experience years ago was brought to mind quite recently at a very different sort of mountain retreat, an East Coast gathering in the Poconos. The assemblage of this retreat consisted of college presidents, and the leader of these discussions—deeper, more meaningful, and more mature discussions than college presidents are normally allowed to have—was Adam Yarmolinsky, in his seventies the Regents Professor of Public Policy at the University of Maryland. Yarmolinsky is a distinguished lawyer and former Harvard Law School professor. He was also an accomplished public servant in the Lyndon Johnson administration, serving as Deputy Director of the President's Anti-Poverty Task Force, Chief of the Emergency Relief Fund to the Dominican Republic, and Deputy Assistant Secretary for International Security Affairs.

In the course of one morning's debate over an abstruse point of comparison between Alexis de Tocqueville's views on American democracy and Max Weber's beliefs about the prerequisites for a life in politics, the conversation some-how turned to course syllabi, faculty responsibility, and, eventually, course evaluation forms. With great innocence one of my colleagues around the table made reference to a canonical question on such forms, that staple, that all-purpose question, "Did this course meet your expectations?"

"That is precisely the wrong question!" Yarmolinsky exclaimed. He went on to explain: it may not so much be the wrong question, but that the conventional use of the question is always accompanied by an expectation for precisely the wrong answer. What intellectual value is there in a course, he argued, that blandly goes about meeting your expectations? The best courses, he said, are those that do precisely the opposite—disregard your expectations and carry you off to the unexpected. Where is the stimulation, the intellectual growth, in get-ting just what you expected? Why even take a course in which everything gotten is expected? In question after question, Yarmolinsky sliced away at the conven-tional wisdom of course evaluations. The best courses, he concluded, are often those that explode your expectations.

That carried me back to the California mountains. It immediately brought to mind my experience with eighth graders, nearly forgotten until then. I recalled how visibly the eighth graders had experienced an explosion of expectations. But I also was confident that in this revelation about human motivation, in the explosion and the figurative fire that followed, a seed had been planted that would grow in them to become a much deeper understanding of what goals matter in life and what one should ultimately be working toward.

That picture, the image of exploded expectations, has stayed with me since. Emboldened by Yarmolinsky's passionate argument and by the satisfaction of eighth graders' transformation, I am led here to take on a larger task.

The expectation I wish to explode belongs to Peter Drucker, for the past forty years a universally recognized guru on management and on business success. Every M.B.A. student in every graduate program is well schooled in Peter Drucker's insights. And from his many books and other writings and his enor-mous appetite for analyzing historical developments, he has been called the most perceptive observer of the American scene since de Tocqueville.

In early 1997, Drucker began to paint an expectation which, in the words of the President of the American Council on Education, sent a shock wave through the higher education community.

- In an interview in the March 10, 1997 issue of *Forbes* magazine, Drucker predicted: "Thirty years from now the big university campuses will be relics. Universities won't survive. . . . The current set-up is doomed. . . . The college won't survive as a residential institution." He has returned repeatedly to this theme:

- In a June 1997 *Forbes* article on the emergence of the cyberuniversity, he is again quoted as saying: "Universities won't survive. The future is outside the traditional campus, outside the traditional classroom. Distance learning is coming on fast."

- And in an August 24, 1998 *Forbes* article, "The Next Information Revolution," he comes closer to home with the assertion that "long distance learning . . . may well make

obsolete within 25 years that uniquely American institution, the freestanding undergraduate college."

So the culprit is distance learning, the new technological combination of television and computers making a virtual classroom out of dozens of different
individual locations scattered widely. Now distance learning may be ideally
suited as a tool for what John Henry Cardinal Newman sees as one sort of
education—instruction in the mechanical as opposed to cultivation of the
philosophical. It overcomes space, even time, to bring instruction, particularly
instruction in particular skills, to those who require those skills and whose
own lives do not allow any other means to gain them. Even for liberal arts
colleges, distance learning may eventually allow certain instruction, say in less
widely spoken languages such as Arabic, that would not be available otherwise.

But Newman, in his still powerful 1853 piece, *The Scope and Nature of
University Education*, correctly identifies the true value of the university precisely as a way of life, a real place, a place where twenty-four hours a day,
seven days a week one is immersed in an atmosphere of philosophical habit,
encountering daily the great outlines of knowledge, absorbing by a sort of os-
mosis an enlarged range of ways of knowing and thinking, even if one does not
formally study them all.

Moreover, Alfred North Whitehead makes the telling argument in "Universities and Their Function" that if imparting information is all that constitutes
education, no university has been justified since the invention and popularization
of printing in the fifteenth century. Colleges and universities, as whole places,
as learning communities, as dedicated battlegrounds of ideas, are the most effective, if not the only, instrument with which, through constant confrontation
of philosophy and oratory, the real leaders of a society can be fully formed and
tested.

And this leads to the particular explosion I wish to ignite, one which Drucker
sets himself up for within his own arguments. In a January 1998 article in
Society, Drucker laments two fifty-year reversals in education. Fifty years ago,
he argues, colleges and universities were not power centers but only marginal
institutions, because the B.A. was not a necessity. Yet the individual professors
in these institutions were opinion leaders: visible, prominent, and in constant
demand. All coming out of the great liberal arts tradition, they mattered because
their disciplines mattered.

Now, he argues, there is a double reversal. With the B.A. a virtual necessity
for upward mobility, the colleges and universities have become power centers,
yet there remain few if any true, recognized public "personages" in their faculties, the faculty having abandoned societal leadership for obscure scholarship.

Regardless of how we individually view this leadership-scholarship debate, I
would argue that the "personages" of our society, the leaders that every society
needs in every field, will of necessity come from the focused, intense experience

of a broad education at a place, a campus, rather than from the haphazard experience of narrow instruction a few hours a week, sandwiched between a work shift and other responsibilities.

In their book, *Passionate Minds: The Inner World of Scientists*, Lewis Wolpert and Alison Richards reveal the source of inspiration and passion that drove a key collection of senior scientists to stunning discoveries. The role of passion and inspiration is dominant in science. How is this passion best transmitted to students: a few hours a week over the screen and speakerphone, or side by side, day after day, together in a laboratory?

Distance learning is claimed as being magically able to bring the learning to the student. How does one bring the true learning of teamwork—such as in an athletic team or a marching band—to individuals scattered far and wide? How does one bring the essential experience of living and learning together in a consciously diverse community to people who do not live together?

There is no more important outcome of a real education than the steady broadening from being merely a technically competent practitioner of some skill to becoming a real citizen. Education taken a bit at a time, by one's self, without the opportunity to carry on immediately after class an important debate over lunch or dinner, hardly gives one the ability to do what Todd Gitlin calls out for in a recent article in the *Chronicle of Higher Education*: to "anchor a high-velocity, reckless, and lightweight culture." In what setting is one more enabled to "take one's time . . . and learn about what endures": a place of quiet beauty, filled with intellectual activity, or in one's kitchen with the TV?

If this society, this culture, is to produce the visionaries, the leaders, the "personages" whose demise Drucker himself has lamented, it will depend, I argue, precisely on the existence of those institutions that he predicts will vanish.

What expectations do you have for your life? Which expectations need to be nourished, and which need to be exploded? The magic of the human, intellectual community that exists in a true college is the richness and the excitement that accompanies the giving of nourishment and the igniting of explosions—figurative ones, of course!

May each of us have the generosity to nourish the expectations that require it, the courage to explode the expectations that deserve it, and, of course, the wisdom to know the difference.

NOTE

Adapted from the Opening Convocation at the College of Wooster, September 1998.

WORKS CITED

Gitlin, Todd. "The Liberal Arts in an Age of Info-Glut." *Chronicle of Higher Education*, 1 May 1998:B4–5.

Newman, John Henry. *Discourses on the Scope and Nature of University Education, Addressed to the Catholics of Dublin*. Dublin: James Duffy, 1852.
Whitehead, Alfred North. "Universities and Their Function." In *The Aims of Education and Other Essays*. New York: Macmillan, 1929.
Wolpert, Lewis, and Alison Richards. *Passionate Minds: The Inner World of Scientists*. New York: Oxford University Press, 1997.

Chapter 2

Using the Internet for Teaching and Research: A Political Evaluation

Michael Margolis

Old Main's scholars still ain't heard the news.
The professors meet their class once more,
Enrollments there had better soar.
Tenure's got to disappear; it's collegial blues.
              (Sung to the tune of Steve Goodman, "City of New Orleans")

BRAVE NEW UNIVERSITIES

Once upon a time, not so long ago, there were communities of scholars who thought the American academy provided refuge from most vicissitudes of the market economy. These scholars dwelled largely at institutions of higher learning: universities and liberal arts colleges. Most immersed themselves in study and in teaching. Occasionally they might publish a scholarly article, book, or review, but a rather small minority produced the bulk of scholarly publications (Ladd and Lipset). For most, the mission of the university remained "the diffusion and extension of knowledge rather than the advancement" of it (Newman 3). Rhetorically, scholars in the liberal arts and sciences generally embraced the idea that their institutions were places that valued education for its own sake, not necessarily for its immediate utility. A university was a place where students and faculty might learn together and reflect upon the philosophical implications of that learning for the conduct of private and civic affairs of the broader society.

Of course higher education had a practical side. Specialized programs, schools, or colleges found within and without the universities provided training for various occupations and professions, from farming and business through engineering, law, and medicine. Moreover, patrons and clients of these institutions—governments, businesses, churches, and philanthropies—expected some useful returns. Ideally, graduates would combine the virtues of educated citizens with the practical skills or knowledge necessary to secure their desired livelihoods. And from the last decades of the nineteenth century American universities themselves began to combine the continental European idea of academic research to advance knowledge with the Anglo/American ideas that emphasized teaching, learning, and citizenship (Sullivan).

Much of this has changed in recent decades. In the aftermath of a great expansion in the 1960s and early 1970s to accommodate the influx of postwar baby boomers, universities and other higher educational institutions found themselves facing increased costs. They had new facilities and infrastructure to maintain, and they had bid up salaries to staff courses for their larger student population or to recruit scholars and researchers of great repute. When the American economy entered a long period of "stagflation" in the mid-1970s, therefore, higher education faced new financial problems. Increases in public appropriations lagged behind inflationary increases, as did profits and asset values of corporate and philanthropic donors. Moreover, the baby boomer population bulge was moving beyond the traditional college age.

To support their expanded programs and operations, universities had to seek additional sources of revenue. Their efforts included recruiting and retaining new and nontraditional students, increasing alumni financial support, and promoting revenue-generating activities such as basketball and football teams or nondegree programs such as alumni travel or education in retirement. They also implemented businesslike evaluations of the revenue streams that stemmed from enrollments in particular academic programs, from research projects, from clinical income, or from other contracts for services.

The upshot of these developments gradually transformed higher education from a collegial to a corporate enterprise. Institutions of higher learning, particularly colleges and universities, had customarily been thought of as bodies of faculty and students primarily engaged in scholarly activities. Faculty committees and a few full-time officers generally had administered these activities. Now there arose a separate class of career academic administrators who oversaw the enterprise. Even though the educational enterprise had always had a central role in preparing a skilled and adaptable work force, educational administrators came to stress its economic benefits, both personal and societal, as the main justification for its receiving public and private subsidies (Bok; Galbraith; Sullivan). Functionally, faculties began to fall into the role of employees, and students into the role of customers.

Still, faculties remained an unusual class of employees, for most of their members, after a six-year trial period, had been granted career-long tenure in their positions. Tenure of course had been established as protection to encourage free inquiry in scholarly endeavors, especially teaching and research. As the need for new revenue became more pressing, however, the criteria for granting tenure tended to weight published scholarship and research supported by external funding more than factors like the quality of instruction or the impact of scholarly activities on communities outside the university. Indeed, the rewards for producing good research were often a diminution of responsibilities for teaching regularly scheduled classes (Bok Chapter 8).

Ironically, therefore, the surest way to gain tenure at research-oriented institutions was to demonstrate that one's research was not merely of sufficient quality to merit publication but that it also satisfied the priorities of external funders. Exercise of independence in teaching and research, the original justification for tenure, was hardly a consideration.[1]

During the 1980s the academy itself was affected by the conservative turn in American politics. Many of the new private foundations were conservative, as were the policies of the Reagan and Bush administrations. Although American universities were sometimes characterized as bastions of political liberalism during the 1960s and 1970s, this was true only of the social sciences, law, humanities, and, to a lesser extent, fine arts. Faculties of the physical and biological sciences, medicine, business, engineering, agriculture, and other applied fields were substantially conservative; and overall, the political orientation of the faculty of the "divided academy" was, if anything, slightly conservative (Ladd and Lipset 60).[2] In short, conservative governmental agencies and foundations found plenty of academics eager to take up their research agenda, and to the extent that they funded young, dynamic faculty members seeking tenure, they might indirectly have tipped the ideological scales further to the right.[3]

By the mid-1990s signs of a corporate culture pervaded most research and doctoral universities.[4] The ratio of full-time administrators to full-time faculty had risen. Retiring faculty were replaced by part-timers and graduate students, especially in disciplines that brought in fewer research dollars from external sources. Universities not only encouraged faculty to bring in research dollars and contracts, but they actively lobbied state legislatures and Congress to receive funds earmarked for their specific institutions (Brainard and Cordes). [5] Administrators commonly likened students to "customers" whose patronage their institutions needed to attract and retain. Pressures increased to raise the teaching load of scholars who failed to bring in research dollars, and politically conservative academics attacked the professorate in general and the institution of tenure in particular (Huber; Sykes). Perhaps in response, efforts to unionize faculties also increased.

When popularly accessible computer-mediated communication through the World Wide Web and multimedia browsers like Netscape Communicator and Microsoft Internet Explorer arose in the mid-1990s, the corporate culture was the catalyst for profound changes in higher education. Higher education had always been a labor-intensive task, but heretofore there had been no fully acceptable way to cut labor costs by eliminating lectures and classroom discussions. The new technology had the potential to overcome this limitation and perhaps could at long last break the professorial guild. Indeed, the very manner in which the educational product had been marketed provided the justification for such changes. The anticipated savings, combined with high-tech delivery of the product, would certainly please their hard-pressed customers; and if the product still resulted in a sufficiently trained work force, those savings alone would also please their patrons and clients (Taylor).

In sum, the stage has been set for the adoption of Internet technologies to bring about profound changes in the conduct of teaching and research in higher education. The next section examines the likely changes. The final section assesses their likely consequences.

THE INTERNET AND HIGHER EDUCATION

The Internet and related media provide the opportunity to alter, enhance, and otherwise improve traditional forms of instruction and research. Enthusiasts have urged faculty to use these new media in their courses, especially those for undergraduates. Suggested uses include placing syllabi and assignments on-line; developing Web sites for teaching and student research; computerizing classroom presentations to enhance or replace lectures and discussions; using distance learning, e-mail, and on-line discussions (synchronic and asynchronic) to improve communication with traditional students and to reach nontraditional students; and using the digitized library to enhance or replace the on-campus institution (Atieh; Harknett and Cobane; Connick).

In a perfect world, incorporating these media would be largely unobjectionable. We can imagine idyllic campuses where mentors guide students through the fundamentals of their academic disciplines, where rigorous study builds good character, and where students and mentors use the knowledge gained to contemplate questions of philosophic import. Combining this setting with access to the Internet's vast stores of information could lay the basis for an unusually well informed and well educated citizenry of good character, who, according to liberal democratic theory, would work toward producing a better life for all.

The most obvious problem with this scenario is its cost. No modern society has offered so rich an education to any but its elite, and, arguably, none could do so without diverting substantial resources from other public and private commitments. In the United States an intimate association of students and teachers "without the distractions of family responsibilities, outside work or other competitive involvements" can be found only at leading private liberal arts colleges or at select undergraduate colleges of major public and private research universities (Trow 294). It is safe to suggest that the costs of information technology will not be the primary concern at these institutions and that they will use the technology largely to enhance the value of the education that results from the close student-teacher relationships already in place.

Higher education for the masses takes place mostly at public institutions and generally focuses on the transmission of knowledge. It has relatively little concern for building character or shaping society's leaders through personal interaction between students and mentors. Studies are less intense than at elite institutions, student to faculty ratios are higher, and most students combine their studies with substantial outside employment during the school year in order to meet educational and other expenses. Outside employment may enrich their studies, but that usually is not a requirement. The key concern is for students to gain skills and knowledge necessary to certify them as trainable employees in their chosen fields. While adopting information technology can enrich the curricula at these institutions, it costs money to do so. Adoption, therefore, tends to be justified as providing wider access to courses and, inevitably, as cutting the per capita cost of delivering the educational product.

The second problem is that the great majority of undergraduates, the customers so to speak, are interested mostly in securing employment and a good income directly upon graduation or in gaining entry to graduate or professional programs to enhance their prestige and income. They are far less concerned about honing their study skills, developing philosophies of life, improving social and political values, becoming community leaders, participating in civic or cultural affairs, or realizing other benefits of a rigorous education. To gain a general education and appreciation of cultural ideas will suffice.[6] That the majority of undergraduates view education as a personal economic investment comports with the corporate marketing of education as an investment product.

This brings us to the third problem involved with simply adopting information technologies to enrich established curricula: the technologies themselves provide a means for new enterprises to upset the near monopoly that traditional institutions have enjoyed as providers of higher education. Whereas the current norms of mass education still bring students to a physical campus, instructional technologies that use the Internet do not require a traditional campus. Virtual institutions can maintain scanty physical plants devoid of expensive laboratories, classrooms, libraries, dormitories, or offices. By employing only a few full-time (let alone tenured) faculty or librarians they can drastically reduce the customary labor costs of instruction. At the same time they can hold out the promise of access to higher education for everyone who can log on to the Internet (Olsen).

The United States is a market-dominated society where citizens commonly express an ideological bias against economic planning and regulation by government. Adopting information technologies for instruction via the Internet allows university administrators to respond to pressures from politicians, taxpayers, and students-cum-customers to decrease the cost of delivering higher education. Moreover, these technologies provide opportunities for new types of higher learning enterprises—private and public, for profit and not-for-profit—to emerge. Most of these enterprises strive to deliver higher educational products comparable to those of traditional university programs of mass education, but with greater efficiency and at less cost (Atieh; Baker; Blumenstyk, "Entrepreneur," "Banking"; *Chronicle*; NASULGC; Olsen; Shea; Strossnider). Others have branched out into the information technology support business, developing administrative and communication software, on-line courseware, and supporting materials for distance learning adaptable to needs of a diverse and growing number of on-line educational institutions. Some, such as Knowledge Universe and CBT Systems, are relatively new ventures. Others have arisen as established distance learning institutions, such as the Open University or the University of Phoenix, placing many of their operations on-line. Yet others, including traditional institutions such as Duke, Stanford, Penn State, NYU, and the University of Illinois, have created new programs or schools for on-line distance learning (Applebome; Baker; Blumenstyk, "Distance"; Olsen).

In the United States today, on-line institutions that offer certificate or degree programs usually see "nontraditional students"—men and women aged twenty-five and over who are regularly employed—as their primary customers. The arguments for enrollment commonly focus on economic advantages:

1. The job market is changing rapidly: most jobs that will be available in ten years do not now exist.
2. The U.S. Department of Labor (or some other authority) predicts that the great majority—perhaps as many as 80 percent—of these new jobs will involve information technology.
3. In order to qualify for these jobs, today's workers will have to keep acquiring new skills and knowledge.
4. Even though we have greatly expanded the opportunities for higher education, the costs of matriculation have been rising faster than have workers' incomes since the 1970s.
5. Distance learning via the Internet saves students time and money by pricing tuition competitively and by decreasing or eliminating indirect costs—transportation, home help, wardrobe, room, board, and the like.
6. On-line courses are less disruptive of students' family and social lives than are traditional programs because they offer flexible hours and self-paced learning.
7. On-line education integrates expertise from business and industry into its programs and caters to the needs of people who must work for a living.
8. Students who successfully complete courses on-line learn as much as or more than students who complete similar courses in traditional college settings. (Atieh; Connick)

Reputable on-line institutions present information about institutional accreditation and about the quality of their courses and programs. They also explain access to library and reference materials. Information about faculty, virtual office hours, and how to communicate with student support services may also be presented, as may testimonials from students who have successfully completed the courses or programs.

Missing, however, is the idea of a college or university as a place where learning extends much beyond formal coursework. There is little concern for developing leadership and character, for examining the nature of society, or for pondering deeper philosophical questions. Nor is there much concern for the modern university's role in the research to expand our knowledge. The appeal, after all, is to "people whose geographic location, work demands, physical or social conditions, personal circumstances, or family and community responsibilities impede their access to traditional university-level education" (Atieh 9). Distance learning via the Internet is presented as the quintessential means of achieving success by fitting oneself to the job requirements set by corporate America.

An on-line education may be found lacking in comparison to the traditional programs at elite colleges or universities, but it may hold up in comparison to standard programs for mass education. While some studies cast doubt on claims that students learn as much or more on-line as in standard programs, on-line instruction is relatively new, and there is good reason to believe that it will improve. Similarly, even though claims that instruction on-line really costs students less than does standard instruction also remain to be proved, we can expect competition and economies of scale to drive down the costs of hardware and software once we move beyond the present stage of heavy capital investment (Gladieux and Swail; Phipps and Merisotis; National Center for Education Statistics; White).

If faculty and administrators at institutions that offer mass education fear that on-line learning may soon make significant inroads into the traditional student base, they must share part of the blame. Having marketed a college degree as an investment designed to produce a profitable return, they have helped to destroy the idea of a university as a gathering place where scholars and students engage in a mutual enterprise of learning and research, regardless of the immediate economic benefits. The idea of a university has begun to resemble that of an education factory designed to produce and disseminate knowledge with maximum efficiency. The immediate consequences will probably make little difference for the education of most students. They portend great changes for the professoriate, however, and possibly for the nation.

ASSESSING THE CONSEQUENCES

Mindful that their patrons and clientele desire more bang for their educational dollar, yet faced with increased costs, institutions of higher learning have adopted more businesslike practices. Differential markets for higher education are openly acknowledged. The best students clamor to gain admission to the most prestigious—and often most expensive—undergraduate programs. Although some scholarships are available, those with both the skills to qualify and the money to pay have the best chances of gaining admission.

Institutions that offer programs primarily for the mass of traditional students are harder pressed to make ends meet. Increasingly, they evaluate the quality of courses or programs by the number of students enrolled and retained. Productivity involves achieving higher ratios of students to full-time faculty, often using low-paid teaching assistants to break large classes into smaller discussion sections. Threatened by the potential loss of many traditional students to less expensive two-year community colleges or to virtual educational institutions, they have sometimes ignored or lowered their standards for admission to maintain enrollments.[7] Alternatively, they have begun to offer distance learning courses on their own or in partnership with other educational providers (NASULGC; Olsen; Young).

Stuck with maintaining both their physical plants and a semi-permanent labor force, however, campus-based educational institutions with traditional four-year degrees cannot match the prices that efficient competitors—well-managed two-year community colleges and on-line educational providers—can offer the mass education market for accredited courses, certificates, and degrees. The good will and prestige that accrue to graduates of traditional programs at established non-elite institutions justify some premium for their tuition, but accrediting boards and systematic studies have concluded that competing institutions offer satisfactory course content and instruction. In short, those that provide distance education to nontraditional students cannot be dismissed as "digital diploma mills" (Noble; Olson; White).

To survive—perchance to thrive—in the new environment, traditional institutions have two general strategies. The first is to emphasize the "quality of life" values rather than the direct economic benefits that education ideally fosters in its graduates and in the nation: democracy, equality, diversity, social mobility, scientific progress, cultural enrichment, moral enlightenment, and the like. These hark back to Newman's idea of a university, and they form part of the attraction of elite institutions.

The second strategy is to model institutional practices more closely on the operations of profitable private corporations. This involves deemphasizing non-economic values and adopting hard-nosed businesslike criteria to measure performance.

Nonelite institutions might have succeeded with the former strategy if they had adopted it when faculty still played decisive roles in university administration. It still might succeed for specific schools or subject areas, where nonelite institutions can establish programs of excellence for niche markets. As an overall strategy, however, it stands the proverbial snowball's chance in hell of success. Faculties never made the case that new information technologies should be used primarily to enhance teaching and research, not to eliminate classrooms, undergraduate laboratories, libraries, and personnel. How could they? They had for the most part accepted the economic rationalization that institutions of higher education deserved public and private subsidies because they provided skills that increased the earning power of their graduates and made the nation's economy a more successful competitor in the global market.

Congruent with this rationalization, student loan programs expanded while public funds for scholarships and institutional subsidies shrank as proportions of higher educational budgets. Higher education had been marketed as an economic investment, and, as we have seen, surveys indicate that most students have accepted this view.

Even though lip service is still paid to the idea of a university as a special place for study and thought, most educational institutions already have adopted aspects of the second strategy. They have revamped criteria for evaluating research, teaching, and community service to reflect their impact on university budgets. They have downsized full-time faculty through attrition and relied increasingly upon low paid part-time instructors and graduate students to teach undergraduate courses. They have begun replacing classroom lectures with interactive sessions on the Internet. They have cut research costs through use of digital libraries and networked computers, reduced support for nonlucrative scholarship, and begun to charge a fair price for services they formerly provided for free, such as computer setup and maintenance or access to special databases. Finally, they have expanded investment in revenue-producing enterprises, such as conference centers, alumni programs, university paraphernalia, varsity athletic enterprises, and exclusive contracts for on-campus sales with food, beverage, and clothing vendors.

As this strategy's aim of reducing costs comports with the economic values held by most students, public officials, and conservatively inclined corporate and philanthropic donors, it has a better chance than the first to win the university plaudits for good management and to gain it capital investment for technological development. Whether or not extensive adoption of information technology for instruction actually produces the same or better educational results more cheaply than does modest adoption remains uncertain. But it certainly redirects extensive sums paid for labor supplied by faculty and staff to capital goods, consumer durables, and other services supplied by business. In any case, most traditional campus-based universities have begun to implement this strategy, and the wild popularity of the Internet gives every reason to expect that the trend will continue (NASULGC).

The next stage in the evolution of higher education for the mass public will most likely result from full adoption of the corporate model of education as an investment product. We already have for-profit institutions like the University of Phoenix, Jones International University, and Knowledge Universe using information technologies on-line for degree programs or implementing such on-line programs for other institutions. As undergraduate courses at traditional universities adopt more and more of the characteristics of those offered by on-line institutions, we can expect greater standardization. Why spend money for faculties at many institutions to develop and teach introductory courses that have essentially the same content? Wouldn't it be cheaper to develop on-line courses that not only could be accessed at the students' convenience but also could be taught by the world's best teachers? Nonelite institutions no longer would need to limit their course instruction to their own—and let's face it—sometimes undistinguished faculty. Eventually, many of their undergraduate programs—perhaps even entire schools or colleges—could be marketed as franchises of greater, more distinguished institutions (Blumenstyk, "Company").

Inexorably, the strategic logic of corporate management of the higher education market leads to ending professorial tenure as we know it. As competing institutions spend more and more money to recruit and retain their most profitable undergraduate customers, they cannot be expected to carry their workers through lean times as well as fat. Academic freedom needs to be protected, but in a competitive market economy tenure must be balanced against economic exigency. When a department or program cannot produce sufficient income to cover its costs, its payroll must be downsized. This could be accomplished in a flexible decentralized fashion that would hardly compromise academic freedom. The faculty members affected by the order to downsize could decide for themselves how to meet the cuts: whether to lay off colleagues, to retain everyone at reduced salary, or to implement some other creative solution (Lively; Margolis; Wilson).

Barring an unexpected resurgence of support for quality of life strategies to preserve the traditional campus-based university model, the lines between most traditional higher educational institutions and the upstart educational enterprises that rely upon information technology will soon disappear. While the particular mix of partnerships, mergers, buyouts, consolidations, spin-offs, and the like cannot be specified as yet, established institutions will restructure their delivery of higher education in businesslike manners that maximize efficient use of information technologies for instruction and minimize the need for personal instruction by high priced professors. As basic courses in most disciplines will be available in a limited number of standardized forms, factors like ease of access and convenience of information delivery will be stressed. Institutions will strive to become the students' portal to higher education, the only connection they'll ever need, at least for their undergraduate training. A good local or branch campus will stress advantages like the availability of personal consultation, meeting rooms, laboratory facilities, entertainment centers, low priced health clubs, and similar services and facilities, not unlike stressing the advantages offered by a good local or branch bank. Nontraditional students will find that the restructured institutions also offer plenty of programs that employ information technologies suited to part-time study. All of this will be offered at a suitably affordable price, at least according to the advertising campaigns.

Outstanding professors and researchers will still be found in the best undergraduate colleges and universities and in the best graduate programs. Gifted students will still be able to attend select undergraduate institutions on scholarship or for a higher price, but the public will have been relieved of most of the burden of supporting a tenured professoriate. That intellectual class will no longer be allowed to draw pay to support its inclination to study and to think. Graduate and professional studies, which offer increased economic benefits to those who earn advanced degrees, will be supported by tuition and by grants or contracts for research. Students, politicians, donors, and taxpayers will be happy.

The campus of the future will be hailed as a triumph of the free market. Why would anyone object?

NOTES

1. An expansion of the size and number of academic journals followed the expansion of faculties as more researchers began to turn out more research, driven in part by new requirements for tenure. Whether or not this expansion has increased the total value or overall quality of scholarship is a matter of debate, not unlike the debate over whether or not the expansion of major league franchises has contributed to the overall quality of baseball.

2. These generalizations are based on aggregate distributions of a sample of 60,028 faculty members at 303 universities, four-year colleges, and junior colleges. They do not account for differences within and among particular educational institutions (see Ladd and Lipset 4).

3. This resembles the cumulative effect of Reagan and Bush appointing relatively conservative judges to the federal bench from 1981 through 1992. Federal judges have career-long tenure and can be removed against their will only through impeachment by the House of Representatives and conviction by the Senate.

4. See Carnegie Foundation for the Advancement of Teaching for definitions of research and doctoral universities.

5. The *Chronicle of Higher Education* also has a searchable database of earmarked academic grants from 1995 to 1999.

6. These assertions are based on the annual survey of freshmen conducted by the UCLA Higher Education Research Institute and the American Council on Education taken in the fall of 1998; 275,811 freshmen entering 469 two- and four-year institutions were surveyed. (See Table 2.1.) No other reasons or objectives were cited by more than 40 percent of those surveyed. These included influencing social values, promoting racial understanding, becoming a community leader, keeping up with political affairs, running one's own business, having administrative responsibility for the work of others, and engaging in various community, environmental, and artistic endeavors.

7. The controversy over whether or not such admissions have led to increased costs for remedial courses or to a general "dumbing down" of standards is beyond the scope of this chapter. So too are the controversies over the impact of affirmative action on admission standards.

WORKS CITED

Applebome, Peter. "Education.com." *New York Times, Education Life*, 4 Apr. 1999:26+.

Atieh, Sam. *How to Get a College Degree via the Internet: The Complete Guide to Getting Your Undergraduate or Graduate Degree from the Comfort of Your Home*. Rocklin, CA: Prima Publishing, 1998.

Baker, Russ. "The Education of Mike Milken: From Junk-Bond King to Master of the Knowledge Universe." *The Nation*, 3 May 1999: 11–18.

Blumenstyk, Goldie. "Banking on Its Reputation, the Open University Starts an Operation in the U.S." *Chronicle of Higher Education*, 23 July 1999. 5 Aug. 1999 <http://chronicle.com/weekly/v45/i46/46a03601.htm>.

Table 2.1
UCLA Higher Education Research Institute 1998 Freshman Survey

Reasons noted as very important in Deciding to go to college	All	Men	Women
Get a better job	76.9%	76.6%	77.1%
Make more money	74.6%	78.5%	71.3%
Gain a general education & appreciation of ideas	62.0%	55.9%	67.2%
Prepare for graduate or professional school	49.0%	42.6%	54.5%
Make me a more cultured person	45.1%	39.4%	50.0%
Improve reading and study skills	41.5%	37.5%	44.9%
Objectives considered essential or Very important			
Being very well-off financially	74.0%	76.0%	72.4%
Raising a family	73.0%	71.1%	74.6%
Becoming an authority in my field	60.2%	61.8%	58.8%
Helping others who are in difficulty	59.9%	49.9%	68.3%
Obtaining recognition from my colleagues	49.8%	50.85%	49.0%
Developing a meaningful philosophy of life	40.9%	40.2%	41.5%

―――. "A Company Pays Top Universities to Use Their Names and Their Professors." *Chronicle of Higher Education*, 18 June 1999. 5 Aug. 1999 <http://chronicle.com/weekly/v45/i41/41a03901.htm.>

―――. "Distance Learning at the Open University: The British Institution's Success Has Inspired Imitators in the United States." *Chronicle of Higher Education*, 23 July 1999. 5 Aug. 1999 <http://chronicle.com/weekly/v45/i46/46a03501.htm>.

―――. "An Entrepreneur Sees Profits in the Future of His 'Power Campus.' " *Chronicle of Higher Education*, 2 Oct. 1998. 5 Aug. 1999 <http://chronicle.com/ weekly/v45/i06/06a04101.htm>.

Bok, Derek. *The Cost of Talent: How Executives and Professionals Are Paid and How It Affects America*. New York: Free Press, 1993.

Brainard, Jeffrey, and Colleen Cordes. "Pork-Barrel Spending on Academe Reaches a Record $797-Million." *Chronicle of Higher Education*, 23 July 1999. 5 Aug. 1999 <http://chronicle.com/weekly/v45/i46/46a00101.htm>.

Bromley, Hank. "Data-Driven Democracy? Social Assessment of Educational Computing." *In Education, Technology, Power: Educational Computing as a Social Practice*. Ed. Hank Bromley and Michael W. Apple. Albany: SUNY Press, 1998. 1–25.

Carnegie Foundation for the Advancement of Teaching. *Definitions of Categories*. 1 Aug. 1999 <http://www.carnegiefoundation.org/cihe/cihe-dc.htm>.

CBT Systems. Home page. 1 Aug. 1999 <http://www.cbtsys.com/>.

Chronicle of Higher Education. "Major For-Profit Higher-Education Companies." Table. 23 Jan. 1998. 5 Aug. 1999 <http://chronicle.com/che-data/articles.dir/art-44.dir/issue-20.dir/forprofit.htm>.

Connick, George, ed. *The Distance Learner's Guide*. Upper Saddle River, NJ: Prentice-Hall, 1999.

Galbraith, John Kenneth. *The Good Society: The Human Agenda*. Boston: Houghton Mifflin, 1996.

Gladieux, Lawrence E., and Watson Scott Swail. *The Virtual University and Educational Opportunity: Issues of Equity and Access for the Next Generation*. Washington, DC: College Board, 1999.

Harknett, Richard, and Craig Cobane. "Introducing Instructional Technology to International Relations." *PS: Political Science and Politics* 30 (1997): 496–501.

Huber, Richard M. *How Professors Play the Cat Guarding the Cream: Why We're Paying More and Getting Less in Higher Education*. Fairfax, VA: George Mason University Press, 1992.

Knowledge Universe. Home page. 1 Aug. 1999 <http://www.knowledgeu.com/>.

Ladd, Everett C., Jr., and Seymour Martin Lipset. *The Divided Academy: Professors and Politics*. New York: McGraw-Hill, 1975.

Lively, Kit. "Northwestern U. Professor Loses Breach-of-Contract Lawsuit over Pay." *Chronicle of Higher Education*, 31 July 1998. 1 Aug. 1999 <http://chronicle.com/che-data/articles.dir/art-44.dir/issue-47.dir/47a00902.htm>.

Margolis, Michael. "Brave New Universities."*First Monday* 3.5 (1998). 1 Aug. 1999 <http://www.firstmonday.dk/issues/issue3_5/index.html>.

NASULGC (National Association of State Universities and Land-Grant Colleges). *NASULGC Universities Connecting to the Future: How Do They Do IT? How Do They Pay for IT?* Washington, DC: Office of Public Affairs, NASULGC, 1999.

National Center for Education Statistics. *Distance Education in Higher Education Institutions.* NCES 98–062. Prepared by Laurie Lewis, Debbie Alexander, and Elizabeth Farris; Bernie Greene, project director. Washington, DC: U.S. Department of Education, 1997.

Newman, John Henry. *The Idea of a University.* New Haven: Yale University Press, 1996.

Noble, David F. "Digital Diploma Mills: The Automation of Higher Education." *First Monday* 3.1 (1998). 1 Aug. 1999 <http://www.firstmonday.dk/issues/issue3_1/noble/index.html>.

Olsen, Florence. " 'Virtual' Institutions Challenge Accreditors to Devise New Ways of Measuring Quality." *Chronicle of Higher Education,* 6 Aug. 1999. 6 Aug. 1999 <http://chronicle.com/free/v45/i48/48a02901.htm>.

Phipps, Ronald, and Jamie Merisotis. *What's the Difference? A Review of Contemporary Research on the Effectiveness of Distance Learning in Higher Education.* Washington, DC: Institute for Higher Education Policy, 1999.

Shea, Christopher. "Visionary or 'Operator'? Jorge Klor de Alva and His Unusual Intellectual Journey: Controversial Anthropologist Gives Up a Chair at Berkeley to Lead the U. of Phoenix." *Chronicle of Higher Education,* 3 July 1998. 5 Aug. 1999 <http://chronicle.com/che-data/articles.dir/art-44.dir/issue-43.dir/43a00101.htm>.

Strossnider, Kim. "For-Profit Higher Education Sees Booming Enrollments and Revenues." *Chronicle of Higher Education,* 23 Jan. 1988. 5 Aug. 1999 <http://chronicle.com/che-data/articles.dir/art-44.dir/issue-20.dir/20a03601.htm>.

Sullivan, William M. *Institutional Identity and Social Responsibility.* Washington, DC: Council on Educational Policy, 1999.

Sykes, Charles J. *ProfScam: Professors and the Demise of Higher Education.* New York: St. Martin's Press, 1988.

Taylor, Kit Sims. "Higher Education: From Craft-Production to Capitalist Enterprise?" *First Monday* 3.9 (1999). 1 Aug. 1999 <http://www.firstmonday.dk/issues/issue3_9/taylor/index.html>.

Trow, Martin. "The Development of Information Technology in American Higher Education." *Daedalus* 126 (1997): 293–314.

UCLA Higher Education Research Institute and American Council on Education. Survey. 1998. 1 Aug. 1999 <http://chronicle.com/weekly/v45/i21/ff4521freshmen.htm>.

Waltz, Scott B. "Distance Learning Classrooms: A Critique." *Bulletin of Science, Technology and Society* 18.3 (1998): 208–16.

White, Frank. "Digital Diploma Mills: A Dissenting Voice." *First Monday* 4.7 (1999). 1 Aug. 1999 <http://www.firstmonday.dk/issues/issue4_7/white/index.html>.

Wilson, Robin. "Georgia State U. to Replace Part-Timers with Full-Time, Untenured Professors." *Chronicle of Higher Education,* 2 June 1999. 1 Aug. 1999 <http://chronicle.com/weekly/v45/i40/40a01801.htm>.

Woody, Todd. "Higher Earning:The Fight to Control the Academy's Intellectual Capital: Universities Are Facing a Revolution over Intellectual Property as Technology Blurs the Lines Between Good Business and Good Education." *The Industry Standard,* 28 June 1998. 1 Aug. 1999 <http://www.thestandard.net/articles/article_print/0,1454,874,00.html>.

Young, Jeffrey R. "Research Universities Team Up to Create a 'Portal' to On-line Education." *Chronicle of Higher Education:Daily News,* 10 June 1999. 1 Aug. 1999 <http://chronicle.com/>.

Chapter 3

The Web, the Millennium, and the Digital Evolution of Distance Education

David C. Leonard

THE DIGITAL AGE IS UPON US

The World Wide Web has become a ubiquitous electronic medium of communication. It is also becoming a Universal Electronic Campus, a global "academical village" (Curry School of Education) where thoughts, ideas, and processes are shared, and where people learn and produce in bits, not in atoms (Negroponte). However, a significant number of university administrators and faculty persist in focusing their vision on the physical campus, on bricks and mortar. They remain fixed in the world of atoms and nearly oblivious to the new virtual learning world being built within their midst.

The problem is that the educational paradigm of the Industrial Age is no longer a valid learning model in the Digital Age (Resnick and Klopfer). Despite the lack of foresight among many of the decision makers in academe, the networked computer infrastructure for the Universal Electronic Campus continues to be built and populated with useful educational and research content. As the trend toward the digitization of knowledge continues in our society and in the workplace (Tapscott, *Growing*), the movement from campus-based learning to Web-based distance education will be an inevitable result within and outside of academe. Concomitantly, the expansion of technical communication to include knowledge management and knowledge transfer is an important aspect of the overall trend toward the digitization of knowledge and the growth of electronic communication within "learning organizations" and within society (Senge).

OVERVIEW OF TOPICS COVERED AND APPROACH TAKEN

In this chapter, I first discuss the educational paradigms of the Industrial and Digital Ages and then the needs and expectations of adult learners and traditional campus-based learners within the context of Web-based education. Next, I define knowledge management and its impact on technical communication in relation to the rise of knowledge sharing on the World Wide Web. Then, I project the development of the Universal Campus Network and Web-based education in the near future, both in general and in relation to technical communication. I end by defining the elements for success for Web-based distance education in technical communication and provide conclusions about where we are headed.

In taking a "big picture" view of Web-based instruction, this chapter makes broad generalizations that could easily be refuted in the particular. While it expresses a broad commitment to Web-based instruction in general, I am aware that Web-based instruction may not be the superior learning method in all situations.

THE INDUSTRIAL AGE SCHOOLHOUSE AND WORKPLACE

The Industrial Age modeled its schools after the factory. The administrators managed the buildings, the faculty, and the staff. As "overseers" in this factory, the faculty made sure that the workers, that is, the students, produced and were tested to meet certain educational objectives. The staff supported the administration by taking care of the buildings and the administrative infrastructure. Operant conditioning and Skinnerian behaviorism provided a good foundation for this industrial and educational philosophy, which rewarded the producers and punished the nonproducers (Wertheim).

Following this model, a successful school administrator in higher education built more buildings, brought in more students, and hired more teachers—as well as more administrators and staff to manage the process. At the university level, course instruction was often limited to teaching the basic theories and practices of particular disciplines, in which conceptual knowledge predominated over putting ideas into action. The predominant method of knowledge transfer was the instructor using chalk and chalkboard, reciting ideas taken down by students using pen or pencil and notepad.

In the factory and in the schoolhouse, this organizational structure provided a great social conditioning process for lower-level managers and workers who needed to process atoms and bits now handled for the most part by the computer. In the work environment of the Industrial Age, most tasks were done by rote and repetitive in nature. More creative activities were the domain of the middle- and upper-level managers who directed the workers on the factory and data processing floors. The need did not exist then, as it does now, for workers to share knowledge, think critically, and exercise creative problem solving.

THE DIGITAL AGE SCHOOLHOUSE AND WORKPLACE

In the Digital Age, success in higher education is not a result of building more buildings, hiring more faculty, or attracting more students to the physical campus. In the Digital Learning Age, colleges focus their expenditures on using technology as integral to the process of learning and sharing information in their virtual "academical village" and within all schools and academic disciplines. Colleges and universities moving into the Digital Learning Age are

• reviewing their present faculty makeup, educational philosophy, and orientation;

• retraining existing or hiring new faculty;

• evaluating what constitutes good methods of knowledge transfer in this Digital Age;

• focusing on providing their faculty with the necessary resources and support to build and maintain the electronic campus; and

• investing in the electronic campus digital library. (Graubard and Leclerc)

Many faculty would be ready to make the change to the digital learning world if they were provided with the right tools, infrastructure, and rewards. Too often, however, innovative and entrepreneurial faculty are given little support or encouragement to create and implement a truly cohesive and well-supported virtual campus environment (McCormack and Jones).

Of late there is much ado about "integrating technology into the curriculum." What this often means, however, is "technologizing" traditional teaching methods that worked well in the Industrial Age, but not now (Sacks). In the current work environment, most knowledge workers are not producing widgets, nor are they creating atoms. Instead, they are working with bits. Their work is a result of a collaborative effort of a team of knowledge workers who use technology to produce processes and programs that transform the business itself and provide knowledge to customers who, more often than not, are business partners (Tapscott, *Digital*).

Most companies in the private sector already have curtailed the growth of their physical infrastructure and the organization that supports it, and have integrated technology to transform the way they do business. Many college and university administrators are not fully aware that the primary focus of corporate executives is the care and tending of knowledge workers. Currently, a huge and unfulfilled demand exists for skilled knowledge workers with math, science, and engineering backgrounds. The higher education system has not been able to produce these types of knowledge workers in sufficient numbers to meet the needs of high-tech companies. In such a talent-starved environment, the main corporate goal is to provide the knowledge worker with the best networked technology available to promote better sharing of knowledge and increased dialogue in which new ideas are generated and innovations are brought to market (Tapscott, *Digital*).

EXPECTATIONS OF LEARNERS IN THE DIGITAL AGE

Whether we call it Web-based distance education, or just plain Web-based education, our media are integral to our message. The environment for utilizing instructional learning theories and methods for effective electronic communication in the Digital Age should parallel the digital networked environment that our students currently are or soon will be working in (Schank).

The Adult Learner

Adults in the current business environment must learn all of their lives. Learning is integral to their success on the job (Senge). Companies encourage their employees, through tuition reimbursement and other educational assistance programs, to start or finish their undergraduate degrees or to obtain graduate degrees. These companies expect some sort of positive change in their employees, primarily in cognitive development, along with new skills and attitudes. Team goals and team effectiveness are also important aspects of the current business environment. Companies thus anticipate that universities will address team learning and have the students use state-of-the-art collaborative tools in the class activities.

The Traditional Campus Learner

Even among college-age students (the traditional campus-bound learner), companies expect that their new hires will be savvy about team activities and have experience using computer-based collaborative tools. Without testing the hypotheses, without actively shaping course content, without sharing ideas among peers, and without putting ideas into action, learning is of little value to both the college-age learner and the adult learner (Lieberman).

Our notion of how we teach traditional learners on campus is in need of drastic revision. Incorporating aspects of the virtual learning environment through a campus-based knowledge sharing network will help faculty (and administrators) break free from their traditional notions of how to teach and how students can best learn in a campus environment.

Learner-Centric Versus Teacher-Centric Instruction

Before embarking upon any course of action regarding Web-based distance education, it is important to understand current learner-centric theories of instruction in which content is manipulated by the learner rather than by the instructor. Learner-centric theories focus on the importance of the learner over the instructor to the instructional activity. In this educational paradigm, the instructor is no longer a primary intermediary between the learner and the learning experience. All knowledge need not pass first through the instructor. The instructor must be a catalyst, a coach, and a program manager directing projects, not an intermediary or a barrier between the information and the student. Otherwise, we are revisiting the Industrial Age education model in which the student is the bench-bound listener passively absorbing content, the body of which is available only via the primary knowledge gatekeeper, the instructor (Schneider).

Any attempt to build truly functional and useful content that the learner can interact with and shape on the Web will fail under the Industrial Age learning paradigm. To succeed at building a digital campus, one must be knowledgeable about and able to implement current learner-centric theories of instruction and provide an electronic learning environment that embodies those theories (Sherry).

TECHNICAL COMMUNICATION REDEFINED

Following the trend occurring in industry, education in technical communication is undergoing a transformation and an expansion. Part of this transformation is a result of a new area that is shaping the way knowledge itself is being disseminated. This new area, defined for years as technical communication, is beginning to be referred to in industry as *knowledge management*. Knowledge management involves primarily three areas: (1) business transformation, (2) organizational learning, and (3) Web knowledge transfer enablement.

Business Transformation

Business transformation involves using technology, especially communications technology, to enhance every aspect of how the enterprise operates. Business transformation is different from process reengineering because it is less concerned with departmental cost reductions and more concerned with spearheading enterprise-wide learning, innovation, and the application of breakthrough digital technologies to create new products and services. In the recent past, data processing primarily handled structured information to run the financial and accounting aspects of the business. With the rise of the Web and the digitization of rich data types (such as image, audio, video, and animation) and electronic document-like objects (such as white papers, design documents, policies and procedures, and technical specifications), enterprises can process unstructured knowledge objects and shift their product focus from physical assets to knowledge assets (Hibbard and Carrillo).

In both high-tech and low-tech industries, technical communicators working with computer hardware and software engineers provide the "digital" epoxy that helps link the bits—the rich data types and the electronic document-like objects—to the physical products (automobile, airplane, software programs) being created. Technical communicators are on the front lines of companies' knowledge management initiatives. Technical communicators are helping move enterprises from the Industrial Age to the Digital Age by their involvement in the creation of a vast library of electronic information that supports the products and services offered by these enterprises.

Organizational Learning

Organizational learning is a result of an enterprise reaching a point of meta-cognition, of becoming conscious of its own processes and decisions and aware of the skills of its knowledge workers. In the recent past, many predigital companies were not consciously able to identify how they satisfy their customers (Malhotra).

Vannevar Bush's vision of a global electronic research library is closer to being a reality today with the rise of the Internet as an information-sharing and distribution "collaboratorium" that helps the enterprise better understand itself and transform itself. Educational institutions have the same potential to build an electronic campus infrastructure and to build their own knowledge networks so that their customers—their students—can share information electronically with faculty and peers alike, whether they are on-campus students or distance learners. Thus, educational institutions need to be learning organizations as well. They need to be more conscious of how they transfer and share knowledge and how effectively they are using technology to do so.

Before Gutenberg, information was shared primarily by monks in medieval monasteries. Retrieval of this information was difficult, copying was laboriously slow, and cataloguing of information was virtually nonexistent. After Gutenberg, information was published and disseminated more readily, but the cataloguing and indexing of information was still slow and laborious, making information retrieval difficult at best. In more recent predigital times—the era of print publishing, analog media, and manual cataloguing—information is still not easily catalogued, indexed, and shared.

In this early Digital Age in which we are working and learning, a vast array of unstructured digital information is available via the computer. The problem is that most high-tech organizations that seek to be learning organizations are choking on "infoglut"—too much information that is not easily indexed, catalogued, retrieved, or shared by the knowledge workers. Unfortunately, in education, many institutions are still in the pre-Gutenberg stage where information is not yet in digital form. Nevertheless, in the more mature phase of the Digital Age (a state that no one in industry or education has quite reached yet), infoglut will be alleviated as media objects are catalogued, indexed, and "pushed" to the knowledge worker (and student) as needed.

Web Knowledge Transfer Enablement

With the rise of the digital economy, the Internet, and the World Wide Web knowledge network, enterprises are better able to disseminate and share information within and outside of the corporation on a global scale. They become cognizant of who they are and who their customers are.

In the world of electronic work teams, knowledge workers are manipulating bits more and atoms less. Companies like 3M, Boeing, Ford, Chevron, and BP are actively building knowledge-sharing cultures internally. Others like IBM, Pfizer, Hewlett-Packard, Honda, and Xerox are providing financial rewards for employees who follow competence models for knowledge sharing. Externally, GE, Netscape, Ritz Carlton, and many others are collecting customer knowledge and using it to create new products and services (Sveiby).

As knowledge managers, our roles should be focused on the evolution of knowledge objects from analog to digital, from paper-based information to electronic information that is indexed and catalogued—not only in industry, but also in academia (Davenport and Prusak). In short, the goal of knowledge management is to capture individuals' tacit knowledge, store it, spread it, and reuse it. Our goal in technical communication education must be to teach students how to be effective knowledge managers in this new digital environment. An important goal in both industry and academia is to build the digital data bank or library, the active storehouse of knowledge that comprises the electronic corporate memory in industry and the electronic campus curriculum and content in education.

THE UNIVERSAL CAMPUS NETWORK

In the near future, the marketplace may well demand a tighter educational certification process for technical communication and other professions, much as there is in law and medicine, thereby forcing colleges and universities to provide more standardized courses. In so doing, the universities will be setting up a structure for knowledge sharing and degree sharing between schools. Multiple universities offering the same degree may begin to see the wisdom of establishing partnerships with each other to give students the best possible curriculum and instruction in the areas that make up a discipline.

The Economic Realities of the Electronic University

Once local geographic boundaries are broken down by Web-based distance education and students are no longer restricted to particular geographic areas to obtain their education, we will experience a more capitalistic approach to education and the birth of a Universal Campus Network. The Universal Campus Network will allow students to consume the best possible interactive courses and content via the Web, no matter what their parent institution is. Professional or regional associations may take the lead regarding certification and promotion of partnerships between industry and education and between educational institutions working together to build the electronic content and the electronic sharing of information within the disciplines. The driving force behind this interaction among the educational institutions will not be great faculty lecturers, but great facilitators who can work with students in a truly collegial, interactive, entertaining, and participative style.

As colleges and universities come to realize that education need not be restricted to a particular place and time, the focus of spending will change dramatically at each institution. Schools that charge too much tuition may experience decreased enrollments because their customers will be able to obtain equally good content and interaction elsewhere for less. Schools that do not invest in their technology infrastructure will lose business in this universal campus environment. It will not matter if a new building is erected, if a new student center is built. What will matter is how much money and support and how many resources are focused on the electronic campus network and on faculty development and staff to support the network.

The digital revolution in the workplace has already happened. It is time for education to participate in the revolution and to transform its vision of learning and consequently its campus into an electronic one.

The Electronic Discipline and the Death of the Academic Department

The organizational structure in high-tech knowledge industries is generally flat; thus, departments have become a thing of the past. Though practically obsolete in industry, departments are still extant in education. However, in the Digital Age, the number of faculty in a particular department is about as valuable and important an accreditation criterion as the number of books in a physical campus library. It is much less important in the Digital Age how many books are in the campus library when an increasingly vast library of electronic research information is available via the Web.

In an electronic educational environment, faculty resource sharing between disciplines becomes commonplace. Why not have instructors from different disciplines (including technical communication) within a school of engineering, for example, teach classes in which there are cross-functional teams of students learning and working together on interdisciplinary projects that cross old departmental boundaries?

The knowledge industry is changing. Unless we, within institutions of higher education, wish to become obsolete as knowledge-sharing and knowledge-dissemination vehicles, we must change too. A viable alternative, from a business perspective, is the rise and proliferation of the Microsoft or Novell Certified Engineer, the IBM Certified Technical Communication Specialist, or the Arthur Andersen Certified Knowledge Transfer Specialist. If we in education do not satisfy the needs of industry, industry will set up its own virtual campus and replace us (Schank).

THE FUTURE IS NOW IN VIRTUAL EDUCATION

For institutions of higher learning, there is an alternative to an engineering certificate from Microsoft University or to a technical communication certificate from IBM University—not through competing with industry, but through joining forces with industry.

California Virtual University

California Virtual University (CVU) serves as a virtual campus, an electronic interface to distance education programs and courses at the member institutions in California. The mission of CVU is to expand access beyond the traditional campus by providing quality, certified distance education, and to make California a global leader in research and development of distance education methods, practice, and delivery via the Internet. CVU itself offers no degrees. As of 1999, nearly one-third of the 300 accredited colleges in California have joined. Corporate sponsors of CVU currently include International Thomson Publishing, Cisco Systems, Sun Microsystems, and Pacific Bell, among others. (For more information and the latest updates on this "cooperative," see the California Virtual University Web site.)

Western Governors University

Another significant example of a "virtual university" via the Internet is Western Governors University (WGU). A collaboration of industry and higher education, WGU provides educational access by means of a virtual university to a widely dispersed student body and to employees who need workplace training. Incorporated in January 1997, WGU continues to grow rapidly. With nearly twenty governors participating, and with corporate sponsors including IBM, Microsoft, 3Com, Apple, International Thomson Publishing, AT&T, Sun Microsystems, and MCI, WGU had an initial budget in 1998 of over $12 million. IBM has constructed a prototype virtual campus interface to WGU, accessible via the Web.

Unlike CVU, WGU students access distance education from nontraditional providers of education services, including large and small corporations. This interjects an element of competition for universities, ensuring that they provide what the customers need at a price they can afford. Students can access a broad range of educational opportunities through WGU from traditional and nontraditional educational sources. In its pilot phase, WGU is offering associate's degrees only. It plans to offer bachelor's degrees and beyond through its member schools. (For more information and the latest developments on this initiative, see the Western Governors University Web site.)

Implications for Education

It is likely that these virtual universities and others not yet in existence will change the nature of education in the twenty-first century. Certainly the existence of these virtual "cooperatives" may foster what many consumers of education have been seeking for a long time: lower-priced, better-quality, and more accessible educational products.

ELEMENTS FOR SUCCESS IN THE DIGITAL AGE

From an educational perspective, one of the major handicaps of our technical communication discipline is that we have not yet rid ourselves of our English department roots. The result is that, based on factors such as faculty promotion and tenure requirements, our curriculum focuses heavily on rhetoric and writing and not enough on software development, electronic communication, and the other technology aspects of our discipline that are integral to the success of the professional technical communicator. Knowing your audience is certainly an important aspect of our field, but it need not be the main focus of every course in the technical communication curriculum.

Based on my experience developing and implementing the Master of Science-Technical Communications Management (MSTCO) program at Mercer University, what follows are questions to consider regarding the technical communication program at your institution of higher learning and its readiness for the twenty-first century:

- Is content oriented toward knowledge management and electronic communication methods and technologies; or is it oriented toward rhetoric and the writing of linear, paper-based information?

- Is the program located in a school or college of engineering; or is it located within an English department?

- Do the faculty have extensive industry experience (not just one or two "consulting gigs" at one or two companies)?

- Have the curriculum and courses been upgraded to reflect the emphasis on electronic communication methods and technologies and the use of the Web as a communication and instructional medium?

- Do students collaborate with each other electronically via the Web, using chat rooms and e-mail?

- Are your instructors using active learning strategies for facilitating knowledge management and transfer; or are they following the traditional teaching paradigm of lecture, discussion, and conventional written assignments?

- Are the student activities and deliverables team-based, with electronic peer review, revision, and posting via the Web; or are the deliverables paper-based and individually written, with evaluations prepared only by the instructor?

As you might suspect, your answers to these questions will likely determine whether you are successful as an educational institution in the discipline of technical communication in the twenty-first century.

CONCLUSION

Our future depends upon our willingness to change as technology changes. We now have the opportunity to undergo a business transformation, to redefine and revitalize our role and mission as educators and as knowledge sharers and disseminators through the use of communication technologies. Those educational institutions unwilling or unable to transform themselves may simply not survive the next wave of change brought about by further advancements in communication technologies. In technical communication education, we have every reason to undergo this transformation, for our discipline is inextricably intertwined with the knowledge management revolution. Our future is tied directly to the electronic dissemination and sharing of knowledge via the Internet and its successors.

NOTE

Originally published in *Technical Communication Quarterly* 8.1 (Winter 1999): 9–20. Reprinted with permission.

WORKS CITED

Bush, Vannevar. "As We May Think." *Atlantic Monthly* 176 (1945): 101–8.

California Virtual University Design Team. "California Virtual University." 1998. 1 Aug. 1999 <http://www.california.edu/>.

Curry School of Education. ". . . On the Term 'Academical Village.' " 1998. 1 Aug. 1999 <http://curry.edschool.virginia.edu/go/academical/>.

Davenport, Thomas H., and Laurence Prusak. *Working Knowledge: How Organizations Manage What They Know*. New York: McGraw-Hill, 1997.

Graubard, Stephen R., and Paul Leclerc, eds. *Books, Bricks and Bytes: Libraries in the Twenty-First Century*. New Brunswick, NJ: Transactions Publishing, 1998.

Hibbard, Justin, and Karen M. Carrillo. "Knowledge Revolution." *Information Week Online*, 5 Jan. 1998. 1 Aug. 1999 <http://www.informationweek.com>.

Lieberman, Debra A. "Learning to Learn Revisited: Computers and the Development of Self-Directed Learning Skills." *Journal of Research on Computing in Education* 23 (1991): 391–95.

Malhotra, Yogesh. "Organizational Learning and Learning Organizations: An Overview." *@Brint.Com*. 1996. 1 Aug. 1999 <http://www.brint.com/papers/orglrng.htm>.

McCormack, Colin, and David Jones. *Building a Web-Based Education System*. New York: John Wiley and Sons, 1997.

Negroponte, Nicholas. *Being Digital*. New York: Alfred A. Knopf, 1995.

Resnick, Lauren, and L. E. Klopfer, eds. *Toward Rethinking the Curriculum.* Alexandria, VA: Association for Supervision and Curriculum Development, 1987.

Sacks, Peter. *Generation X Goes to College: An Eye-Opening Account of Teaching in Postmodern America.* Chicago: Open Court Publishing, 1996.

Schank, Roger C. *Virtual Learning: A Revolutionary Approach to Building a Highly Skilled Workforce.* New York: McGraw-Hill, 1997.

Schneider, Daniel. "Teaching and Learning with Internet Tools." *TECFA Education and Technologies.* 1994. 1 Aug. 1999 <http://tecfa.unige.ch/edu/-comp/edu-ws94/contrib/schneider/schneide.book.html>.

Senge, Peter. *The Fifth Discipline: The Art and Practice of the Learning Organization.* New York: Doubleday, 1994.

Sherry, Loraine. "Issues in Distance Learning." *International Journal of Educational Telecommunications* 1.4 (1996): 337–65.

Sveiby, Karl E. "What Is Knowledge Management?" 1998. 1 Aug. 1999 <http://www.sveiby.com.au/KnowledgeManagement.html>.

Tapscott, Don. *The Digital Economy: Promise and Peril in the Age of Networked Intelligence.* New York: McGraw-Hill, 1995.

———. *Growing Up Digital: The Rise of the Net Generation.* New York: McGraw-Hill, 1997. Wertheim, Edward. "Learning and Behavior Modification: A Technical Note." 1997. 1 Aug. 1999 <http://www.cba.neu.edu/~ewertheim/indiv/learn.htm>.

Western Governors Association, Western Governors University. 1998. 1 Aug. 1999 <http://www.wgu>.

Chapter 4

Critical Reflections: Political Philosophy and Web Technology

John Steel

INTRODUCTION

Discourses on Web technology range from nightmare visions of the future in which we become enslaved by technology and its drivers, to utopian panaceas for our complex dialogues and interactions. Issues that shape and inform these discourses, however, carry with them familiar overarching themes: ownership, control, utility, content, and access, to name but a few. Also, in an age where philosophical reflection is perceived as less and less relevant to our existence, and real critical debate is in effect "dumbed down"—consensual politics is the norm—I argue that in this post-millennium world, the notion of critical appraisal should be reestablished.

One way of initiating this process is by looking afresh at a number of key issues and considering different modes of analysis and critique. This chapter is an attempt at the critical reappraisal I argue for. I intend to take a unique look at Web-based pedagogy from the viewpoint of competing philosophical perspectives: Utilitarianism, Liberalism, and Marxism. As these three philosophical positions provided analyses of aspects of the Industrial Revolution, it is my contention that they each have something to offer the new "Information Revolution." Also, each of these perspectives provides the opportunity to scrutinize the merits and values of Web technology in relation to pedagogy, from uniquely different theoretical standpoints.

In sum, this chapter offers a different way of thinking about education and technology and its place in education structures and processes. By providing an analysis of the World Wide Web from a selection of competing political theories, I hope to add useful insight and stimulate a novel way of thinking about issues concerning democratization, liberty, equality, technology, education, and censorship as they impact teaching and learning on the Web.

CONTEXT

Technology in one form or another, since at least the time of Socrates, has impacted on our experiences and perceptions of learning and what it means to acquire and disseminate knowledge. This was accelerated by the advent of the printing press in 1476. Since its invention, information technology and its gradual proliferation has impacted on such discourses in a multitude of situations and contexts to varying degrees. These discourses are not abstract Platonic forms; they do not exist in some philosophical ether, but are part of the real living social world, where technology impacts on real social and political structures, movements, events, and ideas. The way we think about knowledge and its uses and values, particularly in the sphere of education, is being redefined and reformulated. Also within these discourses are notions of the social, political, and economic value of education set against notions of education as some higher goal. Utilizing a select analysis from political philosophy within these contexts can enlighten our understanding of the issues and stimulate debate.

COMPETING PERSPECTIVES

Utilitarianism

Utilitarianism was a product of seventeenth and eighteenth century Enlightenment thinking. The principal intellectual contribution to Utilitarian philosophy was made by Jeremy Bentham (1748–1832). Often considered a nineteenth century thinker, Bentham was a child of the eighteenth century Enlightenment, and his philosophy displays this emphatically. However, in order to make sense of Bentham's contribution and how it can be applied to Web-based pedagogy, it is necessary to briefly analyze the foundations of Bentham's political philosophy and its methodological structure.

The main (but by no means only) focus of Bentham's life was political and legal reform. In short, Bentham was concerned with the organization and structure of social institutions in the context of formulating a critique of existing (and as he saw it) inadequate law, and with developing the blueprint for a state and its institutions which would operate on a purely rational basis.

Influenced by writers such as John Locke, David Hume and Montesquieu, Bentham formulated possibly his most famous contribution to political philosophy, the "principle of utility" or the "greatest happiness principle." Bentham hoped that the formulation and application of this principle would make him

"the Newton of the moral world" and "provide a philosophy for radical reform-
ers" (Plamenatz 179, 214). For Bentham, there was only one criterion for evaluating or even analyzing legal and constitutional systems, that being the
maximization of happiness of the greatest number under that law. Simply put,
for Bentham it is only natural for humans to seek that which will provide pleasure and avoid that which will induce pain. From this starting point, it is possible
to view actions as either good, in that they promote pleasure or happiness, or
bad, in that they bring about pain or displeasure. For him, all human actions
seek to promote pleasure and avoid pain. Famously, Bentham states:

Nature has placed mankind under the governance of two sovereign masters, *pain* and
pleasure. It is for them alone to point out what we ought to do, as well as to determine
what we shall do. . . . They govern us all in all we do, in all we say, in all we think:
every effort we can make to throw off our subjection, will serve but to demonstrate and
confirm it. (11)

Bentham argues that in acting according to the principles of utility, we are not
acting against the essential nature of man, but the opposite. For him, then, it is
clear that all rational people, by the "natural constitution of the human frame,"
defer to the principle of utility in everyday life (Bentham 13–14).

Education and Progress

Progress and innovation, motivated by the desire to maximize "happiness" in
the individual and society as a whole, represent a strong current within the
Utilitarian creed. So what does this mean for a Utilitarian consideration of Web
technology in the context of education? Let us consider the latter first. For
Utilitarianism, education and its diffusion was *the* crucial factor that would enable society to progress—the foundation of Utilitarianism's radicalism lay in
the social and moral weight it places on the value of education. Education
was the cornerstone of a "good society" both morally and rationally; education
for the masses would enable them to overcome the servitude and ignorance in
which they were placed by the aristocracy and government. It would mean that
the people would be in possession of the knowledge of the causes of their misery
and respond accordingly by spreading "reason among their subjects to grant
arrangements more calculated to serve the general good" (Bentham 120). It was
logically necessary that a greater number of individuals be made aware of their
ignorance and greed, and shown the specific factors that would greatly increase
their long-term happiness. They could not, it was argued, hesitate but to act
upon their better judgment and rational faculties.

According to Utilitarianism, the foundation of human error lay in the lack of
education and people's ignorance of their best interests. Thus, unhindered expansion and extension of education are more than merely useful to society: they
are necessary to maximize the stock of happiness of all, by eradicating ignorance. It was generally argued by Utilitarians such as Bentham, John Roebuck,

and Francis Place that if society as a whole became better educated and free to access and judge opinions from whatever quarter, the net benefit to all of society would be great. This is because if the diffusion of knowledge were to go ahead unhindered, then a movement toward some greater understanding could be achieved.

Web Technology as a Contribution to Moral and Social Good?

From this outline of the Utilitarian perspective on education, it should be reasonable to assert that with the prevalent utilization of technologies such as the World Wide Web, the diffusion of education is enhanced and the net gains for society are great. Would Bentham and his followers agree?

Any technological innovation that can increase the "diffusion of knowledge" would be embraced by the Utilitarian perspective on the grounds that the more knowledge available for society to access the better. However, knowledge for Utilitarians has to be "useful" knowledge. The Web is crammed full of spurious material that "sells" itself as "useful information." Even the discerning surfer cannot avoid being confronted by crass and hollow material "out there" on the Net.

So how would Utilitarianism cope with this factor? It is my contention that Utilitarians would view the Web and its beneficial effects on society as outweighing the negative effects. In true Utilitarian style, if the good effects outweigh the bad, then the choice is easy. Ideally, a society that has better access to a wide range of information is far better equipped to make rational judgments than one with no such access. Also, because people are better educated, this would encourage increased levels of participation in the social, cultural, economic, and political spheres of society.

For Utilitarians this can only be beneficial for society as a whole. Moreover, Utilitarians would argue that given the fact that people are better educated and better informed, the process of democracy works much more effectively and there is less likelihood of misrule by government. Utilitarians would argue that law and order would prevail, as social disorder is largely a consequence of ignorance, which would be eradicated through increased levels of communication and education brought about by the World Wide Web and the Internet. Also, given that channels of communication should be open and democratic, control of the medium should be minimal and not subject to censorship. The benefits for education and society as a whole would be great; more education and increased levels of participation can only be good for society as it becomes more enlightened and the common good prevails. Is the Web the utopian technological realization of Utilitarianism? A consideration of pedagogical processes from a Utilitarian perspective may help answer this question.

New and emerging pedagogical styles that are increasingly related to Web-based learning would, I think, present Bentham and his Utilitarian colleagues with a number of problems. Late twentieth century approaches to teaching and learning are now more concerned with the learner and the learning than with the teacher and what is taught. Essentially, teaching and learning are now being theorized as a "dialogue" in which the process of learning is situated or mediated (Laurillard). This is in sharp contrast to traditional, so-called transmission modes of teaching and learning in which pedagogy is essentially the practice of agents (teachers) passing knowledge to other agents (students). Moreover, it is increasingly argued that "student-centered" approaches lend themselves to Web technology in the sense that learning is directed by students and is relevant to their personal contexts and understanding (Forsyth).

Given the above considerations regarding learning and teaching methods, what impact does this have on Utilitarianism? One major criticism of Utilitarianism lies in its didactic approach to knowledge wherein if facts cannot be known, then some movement toward a greater understanding of those facts is desired. The educational process that Bentham advocated is somewhat different from that which lends itself to the Web and the mode of teaching most suited to its application. For the Utilitarians, mediated learning would, I argue, be perceived as betraying Enlightenment principles in that facts, as with utility in general, are objective "things" that can be measured and quantified. Learning that comes about as a result of subjective reflection, or which is student-centered, is a very different form of learning than that which Utilitarianism would advocate. This is because knowledge is conceived in different terms, that is, facts that have to be discovered and known, rather than emergent subjective reflective practice—the mode of learning perceived as fitting in neatly with the Web paradigm. (See Forsyth; McCain; Sandholtz, Ringstaff, and Dwyer; Tait.)

This is not the only difficulty with Utilitarianism. Obviously, the connection it makes between enlightenment and social harmony is, to say the least, somewhat spurious and paternalistic. What then are we left with? From a Utilitarian perspective, Web technology as an entity would be seen as beneficial for society as a whole, as its bad effects are outweighed by its good—that is, increased access to and democratization of information, enhanced communication, and, importantly, as a result of these factors, greater participation, if only on an intellectual level, in the affairs of society.

In terms of the criticisms of Web technology and its impact on education, the pedagogical process to which Web technology lends itself (mediated and student-centered) is more difficult to accommodate within the Enlightenment, Utilitarian concept of understanding and knowledge dissemination. However, what we are left with is a notion of learning and discovery of knowledge, in whatever form, as somehow contributing to a notion of the "greater good."

Liberalism

Philosophical arguments for "freedom of learning" stem from the Renaissance and the Reformation. Such ideas, which stressed freedom of thought and conscience of the individual, formed the precursor to modern Liberalism; and it is on notions of freedom of thought, or, more precisely, freedom of speech from a Liberal perspective, that Web-based pedagogy is to be considered. The first systematic articulation for freedom of speech was made by John Milton (1608–1674). In *Areopagitica: A Speech for the Liberty of Unlicensed Printing*, Milton argues that censorship entails "the discouragement of all learning and the stop of truth, not only by dissexercising and blunting our abilities in what we know already, but by hindering and cropping the discovery that might yet be further made, both in religious and in civil wisdom" (quoted in Bury 78).

The argument that censorship impedes "civil" wisdom, or what in modern terms can be called human progress, has been further developed by a number of other philosophers since Milton, the most notable of which was made by John Stuart Mill in his most famous work, *On Liberty*. Published in 1859, *On Liberty* gave a philosophical defense of individual liberty, in which a defense of free speech was made that, at first glance, sits well with the ethos that surrounds Web technology and the Internet, that is, freedom of information, unfettered debate, and freedom of expression.

Free Speech and the Argument from Truth

For Mill, true understanding can only be achieved if all restrictions on inquiry are absent. He went to great lengths to formulate his arguments, which have significantly contributed to modern conceptions of "the argument from truth." For Mill and other Liberal defenders of free speech, it is only in the marketplace of ideas that we can gain any understanding that can lead us toward some approximation of "the truth."

[T]he peculiar evil of silencing the expression of an opinion is, that it is robbing the human race; posterity as well as the existing generation; those who dissent from the opinion, still more than those who hold it. If the opinion is right, they are deprived the opportunity of exchanging error for truth: if wrong, they lose, what is almost as great a benefit, the clearer perception and livelier impression of truth, produced by its collision with error. (Mill 16)

The argument from truth therefore allows a set of processes that activate a movement toward some greater understanding. With understanding unveiled and open to all, society will benefit. Also, once understanding is gained, unfettered debate is still necessary in order to test and ensure the validity of the arguments. The basis of this claim can be found in a notion of individual rights. For Liberalism the focal point of society is the realm of the individual. Individuals' rights are inviolable, whether they speak freely on the right to gain profit from another's labor, the right to own property, or the right to free speech. Mill's argument from truth, then, has at its core the rights of the individual, over and above those measures that might be used to stop the search for knowledge and understanding, and its dissemination.

In terms of an analysis of technology, at face value, the advent of the Web and the freedom of speech that it yields fit well with a Millian justification for freedom of speech. Increased levels of communication brought about by the Web would be seen as desirable within the marketplace of ideas, as no single opinion would dominate and all beliefs and opinions would be contestable.

It is clear that Mill's strong Utilitarian influence would emerge and that the marketplace of ideas would be seen as a benefit to society. Mill would embrace the Web, but with concerns about those who exercise the most power over the medium and possible ramifications should this power go unchecked. Most obvious are concerns over censorship and the "dumbing down" of the content.

However, is it safe to assert that Mill's defense of free speech based on the argument from truth is a valid one, particularly in relation to Web-based pedagogy? Frederick Schauer notes that the argument from truth (and variations thereof) "all share a belief that freedom of speech is not an end but a means, a means of identifying and accepting truth" (16). The main problem with this justification of free speech is that of the *supposed* connection between free and open discussion and "knowledge." Is it correct, then, to assume that open and rational discussion is the only method of inquiry? Schauer correctly asserts that the "rational" search for some approximation of truth is optimistic, as history shows us that rationalism sometimes loses out to other human traits—fallibility and emotion, to name but two.

Also, why should we place truth or the search for knowledge above other social values? Even if truth and falsehood confront us side by side, it does not necessarily follow that falsity be rejected. Should we assume, as Mill does, that all knowledge must be rational and that rationality will always triumph over irrationality? If one spends any time on the Web, one soon finds that this is not the case.

Does it follow, then, on these terms, that the Web, particularly Web-based pedagogy, is counter to Liberalism? An analysis of Liberalism and its consideration of Web-based pedagogy need not be restricted to a Millian analysis. However, given the historical importance of the struggle for freedom of speech and its relationship with human understanding and learning, a reconciliation with Liberalism should be possible. Indeed, if one turns to the notion of democracy, that reconciliation can be articulated.

Free Speech, Democracy, and the Web

One of the key components of Web technology in terms of its perceived social good is often stressed in terms of its democratizing nature. In sum, the use of the Web is understood as potentially providing everyone (with the means to access it) the opportunity to express their opinions and values and to contribute to social, cultural, and political discourse and debate. In terms of such technology applied to education, the process is similar, as information flows freely and is as unfettered as the technology allows.

In order that a democratic system operate effectively, two fundamental prerequisites need to be in place, both of which (incidentally) depend upon freedom of speech. First, "free speech is crucial in providing the sovereign electorate with the information it needs to exercise its sovereign power, and to engage in the deliberative process requisite to the intelligent use of that power." Second, "freedom to criticize makes possible holding government officials, as public servants, properly accountable to their masters, the population at large" (Schauer 36).

Although this particular principle may sound attractive at first glance, it does present us with some particular problems. The argument from democracy is based on a notion of sovereign power. However, if the sovereign people so wished, they could restrict freedom of speech as they could any other liberty. They could, in theory, delegate their power to a single authority and negate its power altogether. Also, the "will of the people" could have authoritarian consequences as individual freedom and choice are stifled.

Mill anticipated this particular problem, as we see when he warned of the "tyranny of the majority." However, Schauer points to a possible solution by introducing the notion of equality. If we look at a situation in which every person is able to participate freely and equally, with equal respect for individual dignity and choice, we can see a move away from democracy as majority rule. Implanted in this conception is a notion of equal respect for opinion and choice. However, vast and complex societies make such an ideal difficult to comprehend and problematic in practical terms.

Thus Web technology, if one is to analyze it from a Liberal perspective, is beneficial in that it allows for information to be processed and delivered across the spectrum of society. Society has to be educated in order for a true democracy to operate, as noted by the eighteenth and nineteenth century Utilitarians. In terms of the argument from democracy, it is important that Web content not be subject to censorship, as censorship of the Web, as with censorship of free speech, can only act to disenfranchise and alienate. In this sense education and democracy are linked together, and the Web can be seen as an active component in the educational and democratic processes. Yet, does the Internet make education truly democratic? I shall consider this question in the next section.

Marxism

It seems now in the post–Cold War world that Marx's thoughts and the ideologies that called themselves Marxist have little relevance in this fast-closing millennium (Fukuyama). I argue, however, in the spirit of this chapter, that some innovative understanding might be gained of the Web and its relationship with education and pedagogy from a reassessment of Marx's ideas and their influence. In terms of the focus of this discussion I will concentrate on a Marxian critique of Web technology as well as pointing to the possible liberating potential of the World Wide Web in learning and teaching.

From a Marxian perspective the recent Information Revolution as a phenomenon can be understood as part of the ongoing changing nature of capitalist accumulation which is transforming an industrial society into a post-industrial information society (see McChesney, Meiskins Wood, and Bellamy Foster; Davis, Hirschl, and Stack). One would think that Marxists should challenge and resist this trend at all costs; indeed, a Marxian analysis would find much to criticize in the new information age, and some of these criticisms are highlighted below. However, it is my contention that a Marxian analysis of Web technology, particularly in relation to Web-based pedagogy, may not be as damning as one might expect.

Education as Ideology and the Fetishization of Technology

Marx himself had very little to say about education. However, if the conceptual method Marx employed to analyze social relations and political economy is applied to education, a strong critique of the system of education under capitalism emerges. In Marxian terms, a capitalist system of education is perceived as a process of a particular form of production and thus, as with all forms of production under capitalism, is dehumanizing and alienating (see Marx; also Mandel and Novack). In *Marxism and Education*, Sarup cites Illich, Reimer, Postman and other "de-schoolers" when he discusses the alienating character of education in capitalist society (129–47).

For example, students can be perceived both as workers—competing against one another for better grades or higher merit—and as commodities which, through the educational process, are transformed into products for the market, that is, the workplace after the completion of their studies. The teacher also can be understood in similar terms. The teacher is, however, also a producer of a commodity (the student, and in part, the curriculum) as well as being a product of the capitalist educational system.

Importantly, knowledge and information are also significant commodities under capitalism, and these are represented in Marxian terms as ideology. Sarup notes that this ideological product is essential for capitalist development, as it is used as a commodity in the capitalist market (Sarup). Furthermore, this commodity acts as a key cohesive element of the capitalist system. Given that industrial societies are dependent on ideology, education performs specific functions, the most valuable of which is the production of knowledge and information as a commodity or capital, and one that helps reinforce divisions within society, as the status quo is left largely unchallenged. On these terms, democracy is in fact an illusion.

Obviously, in terms of the production and delivery of information and knowledge, technological developments have an important part to play. However, technology can be perceived not only as an "ideological transmission tool" in terms of education and the Web, but also as a fetishized entity in itself. Technology, or more appropriately for this discussion, technological innovation, in the context of Web technology can be analyzed also in terms of a commodity and as part and parcel of commodity production.

Robins and Webster argue that the so-called IT Revolution, with its increased emphasis on technology skills acquisition, is occurring at the expense, and to the detriment, of other more traditional educational values. They argue that rather than teaching students skills for the world of work, educators engender the limitation of key skills. They question for whom and for what purpose the IT Revolution is taking place, arguing that big business will inevitably benefit the most. They also argue that there is "a role for the critical disciplines of sociology, political theory, history, cultural studies, to demystify the ideology of the 'IT Revolution' " (156).

Educational Technology and Pedagogy: Toward Emancipation?

Given the criticisms noted above, is it possible that educational technology has any emancipatory qualities, or does the Web and its use within the classroom or lecture theater, while it operates within capitalist society, offer no hope to the Marxian creed? Clearly Marxists do have a number of fundamental problems with the new information revolution and its effects on the disadvantaged and disenfranchised. However, I intend to show that this need not be the case. Indeed, the opposite view, that of educational technology as instrumental to any emancipatory project, shall be outlined below, with specific reference to critical pedagogy.

The roots of critical pedagogy can be traced back to the intellectual legacy of Walter Benjamin, Max Horkheimer, Theodor Adorno, Herbert Marcuse, later Jurgen Habermas, and other "critical theorists," also known as the Frankfurt School. The thrust of the movement centered on thought and action in order to achieve emancipatory and democratic ends.

Critical theorists argue that an understanding of historical thinking coupled with a progressive critique of existing power structures is necessary in order to break down the mystified social relations of capitalist society. Historical memory was significant in that, for Adorno in particular, "the loss of historical memory was the precondition for all forms of domination" (Giroux and Freire xi). In forgetting past instances of struggle and domination, current processes of domination seemed "natural."

In addition to historical awareness, critique was necessary, as it would "unmask" power relations within structures and lay bare domination and oppression. Coupled with this critique—and imperative for the negation of cynicism—was the emphasis upon developing a "programmatic discourse for building alternative hopes and realizable visions" (Giroux and Freire xii). For theories of critical pedagogy this discriminating aspect is crucial, as, in education in particular, learning contexts are created where "learning is actively pursued as part of a radical project for new forms of ethical and political community" (Giroux and Freire xii).

Critical pedagogy is most notably associated with Paulo Freire. Freire argued that "education could improve the human condition, countering the effects of a psychology of oppression, and ultimately contributing what he considered the ontological vocation of humankind: humanisation" (Gadotti and Torres 1). Throughout his life, Freire attempted to apply his approach to teaching practice.

The process of learning for Freire is mutually supportive and not only leads to greater understanding, but is connected to empowerment. Learning is placed within a community context and practiced within an arena of cooperation and mediation between learners and educators. The process is "dialogical" in which the "approach to learning is characterized by co-operation and acceptance of interchangeability and mutuality in the roles of teacher and learner, demanding an atmosphere of mutual acceptance and trust. In this method, all teach and learn" (Heaney).

The analysis of the Frankfurt School has been adopted by a number of innovative theorists. For example, Olsen notes the "schizophrenic" nature of educational technology in that the positive aspects of using education technology are equal to the negative. He raises questions such as do computers lead to greater independence or *de*pendence on prescribed teaching formulae? Do they increase or decrease the perceived skillfulness of users, etc.? Even writing in 1987, Olsen notes the unbiased nature of literature on teaching and learning technology, with an emphasis on technology as an entity in its own right, with virtually no mention of the social aspects or impact of the technology on other spheres of life. He notes that such an emphasis emerges from a pro-technologist or "millennialist" perspective. He outlines a polemic discourse that identifies millennialist approaches set against so-called anti-technologists, or a "cataclysmic" viewpoint which observes "technical innovations as hyperextensions of dehumanizing processes of social, state, bureaucratic and mechanized control" (181). What emerges is a de facto moral debate on intentional action instead of engaging in debates about "overt technical effects," or processes of engagement with the media.

Olsen argues that in order to demystify the use of computers in education, it is important to thoroughly examine context, particularly in relation to differing individual and social interests and how these are served by the deployment of technology within education. Also, we should examine how group and individual intentions are represented in the relationship between educational institutions and industry, job markets and private consumption. He continues by noting that debates concerning the introduction of technology into education raise familiar questions around whose interests are served and at what expense.

Is it the interests of the students and teachers, the managers and administrators, or the software and hardware manufacturers and other associated businesses that are served? An interesting parallel is made to the similar impact of the Industrial Revolution and the subsequent "dislocation" of technology and social organization, in that the profound side-effects of such a revolution were wide. In locating technology within these parameters, the analogy is apt because of the extent to which technology impacts upon the production and work processes and their associated social phenomena. Historically, increased material gains have been made, but with devastating effects on old social forms, thus creating new inequalities.

According to Olsen, there is a second (and in my view more important) feature of the introduction of computers into education:

[I]t is the effect on our understanding of ourselves, others and the wider society and of how these find human agency and expressions as instances of volitional control. From this subjective vantage point, the reaction to and conceptualization of computers are important not just in terms of computers' real or potential *technical accomplishments* but also in ideals and ideas about them. These latter *function* personally and ideologically, as icons of our fears and dreams. In this usage, the discourse on computers arouses questions of a moral vision of society. (184)

The computer (and the Web in particular), then, gives us immense opportunities in education, but we must be wary to avoid the pitfalls that have surrounded education in the past. As Olsen notes, "On the one hand, the computer offers an almost assured increase to our real wealth, by giving us access, control and processing information with unprecedented speed and efficiency. Yet on the other hand, in the area of distribution, it is potentially a multiplier of the inequalities that stratify classes, genders and First and Third worlds" (203).

That said, the potential for egalitarian movements to develop and challenge the status quo is increased, particularly via a discriminating approach as illustrated by critical pedagogy. The debate around Web technology in teaching and learning, if this perspective is adopted, broadens and has the potential to be inclusive rather than exclusive as barriers to communication are broken down.

CONCLUSION

It has been the purpose of this chapter to stimulate new thinking on the role of Web technology and the Internet in learning and teaching from particular philosophical positions. The stimulus for this is to reflect on a number of key issues related to Web-based teaching and learning in a novel and perhaps useful manner. It is the case that the ideologies discussed above play a less important role in the modern world than in days gone by. Utilitarianism in its nineteenth century guise is generally only discussed in academic circles with regard to its internal coherence or incoherence. Liberalism also, by and large, has been supplanted by neo-Liberal social democracy in the West, which has within it elements of classical Liberalism and strands of a variegated form of Utilitarianism. Marxism also has been widely discredited as a political end, but still provides useful analyses in certain instances.

In terms of what the discussion has left us with, day-to-day problems of Web-based learning and teaching can be considered in a different light. For example, issues related to moral and social good, democracy, equality, empowerment, censorship, and free speech have all been touched upon in sections of this chapter. It is my hope that the discussion has provided the means to consider or reconsider aspects of Web-based learning from these philosophical perspectives.

Indeed, it is my hope that this brief analysis might stimulate further deliberation and research on fundamental precepts.

For example, we can see from the above discussion that a Utilitarian analysis, although at odds over the nature of knowledge, views mass education and any means to its optimum delivery as a social good. How often is education considered in these terms on a public platform? Also, the Liberal analysis allows us to approach Web-based learning as being part of the marketplace of ideas, which, if allowed to flourish, provide the means for individual fulfillment.

However, how far can such a principle be realized when the "marketplace of ideas" is monopolized by such a narrow field of debate? This is answered to some degree by the Marxian position, which sees education and technology as instruments and products of capitalist domination, but also views education as a means to emancipation whose project is enhanced with the adoption of technology. Still, in the post–Cold War world, has the notion of emancipation now evaporated?

What I have done in this chapter is attempt to stimulate thinking around the values of education—social, cultural, moral, and political. I see this as an important task since increasingly in educational institutions, particularly with regard to educational technology, the debate is less and less about the moral and social value of education, as has been highlighted above, and more about the fiscal priorities of educational managers and the cost-effectiveness of educational technology. If we start to think critically about the nature of education and its function in our society, then the problems we face as we enter the next century may seem a little less daunting.

NOTE

I would like to thank Professor Robert Cole, Dr. Stuart Horsman, Dr. Darren Webb, Alison Hudson, and Debra Tickle for their useful comments and support.

WORKS CITED

Adorno, Theodor, and Max Horkheimer. *Dialectic of Enlightenment*. London: Verso, 1979.

Benjamin, Walter. *Illuminations*. Ed. Hannah Arendt. New York: Schocken Books, 1986.

Bentham, Jeremy. *An Introduction to the Principles of Morals and Legislation*. London: Methuen, 1970.

Bury, John Bagnell. *A History of Freedom of Thought*. London: Oxford University Press, 1952.

Davis, Jim, Thomas Hirschl, and Michael Stack, eds. *Cutting Edge: Technology, Information, Capitalism and Social Revolution*. London: Verso, 1997.

Forsyth, Ian. *Teaching and Learning Materials and the Internet*. London: Kogan Page, 1996.

Fukuyama, Francis. *The End of History and the Last Man*. London: Hamish Hamilton, 1992.

Gadotti, Moacir, and Carlos Alberto Torres. *Paulo Freire: A Homage*. 1 Aug. 1999
    <http://nlu.nl.edu/ace/Homage.html>.
Giroux, Henry, and Paulo Freire. Series introduction to *Critical Pedagogy and Cultural
    Power*. Ed. David Livingstone. South Hadley, MA: Bergin and Garvey, 1987.
Habermas, Jurgen. *Knowledge and Human Interests*. Boston: Beacon Press, 1971.
———. *Theory and Practice*. London: Heinemann, 1974.
Heaney, Tom. "Issues in Freirean Pedagogy." 20 June 1995. 1 Aug. 1999 <http://nlu.
    nl.edu/ace/Resources/Documents/FreireIssues.html>.
Horkheimer, Max. *Critical Theory: Selected Essays*. New York: Herder and Herder,
    1972.
Laurillard, Diana. *Rethinking University Teaching: A Framework for the Effective Use
    of Educational Technology*. London: Routledge, 1993.
Mandel, Ernest, and George Novack. *The Marxist Theory of Alienation*. New York:
    Pathfinder Press, 1970.
Marcuse, Herbert. *One-Dimensional Man: Studies in the Ideology of Advanced Industrial
    Society*. London: Routledge and Kegan Paul, 1968.
Marx, Karl. *Economical and Philosophic Manuscripts of 1844*. London: Penguin, 1981.
Mill, John Stuart. *On Liberty*. Ed. Alburey Castell. Arlington Heights, IL: Harlan Da-
    vidson, 1947.
McCain, Charles H. *Plugged In and Turned On: Planning, Coordinating, and Managing
    Computer Supported Instruction*. Thousand Oaks, CA: Corwin Press, 1996.
McChesney, Robert, Ellen Meiskins Wood, and John Bellamy Foster, eds. *Capitalism
    and the Information Age: The Political Economy of the Global Communications
    Revolution*. New York: Monthly Review Press, 1998.
Olsen, C. Paul. "Who Computes?" In *Critical Pedagogy and Cultural Power*. Ed. David
    Livingstone. South Hadley, MA: Bergin and Garvey, 1987.
Plamenazt, John. *The English Utilitarians*. Oxford: Basil Blackwell, 1966.
Robins, Kevin, and Frank Webster. "Dangers of Information Technology and Respon-
    sibilities of Education." In *Information Technologies: Social Issues*. Ed. Ruth
    Finnegan, Graeme Salaman, and Kenneth Thompson. London: Open University,
    1990.
Roebuck, John Arthur, Francis Place, Henry Chapman, et al. *Pamphlets for the People*.
    Vols. 1 and 2. London: Charles Ely, 1835–1836.
Sandholtz, Judith, Cathy Ringstaff, and David Dwyer. *Teaching with Technology—Cre-
    ating Student-Centered Classrooms*. New York: Teachers College Press, 1997.
Sarup, Madan. *Marxism and Education*. London: Routledge and Kegan Paul, 1978.
Schauer, Frederick. *Free Speech: A Philosophical Enquiry*. Cambridge: Cambridge Uni-
    versity Press, 1982.
Tait, William. "Constructivist Internet Based Learning." *Active Learning*, 7 Dec. 1997:
    3–8.

Chapter 5

Communication Technologies in an Educational Environment: Lessons from a Historical Perspective

Patrick B. O'Sullivan

INTRODUCTION

New technologies have begun to transform business, politics, social relationships, and culture in the industrialized world. One area that has received tremendous interest is the ways in which new technologies are transforming education. From the national government policy initiatives to local school board decisions, greater incorporation of technology is viewed as a "technological fix" for low test scores and disappointing achievement levels. Sometimes, technology is introduced into classrooms based on the vague notion that "students need to be prepared for careers of the future" or because of a belief that more technology is always better. This utopian vision of how technology can improve education has been rightly critiqued as overly simplistic and misdirected even as spending is reallocated from traditional school supplies to computers and Internet connections.

What is often lost in the discussion about educational technology is a close examination of "appropriate" use of technologies in the classroom. Uncritical adoption of various technologies means that, too often, the tail wags the dog: pedagogical goals, curricula, and lesson plans are made subservient to technologies that were adopted to implement educational goals. Language, tone, and content of discussions about technology in the classroom suggest a relatively unsophisticated understanding of the complex nature of various technologies. Technology is almost always assumed to bring improvements, and critical assessment of possible tradeoffs is rare. This lack of understanding can lead to decisions about technology in education that are inefficient financially and ineffective pedagogically.

The goal of this analysis is to provide a framework for evaluating the "appropriateness" of technology uses in the classroom that can lead to better decisions about when, how, and with whom to incorporate various educational technologies. Scholars of communication technology, defined broadly, have developed perspectives on the relationships between technologies and the humans who create them. This provides a foundation for a deeper understanding of technology in general and educational technology in specific. Examining communication technology in particular is appropriate since, at its essence, the education process is a communication process. Applying this perspective to the narrower topic of educational technologies provides a framework for evaluating technology selection and implementation for effective and appropriate uses. This chapter incorporates three major sections: (1) a historical perspective on technologies to encourage a rethinking about, and a redefining of, technology itself; (2) a review of a growing body of research and theorizing about the implications of technology use for human interactions; and (3) an exemplar of how applying these ideas to analysis of educational technologies can provide insights to guide decisions shaping the selection and applications of the technologies.

UNDERSTANDING "TECHNOLOGY": HISTORICAL PERSPECTIVES

It has been fairly common in the American "now" culture to assume an ahistorical approach to modern problems. Nowhere is that tendency more prominent than in perspectives on new technologies. For many, it appears that computers burst onto the national scene in the 1980s, and the Internet came out of nowhere in the 1990s to dominate news and culture. For them, the term "technology" encompasses sophisticated electronic hardware such as computers, faxes, cellular telephones, pagers, modems, satellites, digital cameras, and the like. Thus, for many, the term "technology" is synonymous with "new, high-tech electronic gadgets."

An alternative view challenges this conceptualization, including the necessity of "newness" and even the necessity for some hardware, whether electronic or not. In contrast to the popular view, a conceptual and historical view suggests a far broader approach to the term "technology." A close examination of the term suggests that technology is a human construction that may—or may not—actually involve some form of hardware or artifact.

Defining Technology

From its linguistics roots, the term is fairly explicit: "techno" comes from the Greek word "techne," which means art or skill, and "-logy" means "the science of" or "the study of." Similarly, the *Oxford English Dictionary* defines technology as "the scientific study of the practical or industrial arts." In its broadest sense, then, "technology" has long been defined as the study of how things get done. Neither of those definitions implies that a tangible piece of hardware or equipment—an artifact—is necessary for a technology to exist, although they do not rule them out either. The focus is on goal-directed human activities. This suggests a shift in focus from the artifact to the ways in which humans accomplish their goals (perhaps, or perhaps not, using an artifact).

Other definitions also reflect the idea that "technology" cannot exist in isolation from human social constructions. Perrolle's view is that technology "is more than tools. It involves the social processes that produce tools, the social behaviors involved in using the tools, and the socially defined meanings of tools" (22). Similarly, Ball-Rokeach and Reardon note, "It is not so much the formal characteristics of a technology that determine its significance . . . but how it is used and whether it is used by people to, in some fashion, extend what they already do via other forms" (135).

If one accepts this view, then the term "technology" is no longer limited to computers or electronic equipment. Technology is a technique, a way of accomplishing a goal. Thus, "medical technology" can refer to surgical techniques developed to decrease the risk of infection or to administering combinations of drugs that reinforce each drug's effectiveness. "Agricultural technology" can refer to planting strategies developed to increase production and to plowing practices developed to reduce erosion. "Educational technologies" can refer to a wide range of techniques and practices in the classroom such as introducing group work strategies to facilitate collaboration and peer learning, sequencing of topics, and procedures to reinforce key ideas across content areas. Any one of these may—or may not—incorporate tangible artifacts. In essence, this view would argue that the broad group of activities that we call "education" itself is a technology for developing individuals and evolving society. The implications of this view will be discussed below.

"New" Versus "Old" Technologies

A historical perspective also argues against the notion of "newness" as being essential to a conceptualization of technology. The term "new" is, of course, a relative indicator that has different meanings in different historical settings. As historians of communication technologies have illustrated (e.g., Marvin), what we consider "old" was once new.

For example, most would not think of writing as a technology. However, thousands of years ago, written communication and the development of phonetic alphabets were revolutionary developments that allowed people to transcend time and space in their interactions, with significant consequences for the development of civilization (Fidler; Logan; Manguel). In this example, writing technology includes the artifacts of various materials used to make marks of some sort (scratches on bone, impressions in clay, carving in stone, pigment on papyrus, etc.) (Fidler; Schmandt-Besserat). But it was the system of symbolic communication that generated shared meanings to the markings that is at the center of what we consider "written communication."

An even earlier example of a communication technology, however, involves no artifacts at all. The development of spoken languages emerged as a means of accomplishing more efficient communication than was possible via signals and nonlanguage vocalics that anthropologists speculate were used prior to language. Thus, spoken language constitutes one of the earliest communication technologies ever created—and perhaps the most important technology, since every other form of communication (indeed human civilization) has built upon that foundation (Bickerton; DeFleur and Dennis; Fidler).

A bias toward "new" technologies is apparent even among scholars today. "Old" technologies, such as letters and the telephone, have been overlooked in the technology research (Fischer; Pool) even though everyday experience tells us that they are ubiquitous in social interactions. Thus, a historical perspective conceptualizes communication technology to include "old, low-tech" as well as "new, high-tech" forms.

The notion that older technologies are validly considered "technologies" suggests a need to reframe how to think about these technologies. If one sees a continuity through history of various technologies created to further human goals, then understanding the consequences of using older, established technologies may help illuminate consequences of newer, exotic-appearing technologies.

For example, Standage has documented how the development of the telegraph, and popular reaction to this then-astounding new technology, have strong parallels to current fervor surrounding its successor—the Internet. We may find that new and old technologies may be more alike than they are different, particularly in users' eyes. In addition, users may tend to use newer technologies in many of the same ways they did the older technologies, which suggests insights into current and future uses of newer technologies. Anyone who has followed the emergence of so many new innovations in various communication technologies has a sense of how difficult it is to predict which ones will be successful and which will not. To be able to make informed predictions, with some degree of probability, is a valuable contribution.

Relationships Between Older and Newer Technologies

Another lesson from the history of technologies is instructive here as well. A tendency is to view the history of technologies as a series of revolutions, in which a new form emerges to conquer and replace an older form. For example, it has been argued that the emergence of the printing press sparked a revolution in communication that had sweeping consequences for social upheaval and cultural development (Eisenstein; Fidler) and led to the age of print (McLuhan). Similarly, in the 1950s the rapid spread of television ended the dominance of radio, almost extinguished the movie industry, and has been an overwhelming cultural influence ever since (Fidler).

However, a closer look reveals that the persistent pattern is that older technologies tend to endure and to coexist with newer technologies rather than becoming extinct (Fidler). Key here is that the emergence of newer technologies can prompt a redefining of older technologies' ongoing roles and meanings in society. Although the roles of older technologies are often greatly reduced, they are not necessarily inconsequential. This theme can be traced throughout the history of communication technologies.

For example, written communication did not (and has not) replaced oral communication, although some of the prior functions of oral communication (e.g., exchanging ideas, preserving history and knowledge) were taken over by written forms to some degree. Yet, even today, oral forms of communication are not only essential to human communication but, in some instances, are imbued with particular reverence and significance (e.g., wedding vows, oaths and oral testimony in court). Similarly, the emergence of the printing press and the rise of printed forms did not totally supplant handwritten forms. While printed matter replaced many functions of written communication and put most public scribes out of business (Troll), throughout the centuries there has still been a role for handwritten documents that extends into today. Handwritten letters, although certainly rarer than they were in the past as typewriters and word processing developed for business uses, can carry an even more powerful symbolic impact—precisely because they were created *without* using the efficiency and ease of newer technologies, as well as for their ability to display the personal touch that handwriting can convey.

This analysis also suggests that, in many instances, the introduction of new technologies can prompt a reassessment—and often a reappreciation—of older technologies. The emergence of an alternative to an existing technology can provide an opportunity to recognize more clearly specific attributes and consequences of the existing technology that has long been fully integrated into a culture and thus become almost invisible. It may seem odd to recommend looking back at older forms when the tendency is to look ahead to all the benefits that the newer forms would (presumably) provide. It runs against the utopian tendencies in American culture to embrace the newest and latest idea or development. Any reappraisal, if it happens at all, might occur only after initial excitement and hype surrounding the newer forms begin to wane and the full array of implications of implementing the newer forms into existing patterns of activities is assessed. The new environment created by the newer technology can cast the older technology in a new light, sometimes highlighting benefits that were not as apparent before different ways of accomplishing goals emerged.

ASSUMPTIONS REGARDING TECHNOLOGIES

Basic assumptions that people hold about technology shape their perceptions of, and attitudes toward, technology. These can be characterized in several ways:

technological determinism versus social determinism, and utopian versus dystopian perspectives. These perspectives can intersect to produce four possible combinations of views regarding the nature and consequences of technologies: (1) utopian technological determinism, (2) dystopian technological determinism, (3) utopian social determinism, and (4) dystopian social determinism.

Many in American culture hold a "technological determinist" view that sees technology as almost an independent, willful entity that imposes itself on human social dynamics. They believe that technology itself will determine the ways in which it will affect society, and understanding the technology means that one can reliably predict the effects of that technology on society. This view is apparent in much of the language used regarding technology. For example, it is not uncommon to read or hear such technological deterministic statements as "Computers will revitalize education" and "The Internet will make our children smarter."

As the above examples suggest, technological deterministic views are often combined with the assumption that outcomes associated with technologies will be positive. American culture in particular, as the source of many of the most influential innovations of the last few centuries, persistently has embraced a utopian perspective toward technology. Technological advances, whether they be in medicine, agriculture, aerospace engineering, or household products, are believed to make our lives less work-filled, more convenient, less dangerous, and more comfortable. After all, why would someone develop a technology (usually viewed as a product) that was not intended to be an improvement? In many eyes, and in many instances, technological developments have indeed benefited humanity in many ways (e.g., Dertouzos; Negroponte; Rheingold). The utopian technological determinist view is perhaps the most prevalent. However, assuming that technological developments are inevitable and resistant to change or adaptation, and assuming that these developments are always an "advancement" or an "improvement" can lead to uncritical acceptance of technologies and their consequences.

However, just as there are strong proponents of the newest technologies at one end of the continuum, there are strong opponents at the other end representing dystopian views. Technology, by its nature, is not necessarily an advance, an improvement, or a sign of progress, they argue. They point to the many destructive consequences of various technological advances developed in the name of progress: the development of nuclear energy leading to the threat of nuclear war; development of chemical fertilizers and pesticides leading to water and soil pollution; the development of the automobile leading to smog and urban sprawl. There are critics of the newer communication technologies as well, those who say that the implications of the Internet will be far more negative than positive (e.g., Postman; Stoll). Positions such as "Electronic mail depersonalizes human communication and isolates people" and "The Web pushes commercialism and pornography" reflect this perspective.

Technological determinism can be contrasted with the "social determinist" view, which instead argues that the technology itself is less important than people's ways of using a technology. Rather than the technology driving change, technologies are human creations for human uses. We developed the technologies to solve problems, and we make decisions about how to use them. Understanding people's motivations and goals, rather than the characteristics of a technology, will lead to reliable predictions about the consequences of technology uses, according to this view.

As with technological determinism, social determinism can reflect utopian or dystopian perspectives. The utopian social determinist position would assume that individuals will use technologies in positive ways. They will make decisions in applying technologies to social needs and challenges that, for example, bring people together, reduce misunderstandings, and increase the breadth and scope of information available to people. The dystopian social determinist view would focus on people's use of technology for antisocial and destructive goals. For example, people will use the relative anonymity of the Internet to misrepresent themselves and manipulate others. Similarly, people will exploit the access that the Internet provides to distribute "spam" (electronic junk mail) to millions of people, or they will develop new ways of invading others' privacy through computer databases and tracking on-line activities (e.g., "cookies").

These views can be identified in the debate regarding the role of technologies in education (see Figure 5.1). A close read of the popular literature on educational technologies will likely find representations of each view. Which perspective is dominant is likely subject to debate, although there seems to be a fairly strong voice among the utopian technological determinists promoting computers and the Internet as inevitable and positive developments in education. Consistent with the prevailing view in American culture that more technology (new, high-tech hardware) is always better, many prominent voices have been pushing for more computers and Internet connections in classrooms (Mendels, "Can"). This includes such individuals as Richard Riley, Secretary of Education in the Clinton administration, and Reed Hundt, former chair of the Federal Communications Commission. However, there also appears to be a significant cadre of dystopian technological determinists challenging the assumption that more technology is always better. They question the apparent assumption that new, high-tech equipment is the answer for what ails American education (e.g., Healy; Mendels, "Once," "Educator"; Oppenheimer).

There is, of course, some truth in each of these perspectives. The "mutual influence" model recognizes the potential contributions of all of these views. Technology does, in fact, impose certain biases, restrict or prevent certain capabilities, and facilitate other capabilities. This is true when considering the various communication technologies used in education. For example, when interacting via electronic mail, people cannot hear each other's voice. When viewing television, the person on the screen cannot receive communication from audience members, nor can audience members affect the activities on the program (call-in shows, which combine two communication technologies, are an

Figure 5.1
Perspectives on Educational Technologies

	Technological Determinism	Social Determinism
Utopian Perspective	Technology will improve education by reshaping the educational process, encouraging more and better interaction, and making more useful information available to students.	Teachers and students will use technology to improve education by reshaping the educational process, interacting more with each other in positive ways, and by being able to find more useful information.
Dystopian Perspective	Technology will degrade education by reshaping the educational process, discouraging interaction, and making more unwholesome information available to students.	Teachers and students will use technology to undermine education by reshaping the educational process, interacting less with each other and in negative ways, and by being able to access more unwholesome information.

exception). As the technological determinist view argues, these characteristics of the technology *do* shape the uses and outcomes.

However, individuals are not hapless victims or beneficiaries of autonomous technology—they can make choices about how to use various technologies' characteristics. In this view, individuals have the ability to evaluate various technology options, select the one perceived as best suited to their goals, and use the technology's characteristics in ways that further those goals. Whether those goals, and the outcomes of technology use, are constructive or destructive, beneficial or detrimental, pro-social or antisocial is a subjective evaluation that can depend on contextual factors such as one's standpoint, the historical setting, and short- or long-term timeline. So the mutual influence model encompasses both types of determinism and the potential for positive and/or negative outcomes depending on individuals' actions with the technologies, as illustrated in Figure 5.2.

An alternative to extremes of advocacy and opposition is a balanced view of technologies, which recognizes that technologies are not inherently "good" or "bad." Technologies, as human creations, have the capacity to facilitate change of various types, but an evaluation of their use may depend on the specific applications as well as the evaluator's perspective. One person's "constructive" application of technology (teachers' use of computers with software to provide

Figure 5.2
Perspectives on Educational Technologies

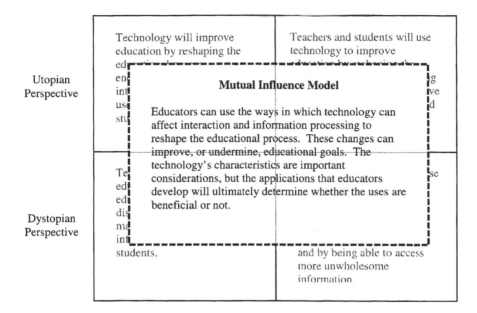

Technological Determinism   Social Determinism

Utopian
Perspective

Dystopian
Perspective

Technology will improve
education by reshaping the
ed...
en...
int...
us...
stu...

Te...
ed...
ed...
dis...
ma...
int...
students.

Teachers and students will use
technology to improve
...
...g
...ve
...d

...se

and by being able to access
more unwholesome
information.

Mutual Influence Model

Educators can use the ways in which technology can
affect interaction and information processing to
reshape the educational process. These changes can
improve, or undermine, educational goals. The
technology's characteristics are important
considerations, but the applications that educators
develop will ultimately determine whether the uses are
beneficial or not.

students with self-paced instruction) can be "destructive" to another (the student
who thrives on personal contact with teachers and peers in instructional settings).
In addition, a thorough evaluation is unlikely to be a simplistic "good" or "bad"
dichotomy. More likely an evaluation will reveal a mixture of positive and
negative potentials, and different mixtures for different applications and users.
Thus, there is a potentially complex array of assessments regarding various
aspects of a particular technology put to use in specific contexts for specific
goals with specific individuals.

A FRAMEWORK FOR WEB-BASED INSTRUCTION

Overlaying this historical framework onto issues surrounding Web-based instruction suggests a need to reassess conceptualization of technologies used for
educational purposes and different ways of evaluating various technologies for
their possible use in educational applications.

Redefining "Educational Technology"

In contrast to much of the current discussion about computers in the classroom, educational technologies can be defined much more broadly than just

"new, electronic, computerized devices." Discussions of educational technologies, then, should include older, low-tech forms such as oral interaction (one-on-one and group; one-way lectures and two-way discussions), written communication and its artifacts (pencils and paper, chalk and chalkboards, books), and visual communication and its artifacts (pencils and paper, paints and paintbrushes, paper, pictures, photographs, overheads). These educational technologies have been essential to education from the outset, and have been so deeply embedded in the classroom that they are often overlooked as important resources. As has been true in many other arenas, newer educational technologies have not replaced the older forms—they exist side by side in educational contexts. However, attention is showered on newer, flashier technologies with little close consideration of the strengths and weaknesses of each specific technology in relationship to the specific educational goals or with recognition of the potential contributions of older, lower-tech forms. The newer forms can prompt a reappreciation of older forms for their distinctive characteristics and applicability to educational goals.

Internet-Based Education in Context

Internet-based education is the latest and most intriguing application of new communication technologies to educational goals. It represents the latest and most advanced application of new technologies to the classroom. Utopian and dystopian viewpoints abound. Proponents have touted the Internet and its multifaceted capabilities for supporting dyadic and group interaction and for making vast amounts of information available "at your fingertips" as the next great advance in education. Critics argue that Internet-based education undermines human contact that is essential to effective educational processes. On-line courses, they say, are but a poor facsimile of real, on-site courses and threaten the legitimacy of what it means to be "educated."

Applying the historical framework described above transcends the polarized debate represented by the utopian-dystopian dichotomy. It argues for the importance of basing applications and evaluations of various types of educational technologies on a close understanding of the nature of the technologies and the appropriateness of specific applications for furthering educational goals. The key is to promote pedagogical strategies through the informed selection and use of various educational technologies and technological artifacts. By understanding the characteristics of the technologies (incorporating technological determinism) and the ways in which those characteristics can be applied to shape educational experiences (incorporating social determinism), choices can be made to presumably minimize potentially negative consequences (incorporating dystopian perspectives) and to maximize potentially positive consequences (incorporating utopian perspectives). These choices will not be the same for every instructor, much less for every course. Just as the nature of the material, the pedagogical strategies deemed most effective, the characteristics of the students, the context of the curriculum, resource limitations, and other such factors shape the design and implementation decisions for each on-site course, similar issues will shape on-line courses as well. The goal here is to provide instructors with a framework for making such decisions as they balance many different needs, goals, and considerations.

Synchronicity and Educational Technologies

First, it is important to recognize that even for Internet-based courses, older, low-tech forms of technology are not necessarily displaced. Depending on the instructional goals, they can be highly relevant. For example, instructors can incorporate printed material (e.g., textbooks) into Internet-based courses just as they do for on-site courses. Students will likely continue to use paper and ink (or pencil) for note taking even while using the Internet connection. Conversation (even if it is not face-to-face) between instructors and students and among students will likely continue to be an important element in classroom experiences.

A concept useful for rethinking the "newer" versus "older" technology typology and sorting out the available artifacts is synchronicity. Synchronicity is an assessment of time factors in communication processes, a concept that transcends new/old technology distinctions. Communication can be "synchronous," meaning that both (or all) participants are directly involved in the interaction simultaneously. Examples include face-to-face talk, telephone conversations, electronic chat room interactions, "instant messaging" one-on-one chat rooms, videoconferences, and live broadcasts. Communication can be "asynchronous," meaning that there is some degree of delay in reception and response in the interaction. Examples include letters, Post-it notes, leaving messages on an answering machine, electronic mail, on-line discussion groups, recorded broadcasts, live broadcasts that are recorded (e.g., via videocassette recorder), video or audio taped messages, books, and newspapers.

Considering the synchronicity of various educational technologies on Web-based instruction can help clarify the relationship between new and old technologies. Comparing various technologies for specific elements of a course demonstrates that course designers can incorporate many "older-tech" elements if they fit pedagogical strategies and course goals.

An application of these proposals can illustrate the possibilities. For example, one way to approach on-line courses is to provide experiences that parallel on-site courses as much as possible in terms of synchronicity. In every course there are both synchronous (e.g., lectures, discussions, exams) and asynchronous (reading assignments, homework problems) elements. One of the key advantages to an on-line course, according to many proponents, is that students can take the class to fit their own schedule—that is, the majority or all of course experiences would be asynchronous. Others question whether making use of that capability is equivalent to, or even is a minor divergence from, what students experience in on-site courses. Synchronous elements of courses can be seen as the essence of what it means to "take a class" or "be in school." It is experiencing a greater sense of others' presence that generates a personal connection between instructor and students and among students. The asynchronous elements of on-site courses are familiar to students and arguably effective, so retaining those might also be desirable. Therefore, for those instructors who adopt this approach, their macro goal to maintain synchronous elements of a course would guide decisions regarding possible use of various synchronous and asynchronous technologies. Table 5.1 provides a schematic for comparisons.

Four pedagogical processes in the course can be identified: (1) information presentation, (2) comprehension enhancement, (3) experiential application, and (4) assessments. Each process can be examined in terms of synchronous and asynchronous approaches for both traditional on-site courses and Internet-based on-line courses. For example, in on-site classrooms, synchronous information presentation is the traditional oral lecture, while synchronous comprehension enhancement might involve oral question and answer opportunities as well as oral group discussions and exercises and face-to-face conversations during office hours. Synchronous experiential application could be group exercises and group or full-class discussions, and synchronous assessments would be in-class quizzes and exams (oral or paper-and-ink), in-class papers, oral presentations, and so on.

For on-line courses, many of these elements can also be offered synchronously. Live Web broadcasts of lectures or live closed-circuit television lectures could be incorporated for information presentation. Comprehension enhancement could be accomplished synchronously using chat rooms for scheduled question-answer sessions and group discussions. On-line forums could be utilized for synchronous group exercises and office hours. Experiential application could be handled through group discussions in electronic chat rooms or exercises using electronic forums. Synchronous assessments are possible on-line but may not be used since most assessments are individually based and interaction between classmates is discouraged. Note too that the content of most of these experiences can be archived for later retrieval and review. Although the ability to participate directly in the process is lost, the synchronous elements can also become an asynchronous resource available as a reference—which is difficult and rare for on-site courses.

Traditional, on-site courses usually include asynchronous elements. Information presentations often include textbook or other reading assignments and, increasingly, Web page reading assignments. Asynchronous comprehension enhancement has long taken the form of homework assignments but could also include instructors and students trading telephone messages or written notes. Similarly, asynchronous experiential application could be accomplished through homework problem solving or other out-of-class assignments. Take-home quizzes, exams, and papers can provide asynchronous assessments in traditional, on-site classrooms.

Table 5.1
Synchronicity in Traditional and On-line Courses

Pedagogical Processes	Synchronous		Asynchronous	
	On-site Course: "In-class"	On-line Course: Scheduled	Traditional Course: "Out-of-Class"	On-line Course: Unscheduled
Information Presentation	* Lectures (oral presentation, visual reinforcement through overheads/images)	* Live broadcasts of lectures (Web-based or closed-circuit television)	* Textbook readings * Web page assignments	* Lectures (on-line video clips, web-based lecture notes, links to on-line resources) * Textbook readings (offline at home) * Web page assignments
Comprehension Enhancement	* Q/A sessions * Group discussions * Group exercises * Office hours	* Scheduled Q/A sessions (chat room) * Group discussions (chat room) * Group exercises (on-line forum) * Office hours (on-line forum)	* Homework assignments	* Homework assignments (email or A/V file distrib/ collection) * Virtual office hours (email)
Experiential Application	* Discussions * Group exercises	* Group discussions (chat room) * Group exercises (on-line forum)	* Homework assignments	* Homework assignments (email distribution/ collection)
Assessments	* Weekly quizzes * Exams * Papers * Oral presentations	* Quizzes (Web-based) * Exams (Web-based)	* Take-home quizzes, exams, papers	* Quizzes (Web-based) * Exams (web-based) * Homework assignments (email distribution/ collection)

Many of these elements can also be provided asynchronously for on-line courses as well. As with the traditional, on-site courses, information presentation could include textbook readings and Web page reading assignments. However, archived audio-video lectures could provide access to lectures to fit the students' schedules as well as the capability of repeated exposures and review. Asynchronous comprehension enhancement could be accomplished similar to traditional classrooms through distribution and collection of assignments on-line (text, audio, or video—or all formats) and through instructors exchanging telephone, written, and e-mail messages with students during "virtual" office hours. Similar to on-site classes, experiential application can be done asynchronously using e-mail for distribution and collection of exercises or assignments and on-line forums. Finally, Web-based quizzes and exams, as well as electronic mail distribution of homework and term paper distribution and collection, would serve as asynchronous means of assessment.

This demonstrates not only that various new and old technologies can substitute for one another, but that both can be utilized for on-site and on-line courses. Which course elements are designed as on-line elements and which are "off-line" (e.g., books and printed articles) will be guided by each instructor's macro goals for the course as well as micro goals for a particular module or topic.

CONCLUSION

This chapter offers a historical and conceptual framework of technology, intended to bring insights from technology studies to bear on issues relevant to educators. The hope is that it can help educators make better-informed decisions about appropriate roles and effective uses of various communication technologies in the classroom in pursuit of specific pedagogical processes and goals. The intent is to contribute to critical evaluations of educational technologies by providing educators with analytical tools to assess various technologies and uses in terms of appropriateness for explicit educational goals. This approach argues that technology should be employed in service of educational goals and pedagogical strategies, rather than having educational processes be forced to adapt to technologies. The hope is that, when it comes to educational technology, the dog will (more often) wag the tail.

WORKS CITED

Ball-Rokeach, Sandra, and Kathleen Reardon. "Monologue, Dialogue, and Telelog: Comparing an Emergent Form of Communication with Traditional Forms." In *Advancing Communication Science: Merging Mass and Interpersonal Processes.* Ed. Robert P. Hawkins, John M. Wiemann, and Susan Pingree. Newbury Park: Sage, 1988. 135–61.

Bickerton, Derek. *Language and Species*. Chicago: University of Chicago Press, 1990.

DeFleur, Melvin L., and Everette E. Dennis. *Understanding Mass Communication*. 4th ed. Boston: Houghton Mifflin, 1991.

Dertouzos, Michael. *What Will Be*. New York: HarperCollins, 1997.

Eisenstein, Elizabeth. *The Printing Revolution in Early Modern Europe*. Cambridge, England: Cambridge University Press, 1983.

Fidler, Roger. *Mediamorphosis: Understanding New Media*. Thousand Oaks, CA:Pine Forge Press, 1996.

Fischer Claude S. *America Calling: A Social History of the Telephone to 1940*. Berkeley, CA: University of California Press, 1994.

Healy, Jane M. *Failure to Connect: How Computers Affect Our Children's Minds—for Better and Worse*. New York: Simon and Schuster, 1998.

Hundt, Reed. "Computers Are a Necessary Resource for Schools." In *Computers and Society*. Ed. P. A. Winters. San Diego, CA: Greenhaven Press, 1997. 149–52.

Logan, Robert K. *The Alphabet Effect: The Impact of the Phonetic Alphabet on the Development of Western Civilization*. New York: William Morrow, 1986.

Manguel, Alberto. *A History of Reading*. Penguin: New York, 1996.

Marvin, Carolyn. *When Old Technologies Were New*. New York: Oxford University Press, 1998.

McLuhan, Marshall. *The Gutenberg Galaxy*. Toronto: University of Toronto Press, 1962.

Mendels, Pamela. "Can New Technologies Revitalize Old Teaching Methods?" *New York Times on the Web*. 24 March 1999 <http://www.nytimes.com/library/tech/99/03/cyber/education/24education.html>.

———. "Educator Questions Need for Computers in Classrooms." *New York Times on the Web*. 19 May 1999 <http://www.nytimes.com/library/tech/99/05/cyber/education/19education.html>.

———. "Once a Champion of Classroom Computers, Psychologist Now Sees Failure." *New York Times*. 16 Sept. 1998 <http://www.nyt.com/library/tech/98/09/cyber/education/16education.html>.

Negroponte, Nicholas. *Being Digital*. New York: Vintage, 1995.

Ong, Walter. *Orality and Literacy: The Technologizing of the Word*. London: Methuen, 1982.

Oppenheimer, Todd. "The Computer Delusion." *The Atlantic*. July 1997 <http://www.theatlantic.com/issues/97jul/computer.htm.>.

Perrolle, Judith. *Computers and Social Change*. Belmont, CA: Wadsworth, 1987.

Pool, Ithiel de Sola. *Technologies of Freedom: On Free Speech in an Electronic Age*. Cambridge, MA: Harvard University Press, 1984.

Postman, Neil. *Technopoly: The Surrender of Culture to Technology*. New York: Alfred A. Knopf, 1992.

Rheingold, Harold. *The Virtual Community: Finding Connection in a Computerised World*. London: Secker and Warburg, 1994.

Riley, R. "Computer Education Is Vital for Students of the Future." In *Computers and Society*. Ed. Paul A. Winters. San Diego, CA: Greenhaven Press, 1997. 143–48.

Schmandt-Besserat, Denise. "Symbols in the Prehistoric Middle East: Developmental Features Preceding Written Communication." In *Oral and Written Communication*. Ed. Richard Leo Enos. Newbury Park, CA: Sage, 1990. 16–31.

Standage, Tom. *The Victorian Internet*. New York: Walker and Co., 1998.
Stoll, Clifford. *Silicon Snake Oil: Second Thoughts on the Information Highway*. New York: Anchor Books, 1995.
Troll, D. A. "The Illiterate Mode of Written Communication: The Work of the Medieval Scribe." In *Oral and Written Communication*. Ed. Richard Leo Enos. Newbury Park, CA: Sage, 1990. 96–123.

Chapter 6

When and Where Appropriate: Lessons from "Foreign" Contexts for the Pedagogical Use of Web-Based Technologies in the United States

Julian Kilker

Back in 1880, Ella Thayer published *Wired Love: A Romance of Dots and Dashes*, featuring an innovative technology—the telegraph—and a script that predates Hollywood's movie *You've Got Mail* (Ephron) by more than a century: The lovers meet "on-line," chat while attempting to guess each other's sex, and flirt at the anonymity-preserving (for the era) distance of fifty miles or so. This romance novel was subtitled " 'The old, old story'—in a new, new way," a phrase that resonates with Web-based pedagogy when earlier attempts to use emerging technologies are considered.

Do Web-based technologies encourage new and improved teaching, and are their benefits worth the inevitable challenges?[1] Educational technology has a long history of promise, often unfulfilled, and as with other debates involving notions of tradition and progress it attracts polarized commentary. In this chapter, I argue that a core challenge in using an emerging technology such as the Web for pedagogical purposes is understanding the context of its use, and matching the specific form and function of the technology to this context. The challenges encountered by those designing, implementing, and evaluating the pedagogical use of the Web parallel those encountered earlier in the use of communication and information technologies in developing country contexts, in which successive notions of what technologies and technology transfer methods were appropriate have been debated. We can benefit greatly from examining the practical experiences with, and the successes and failures of, both the technologies in such "foreign" contexts and the theoretical frameworks in which they were used.

This chapter was prompted by my observation that many of the challenges faced in Web-based learning contexts echo those encountered earlier in developing countries. Although the specific contexts do differ greatly, examples of "appropriate technology" from developing country contexts resonate with examples faced today by practitioners in developed countries such as the United States. Examples include concerns about overly complex technology, limited availability of resources for emerging technologies, and inequitable access to information and technology (National Telecommunications and Information Administration).

In the 1970s and 1980s, Western practitioners of international development, in reaction to uncritical transfer of technology and the failure of large-scale and expensive projects, created the concept of "appropriate technology." This term has since fallen into disfavor for a variety of reasons, including the lack of a clear definition of the concept beyond its apparently trivial contrast with "inappropriate technology," a lack of support for the concept in developing countries because of its "implicit association with low-grade, second-class technologies" (Cassiolato 60), and a dramatic change in funding priorities for international development as a consequence of the end of the Cold War.

While "appropriate technology" has largely disappeared from development literature—although the core issues survive under different names and the odd textbook continues to present a simplified version (Hazeltine and Bull)—its history holds important lessons for those interested in designing and implementing relatively advanced technologies in pedagogical contexts. Just as it was tempting during the early decades of international development to advocate the use of communication and information technologies without regard to the specific context of use, at present, advocates of Web-based technologies too often neglect to reflect sufficiently on the technology's possible consequences, challenges, and potential alternatives.

Thus, I argue for reexamining "appropriate technology," conceptualized over the past four decades, and relating it to the design, implementation, and evaluation of Web-based pedagogy in the United States today. It is particularly important to benefit from the expertise developed during efforts to define appropriate technology in order to critically examine assumptions for Web-based pedagogy.

CONCEPTUALIZING APPROPRIATE TECHNOLOGY

Web-based technologies have increasingly important and expensive roles in pedagogy. But while they clearly have benefits, including cost-effectiveness for students spread over large (or inaccessible) regions, efficient use of valuable experts' time, consistent program content, and the possibility of self-paced learning, such systems do present important challenges. For example: How do people, especially those who are less technically or linguistically literate, collaborate in impersonal on-line situations? Are high-technology systems accessible to a wide range of students? Can such technologies support a participatory model of education? Should institutions acquire the most advanced technologies, and, if so, how should they be used?

Conceptualizing "appropriate" in relation to technology, which requires a detailed process known in formal terms as "explication" (Chaffee), provides a valuable perspective for examining such issues because attempting to define the concept raises questions such as "Appropriate for whom?" and "Appropriate in which contexts?" In addition, the concepts of "appropriateness" and "context" are closely linked to that of expertise. Who are the experts of pedagogical technologies: those who are familiar with the technology, or those who are familiar with the pedagogical context in which it will be used, such as faculty or students? If a combination of these conceptualizations is to be synthesized, then how can this process be encouraged? Defining the role of the expert is especially challenging in situations in which expertise appears commonsensical or unnecessary; in these cases, the views of the technology "user" are often neglected. Even the use of a definite pronoun with "user" is, of course, problematic, given that technologies are used by a variety of people from various backgrounds and in various contexts (Agre). I discuss the critical importance of examining users—faculty and students—in determining appropriateness later in this chapter.

Expertise and the conceptualization of appropriate technology have been closely linked in international development projects. During the 1950s and 1960s, for example, those promoting health or agricultural techniques in countries such as India, Egypt, and Brazil, the emphasis for development communication was on unidirectional, top-down mass media, primarily instructional television and radio. A major criterion of appropriateness was efficiency, which meant the number of people reachable for a specific cost. Such technologies, however, did not gracefully support participation and collaboration among students and faculty.

In contrast, development notions in the 1970s encouraged a "bottom-up" self-reliance; "little media" such as radio and cassette were recommended for rural areas. Appropriateness during this era meant more interactive and feedback-oriented media. Schumacher's influential *Small Is Beautiful* was a catalyst for redefining the appropriate technology for this era; he encouraged the use of intermediate technology—a combination of indigenous and advanced technology with an emphasis on labor rather than on expensive technology. But as the emphasis of appropriate technology broadened from technical considerations to include social ones, critics pointed out serious problems with the concept. Most important were the lack of specificity (Eckaus), lack of direct applicability (Betz), and a perception that appropriate technology was demeaning because it was inherently inferior to the technologies used in "developed" countries (Cassiolato). When the U.S. National Technical Information Service released its *Ap-*

propriate Technology Information for Developing Countries report in 1979, however, its introduction noted simply that appropriate technology is "now often associated with technologies best suited to meet the needs of low-income communities" (ix–x).

Recent international development experiences in the 1980s and 1990s, which generally acknowledge that there is no universal model for development, have produced a more complex definition of "appropriate." The resulting conceptualization of "appropriate" can be divided into four areas: technical, economical, institutional-political, and sociocultural (Matta and Boutros). Below I have summarized factors of "appropriateness" using definitions of appropriate technology found in the literature of international development studies (Bunch; Eckaus; Oxfam; Werner and Bower), communication (Epskamp and Boeren; Matta and Boutros), and library sciences (Baark; Davies; Froehlich). To be considered appropriate *in international contexts*, technology should meet many, but not necessarily all, of these factors (some of them might even be in conflict in specific contexts):

- Technical factors: The technology should work consistently in local surroundings; be simple to understand and use (Baark; Werner and Bower); be interesting to use; be locally repairable (Oxfam); be adaptable (Bunch; Schumacher); be easily abandoned (if it does not work well) (Samarajiva); require little support and operate independently of other systems (Davies; Matta and Boutros); and be able to store and transmit the "local language" (for example, if the language uses non-Roman characters) (Davies).[2]

- Economic factors: The technology should be low-cost, demand little investment to acquire and maintain, depreciate slowly, have low import, export, and transportation costs (Matta and Boutros); use available local resources, require few and inexpensive supplies (Bunch); be labor- rather than capital-intensive (Baark; Bunch; Werner and Bower); and have incremental costs related to usage rather than a high start-up cost (Samarajiva).

- Institutional-political factors: The technology should reduce the gap between the information-rich and -poor, and help students gain greater control and become more self-reliant (Werner and Bower); be relatively risk-free (Bunch); meet policies on information dissemination, and be visible and viable—it must compete favorably for funds with other projects (Matta and Boutros).

- Sociocultural factors: The technology should incorporate local opinions and suggestions (Werner and Bower); meet the communication style of the culture (Matta and Boutros); fit into existing social and status structures (Davies; Matta and Boutros); meet actual local needs (Baark; Davies); and encourage people to produce their own content (Oxfam).

Based on these factors, the specific context influences the conceptualization of "appropriate." In practice, appropriate technology might mean doing nothing (Froehlich), using a nontechnical solution (Oxfam), using multiple complementary technologies (Goulet), using a leading-edge technology (FAO), or, conversely, using "traditional" (meaning well-established) media (Betz; Epskamp and Boeren). Because of subtle interactions among the factors listed above, the same technology can be appropriate in one context yet disastrous in another context.

Appropriate is difficult to define because the concept is contextual and subjective (Davies; Samarajiva). Baark wryly notes that "while the inappropriateness of much modern technology for Southern countries has been amply demonstrated, the criteria for identification of appropriate solutions have been far more difficult to define" (264). Goulet concludes that "no single technology is 'appropriate' for all development purposes, but every technology is 'appropriate' for reaching some objectives" (174). It cannot be overemphasized that examining overall pedagogical objectives as well as the context is essential to defining "appropriate" for Web-based pedagogy.[3]

Whether a technology is appropriate is influenced not only by the physical hardware (computer, network, and so on in Web-based contexts), but also by the content (or software) used with it, and the physical and intellectual context in which the technology is used. A case in point: Many Web-based classrooms use a lecture-style physical layout, with rows of students at computer desks facing the instructor; the tables and the computer monitors obstruct interactions among students and instructors. The same classroom technologies—computers, tables, and chairs—can be reconfigured using a central seminar table and placing the computers on tables along the perimeter of the room. This configuration literally and figuratively renders the computers peripheral to the class, and encourages discussion and collaboration.

CONTEXTUAL DEFINITIONS OF "APPROPRIATE"

How does "appropriateness" operate in the context of Web-based pedagogy in the United States? Clearly some of the technical, economic, institutional-political, and sociocultural factors listed above are directly applicable, while others, at least at first impression, are less useful. To examine different notions of what "appropriate" might constitute in U.S. settings, I examined two sets of courses. One set was taught at an urban "commuter" university to which approximately 80 percent of the student body commutes, and the second set at an Ivy League university during the fall semester of 1998 (both institutions are on the U.S. East Coast). The two professional communication course sections surveyed at the commuter institution were taught in a traditional lecture hall by the same faculty member; while a portion of the syllabus addressed on-line research, students had to locate and use computer resources on their own time. In contrast, the three courses surveyed at the Ivy League institution used a "wired" classroom—a hybrid computer lab and discussion room having one networked computer per student and an instructor's computer-projection system—for at least half of the class meetings. Of these three writing courses, each taught by a different faculty member, two addressed the social impact of Internet technology, and the third examined social identity and the Internet. A large portion of each course's assignments relied on students using the computers during class for collaborative writing and editing, on-line research, participating in textual adventure and chat environments, and creating personal Web pages.

Based on an examination of questionnaires about computer experience completed by undergraduate students at each location at the beginning of their courses, it is apparent that the "appropriate" use of Web-based pedagogy must be conceptualized differently in these two settings.[4] The primary goal in administering these questionnaires to students was to examine their experiences with, and attitudes toward, computers in order to understand specific groups of students as users of computer technology and thus assist in planning the use of computers in the context of specific courses. This example concentrates primarily on the students as "end-users" of Web technology—an issue encompassed by the sociocultural factor described above. A complete analysis would consider additional relevant social groups such as faculty and administrators, and would examine the technical, economic, and institutional-political factors listed earlier.

Given a summary of the students' experiences with computers (see Table 6.1), what are appropriate uses of Web and Internet technologies for these two classes? A summary of the students' responses indicates that while the mean age of the commuter students was higher than that of the Ivy League students by over four years, the commuter students had *fewer* years of experience using computers for sending e-mail, Web site development, and word processing (this finding is probably related to the socioeconomic status of the students). In addition, far fewer of the commuter students owned computers (although some students reported having access to other people's computers at work and home). Institutional support for student access to the Internet varied: the Ivy League institution had numerous computer labs that provided Internet access for students in campus dorms and off-campus, and with relatively little effort on the part of faculty, "wired" classrooms could be reserved during class time. The commuter institution, with more limited resources, provided on-campus network access in computer labs, but its students were expected to use a commercial Internet service provider when they were off campus.

Not surprisingly, the commuter students were a more heterogeneous group than those in the Ivy League course. The variations in ages and length of experience with word processing, for example, were both greater among the commuter students than the Ivy League students, as indicated by the wider ranges for these values in Table 6.1. The commuter students also rated computers more negatively on an attitude scale than did the Ivy League students.

The differences in these two groups are no doubt partly due to different course topics and the self-selection of students taking these courses (the Ivy League courses, which addressed computers and society, probably attracted more computer-literate students). It must also be stressed that these differences cannot

Table 6.1

Comparing a "Commuter" and an "Ivy League" Institution

	Commuter institution	Ivy League institution
Courses	Two sections of a Junior-level Professional Communication course	Three Freshman-level writing courses on computers and society
Students	41	50
Women / Men	20 / 21	6 / 44
Computer owners	17 (42%)	46 (92%)
Mean age	22.5 (17 to 40)	18.1 (17 to 21)
Computer experience (mean years; min to max)		
E-mail	3.0 (0 to 15)	4.2 (0 to 12)
Word processing	6.6 (3 to 20)	8.3 (2 to 14)
Web site development	0.5 (0 to 2)	1.2 (0 to 6)
General attitude towards computers *	More negative than students at Ivy League institution	More positive than students at Commuter institution
Use of computer technology	Minimal and optional: Few students used tools more complex than word processors and Web browsers	Intensive and required: Each student was expected to develop a simple Web site containing writings

*Attitude was measured using a nine-item semantic differential scale in which students rated computers as being, for example, easy or difficult to use.

be generalized to the broader student populations at each institution. Still, three important differences are immediately apparent from this comparison.

First, the combination of higher mean age, lower mean computer experience, and less access to networked computers among the commuter students suggests that a course designed for them would, if using Internet-based technologies, require much more attention to introducing computer technology and concepts, and that the specific examples and exercises should address topics of interest to an older audience.

Second, the greater heterogeneity among the commuter students in terms of computer experience means that Web-based tasks must take into account a greater variation in the students' experiences with computer technology. Faculty will likely encounter classes in which the tendency for students to be over- and under-challenged—present in most classes—is especially exaggerated. Under such conditions, some students finish their assignments rapidly and lose interest, while others cannot finish them and become frustrated. In these circumstances, the technology (which in the broad sense of the term combines the computer and the course assignment) might not be appropriate for many students, and creative solutions are necessary. For example, faculty can pair knowledgeable students with novices and hold extra training sessions for students who request them.

Another striking difference between the two sets of courses is their differing ratios of women to men; the possible reasons for such differences are both complex and suggestive of broader challenges in introducing technology into the classroom. The three Ivy League courses were part of a required freshman writing program in which students selected courses based on brief descriptions from a large number of possibilities. Few women may have been interested in the course topics based on their descriptions as addressing computers and society (although there was no indication that computers would actually be used in class), or there may have been scheduling reasons that increased the chance that men would take these courses. However, when two of the three courses were repeated the subsequent semester with the same schedule, but with one having an identical description and the other with a modified description emphasizing the women authors read in the course, the ratio of women to men was balanced in both. This experience suggests that the composition of elective courses—in this case the relative ratios of women and men—can vary dramatically when a course includes, or even appears to include, technology-based content.

Third, the decreased computer and network access by the commuter students influenced the design of assignments. The commuter students were less able to complete assignments outside of the classroom or computer labs, while the Ivy League faculty could assume that their students had both ready access to computing resources outside of the classroom and extensive computer skills, and could thus require that students use word processors and even develop basic Web sites. Even if all Ivy League students did not have these skills, the expectation of computer expertise was high enough that students could seek help from campus facilities or other students in the class.

It would be a mistake, however, to assume that the Ivy League institution, with its easier computer access and more computer-literate students, provided an ideal setting for Web-based pedagogy. The advanced skills of the young students sometimes resulted in criticism of perceived shortcomings in the technology used in the classroom. For example, when the Ivy League course faculty used textual adventure games to encourage students in their writing—an appropriate use of the technology from the faculty's perspective considering the goals of the writing assignment—several students criticized the "boring 80's-style computer text" (in the words of one student) and instead requested more familiar games with point-and-click graphics—a technology that would not have met the pedagogical goals of the writing assignment.

The homogeneity in the Ivy League students' experiences, both with respect to computer technology and in life experiences, also meant that there was a relatively narrow range of perspectives from which to draw during class discussions. This proved to be a challenge in the three "technology and society" courses, in which few "nontraditional" students were present to describe, for example, experiences with early personal computers or critical perspectives on current computer technology.

Finally, although this was not the case in these courses, ready access to Web-based technologies could mean that faculty must resist expectations that such technologies are always appropriate. These expectations may be held by students (who are familiar and enjoy working with the tools) or by administrators (who arrange funding for and naturally wish to promote their institution as a leader in advanced technology). In addition, faculty might rely on technology too heavily because it is available or because there are incentives to do so, not because it has an appropriate pedagogical goal. Clearly, in certain contexts and for certain goals, traditional technologies such as pen and paper, overhead projectors, and so on are more appropriate. The Ivy League students, for example, relied on Web-based information resources to the exclusion of traditional library resources, foregoing opportunities to develop critical research habits using the library holdings.

From this comparison of students in two different contexts that emphasized social-cultural (and implicitly economic factors), it is apparent that institutional capacities and students' experiences must be taken into consideration when planning appropriate Web-based courses or when integrating Web-based assignments in existing courses.

WHOSE NOTION OF APPROPRIATE?

My focus on students in the previous section raises the question of whose views should be emphasized when defining appropriate. In the example, I briefly described the commuter and Ivy League courses; these courses were designed by the faculty to take into account both their pedagogical goals and the students' familiarity with computer technology (based on the faculty's interpretation of the questionnaire responses). Thus, the faculty were largely responsible for conceptualizing the form and function of Web-based pedagogy appropriate for their specific contexts. Determining who should influence such conceptualizations is a challenge faced by both those involved in education and those in international development. As noted earlier, concerns about defining expertise in international development resulted in a shift in conceptualizing appropriate from "top down" to incorporating local knowledge.

Similarly, those developing technology have increasingly incorporated the expertise of users. Users' conceptions of a technology's appropriateness can differ from those of its planners, and it is critical to understand such differences early on. The AT&T Picturephone in the early 1970s, whose conceptualization was based on the simple—but incorrect—notion that more bandwidth is inherently better for interpersonal communication, is an example of an expensive failure to adequately negotiate planner and user conceptualizations. After a $500 million investment, an engineer eventually discovered one reason behind user resistance to the technology: a "surprisingly large number of people . . . seem willing to pay extra *not* to have Picturephone service" because they valued the privacy afforded by existing telephone technology (Noll 316, original emphasis).

The nature of planner-user collaboration varies with the strategy used to define the appropriate technology. Traditional technology development methods, such as those used during the Picturephone's design and currently in the early rush to implement Web-based solutions, sometimes neglect user perspectives. Traditional methods involve planners envisioning a composite, stereotyped group of users. However, a more accurate notion of users can be imagined through discussions with and observations of group members, as in user-centered participatory design approaches (Ehn; Muller and Kuhn; Norman). These approaches mirror the participatory focus of later conceptualizations of "appropriate technology." Whether using stereotyping or participatory techniques, the notion of "user" must be explicitly or implicitly negotiated as part of the conceptualization of appropriate.

User-centered methods often adopt an iterative cycle in which evaluation is a critical repeated component of a design-build-evaluate-analyze spiral (Butler). After several iterations of using a technology—for example, using Web-based systems in several courses—planners and users such as faculty and students have a chance to repeatedly refine (and synthesize) a conceptualization of appropriate based on their interactions with the technology. By expanding the notions of user-centered design to include other groups who are pedagogical "users" but often neglected—such as teaching assistants, students, and faculty—the process of defining "appropriate" is placed in the foreground.

While user-centered, iterative methods are an improvement over traditional strategies in which technologies are created and implemented without collaboration with the eventual users, they cannot identify future uses, needs, and problems that users and planners do not independently envision. This is a challenge in attempting to predict any nascent technology's strengths and weaknesses, and the reason for which I advocate examining appropriate technology literature for cautionary tales from earlier technologies.

WHICH OTHER CONTEXTS?

Perusing development communication and appropriate technology literature reveals familiar challenges encountered by those advocating the introduction of advanced technologies in other contexts. At first glance, the literature will appear to be from another world, literally addressing "foreign" challenges. However, the emphases—the attention to local knowledge, the concern about impact, the consideration of simpler technologies—require only slight modifications to be viewed in terms relevant to present-day academic institutions in developed countries.

Examining "foreign" contexts can often encourage reflection about technology use in education. Those concerned about improving Web-based pedagogy should refer to studies and reports analyzing technology use in other eras (such as the high hopes for radio as an educational medium [Cassidy]) or in other national or institutional contexts using resources such as "Benton's Best Practices Toolkit" and *The Development Communication Report (DCR)* (the latter is, unfortunately, no longer published). For example, *DCR* presented an issue on interactive technologies in 1993 with articles covering "cutting edge multimedia technologies" (Brodman) as well as "traditional" technologies such as the radio (Moulton). While the technologies discussed are dated, these back issues are useful not only for general concepts but also for their descriptions of challenges encountered and solutions developed. For example, Moulton described working within the constraints of interactive radio programs to teach math, while Brodman's summary of the pros and cons of multimedia technologies recalls issues that may now be overlooked in technology selection: "CD-ROMs are slow compared with other multimedia systems [such as the videodisc]. They also offer very limited and primitive motion video. This makes them inappropriate for some applications—such as training in a medical procedure" (6). "Benton's Best Practices Toolkit" includes more current resources in the spirit of appropriate technology; this Web site provides up-to-date resources aimed at helping (primarily U.S.-based) nonprofit organizations make effective use of information technologies.

Academic articles, such as Samarajiva's comparison of print, microform, online, and CD-ROM technologies as information conduits for "Third World" scientists, provide insight into familiar phenomena. He found that the ultimate test of appropriateness is whether people will freely choose to use the technology; in this case he found that researchers in Sri Lanka contacted overseas colleagues for photocopies of articles, bypassing their local libraries, which were considered impractical. This suggests that users can create alternative innovative strategies when faced with inappropriate (from their perspective) technologies. Similarly, Matta and Boutros, in an article that provided the initial framework for my conceptualization of "appropriate," list in detail what they term barriers to the introduction of e-mail in developing countries. The technical barriers they list include poor telecommunications lines, a lack of technical support, and unreliable power; the economic barriers include scarce capital, high unemployment, vendor monopolies, prohibitive insurance rates for equipment, and so on. Many of these same barriers apply to computer technologies in developed countries.

SPECIFIC LESSONS

Examining "appropriate technology" can provide at least three specific contributions for planners of Web-based pedagogy, based on early attempts to use advanced technologies in "foreign" contexts. First, the evolving conceptualization of "appropriate" with respect to Web-based technologies suggests that the process of reflecting on the form and pedagogical role of such technologies is more important than choosing a specific technology, and that their challenges and benefits are strongly context-dependent. Educators should start with pedagogical goals and contextual factors as described earlier in this chapter, *then* choose specific technologies which may include Internet- and Web-based technologies as well as more traditional tools and techniques.

Second, incorporating a wide variety of perspectives during the conceptualization of appropriateness is important for the success of Web-based pedagogy. At the very least, a comprehensive situation analysis and needs assessment should be conducted to assist in planning the technologies' uses. Planners should avoid neglecting the perspectives of end-users, as did the early promoters of technologies in developing countries and early designers of computer software. In both cases, subsequent reconceptualizations actively incorporated such perspectives, in the former case through emphasizing "local knowledge" and in the latter by adopting user-centered and participatory design methods. These experiences reinforce the notion, demonstrated in my comparison of courses at the commuter and Ivy League institutions, that technology-based solutions must take local context into account.

Third, reviewing literature about attempts to conceptualize appropriateness and to implement communication technologies in "foreign" contexts provides planners with relevant expert perspectives on pedagogical technologies. Many common lessons encountered earlier in developing country contexts are being relearned with respect to Web-based pedagogy in developed countries. These include attempts to simplify the delivery of information. After initial experiments with complex, slow-loading graphics and confusing frame-based navigation systems, many Web site designers have reemphasized simple and clear designs, taking into account the continual maintenance and upgrading required for both hardware and software, and the knowledge that emerging technologies might distract both faculty and students from the core pedagogical goals. As with other communication technologies, Web-based systems can facilitate access to information but inhibit pedagogically effective social contacts. Even if Web-based technologies are deemed appropriate, they should be used cautiously, paying particular attention to frequently underestimated issues such as training faculty in their use.

CONCLUSION

Examining the concept of "appropriateness" in relation to technology, which has been thoroughly explored in development communication, encourages us to be reflexive about our own contexts, to learn from research in other specific contexts, and to benefit from existing theoretical frameworks and practical resources. Just as the concept of "appropriate" has been negotiated from the 1950s to the present in development communication, so it must be negotiated today in the differing pedagogical contexts in which it is, and will be, used.

The Web comprises sophisticated technologies capable of supporting and nurturing innovative pedagogical strategies. But if used inappropriately, these technologies are also capable of dulling academic experiences and squandering valuable financial and intellectual resources. As with the traditional classroom technologies of blackboards, overhead projectors, and videocassette recorders, the use of networked computers should be approached thoughtfully with regard to the overall pedagogical goals. Taking into account lessons gleaned from the successes, failures, naïve visions, and sophisticated analyses of appropriate technology in "foreign" contexts provides an important heuristic for planning Web-based pedagogy in familiar contexts.

NOTES

1. Throughout this chapter I use the term "Web-based" technologies, although the issues I discuss apply equally to Internet-based technologies—the latter is a superset of the former and includes e-mail and other networked resources such as on-line library catalogues that are typically used with the Web.

2. Although this last factor would appear to have limited relevance within the United States outside of language pedagogy, broader related concerns are how user interfaces limit access for those with disabilities (Hakken) and how Web-based resources can better accommodate users having language disorders (Singh, Gedeon, and Rho).

3. I am indebted to Yvonne Houy for emphasizing the importance of this point.

4. These questionnaires are part of a larger project examining computer experiences and attitudes of students and faculty toward computers at different institutions. My thanks to Yvonne Houy, Sharon Kleinman, and Shelah Weiss for distributing questionnaires to their students, and to Andrew Emmert for compiling data from Kleinman's questionnaires.

WORKS CITED

Agre, Philip E. "Conceptions of the User in Computer Systems Design." In *The Social and Interactional Dimensions of Human-Computer Interfaces*. Ed. Peter J. Thomas. Cambridge: Cambridge University Press, 1995. 67–106.

Baark, Erik. "Appropriate Information Technology: A Cross-Cultural Perspective." *UNESCO Journal of Information Science, Librarianship and Archives Administration* 4 (1982): 263–68.

"Benton's Best Practices Toolkit." *Benton Foundation*. 7 June 1999. 1 Aug 1999 <www.benton.org/Practice/Toolkit>.

Betz, M. J. "What Technology Is Appropriate?" In *Appropriate Technology: Choice and Development*. Ed. M. J. Betz, P. McGowan, and R. T. Wigand. Durham, NC: Duke Press Policy Studies, 1984. 3–14.

Brodman, Janice. "Cutting Edge Multimedia Technologies: Promise and Pitfalls." *Development Communication Report* 81 (1993): 1, 5–8.

Bunch, Roland. *Two Ears of Corn: A Guide to People-Centered Agricultural Improvement*. Oklahoma City: World Neighbors, 1982.

Butler, Keith A. "Usability Engineering Turns Ten." *IEEE Interactions* 3.1 (1996): 59–75.

Cassidy, Margaret. "Historical Perspectives on Teaching with Technology in K–12 Schools." *New Jersey Journal of Communication* 6.2 (1998): 170–84.

Cassiolato, José E. "Information and Communications Technologies in Developing Countries." In *New Generic Technologies in Developing Countries*. Ed. M. R. Bhagavan. New York: St. Martin's Press, 1997.

Chaffee, Steven H. *Explication*. Newbury Park, CA: Sage, 1991.

Davies, D. M. "Appropriate Information Technology." *International Library Review* 17 (1985): 247–58.

Eckaus, Richard S. "Appropriate Technologies for Developing Countries." Washington, DC: National Academy of Sciences, 1977.

Ehn, Pelle. *Work-Oriented Design of Computer Artifacts*. Stockholm: Arbetslivscentrum, 1988.

Epskamp, K., and A. Boeren. *The Empowerment of Culture: Development Communication and the Popular Media*. The Hague, Netherlands: Centre for the Study of Education in Developing Countries, 1992.

FAO. "Pioneering a New Approach to Communication in Rural Areas: The Peruvian Experience with Video for Training at Grassroots Level." Rome, Italy: Food and Agricultural Organization, 1987.

Froehlich, T. J. "Ethical Considerations in Technology Transfer." *Library Trends* 39 (1991): 275–302.

Goulet, Denis. *The Uncertain Promise: Value Conflicts in Technology Transfer*. 2nd ed. New York: New Horizons Press, 1989.

Hakken, David. "Electronic Curb Cuts: Computing and the Cultural (Re) Construction of Disability in the United States." *Science as Culture* 4.21 (1995).

Hazeltine, Barrett, and Christopher Bull. *Appropriate Technology: Tools, Choices, and Implications*. San Diego, CA: Academic Press, 1999.

Matta, Khalil F., and Naji E. Boutros. "Barriers to Electronic Mail Systems in Developing Countries." *Information Society* 6 (1989): 59–68.

Moulton, Jeane. "Rethinking Interactivity: Lessons from Interactive Radio Instruction." *Development Communication Report* 81 (1993): 9–11.

Muller, Michael J., and Sarah Kuhn. "Special Issue: Participatory Design." *Communications of the ACM* 36.4 (1993): 24–103.

National Telecommunications and Information Administration. "Falling Through the Net: Defining the Digital Divide." 8 July 1999. 1 Aug. 1999 <http://www.ntia.doc.gov/ntiahome/fttn99/contents.html>.

Noll, A. Michael. "Anatomy of a Failure: Picturephone Revisited." *Communications Policy* 16 (1992): 307–16.

Norman, Donald A. *The Design of Everyday Things.* New York: Doubleday, 1988.

Oxfam. *The Field Directors' Handbook: An Oxfam Manual for Development Workers.* Oxford, UK: Oxfam Publications, 1985.

Samarajiva, Rohan. "Appropriate High Tech: Scientific Communication Options for Small Third World Countries." *The Information Society* 6 (1989): 29–46.

Schumacher, E. F. *Small Is Beautiful: Economics as if People Mattered.* New York: Harper and Row, 1973.

Singh, Sameer, Tamàs Domonkos Gedeon, and Youngju Rho. "Enhancing Comprehension of Web Information for Users with Special Linguistic Needs." *Journal of Communication* 48.2 (1998): 86–108.

U.S. National Technical Information Service. "Appropriate Technology Information for Developing Countries." 2nd ed. Washington, DC: U.S. Government Printing Office, 1979.

Werner, David, and Bill Bower. *Helping Health Workers Learn: A Book of Methods, Aids, and Ideas for Instructors at the Village Level.* Palo Alto, CA: Hesperian Foundation, 1982.

You've Got Mail. Dir. Nora Ephron. Warner Bros., 1998.

Chapter 7

From Rhetoric to Technology: A Transformation from Citizens into Consumers

Laura Blasi and Walter F. Heinecke

INTRODUCTION

The classrooms and the libraries of men like Thomas Jefferson held writings by Aristotle and Cicero, with lessons from classical rhetoric. Over the past two hundred years we have seen the study of rhetoric change, be redefined, and virtually vanish from our English classrooms. At the same time, the increasing presence of technology in our classrooms is accompanied by the underlying assumptions of corporate values and goals. We have seen the rise of corporate interests—both in the structure and in the purposes of education—as economic agendas infuse our curricula.

Technology has risen as a focal concern in secondary as well as postsecondary liberal arts and professional education. We seem intent as a society on ensuring that our citizenry, our student body, is technologically literate. What seems disturbing is an implicit shift where education for productive democratic participation is being replaced by education for effective consumption and compliance. Rhetoric was a skill that empowered young students to participate and persuade, to produce. Technology in education is aimed at creating effective consumers of information. In this chapter we explore the tensions inherent in the exchange of the skills once present in the study of rhetoric for the behaviors that are being cultivated through technology education.

It is our belief that the corporate values embedded in technology shape our students into passive consumers, and that this transformation will eventually undermine the social context that corporations rely upon. As it once was a priority for schools to work with the needs of business to fuel the economy, it is in the best interest of both to come together now to strengthen our communities. While on one level this may be accomplished with the infusion of corporate funding to support our schools, financial support alone will not suffice. Concentrated efforts need to be made to educate, rather than train, a diverse citizenship. The economic agenda that we highlight in the transformation of the study of rhetoric is also present as technology increasingly becomes part of our classrooms. After reviewing this transformation of the study of rhetoric over time, we will then visit several current examples to illustrate the corporate presence in our classrooms through technology. We will conclude with the possibility of a new "rhetoric of technology" that would allow for the language and the pedagogy that will require that both teachers and instructional technology designers focus on the interactive and communicative potential of classroom technology.

THE TRANSFORMATION OF RHETORIC

Over two hundred years ago the "Founding Fathers" drafted the Declaration of Independence. Has there been a more auspicious example of collaborative writing in the history of the United States? Fourteen years prior to the drafting of the Declaration of Independence, King George III had appointed Hugh Blair the first Regius Professor of Rhetoric at the University of Edinburgh. Michael Moran has noted that "although Blair did not entirely reject classical rhetoric, he did continue the shift in the theory from the production of discourse to the reading of discourse" (5). Moran notes that style was emphasized over invention. This is not the first time that rhetoric was parsed. Approximately 333 BCE Aristotle defined rhetoric as having three modes of persuasion: logos (appeal to reason), pathos (appeal to emotion), and ethos (by the appeal of our personality or character) (Corbett 37). Contemporary writings by Chaim Perleman, Luci Olbretchs-Tyteca, Steven Toulmin, and Jurgen Habermas have emphasized reason, discourse, and logic in the twentieth century, but as logic was parsed from rhetoric in its definition prior to Blair, the impact was felt in the changing curriculum of American schools. The consequences of this division are still evident in today's English classes, in instances where form is valued over content.

Today we still use the word democracy, and we still abide by the Declaration of Independence, which was written by men who had studied classical rhetoric, but our educational emphasis has shifted. The redefinition of rhetoric had an impact on English classes as logic evolved out of the school curriculum. Left on its own in the curriculum, rhetoric is often viewed as having negative, ornamental connotations. Writing skills are sometimes secluded in composition courses or separated out of the disciplinary areas in postsecondary education. In secondary education, writing and speaking skills are the exclusive domain of

English teachers, who frequently join elementary teachers in helping students meet statewide standards or the benchmarks of national testing aimed at basic skills and competencies, rather than being supported in their efforts to help students become literate in forms of discourse, modes of persuasion, and the ways they can critically listen, read, and create.

As we understand how the split between logic and rhetoric occurred, and how it manifested itself in the classroom, we then can ask if there were elements of rhetoric that encouraged qualities or skills in students that would in turn lead to more active citizenship. As the unintended consequences of educational decisions fueled by economic trends become evident, we predict that the passive acceptance of technology into the classroom may actually damage the social fabric within which corporations are enmeshed. Integrated learning systems and "drill and skill" software move students away from active citizenship toward the intellectual prowess more suited to passive consumerism.

FROM CONTENT TO FORM

In the second century, Corbett notes, "Grammar, logic, and rhetoric constituted the trivium, the four-year undergraduate course of study leading to a bachelor of arts" (546). The master's course was composed of music, arithmetic, geometry, and astronomy—called the quadrivium—and lasted three years. Peter Ramus in the seventeenth century influenced the definition of rhetoric by following the writings of Aristotle, who established rhetorical categories and structure, Cicero (106–43 BCE), who advocated that an orator needed to know a wide range of subjects, and Quintilian (AD 35–99), who emphasized that moral character was also important. The Ramists were those who "assigned invention and arrangement to the province of logic and allocated only style to rhetoric" (Corbett 553; Bizzell and Herzberg 9).

Further illuminating this shift, Bizzell and Herzberg write that Ramus "formally separates invention (and arrangement as well) and assigns it to dialectic . . . rhetoric in Ramus' scheme is confined to style, memory, and delivery" (Bizzell and Herzberg 10; Berlin, *Writing Instruction in Nineteenth-Century* 13). The rise of the scientific academies also signaled a revolt against the logic of Aristotle. "The new logic was empirical—a scientific logic. And in overthrowing Aristotelian logic, the age discarded Aristotelian rhetoric as well, if only for its association with the deductive method" (Berlin, *Writing Instruction in Nineteenth-Century* 17).

The shift from the content of rhetoric to aesthetics has been described by Sharon Crowley. "It is true that modern aesthetic notions made inroads into the new rhetoric, as is witnessed by the inclusion of the term belles-lettres in the title of Hugh Blair's popular *Lectures on Rhetoric and Belles-Lettres.* . . . But the rise of aesthetics and the fall of rhetoric are also linked by their entanglement in a larger cultural change" (Crowley 33).[1] Crowley notes that the shift away from rhetoric soon followed, leading students away from civic virtue and toward "the bourgeois project of self-improvement" partially influenced by Kant's *Critique of Judgement* (1997).

The shift also gathered momentum as Americans sought to distance their education from the British system and from the aristocratic underpinnings of the European model (Berlin, *Writing Instruction in Nineteenth-Century* 18). Prior to Kant and Hume's earlier work, the study of rhetoric included character development and civic virtue. After these writers, we see the decline of rhetoric as education becomes more about cultivating good taste, and is shifted toward the study of literature (Crowley 34). S. Michael Halloran, citing the Declaration as an example, also notes that "through the eighteenth century, individualism was in this country chiefly a matter of political rights, but during the nineteenth century the idea that everyone has a right to rise socially and economically took root" (165).

It is interesting to note that with this movement the rhetorical education that was available only to select men does not disappear completely. As education becomes more prevalent, libraries flourish, and writing implements become less difficult to obtain and use, the elements of rhetoric undergo a transformation of sorts, in terms of access. The rhetorical elements gradually disappear from the undergraduate curriculum, but they reappear for those who can gain entry in the professional schools.

THE DECLINE OF RHETORIC: THE RISE OF CORPORATE CONCERNS

Increasing professionalization transformed the priorities for teaching, and the preferred approaches to writing and communicating. Scientific writing from Francis Bacon (1561–1626) onwards moved writing away from moral topics and toward observations and the extrapolation of theory based on inductive reasoning. The scientific academies were established and professionalism was on the rise. In relation to this rise, Halloran explains, " 'expertise' was rooted in methods of inquiry particular to the profession, a point which helps to account for the often noted decline of invention in nineteenth-century rhetoric. . . . [W]ithin the ethos of professionalism, passion would ideally be eliminated altogether" (168).

The rise of governmental representation and the legal profession at the end of the eighteenth century and into the next, dispersing the role of public speaking to representatives, shifted emphasis away from oratory, which had been intertwined with rhetoric. This shift left only elocution or stylized delivery as the defining element of the school subject. The methods employed in teaching rhetoric were out of touch with the changing society of the eighteenth century and the years that followed. Under medieval pedagogical beliefs students were expected to memorize and model, translate between Latin and English, take dictation from their professors, and recite aloud (Halloran 153).

James Berlin has pointed out that rhetoric at the beginning of the twentieth century saw the rise of instructors echoing John Dewey's belief in pragmatic education toward social reform and a strengthened democracy at the turn of the nineteenth century ("Writing Instruction in School" 194). In his list he includes Fred Newton Scott, Joseph Villiers, and Katherine Stewart Worthington, among others. But he adds that this impulse was subsumed in the implementation of a 1917 report by the Office of Education, titled "Reorganization of English in the Secondary Schools," and a 1944 report titled "Education for All American Youth," released by the Progressive Education Association.[2] The implementation of both reports emphasized efficiency and utilitarian skills, echoing the values of Frederick Taylor, which were being applied to work environments.

Rhetoric continues to be researched and studied by teachers and scholars like Edward P. J. Corbett, Richard Weaver, Sharon Crowley, and James J. Murphy. Composition has evolved through efforts like the National Writing Project toward expressionistic writing, the use of ethnography, and process writing, with students at the center, and often casting the teacher as researcher. Much more thorough examinations of the history and the elements of rhetoric have been written than we intend to detail here (see the Works Cited for references). We have taken a brief glimpse at the shift away from rhetoric in English classrooms. We can now bring some of what we have seen during this shift to bear upon our understanding of the impact technology can have on our classrooms.

MARKETING TO TEACHERS: WILL CORPORATIONS BECOME THE NEW CURRICULUM DESIGNERS?

As the study and practice of rhetoric were further defined by economic agenda in the twentieth century, curricular aims increasingly emphasized efficiency and utilitarian skills, mirroring the values of Frederick Taylor. Sixty years later the drive for "computer literacy" and to "wire" our classrooms has been connected to an underlying corporate agenda. Goodson and Mangan cite Noble's arguments that this technology agenda is "motivated more by the needs of business and the military than by its inherent educational worth" (68).

Along with this drive toward computer literacy, standards are being put in place to hold schools accountable to their communities. While standards help to make the expectations across districts or divisions transparent, we can also see the ripples of "Total Quality Management" (TQM) in these new approaches to education. We see corporate expectations foisted on education, as the language of education is co-opted by business and the military.

For instance, with the recent implementation of the Standards of Learning (SOLs) in Virginia, the state Department of Education is collecting model lesson plans and establishing resource centers. Is this function to be assumed by corporations that take the initiative to put materials on the Web? In this process we should ask: What are the sources of model lessons and resources? What and whose values and interests do these materials reflect? Technology and software reflect the values of their creators (Altheide; Pfaffenberger). If the "information superhighway" is to be treated as a "marketplace of ideas," then who is advantaged and disadvantaged in the production of Internet curricular materials for mass educational consumption?

Edutest, Inc., founded in 1995, claims that its on-line tests and diagnostic information are "being used in Virginia elementary and middle schools, as well as other schools throughout the nation, to provide independent assessment, immediate results and feedback, and critical performance information" (17 Feb. 1999). As this corporation moves to align itself with the newly implemented Virginia Standards of Learning, it provides an example of how the corporate world is using the Web to pander to the fears of teachers, administrators, and parents, while supporting the new curriculum to make a profit. As opposed to the way in which textbook companies plug into these changes for profit, Web-based interactive resources feed off the limitations teachers currently face (such as lack of time and fragmented scheduling), and promote pedagogy based on drills and quantitative data that circumvents the expertise of the teachers and the learning styles of the students. The corporation is reinforcing the drive for "teaching-to-the-test" that is becoming an imperative for many teachers as the scores are linked to statewide school accreditation.

The drive to use drills and quantitative data bears no relationship to the cultivation of citizenship—or does it? It certainly does seem to exist independently of the rising statistics regarding youth violence in today's schools and communities. According to a report from the National Center for Education Statistics, "Violence and Discipline Problems in U.S. Public Schools: 1996–97," 47 percent of elementary and secondary school principals reported incidents such as theft/larceny, vandalism, physical attacks and/or fights without a weapon; 10 percent reported one or more serious violent crimes or acts, such as rape or sexual battery, suicide, robbery, physical attacks or fights with a weapon (the survey was conducted with a nationally representative sample of 1,234 public elementary, middle, and secondary schools in the fifty states and the District of Columbia).

A polite euphemism for the youth violence in schools and communities might be "socialization problems." But in research literature on effective teaching, student achievement does not include social or moral development (Brophy and Good). When student achievement is defined by standardized test scores, then pedagogy becomes tailored to the test, and the students' skills that are cultivated are those which help them efficiently take the test.

Citing earlier research (Soar and Soar), Brophy and Good have shown that high socioeconomic status (SES) students (grades 3–6) relate positively to high-cognitive-level activities, whereas achievement in low SES (fifth grade) classes was associated with recitation or drill. They state that "interactions between process-product findings and student SES or achievement level indicate that low-SES–low-achieving students need more control and structuring: more active instruction and feedback, more redundancy, and smaller steps with higher success rates" (365). Here economic status in combination with other factors like their parents' level of education can preordain the type of education that a student receives. When tracking groups of students according to the abilities they cultivate toward "achieving" on the standardized tests, this practice then sets up a cycle reinforcing particular approaches to pedagogy. In his review of research literature on performance assessment, Tony Lam has pointed out that assessment is unfair if:

1. students are not provided with equal opportunity to demonstrate what they know (e.g., some students were not adequately prepared to perform a type of assessment task) and thus the assessments are biased;
2. these biased assessments are used to judge student capabilities and needs;
3. and these distorted views of the students are used to make educational decisions that ultimately lead to limitations of educational opportunities for them.

When assessment is used as a predetermined benchmark, rather than as a diagnostic, it influences the skills required of students and the pedagogy used by teachers in order to meet that benchmark. Research has shown that technology is being used in some lower SES classrooms to advance lower-order skills, and to reinforce student competency regarding drill and recitation.

Harold Wenglinsky of Educational Testing Service, in his 1998 study, "Does It Compute? The Relationship Between Educational Technology and Student Achievement in Mathematics," has written that "it appears, then, that there is little difference in computer use between advantaged and disadvantaged groups in fourth grade, but great differences in eighth grade. In eighth grade, minority, poor, and urban students are more likely to find themselves learning lower-order skills than their White, non-poor, and suburban counterparts; disadvantaged students are also less likely to find themselves learning higher-order skills."

He notes that "disadvantaged groups do seem to be less likely to have teachers well-prepared to use computers, and disadvantaged eighth-graders seem to be less likely to be exposed to higher order learning through computers." But he goes on to explain that "identifying some disparities does not suggest whether these disparities matter. The importance of the disparity for a given indicator depends upon the overall significance of that indicator to academic achievement and other educational outcomes."

Here, too, it seems that the definition of "student achievement" plays a significant role in determining the types of higher- or lower-order skills that a student will be required to learn. Testing and standards heavily influence these skills. Meanwhile, there is little incentive for teachers to cultivate the interactive, communicative, and productive practices that would lend themselves to participatory citizenship. As researchers on student achievement and teaching effectiveness separate out independent variables, they seem to be removed from the quality of life issues and the "socialization problems" that are shaping the environment within which many students are being asked to learn.

Stepping away from assessment and student achievement, we now look at the relationship between technology and content organized and mandated by standards. After looking at educational practices that are driven by corporate values (such as benchmarking) and the role companies like Edutest have in profiting from standards, we can ask if corporations will provide the national linkages between all of the standards—in essence becoming the "new" curriculum coordinators. In searching the Web we can, for example, visit a site on the Declaration of Independence called *founding.com*. The state of California provides this example, linked to its educational standards. The content of the site provides the text of the Declaration with an accompanying interpretation and links to the larger organization that is behind these materials. This organization is called the Claremont Institute.

Here a corporate body is redefined as nonprofit, but has been organized by various corporate officers. In creating Web materials later linked to standards, it has stepped in and designed educational materials that have been given a seal of approval by a state official. The Claremont Institute's site explains that their mission since 1979 has been "to restore the principles of the American Founding to their rightful, preeminent authority in our national life." They further note: "The Claremont Institute believes that informed citizens can and will make the right choices for America's future." Among other resources they offer, the institute names the 1988 book, *The Imperial Congress* (co-published with the Heritage Foundation), and policy proposals such as their 1995 "Contract with California." Their twenty-three-member board boasts four people in higher education, but is composed mostly of corporate figures, including the president of North Central Life Insurance Company, the chairman of Grow Biz International, the president of the Tax and Financial Group, the president and CEO of Phillips Publishing International, Inc., and a member from the Ashbrook Center for Public Affairs.

Without contesting the value of an informed citizenry they emphasized earlier, it is important to note that in the information on this site Claremont's biases are pronounced in ways that those of a textbook or a teacher might not be permitted to be. In other areas of their site they argue for expanded development of weapons, and advocate for presidential impeachment, while listing Rush Limbaugh among their past speakers, and Clarence Thomas and Ronald Reagan as award-winners. Clearly politically active, their materials on the Declaration are accompanied by an interpretation that at some points makes assertions based on the historical context of the Founders, and at other points is unclear about the extension of the philosophy over time. They stress the value of objective truth, for example, contrasting it with contemporary relativism. While textbooks and other educational materials are not considered "bias-free," districts go through a review process. As of 1999 we do not have such a process in place for resources developed on-line. The political undertones found on the Claremont site resonate louder when the site is linked to statewide educational policy.

The site is defined as part of a government requirement under Governor Pete Wilson's California Assembly Bill AB 3086 (Sept. 1996). This law requires

California high school students to know the fundamental ideas and documents from the American Founding before they may receive a high school diploma. Recently, text on the site stated that "the California State Superintendent of Public Instruction recommended [*founding.com*] as an educational tool for teaching these things to students" (Oct. 1998). To this end the site offers an essay titled "The Utility of [*founding.com*] for Teaching History-Social Science in California Public Schools" and a "User's Guide to the Declaration of Independence" to assist history-social science teachers in California public schools. The user's guide includes 10,000 pages of original source material, fully linked and searchable, and explanations of the "essential ideas" contained in the available documents.

The free market approach underlying the Internet advantages some and disadvantages others when it comes to the production and spread of Web-based curricular materials. There are advantages to using the Web to publish educational materials. In contrast to the textbook, the Web can be revised without recalling or reprinting thousands of textbooks. Sites also flow over transnational and disciplinary borders, allowing students to access materials from the cultural perspectives of those who have the access and the resources to create materials for the Web. As we have seen with hardcopy textbooks, the Web can offer primary materials compiled by designers for the ease of the educator. As is possible with a textbook, the materials on the Web are susceptible to political editorializing. This is evident in the *founding.com* site. But unlike the textbook, Web materials can be designed and used in the classroom without drawing from educational literature, schools, and practitioners, and there is no districtwide review process established for sites.

With or without a review process, we need to question the ways in which education literature and schools of education prepare teachers to evaluate, critique, and contextualize educational materials. In the press to integrate technology into classroom instruction, teachers may adopt an uncritical stance toward curricular materials found on the Web. What works may be defined as what is readily available for quick, mass consumption. We also need to return to the idea that, as was evident with the Edutest site, technology is once again being used to circumvent the expertise of the teacher and introduce an agenda, this time involving content, that is independent of the teaching and learning styles of the classroom. It provides content materials that ask teachers and students to simply absorb the Claremont Institute's beliefs, and these materials carry the weight of state mandates when linked to statewide standards.

Lest we take it for granted, the Web itself is a format, and all media formats structure what we come to accept as legitimate sources of knowledge (Altheide). Hence we find corporations advertising on national television presenting their Web addresses as a means for communicating their facility with the new format. The emergence of new players and changed standards for the design of educational materials—due to the incorporation of technology—has consequences for the teaching profession as well as for the immediate classroom. This new role asks educators, who become designers, to market, to package, and to contain their materials within the cognitive limitations of formats available on the Web. For parents who deliberate over their childrens' exposure to media, they may find that their care is usurped within the school system.

In addition to noting the effect the design has on the presentation of the materials, we can also question whether appeasing student inclinations toward the "edu-tainment" appeal of some classroom software should override the role of the school (in conjunction with families) in fostering discipline, a sense of community, and integrity—even if such values contradict the dominant images that saturate us through television and other popular media. The values underlying the ideal of "democracy" need to be developed within classrooms as we seek to help students assume active voices in contemporary U.S. democracy, a potentially participatory structure that is also being shaped by technology. Again, technology and educational standards make problematic the relationship between unbridled capitalism and democracy. Lessons on democracy exist within a format of the free market of ideas.

While the *founding.com* site allows us to look critically at the sources of online materials, it also provides an example of how teachers and parents can raise such issues with their students. In doing so we return to the questions: Who has created this site? What else do they do? Who are the people behind the design? What are their goals? Businesses have access to the money, the time, and the equipment, as well as an inclination toward using technology. These aptitudes are then coupled with an interest and an understanding of policy and education that reflect industrial priorities, rather than purely educational concerns.

Founding.com offers an example for us to think about in terms of the future of the development of educational materials, and the role that education schools will be able to play in this new virtual landscape. How should we prepare prospective teachers to use the Internet and other forms of technology in their teaching?

Technology has an impact far wider than simply changing the way teachers can present materials. In addition to reshaping the way students can navigate through the materials at their own pace, technology enables us to combine media in ways that were not accessible through textbooks. The Web's hypertext format allows the student to click on a term and be provided with a reference while reading the text from the Declaration of Independence. But the construction and the formation of knowledge through technology may redefine who provides the content—and for what purpose—especially when this is linked to educational policy. The introduction of technology is also shifting the job market—potentially creating new curriculum coordinators, and more lucrative employers for educators. This movement occurs at the same time corporations are offering online education, in a mode that competes with current U.S. educational practices. Indeed, some universities are undergoing metamorphoses in which postsecondary education is redefined as information brokerage (e.g., the University of Phoenix). If schools are not invited to this table, we need to carefully ask how we will be able to articulate a voice over and in spite of the rising call of corporations.

THEORIES DRIVE THE DESIGNS

The social efficiency movement's presence in education has had its impact on the definition of instructional technology. Instructional design courses have been called into question for the paradigm that designers are taught to use. The approach is often characterized as the "Dick and Carey" model, based on *The Systematic Design of Instruction: Dick and Carey*, which is in its fourth edition. Their concept map for instructional design follows several steps, which are less suited for the classroom than they are for assembly line tasks related to industry. While changes in instructional design are considered, use of the Dick and Carey model still influences the materials that are designed by people with backgrounds in instructional design.

Those without experience studying instructional design may or may not incorporate strictly behavioristic approaches to learning in their software or sites, but at this time the teacher is the only "translator" for these technologies—asking students to see the technological and cultural limitations of the software or the sites used. Teachers should be aware of the role of theory in instructional design, since these theories influence and direct the pedagogy built into the classroom technologies. An example of teaching beyond the parameters of the software might be to draw from research on the cultural and gender biases that are embedded in the Learning Company's "Oregon Trail" to help students create a historical context that develops beyond the game's goal to survive the journey (Bigelow).

Recognizing and teaching beyond the boundaries of the prescribed software and Web sites means that the context that the teacher creates for students learning with technology should take precedence in the classroom. But the creation and development of such a context, as we have already noted, is not supported in a climate of standards and mandatory testing. The understanding of context and historical background may be useful approaches for citizens to bring into community-building efforts, but these approaches are not valued in an education system that is fashioned on corporate accountability and fed by industrially crafted materials.

TECHNOLOGY AS A SYMBOL: THE VALUES OF CONSUMERS OR CITIZENS?

Behind every set of standards is a set of values about what is important to teach and how to best teach it. As we consider the range of materials available because of technology, we can call for standards just as quickly as publishers and corporations, envisioning controls to be applied (efficiently), perhaps accompanied by a list of acceptable and unacceptable ways of approaching topics and teaching. Naturally these would be "issued"—perhaps by a consortium or a governing body. Perhaps the best defense is a good offense. Perhaps arming students with the skills of rhetoric applied to technology is the best mechanism for guarding against corporate colonization of national, state, and local education curricula.

A revival of some of the values of rhetoric does not mean we need to resume dictation or grammar translation, but it could mean a heightened emphasis on invention and on citizenship. We believe that schools of education and education literature should strive across the curriculum to articulate the critical pedagogies that will ask teachers to help diffuse the corporate voice embedded in technology aimed at students. This would mean turning away from a passive, consumer model of education, while cutting through the chaos of materials available through free market technologies. The Web requires that everyone become an editor. An alternative would be to leave the decisions in the hands of coalitions, often driven by coalitions of universities advancing corporate interests, like Educause, and to wait for someone else to package educational materials.

The adoption of standards may or may not take place, and the decision may involve or ignore the perspective of teachers. As we see the level of influence corporations have on education, we need to remain mindful of the design behind the products and our own responsibilities while teaching with them and integrating them into our lives. If teachers consciously avoid teaching with or through technology, a decision has been made there, too. We need to resist the structures that ply us away from creativity and community building, those that break down the possibility of working toward a participatory democracy. Resisting means more than just standing aside. In this act we can reject the corporate goals of "creating good workers," or the drive for "efficiency" that rules out ambiguity, negotiation, and imagination.

While Goodson and Mangan ask us to scrutinize the connections between our definition of education, our moves to restructure, and the prevalence of computers in society, we cannot turn our eyes away from the values embedded in the technology that is already in our classrooms. While technology is becoming a viable symbolic way for corporate values to flood the classroom, technology also can become symbolic of a commitment for educators to illuminate the schools with their concern for teaching for productive means and against consumer trends. This moment gives universities an opportunity to stop allowing their language to be co-opted by business, to articulate the values and commitments that are unique to education. Our current condition calls out for the revival of the teaching of rhetoric, perhaps a rhetoric of technology. Language remains a powerful source of the means of the production and creation of the individual and communitarian self in a period when the technological drive for efficiency marches past ingenuity, intelligence, and inspiration (Ellul).

In addition to valuing teacher expertise and lessening the emphasis on national standards as a driving force behind learning, we need to acknowledge the relationship between corporations and technology in our classrooms. We can unmask the values and pedagogy that surround students in school as a consequence of that relationship. We can see how these values may later play out in terms of our students' commitment toward building and participating in the communities around them. A rhetoric of technology would be one step toward teaching teachers and then their students to unmask the values inherent in the discourse of technology (the drive for efficiency), the construction of technology (found in software and Web sites), and the ways we can communicate, create, and participate through technology.

NOTES

1. For additional insight into late eighteenth century rhetoricians, see also writings about and by George Campbell and Richard Whately.
2. For fuller details see (Berlin, "Writing Instructions in Schools" 201).

WORKS CITED

Altheide, David. *Media Power*. Beverly Hills: Sage Publications, 1985.

Berlin, James. *Writing Instruction in Nineteenth-Century American Colleges*. Edwardsville: Southern Illinois University Press, 1984.

———. "Writing Instruction in School and College English." In *A Short History of Writing Instruction*. Ed. James J. Murphy. Davis, CA: Hermagoras Press, 1990. 183–222.

Bigelow, William. "On the Road to Cultural Bias." *Social Studies and the Young Learner* 8.3 (1996): 26–29.

Bizzell, Patricia, and Bruce Herzberg. Introduction to *The Rhetorical Tradition*. Ed. Patricia Bizzell and Bruce Herzberg. Boston: St. Martin's Press, 1990. 1–13.

Brophy, Jerry, and Thomas Good. "Teacher Behavior and Student Achievement." In *The Handbook of Research on Teaching*. 3rd ed. Ed. Merlin C. Wittrock. New York: Macmillan, 1996. 328–75.

Corbett, Edward. *Classical Rhetoric for the Modern Student*. 3rd ed. New York: Oxford University Press, 1990.

Crowley, Sharon. *Composition in the University: Historical and Polemical Essays*. Pittsburgh: University of Pittsburgh Press, 1998.

Educause. 1 Aug. 1999 <http://www.educause.edu/>.

Edutest, Inc. 1 Aug. 1999 <www.edutest.com>.

Ellul, Jacques. *The Technological Society*. New York: Vintage, 1964.

Founding.com. 1 Aug 1999 <http://www.founding.com>.

Goodson, Ivor F., and J. Marshall Mangan. "Computer Literacy as Ideology." *British Journal of Sociology of Education* 17 (1996): 65–79.

Halloran, S. Michael. "From Rhetoric to Composition: The Teaching of Writing in America to 1990." In *A Short History of Writing Instruction*. Ed. James J. Murphy. Davis, CA: Hermagoras Press, 1990. 151–82.

Heaviside, Sheila, C. Rowand, C. Williams, and E. Farris. *Statistical Analysis Report; Violence and Discipline Problems in U.S. Public Schools: 1996–97*. Washington DC: National Center for Education Statistics, March 18, 1998.

Humphreys, R. A. "The Rule of Law and the American Revolution. In *The Role of Ideology in the American Revolution*. Ed. John R. Howe, Jr. Atlanta: Holt, Rinehart and Winston, 1970. 20–27.

Kant, Immanuel. *Critique of Judgement*. Trans. J. C. Meredith. New York: Oxford University Press, 1997.

Lam, Tony. "Fairness in Performance Assessment." *ERIC Digest*. ERIC Clearinghouse on Assessment and Evaluation (1995): ED391982.

Mendelson, M. "Declamation, Context and Controversiality." *Rhetoric Review* 13 (1994): 192–97.

Moran, Michael. Introduction to *Eighteenth-Century British and American Rhetorics and Rhetoricians*. Ed. Michael Moran. Westport, CT: Greenwood Press, 1994. 1–10.

Pfaffenberger, Bryan. *Microcomputer Applications in Qualitative Research*. Newbury Park, CA: Sage Publications, 1988.

Wenglinsky, Harold. "Does It Compute? The Relationship Between Educational Technology and Student Achievement in Mathematics." *pic@ets.org*. Princeton, NJ: ETS Policy Information Center, Educational Testing Service, 1988. 1 Aug 1999 <http://www.ets.org/research/pic/technolog.html>.

Chapter 8

Is There a Professor in This Class?

David C. Paris

INTRODUCTION

In his book *Is There a Text in This Class?*, Stanley Fish challenges two views of literary interpretation. The first sees the text as a "self-sufficient repository of meaning." That is, if the text is the datum or object of study, and "if meaning is embedded in the text, the reader's responsibilities are limited to the job of getting it out" (2). This view is often opposed to one suggesting that the meaning of a text is the reader's response(s) to it: "one could not point to this meaning as one could if it were the property of the text; rather one could observe or follow its gradual emergence in the interaction between the text, conceived as a succession of words, and the developing response of the reader" (3). Fish argues that these views are insufficient, for they fail to take into account the role of interpretive communities in determining what is read and how it is understood. It is neither reader nor text that is primary but a much broader, historically situated and evolving community of understandings—"that interpretation is the source of text, facts, authors, and intentions" (16).

Fish's view, like much of contemporary literary theory, tends to reveal and challenge settled assumptions about academic inquiry, particularly by pointing out the cultural perspectives and social contexts that inform them. Something similar seems to be happening as electronic technologies present different pedagogical and institutional possibilities. The role of the professor is certainly likely to change as these technologies develop. Given the development of instructional software, multimedia materials, and distance learning options of various sorts, the question "Is there a professor in this class?" does not seem as strange as it might have at one time. Just as the relationship of reader and text must be put into the context of a broader community, so too the relationship of professor and student must likewise be reevaluated in light of changes in learning communities and institutions made possible by these new technologies.

Much of the recent discussion and debate focuses on the issue of the *pedagogical* uses, impact, and value of the new technologies. The suggestion here is that, as important as pedagogical issues are, they need to be examined in a broader *institutional* context. The immediate impacts of technology at the postsecondary level may be more institutional than pedagogical, and pedagogical questions cannot be fully addressed without seeing their interaction with issues of institutional identity and purpose. I will use my own tentative explorations with the use of the Web in teaching as a kind of case study of what some of these issues are and how they might be addressed.

PEDAGOGY: "DOWN AND INTO" VERSUS "UP AND OUT"

There has been a great deal of discussion in the last decade about the potential for electronic technology to transform education at all levels, but especially in the postsecondary sector. The pace of that discussion has increased in the past five years with the development of the World Wide Web. Technological optimists see the Web as a huge pedagogical asset that provides students and instructors with incredible access to information and people. At its most heated, the rhetoric concerning the new technologies suggests a shift in education analogous to the change from speech to writing in the ancient world or the advent of the printing press several hundred years ago (Young). On the other hand, skeptics point out that the discussion of these technologies mimics a number of previous instances in which technology promised much but delivered little. Thomas Edison's claim that films would replace books was a good example of overselling technology, as were the claims that television would be a revolutionary pedagogical tool (Oppenheimer). Perhaps equally important, doubters suggest that for all the hype there is little or no evidence that technology actually improves instruction. Indeed, the most common finding is that there is "no significant difference" between distance instruction in any medium and more standard approaches (Russell; Verduin and Clark).

Much of the debate about the new technologies is phrased in a familiar idiom of "man vs. machine," whether technology-based instruction can effectively replace face-to-face interaction. But the use of technology can only be evaluated against some specific pedagogical expectations. Even a cursory examination of these suggests that technology is likely to have a profound effect on pedagogy, but perhaps not in a straightforward way. If technology threatens the traditional relationship of professor to students, it implies, ironically, other possibilities that may not be as readily met through technology.

Think of a college classroom and a certain image arises. The professor enters a building, walks through the classroom door, and steps up to the lectern or sits down at the seminar table. A lecture or discussion follows that covers material that students have (presumably) read. The material may be most anything, but certainly literature, history, and other liberal arts come to mind. In addition to this material, the professor brings his or her disciplinary knowledge and experience to the lecture or discussion.

Pedagogically, the key to this image is the centrality of the professor. Just as the text was the central object in the traditional process of interpreting literature, so too the professor is the authoritative representative of a discipline and subject matter to the students. He or she brings the material "down" from the discipline and library "into" the classroom. It is common to speak of "Professor X's course" in this or that subject that the students "take" from him or her. He or she sets the agenda, provides the syllabus, grades the material, and so on. All the instructional roles and functions are bundled into the person of the professor in the classroom. The professor defines what the class is, how it is conducted, what the students "get" by way of material and grades. Studies of classrooms, even those that have a discussion format or are supposedly student-centered, find that they are dominated by "teacher talk."

This traditional model of the "sage on the stage" is, perhaps inevitably, both widely practiced and often criticized. The widely praised, though far less practiced, alternative notion sees the professor as a "guide on the side." It envisions students spending class time working on projects, often in groups, and being more active participants in the construction of their own understanding of material. Chickering and Gamson's often-cited comparison of the two views praises faculty-student interaction, group work, constant feedback on tasks, and individualized treatment. The shorthand way to describe this shift is changing the emphasis from teaching to learning (Barr and Tagg).

Of course, the debate between subject and student-centered pedagogy predates the development of new technologies. But the new technologies transform that debate. First, the necessity of the instructor bringing material "down" and "into" the classroom is obviated by the fact that information of all sorts is available from the desktop. If students can access information/lectures, software packages, and training at a distance, then there seems to be little need for the professor as an intermediary. Similarly, for many simple tasks, such as those that involve more structured or algorithmic problems, the professor can be virtually replaced by software or materials that will guide and grade students through, for example, a set of math problems. In either case the relatively bounded relationship of the professor and student within the classroom, like the traditional reader and text in Fish's formulation, is recast in light of the new technology. The new technologies open up a broader set of relationships to a community of information and materials that go beyond the professor and the classroom. As one observer puts it, "If the data road-warriors are right, students will be able to download any book in the Library of Congress, participate in a geological excavation in

Morocco, interview the Prime Minister of Japan, or call up the latest Nobel laureate to discuss cold fusion. The funny thing is that a lot of these predictions could actually happen" (Salvador 34).

At first glance, then, the new technologies displace the traditional "sage" by making it possible for instruction to be delivered at a distance. The explosion of on-line providers (Marchese), the construction of Western Governors University and other virtual institutions like the University of Phoenix, and the rapid development of on-line offerings by traditional residential colleges and universities strongly suggest that distance learning has a new meaning and legitimacy. If, as is typically found, distance learning offerings are generally as effective as more traditional ones, then the advantages of cost and access would give on-line courses powerful advantages. Eli Noam takes this line of reasoning to a logical, if apocalyptic, conclusion by suggesting that the tasks of the university—the creation, storage, and diffusion of knowledge—no longer require universities as (physical) institutions: "In the past people came to information which was stored at the university. In the future the information will come to the people wherever they are. What then is the role of the university?" (Noam 247). Steven Ehrmann ("What") raises the question more succinctly: "What good is a campus today?"

There are, however, some ironic twists in the scenario of technology somehow replacing the traditional "sage." First, the new technologies may do best what is least desired. "Distance education" now has a new and powerful medium, but it can still be a variation of the traditional model or "transmission belt" of information—just another "sage." As observers are quick to point out, the potential downside of this new medium is that increased access to information may end up being merely an amplification of the traditional model or, worse, the creation of "digital diploma mills" (Noble). The gains achieved in terms of access and efficiency might not correspond to gains in depth of learning and understanding. In fact, there are probably some tradeoffs between these two dimensions (Gilbert). The criteria of improved teaching and learning involving more in-depth and active engagement among students, teachers, and technology are not as readily met simply through electronic delivery.

At the same time, expectations about enhancing teaching and learning have been moving away from traditional forms (the "sage") in part because of electronic technologies. It is now easier to imagine students playing the more active and engaged role anticipated in shifting from "teaching" to "learning." And typically, one of the most promising features and common selling points of computer-assisted instruction has been that it can provide individualized instruction, that it is in important ways student-centered. William Massy and Robert Zemsky call this "mass customization: Technology allows faculty to accommodate individual differences in student goals, learning styles, and abilities, while providing improved convenience for both students and faculty on an 'any time, any place' basis." Moreover, all the promising features of computer-assisted instruction—convenience, engagement, and individualization—are potentially heightened with each improvement in electronic technologies.

Once the professor is no longer the source of information, then "the guide on the side" becomes a more fertile possibility. Instead of bringing information "down" and "into" the classroom, the professor can now become a genuine guide and move students "up" and "out" to materials and information made available through technology. This might be as simple as a "studio" course in which students work on problems in software packages at separate stations. Or it might be the gathering of information from the Web for presentation to the class, communication with other classes, and so on. Students guided by and moving beyond the professor in the classroom to connect to broader communities of information and interpretation is no longer just a technological dream (Means and Olson).

This partial shift in pedagogical focus raises two questions. The first is whether the new technologies "work," in some sense, against certain expectations. The second, related question concerns the role and value of face-to-face instruction in meeting these expectations. We have far more information, if not definitive conclusions, about the former than the latter. But in both cases it is clear that assessment is lacking, and needed.

Many of the studies of the results from using technology in instruction suggest that it can be effective, even though in many instances there are no significant differences (Russell; Kulik and Kulik). But even if the latter is true, then cost savings and access would seem to give an edge to technology-based education. At the same time, despite all the research about the effects of technology-based instruction or college education more generally, there is a widespread sense that our assessment tools are still lacking; we lack confidence about what truly affects students in college (Cross; Pascarella and Terenzini). This is perhaps best captured in Stephen Ehrmann's anecdote about the Harvard graduates who could not say why it was colder in the winter. Lest this be seen as an indictment of Ivy League education, Ehrmann also points out that middle schoolers who had been recently given a unit on the subject did not really understand it even as they appeared to give the right answers to test questions. He notes that "students' preexisting theories remained invisible to the teacher, and often untouched by instruction" ("Asking" 22).

It is interesting to note that for all the talk of assessment in postsecondary circles there is nothing like the arsenal of tests and measures of outcomes in K–12 education in the United States. One of the salutary effects that the new technologies have had on postsecondary education is to bring the question of assessment to the fore. Distance educators have always measured (or claimed to measure) their work by results rather than seat time, and hence assessment has always been an issue. But as on-line courses become a more integral part of, and potential competitor to, more common approaches and institutional arrangements, the question of results becomes more visible and more crucial.

Indeed, one of the promises, as yet unfulfilled, of various on-line universities is that there will be "competency-based credentials" certified by third party or independent assessments of results (Western Governors University; Denning). This kind of assessment might be part of a general "unbundling" of the roles of the professor as design, instruction, mentoring, and assessment can all potentially be handled by different parties through the medium of technology (Massy and Zemsky; Young).

The developing pedagogical issues around technology suggest a renewed focus on student-centered, constructive work. They also point to the importance of assessment, particularly as technology-based education is institutionalized. However, many of these pedagogical discussions perhaps do not go far enough in their move toward student-centeredness or institutional analysis. If we look more closely at the "markets" for postsecondary education, we find a somewhat different notion of student-centeredness that has more immediate institutional consequences.

THE CAMPUS MARKET(S): WHAT GOOD IS AN EDUCATION?

The debate on the pedagogical possibilities and effects of the new technologies is likely to continue. However, what is often missing from that debate is reference to the institutional context in which instruction occurs. The institutional effects of the new technologies are perhaps more visible and profound than their pedagogical ones. That is, just as the new technologies have reshaped the debate about pedagogy, so too are they now reshaping the debate about institutional forms and purposes. Specifically, the new technologies seem to create new possibilities for the student as client or consumer, increase the differentiation of the "market" for postsecondary education, and, again, put a premium on outcomes and assessment. As in the pedagogical arena, each of these developments disrupts the traditional image of the professor in the classroom promoting (liberal) education.

In the case of the traditional classroom discussed earlier, the idea of a college or university evokes a certain image—residential, selective, noninstrumental. The students emerging from the class described earlier might walk out onto the campus and discuss their work with their peers, go to the library or lab, or head off to an athletic or club activity akin to what they did in high school. The residential campus provides the opportunity for students to immerse themselves in their education, as well as providing other opportunities and services. Likewise, facilities for research and teaching—the complex of library, laboratories, and classrooms—are the "infrastructure" supporting faculty and students. The university selects students and brings them into its network of courses and facilities as part of its mission to create and disseminate knowledge. Although that knowledge might be part of some specific prevocational or professional program, the core of the university is the disinterested pursuit and dissemination of knowledge for its own sake. Norms of academic freedom, the institution of tenure, and so on all insulate the university as a self-governing collection of scholars.

This stereotypical image of selective, residential, elite colleges and universities as paradigmatic of postsecondary education probably never fully reflected its more complex realities—perhaps even less so recently. The residential campus is increasingly unrepresentative of postsecondary education, as more and more students are part time and "nontraditional" in terms of age and interests. They are seeking particular kinds of courses or credentials rather than some general or liberal education. Similarly, the vast majority of the roughly 3,300 colleges and universities in the United States have very low rates of selectivity or are de facto open admissions. As a college degree is increasingly seen as akin to what a high school diploma was a generation or two ago, more students are pursuing education beyond high school. Finally, the image of the college or university as disinterested has always been belied by the continual adding on of instrumental functions and programs, beginning with the establishment of land grant universities and continuing through the creation of community colleges.

Taking these realities into account suggests that there are several different markets for postsecondary education. The traditional image of the college or university is taken from the "name brand" institutions, those that compete for top rankings (for example, in *U.S. News & World Report*) and provide for "rite-of-passage students . . . holistic experiences . . . which are preparatory experiences in their continuing pursuit of education" (Zemsky, Shaman, and Iannozzi 35–36). But the vast majority of postsecondary institutions do not compete in this market. There is a growing "convenience/user-friendly" segment that is increasingly customer-driven, instrumental, and specialized, in which students "are more likely to see themselves as shoppers buying their postsecondary education one or two courses at a time. They have learned to search for the best price, the most convenient time, and the most appropriate place to take the next set of courses they think they require" (35).

The idea that education might be thought of as a commodity that is bought and sold in a market or markets is often foreign to most discussions in postsecondary institutions. Much of the discussion of the aims of educational institutions takes a distinctly philosophical tone, with references to student development, critical capacities, reflection, the "life of the mind," and so on. Oddly, for all the talk about the value of student-centered pedagogy, there is, perhaps necessarily, not much attention to what students are seeking from their education. The "guide on the side" is still a guide to a subject matter, and in the traditional picture of the university the subjects and courses of study are established by the faculty, again, in the interests of producing and disseminating knowledge, "prescribing the life of the mind" (Anderson).

If, however, we think in a more radically student-centered way that reflects the "markets" for postsecondary education—if students are considered (or consider themselves) customers or clients—the issue then becomes what students are seeking to purchase in the various markets for postsecondary education. Recently, David Labaree has suggested that many of the institutional developments in postsecondary education, particularly its continuing expansion, can be best understood in terms of credentialism. That is, students are less seeking use value out of education than exchange value. This in turn explains the commonly noted disengagement of students from academic work at all levels of education, "because the primary goal of pursuing an education has become the acquisition of educational credentials—symbolic goods, such as grades, credits, and degrees—rather than the acquisition of useful skills and knowledge" (251). In Labaree's account, market pressure is the primary villain in this drama. As he puts it, "By redefining education as a commodity whose acquisition can help individuals get ahead of the pack, market pressures have led to the reconstruction of the educational system in the service of a private pursuit of individual advantage" (252).

Although one might share Labaree's dismay about the credentialism in education and its pedagogical effects, his analysis does not differentiate between market segments. His argument suggests that, in whatever market, students' hopes are quite similar. They hope that their courses and degrees will help them enter, or advance in, (middle-class) jobs and careers; education is really the accumulating of credentials more than anything else. But the process that Labaree describes may work differently in different markets because of technology, and the new electronic technologies are making more visible the "market" aspects of postsecondary education and thereby sharpening the distinctions in these markets. As in the case of changes in traditional pedagogical notions, the new technologies are altering the stereotypical view of the college or university as an institution. These institutional changes also have some ironic results, especially as they raise questions about outcomes and assessment.

Not surprisingly, the new technologies have had the biggest impact on the "convenience/user-friendly" segment of the market. On-line courses are attractive to part-time and nontraditional students who cannot be full-time and in residence. The notions of "continuing education" and "lifelong learning" are no longer just clichés. Moreover, these programs are often focused on specific professional certification of various kinds; for example, the new programs of the Western Governors University are largely pre-professional in nature. Perhaps most important, the claim for distance learning alternatives and the virtual university, beyond cost and convenience, is that they will be subject to stricter and clearer measures of assessment and accountability. Once "seat time" (in conjunction with grades) is no longer used as one of the primary measures of educational credit and accreditation, then issues of results—skills and knowledge, that is, use value—potentially come to the fore. Absent these traditional input-based measures, the virtual university inevitably faces issues of quality and accountability. However, proponents of distance education see this as a virtue, not a liability; for example, the new for-profit institutions are spending a good deal on assessment as a way of enticing customers and ensuring satisfaction.

Much of the turmoil generated by electronic alternatives has not hit the more traditional "name brand" segments of the postsecondary market. Although there is increasing unease about cost, many upper-middle-class parents, prosperous in a long-growing economy, are willing to foot the bill. The intuition that face-to-face instruction is better than any electronic alternative, that there is social value in the residential experience and the range of services offered on a campus, and above all that the "name brand" schools offer a credential that leads to professional education and attractive job opportunities continues to keep applications up at the most selective schools. The demand for assessment or outcome measures, other than the grades and a degree from a prestigious college or university, has yet to "trickle up" to these institutions.

Indeed, the response to issues of client or customer satisfaction in the "name brand" segment of the market has been typically to focus on inputs, not outcomes, and the issue of assessment is often viewed with skepticism, if not hostility. A study of cost increases at several selective institutions by Clotfelter suggests that in the absence of clear measures of quality, the dominant strategy is one of "buying the best." In order to compete with other comparable institutions and to address "unbounded aspirations" from various constituencies, these schools expand services and existing programs. "[T]here exists a general consensus within institutions that they should strive for excellence . . . each institution carries with it a set of goals that few could actually achieve. Consequently room for improvement always exists, and university leaders can always produce lists of worthwhile projects for which money could be readily spent" (49–50). The striving for excellence involves a product that is "essential, ephemeral" (28).

There are at least a couple of ironies in this situation. The market forces potentially creating "digital diploma mills" that are seen as antithetical to educational values may actually be producing pressure against the prevailing credentialism. That is, the combination of market forces and technology is creating comparable or perhaps even countervailing pressures for educational programs and measurements that are more squarely focused on use as well as exchange value. These pressures are already being felt in the convenience segment of the market. And this produces a further irony. Market responsiveness in the "name brand" sector, supposedly the leaders of the industry, is not to look at results but to increase inputs. Thus the relationship of use and exchange value is (or soon will be) different in different market segments. Educational markets will become increasingly differentiated because of the use of technology and its implications for assessment.

Looked at in one way, the bifurcated market produces comparisons favorable to the convenience segment. These institutions are the wave of the future, it might be argued, because of their businesslike approach and focus on competency-based outcomes (Denning). At the same time, these developments might be seen as creating even greater stratification, and perhaps greater inequity, in postsecondary markets: "[n]on-codified knowledge, interpretative ability, and deeper wisdom will be available mostly to a privileged few (the affluent and the best and brightest)" (Massy and Zemsky). Certainly, there is a widely shared conviction that adding some kind of "human intermediation," whether through face-to-face classroom work or in the residential mix of students and faculty, adds value, but that is still mainly an article of faith and intuitive knowledge rather than a research-supported proposition (Cross 1998).

Like the previous pedagogical discussion, these institutional investigations end up with questions of assessment. The new technologies disrupt the traditional relationships of postsecondary institutions to the market(s) and in so doing raise important questions of outcomes and assessment. Traditionally, the educational results of postsecondary study go unmeasured, other than through individual grades. Few would claim that grades provide a common measure of assessment, and there is little evidence that grades are strongly correlated with future success (Pascarella and Terenzini; Ehrmann, "Asking"). Absent such measures, there is as yet no answer to the question of the value of the traditional institutional setting and infrastructure of the university, and particularly of face-to-face instruction. Again, answers to this question—actually a set of questions about values, aims, cost, and outcomes—are premature. The irony is that these questions are being more directly addressed in the less prestigious segments of an increasingly bifurcated market. Nevertheless, one suspects that as technology advances and cost pressures continue to increase, demands for accountability and assessment will impinge upon all institutions—hence, the following case study.

CASE STUDY: THE "CITIZEN'S GUIDE" AND A PERSONAL TRAINER?

For the past two years, I have attempted to use the Web as a teaching tool in my course on education policy by having students build a Web site, "A Citizen's Guide to Education Reform," as a class project (Paris, *Citizen's*, "Building," "Is There"). The on-line syllabus (Paris, "Politics") had a description of some of the topics in the course with suggested links to sites of interest. After a short introductory section that provided a basic history through lectures and discussion, students were required to take an "entrance exam" to show that they had mastered enough of the basic material to embark on doing projects. Students were then assigned to groups on the basis of interest, and class time for the semester was mainly devoted to groups reporting on their progress to the class. With student help from our technology support services, the sites were "loaded" and placed on the Web.

The pedagogical strategy for these classes should be fairly transparent. Besides seeing the Web as an extraordinary information source, the approach was to have students see it as a medium for presenting and assessing their work in the context of a larger community. Like the shift in focus suggested by Fish, the focus of the class would move steadily away from the professor and toward other groups. Students would work collaboratively in groups and actively engage in constructing something of intellectual value for a nonspecialist audience. After a few weeks of being a "sage," the use of the Web as medium for student work would permit me to "guide" their apprenticeship at producing material of value. The results would be publicly assessable, a kind of performance assessment that goes beyond the classroom. In institutional terms the aim was to demonstrate to any number of constituencies—perhaps most important, the students themselves—the value of their work as part of a liberal arts education.

In general the project has been a success. Students seemed pleased with the opportunity to control their own work and enjoyed the idea of a common class project. The site is, not surprisingly, uneven, but there is a good range of topics and discussion. Interestingly, final exams that required discussion of some broader themes in education policy have been better than in previous courses, suggesting that students move best from the particular to the general rather than vice versa, and that the continuous group discussions and presentations had some positive effects. Thus, a combination of working in this technological environment and ongoing face-to-face interactions seemed to contribute to student learning.

Perhaps the biggest change produced by this approach has been students' conception of the audience for their work. Instead of a private (paper) presentation of individual work or, at most, some short-term, semi-public class presentation, the class was confronted with the prospect that their work would be available for wider, long-term public scrutiny. The students found this prospect both exciting and daunting; such public exposure could and did seem threatening. But it had a positive impact as well in providing a focus and criteria for evaluating student work. Suggesting that students were constructing a "citizen's guide" provided a way of organizing discussions and evaluating materials as part of a larger group enterprise. The constantly repeated question was, "What should we say to an ordinary citizen or visitor to our site about these issues?" The shared burden of answering this question made the project somewhat less threatening.

There are at least three categories of problems with the project. The first involves issues that might arise in any course that followed this strategy. There were technical difficulties of various sorts. It was much harder to smoothly integrate one year's work with another's, and the site is still in two parts. It will be revamped eventually to try to make ongoing changes and additions easy to do. Similarly, for all their familiarity with computers, students have a better sense of how to find and receive information from the Web than how to construct it. Most felt (or knew) that merely putting hypertext papers on-line was not the best way to use the medium, but few, myself included, had a sharp sense of how their work could best be presented. Finally, group work has its inevitable interpersonal frictions and free riders, since students' mode of working for most of their educational lives has been individualized. And the instructor who assigns the groups work may know well how to grade writing or manage a class discussion, but less well how to coach or manage a group.

The second, more interesting category of pedagogical problems follows from the previous discussion and concerns appropriate criteria for evaluating student work. As students discussed how to evaluate their efforts and aims for the site, we discovered what might be called the "Education Week" problem (Education Week). The site connected with this weekly newspaper has accessible descriptions of major problems in public education as well as links to relevant materials. If the aim of the site was to contribute something new to public discussion, it was difficult to imagine adding much to what these and other professionals have already done on other sites. A related problem concerns the adequacy of the information students either present or point out through the site. Given that the Internet materials on education policy are, as with any area of policy, vast, how can students, or even their instructor, evaluate what is an adequate use of the Web? As the much talked about information explosion becomes ever more visible to students and professionals, how should students or faculty manage information they receive or produce in this medium? To follow Fish's suggestion, the answer to these questions may lie in a community of (scholarly? popular?) interpreters of some sort, but who, or what, that community is poses some very difficult questions, particularly given the nature of the Internet.

Looked at in one way these questions of standards, criteria, and audience are not serious issues. These would only seem to be problems, it might be argued, against expectations that are inappropriate for undergraduates. The apprentice woodworker is not expected to craft the perfect table, the student performance of *King Lear* is not judged by the same standards as the professional company's, and so on. Students' work in this or any medium should be judged, as it would be in traditional formats, against expectations appropriate for students. The norms appropriate to undergraduate research or an undergraduate learning community might be informed by the norms of the larger professional community, but they are not the same thing. Of course, this partly begs the question of what are appropriate aspirations for undergraduates, of finding a point between undergraduate research as "glorified homework" and a genuine scholarly or civic contribution (Reisberg).

Striking this balance might be done in a number of ways. One is to make the undergraduate research more manageable by having students do projects that do not merely duplicate existing resources, for example, case studies or applications with which they have some unique or direct experience. Another way might be to rethink the audience for the project, for example by limiting access to the site to campus and other specific groups (faculty or students at other institutions) who form a more limited "learning community" around this and related projects. Similarly, some of the various functions of the project might be unbundled; for example, the compilation of information and links might be separated from the student analysis of issues. Any or all of these might provide a clearer context for doing and evaluating projects.

These pedagogical problems in turn suggest a third category of issues concerning institutional purposes, markets, and assessment. Specifically, how does this kind of technology-based course fit into some larger picture of, for example, Hamilton College as an institution in a certain market? Hamilton is a fairly traditional liberal arts college. Students and families investing in a "name brand" institution have both pedagogical and career expectations. The pedagogical expectation is access to personalized and individualized teaching in the service of a liberal education. The career expectation is that a degree from this kind of institution will open doors to professional jobs or further pre-professional training. For better or worse, technology is less likely to play an immediate, powerful role in such a setting because of these expectations.

First, this course on education policy, and indeed the entire curriculum, is not aimed at preparing students for some specific career or certifying them for an occupation. The question then becomes what the results of liberal education should be. The idea of a liberally educated individual is constantly contested (Orrill), and, as noted previously, often framed in general philosophical terms that are rather elusive ("essential, ephemeral"). The stock answer to the above question is often skill-based—a liberal education improves skills in reading, writing, discussion, and analysis—in the context of study of a variety of specific disciplines. Implicitly, if skills are primary, then their development can presumably be best encouraged and enhanced through the ongoing interaction with a faculty member and students in a class such as this one—with technology providing a medium in which these skills are developed and demonstrated. Thus, the success of this course in terms of some wider institutional aims can be aided by technology, but continues to depend on the ongoing presence of other students and the "guide on the side."

Perhaps another way to describe this context might be by analogy to private lessons or a personal trainer in music or sports. In this course students expect that their projects will be monitored and their work will be guided and coached as a means of developing both an understanding of the subject matter and the skills mentioned above. However, the analogy to personal training is incomplete, again, because of issues of assessment. Given that the result for students, a "liberal education," is more elusive than for some pre-professional training, then the success of this or any particular course, or even the effects of college education more generally, remain somewhat obscure. Similarly, questions about results—for skills, for "liberal education" generally—are also discouraged by the implicit promise that graduates will have access to jobs and further professional education because of the "name brand" credential. Unfortunately this sometimes lends itself to the kind of disjunction between use and exchange value, the pursuit of credentials rather than learning pointed out by Labaree (see also Edmundson).

The potential role and impact of technology in this setting are thus mixed.

On the one hand, there is an expectation that a "name brand" school will be well equipped and make use of technology as part of a personalized education, for example, as in this course. On the other hand, because this education is, nominally or actually, more personalized, the incentives to use technology found in other market segments are muted or nonexistent. Access to educational resources is not an issue on a well-equipped, wired residential campus. Similarly, although cost pressures exist, technology is not seen as a way of reducing cost or otherwise affecting the institutional practice of "buying the best" in a significant way. Moreover, assessment is less an issue in this market setting than in others. The possible uses of technology in assessment are not typically explored because of the vagueness of the "product" and the assumed (exchange) value of the credential. Technology is typically used, as in this case, as an enhancement rather than an alternative.

In conclusion, there can be little doubt that the new technologies are having an important impact on postsecondary education. Pedagogically they open up new possibilities for teaching, learning, and assessment. In so doing they may create pedagogical expectations that may not be easily met through distance learning and comparable approaches. The more immediate impacts of the new technologies are likely to be felt in reshaping and even more sharply differentiating certain markets for postsecondary education, and they are playing different roles in different markets. Ironically, the institutions that are supposedly the leaders in postsecondary education are not the ones most likely to explore or exploit the full range of possibilities presented by technology. As the case study illustrates, the new technologies can promote a more student-centered education in a "name brand" setting, but also sharpen thorny issues of aims and assessment. These issues will increasingly come to the fore as technological possibilities and uses expand in all segments of the postsecondary market.

WORKS CITED

Anderson, Charles. *Prescribing the Life of the Mind.* Madison: University of Wisconsin Press, 1993.

Barr, Robert B., and John Tagg. "From Teaching to Learning: A New Paradigm for Undergraduate Education." *Change* 27.6 (1995): 13–25.

Chickering, Arthur, and Zelda Gamson. "Seven Principles for Good Practice in Undergraduate Education." *AAHE Bulletin*, Mar. 1987.

Clotfelter, Charles. *Buying the Best: Cost Escalation in Elite Higher Education.* Princeton: Princeton University Press, 1996.

Cross, Patricia. "What Do We Know About Students' Learning and How Do We Know It?" June 1998. 1 Aug. 1999 <http://www.aahe.org/>.

Denning, Peter. "Business Designs for a New University." *Educom Review.* May 1998 <http://www.educom.edu/web/pubs/review/>.

Edmundson, Mark. "On the Uses of a Liberal Education: 1. As Lite Entertainment for Bored College Students." *Harper's* 295.1768 (1997): 39–49.

Education Week. *Issues in Education*, May 1999. 1 Aug. 1999 <http://www.edweek.org/context/topics/issues.htm>.

Ehrmann, Stephen. "Asking the Right Question: What Does Research Tell Us About Technology and Higher Learning?" *Change* 27.2 (1995): 20–27.

———. "What Good Is a Campus Today?" Feb. 1996. Online posting. Listserv <aahesgit@cren.net>.

Fish, Stanley. *Is There a Text in This Class?* Cambridge, MA: Harvard University Press, 1980.

Gilbert, Steve. "Making the Most of a Slow Revolution." *Change* 28.2 (1996): 10–23.

Kulik, Chen-lin, and James Kulik. "Effectiveness of Computer-Based Instruction: An Updated Analysis." *Computers in Human Behavior* 7.2 (1991): 75–94.

Labaree, David. *How to Succeed in School Without Really Learning*. New Haven: Yale University Press, 1998.

Marchese, Theodore. "Not-So-Distant Competitors: How New Providers Are Remaking the Postsecondary Marketplace." *AAHE Bulletin*, May 1998.

Massy, William, and Robert Zemsky. "Using Information Technology to Enhance Academic Productivity." May 1998. 1 Aug. 1999 <http://educause.edu/nlii/productivity.html/>.

Means, Barbara, and Kerry Olson. "The Link Between Technology and Authentic Learning." *Educational Leadership* 51.7 (1994): 15–18.

Noam, Eli. "Electronics and the Dim Future of the University." *Science* 270.13 (1995): 247–49.

Noble, David. "Digital Diploma Mills: The Automation of Higher Education." *First Monday*, 3 Jan. 1998. 1 Aug. 1999 <http://www.firstmonday.dk/issues/issue3>.

Oppenheimer, Todd. "The Computer Delusion." *Atlantic Monthly* 280 (July 1997): 45–59.

Orrill, Robert, ed. *Education and Democracy: Reimagining Liberal Learning in America*. New York: The College Board, 1997.

Paris, David, "Building a Web-site as a Class Project: 'A Citizen's Guide to Education Reform.'" Paper/poster presented at the Annual Meetings of the American Political Science Association, Washington, DC, 30 Aug. 1997.

———. "Politics and Ideology in Education Reform." Jan. 1998. 1 Aug. 1999 <http://www.hamilton.edu/academic/Government/gov375/>.

———. "Is There a Professor in This Class?" Paper presented at the Annual Meetings of the American Political Science Association, Boston, MA., 4 Sept. 1998.

———, ed. *A Citizen's Guide to Education Reform*. June 1998. 1 Aug. 1999 <http://academics.hamilton.edu/government/dparis/govt375/spring98/default.html>.

Pascarella, Ernest, and Patrick Terenzini. *How College Affects Students*. San Francisco: Jossey-Bass, 1991.

Reisberg, Leo. "Research by Undergraduates Proliferates, but Is Some of It Just Glorified Homework?" *Chronicle of Higher Education*. May 1998 <http://chronicle.com/che-data/>.

Russell, Thomas. "The 'No Significant Difference' Phenomenon.'" June 1998. 1 Aug. 1999 <http://teleeducation.nb.ca/phenom/>.

Salvador, Roberta. "The Emperor's New Clothes." *Electronic Learning*, May/June 1994: 32–46.

Verduin, John, and Thomas Clark. *Distance Education: The Foundations of Effective Practice*. San Francisco: Jossey-Bass, 1991.

University of Phoenix. Home Page. May 1998 <http://www.uophx.edu/>.

Western Governors University. "Welcome to WGU." 1 Aug. 1999 <http://www.wgu.
    edu/wgu/about/welcome.html>.

Young, Jeffrey. "Rethinking the Role of the Professor in an Age of High-Tech Tools."
    Chronicle of Higher Education, 29 Sept. 1997: A26.

Zemsky, Robert, Susan Shaman, and Mark Iannozzi. "In Search of a Strategic Perspec-
    tive: A Tool for Mapping the Market in Postsecondary Education." *Change* 29.6
    (1997): 23–38.

Chapter 9

Where Is Every-Body?

Paulette Robinson

Clicking through
    links
    of screens
Looking for a place
    that gathers
    every-one
    together
Moving in
    empty spaces
    of information
    barren lines
    of images, words, sounds . . .
Where are
    the digital footprints
    the shadows
    of you being here?
Where is every-body

"Where is every-body?" is a question that captures a crucial dilemma for students taking courses in Web-based environments. The "where" implies there is a place to gather—a specific class location. "Is" suggests an actual reality—an ontological social nexus. "Every-body" complicates the issue for students. "Every-body" implies a group or collection of members who have an identity as a group. And this identity is located in a sense of the body. What is body on-line? What does it mean to be in a place in an on-line classroom? What is an on-line place? Is there a sense of group identity in an on-line classroom? How can we as educators form that identity? How can I know my classmates from their electronic footprints and shadows?

This chapter is based on a phenomenological research project (Robinson) that explores the issues of space, place, time, a sense of body, and group identity for students in Web-based learning environments. Each dimension is part of a whole experience and intertwined like a hypertext environment moving back and forth—between. My exploration slices into the whole to give a sense of the parts. It is, however, the interaction between all of the parts where the experience occurs. It is from these issues that the pedagogical implications of the question, Where is every-body in Web-based learning environments?, arise.

WHERE

Where implies a location. Location can be described in terms of space and place embedded within time. Space and place are concepts that are often used interchangeably, but are they the same concept? How are they different in Web-based learning environments? How does time shape "where," and does that change in on-line environments? How is "where" experienced by students in a Web-based learning environment?

Space

Space comes from the Latin word *spatiari*, to wander. It is a "distance extending without limit in all directions; that which is thought of as boundless, continuous expanse extending in all directions or in three dimensions, within which all material objects are contained" (*Webster's* 1736). Space has no boundary, no shape. It is an abstract container determined by distance, direction, and time. While space is a container for concrete objects, without boundaries it lacks a sense of the concrete. Space in the modernist tradition is a priori to place. Place from this view is formed from space and is the object of localized knowledge. How can I be-in space? Is it possible to have a lived experience "in" space?

McHoul suggests that cyberspace is "between 'as' and 'as-if.' " Heidegger's concept of *Dasein* is "as" because *Dasein* is embedded in the actual, the lived experience grounded in the use of equipment. *Dasein* is described through assertion and deliberation that is occurrent. "As-if" is virtual. It is the art of play. It is the world of imaginary tools that produce art, poetry, literature, and so on. The reality of virtual is described through intuition and feeling. Cyberspace is neither actual nor virtual. It lies between "as" and "as-if." The actual components of cyberspace lie in its physical equipment (e.g., the computer hardware and software, the programming languages, etc). According to McHoul, the actions produced by the interactions between *Dasein* and equipment changes become indistinct. Cyberspace not only facilitates the distribution of the capacity to supplement *Dasein*, but it also carries it out.

Is cyberspace different from the modernist notion of space? When I get on my computer and connect to the Internet, I have a sense of entering a space— I wander within a boundless, continuous expanse that for me extends in all directions in three dimensions. There are concrete images that offer stepping stones within Internet-space, but there is not a sense of connection as I wander. There is only the journey.

In cyberspace, Web-based learning environments offer a space for faculty to create a place for students to learn. In and of themselves, Web-based learning environments are only digital structures that offer an interface—a mask or translation that lies on top of a set of computer instructions. The interface—this face between—is a starting point, a space. From this space, faculty put materials, students discuss, and assignments are submitted. Each space is molded into an on-line environment that is unique to the group who is assigned there. Does the creation of a learning environment make it a place?

When I took a course in a Web-based learning environment, I never felt like it was a place to gather. The student discussions remained for me just text—an object of information. They were formal, textbook-like pieces that did not invite me to explore issues with a fellow seeker. Only once, when our class used a synchronous on-line chat, did I begin to know my fellow classmates as persons, not objects. It was through their stories that I gained a sense of who they were. Objective, formal text-based rhetoric was transformed into the informality of conversation, dialogue.

Hannah, a student participant in a research study (Robinson), describes her experience in a formal on-line learning space:

The professor had posted some great philosophical question and there were one or two answers. One or two responses underneath it were full of great grandiose vocabulary, lofty graduate school quality ideas. Everybody was just polishing their best apples to lay on the teacher's desk and I was just looking at it going, "I'm not smart enough to be in here. I don't know what half of these things mean." So, I went back to my reading and I thought about it. I came up with a carefully composed answer. I typed it in because I wanted to sound just as smart. I wanted to throw in some new twists—some inventive thought that no one else had come up with and they would all say, "Wow, she's really smart, she's a graduate student!"

If the rhetoric is formal text in on-line learning spaces, will students interact with each other or will they pass by without hearing one another? Does the on-line environment become a container for written pieces—a space? Is there a "where" that facilitates the learning process? Is there a qualitative difference between space and place in forming a learning environment?

Place

The ancient Greeks had two words for place: *topos* and *chora* (Walter). *Topos* is the physical location or objective features of the place. *Chora* is the earlier term for place and captures the quality or subjective meaning of a place. Plato understood place as one of the three types of being. For Plato, *chora* is the receptacle of sensory experience and the seat of phenomena, a feminine and nurturing concept. *Chora* is a space that unifies the physical and moral, a location of shapes, powers, and feelings. It can only be known through myth, not pure reason. The myth captures the sensuous feel and energy of place. While place has a *topos* or location, *chora* is the essence of the place (Walter). The essence is tied to the lived experience of the community. Therefore, community exists not merely through shared physical places, but through the sociocultural context. It is *chora*, the sensuousness of the place, that nurtures the community. The sensuousness of the place is articulated through community stories or myths. Myths are the history of place as feeling and energy. *Chora* invests a place with value. Do on-line learning environments have community and value? If not, is it possible to have "a place" in a Web-based learning environment? Can students learn without a sense of *chora*?

Web-based learning environments are predominantly text-based asynchronous spaces (i.e., the space can be accessed at any time from any physical location). The creation of place in these environments relies on textual expressions to relate sensuous information. We are familiar with how a good novel or a sincere personal story can use text to relay a depth of sensuous information. When I read this type of text, I become engaged by the voice in the story. My imagination is the bridge that fills in the sensory gaps. The narrative engages me in my own story as I "listen" to another's story. I know myself connected within a context. The stories become communal stories that form a shared place. A shared narrative speaks of our experiences and values. It is a navigator's map, a hermeneutic bridge from space to place. It gives me access not only to who, but to we. Does a space have to be occupied in an actual sense to form a shared place? Can this hermeneutic bridge of narrative be used to form a place in a Web-based learning environment?

A student shared an example of how the narrative was used in her course's Web-based learning environment.

I think just because people began to talk about classroom experiences and they began to talk about children that they had in their classrooms . . . some they were bothered about because they hadn't found the right way to approach them and get the information through to them . . . and I think because of that, and the circumstances often times were separate . . . that it just . . . I thought it was personal. (Betty)

Levy points to the disconnect that is common when individuals encounter a different orientation to time and space in an on-line environment, noting that when people, information, or communities are "virtualized," they are "not there," they deterritorialize themselves. . . . They are not totally independent of a referential space-time since they must still bond to some physical substrate and become actualized somewhere sooner or later. Yet the process of virtualization has caused them to follow a tangent. They intersect classical space-time intermittently. . . . Virtualization comes as a shock to the traditional narrative, incorporating temporal unity without spatial unity, continuity of action coupled with discontinuous time. Synchronization replaces spatial unity, interconnection is substituted for temporal unity. As soon as subjectivity, signification, and pertinence come into play, we are no longer dealing with a single expanse or uniform chronology, but a multitude of types of space and duration. . . . The contemporary multiplication of spaces has made us nomads once again. We leap from network to network, from one system proximity to the next. The spaces metamorphose and bifurcate beneath our feet, forcing us to undergo a process of heterogenesis. (Levy 29–31)

When I ask my students to create a list of themes in an asynchronous bulletin board environment from stories posted earlier in the same environment, they are confounded by the possibility of talking on-line in a space that is textual and asynchronous—they have to *wait* for a response. They are disoriented by a loss of spontaneous interaction. They usually ask me several questions that suggest their disorientation. How will they know who their partner is? How do they get to know a person when that person is represented in text? How do they "talk" to another student with whom they do not have immediate contact? These questions in turn lead me to question my own instruction. How do I make this space into a place to gather? If students feel disconnected and disoriented, how can I connect them to place and each other?

Casey suggests that places gather. They gather things, experiences, histories, languages, and even thoughts. Casey applies gathering to place as "a particular hold on what is presented (as well as represented) in a given place. Not just the contents but the very mode of containment is held by a place" (25). The hold of a place is described by Casey as: (1) a holding together in a particular configuration; (2) a holding-in within the boundaries of place and a holding-out— a beckoning to inhabitants; (3) the layout of landscape; (4) the holding or keeping of experiencing bodies; and (5) the holding or keeping of unbodylike entities as thoughts and memories. Can on-line learning environments gather? If they can, what does it mean for a place to gather on-line? Can students gather on-line? Can we as educators create places that gather on-line? How does gathering affect the learning process?

Web-based on-line learning environments are held together by the software that creates them. In many learning environments, security login conditions create a doorway for students to enter. The boundary sentry is password and I.D. Students not enrolled cannot enter. The layout of the landscape is shaped by the interface—the look and feel of the software. How does a virtual on-line learning environment hold or keep experiencing bodies? Students can leave just through the click of a mouse. If I enter once a week, read classmates' entries, post a reply, and leave in thirty minutes, has my body been kept? Has my body even entered to be kept? Is it perhaps easier to believe that on-line environments hold and keep thoughts? Students record what they think, but do they record their memories?

Memory is from the Latin root *memoria*, "the faculty of remembering" (*Webster's* 1123). "*Re*" in Latin means "back and again" (1528). Memories are re-membered and brought back—retrieved from the mind. Do students have memories of others shaped in on-line environments? Do I re-member you? Do you re-member me? What is it that students re-member in Web-based learning environments? Is to be mindful the ability to recall facts or is it the facts embedded in a sociocultural context? What is re-membered in a place?

When I bring back to mind Web-based learning environments, it begins with experiences. The specifics of the content have receded—woven into a larger context of meaning. Most of my memories are triggered by feelings connected to interactions with classmates where we glimpsed one another. I re-member chatting with a fellow student in a synchronous textual space. The two of us "talked" about ourselves. I re-member that he was the first classmate that felt real to me. I could not tell you what he looks like or sounds like, but I re-member him. The conversation is brought out of the past into the present— changed through my experiences. How does time affect re-membering in a Web-based learning environment?

Time

Time cannot be separated from place. It is a chain of interlocking "fields of presence" (Merleau-Ponty). Presence is situated in a body perspective—a place.

Time must be understood as a system that embraces everything . . . Although it is graspable only for him who *is there*, is at a present. . . . Time exists for me only because I am situated in it, that is, because I become aware of myself already committed to it. (Merleau-Ponty 423)

To describe our sense of time continuity, Merleau-Ponty uses a river as a metaphor. If I stand on a riverbank, from that perspective, the water is present. Where the water has come from is past; and for me, it will flow downstream toward a future. To another further upstream, the water from my perspective or place in the river would be future. Where I stand in relation to the river determines my perspective of time. The present can also be personally viewed within several time contexts. "I am not, for myself, at this very moment, I am also at this morning or at the night which will soon be here, and though present is, if we wish so to consider it, this instant, it is equally this day, this year, or my whole life" (Merleau-Ponty 421).

My body is situated in a particular place, and the movement and change— the flow of life—is embedded in time. In an on-line environment, what is time? As a student, does one's sense of time affect one's sense of one's body and place on-line? Students have "real-time" interactions—a temporal unity without being in the same place (e.g., chats, two-way video conferencing, etc.) and continuity of action with asynchronous time (e.g., bulletin boards, listservs, and e-mail). Students have become nomads on-line, moving from point to click, logging on and off, wandering onto other sites and pages, lost in time and space. Rather than time and space being annihilated, virtualization "creates qualitatively new velocities, mutant space-time systems" (Levy 33).

In synchronous on-line interactions, time is often lagged—delayed from the moment I submit my response until it is viewed by other chat participants. If I type my response into a text box but do not submit it immediately, is it future? Am I future to my classmates until I post my comment? Are my words present for my classmates when they appear, or when they are read? Am I past or present in my words, or am I imagined as present only when my words are posted and my presence behind the words comes to the foreground?

In asynchronous environments, time becomes space—a location on a screen. If you have ten messages that are posted simultaneously to your e-mail, which message do you think is the most current? How is time perceived in terms of communication? Merleau-Ponty suggests that time and space cannot be considered separately. They form a spatiotemporal world that situates perception within a specific situation. Do students' senses of body and space influence how they perceive time on-line? Students in a typical on-line Web-based computer conference view discussion postings in a linear list where the posting last received by the server is at the top of a list. It is perceived by students as the most current—the present. Postings beneath the top listing are viewed to be progressively past even though they may have been written at the same time. One student described his experience of time in an on-line learning environment:

Well, you know how movie marquees change periodically? Well, I think I had this image of something like that. Although now I'm just sort of putting it into an analogy. Once you've written whatever it is you're going to write and you've posted it into the computer conference [type of bulletin board] site, you're like the headline. This is the one that everyone's going to see so you're like in bright neon. You're there, that's it, you're on. Whereas all the other [computer conferencing] spaces, if you're three days away, you're still there now but you're not like the hot item.

The computer conference sites were all linear—linear over time. Whereas you might have five or six people around a conference table physically, the conversations might be going various ways, but computer conferencing is not spatial at all. It's just like time. If you miss something, you're out of the conversation. Your little comment back here four days ago might no longer apply. Or, if you want to comment about something to the person that commented about your comment three days ago, that might just be completely out of context from the last comment. In other words, you might feel compelled to say something about the last comment on the computer conference space before launching, "Oh, by the way, so and so who said this, three days ago, I find rather interesting and I've been wanting to say something about it, . . ." but that might throw everybody off a little bit. (James)

Time is located spatially on the screen. When the posting is located in an on-line space (i.e., on the computer screen), the student is located in time and space. If a student deletes a message, was the student there? Can there be memory of the student? The relationships between students' replies are governed by this sense of present time. A message located three or four postings from the top is considered past and outside the conversations. Students felt that to reply to "past" messages would disrupt the conversations. If students feel part of the ongoing conversation, does their sense of time in the on-line learning environment establish a place for them? Does time orientation help or hinder a sense of place, drawing in or gathering students to interact in an on-line environment? If students are drawn into an on-line learning environment, where are their bodies?

Body

Merleau-Ponty places the body at the center of ontology. "I am" because I have a body. It is from the body that I perceive the world. Without a body, I have no place from which to perceive the world. "Where is" begins with the location of the body. It locates me in a place. Merleau-Ponty suggests that we

enjoy the use of the body not only in so far as it is involved in a concrete setting, [we] are in a situation not only in relation to the tasks imposed by a particular job, [we] are not merely open to real situations [i.e., actual]; we are open to those verbal and imaginary situations [i.e., virtual or abstract] which we can choose for ourselves or which may be suggested to us in the course of an experiment. (108)

Actual

The actual concrete body is located in-place. Being-in a place as a lived body involves five aspects: (1) the body localizes complex sensations to a place; (2) bodily orientations of up/down, front/back, right/left connect the body to place settings; (3) the concreteness of the body is matched to the concreteness of place; (4) this body presents itself in this place—both in "this-here"; and (5) the porosity of the skin shares the openness of the place in a "common flesh of the world" (Casey 22–23).

When I entered the Web-based learning environment, I sat on a chair, my feet touching the floor, my fingers poised on the keyboard, and my eyes scanning the screen for clues. I was in my office alone. I sat and read the words on the screen, but I did not leave. My imagination did not draw me into the virtual space. It was not a place for me. A student describes his experience of his body in an on-line learning environment:

I think that the conferencing because of the way it works for me it was like writing on a blank page and I don't know as when I'm writing my sense of body changes. I think it's different when I surf the net. It's like you're going places. It's like you're actually physically there. But this [the conferencing] was a little different because it was very similar to word processing in some ways. (James)

Virtual

The virtual body exists, according to Merleau-Ponty, in reflection and subjectivity. My sense of body is not restricted by the concrete; it is where I can imagine myself to be. Levy describes this imaginative sense as a projection of our body image. In our world this projection is associated with the notion of telepresence where "my tangible body is both here and there" (39). Levy gives the example of using the telephone where the voice is separated from the tangible body and projected to another location; "the virtualization of the body is therefore not a form of disembodiment but a re-creation, a reincarnation, a multiplication, vectorization, and heterogenesis of the human" (44).

How do students experience being-in-place in a Web-based learning environment? Is there a place to be-in? What is body in an on-line environment? How does this affect how students learn? A student describes her experience of being-in an on-line learning environment:

Well, I enjoyed it so, I didn't pay that much attention where I was at the time. I was thinking about what I wanted to say and what that other person was saying and how to respond to them and when I was reading the comments on it. It was exciting to me because I like to see other people's opinion and how they reacted to it. No, because I'd sit there for hours sometimes and not realize that my shoulder hurt because I'd been in the same position for so long until it really hurt bad. It was like listening to them talking—especially after I got to know people. I could see their face as I read their comments. (Betsy)

EVERY-BODY

The body locates me in a place. The essence of a place is rooted in its sociocultural context. It is not a single body, but part of every-body who is part of the gathering in a place. "Every" assumes a relationship—a we. The root word of relationship is relation. It comes from the Latin word *relatio*. One of the earliest meanings of the word is "to narrate, account, or tell" (*Webster's* 1525). The suffix "ship" comes from "the Anglo-Saxon-*scipe*, from the base of *scieppan*, to create, make" (1675). A relationship is the creation of a narrative or a telling. Those moments creating stories to tell are the ones I re-member— the ones that teach me about myself. I gather stories to myself. How are these relationships created in educational settings? How are they created in Web-based learning environments? How can narrative be used to establish a sense of relationship and community? Do narratives gather in to community?

In my conversations with students, it is common for them to feel separated from other students in a Web-based on-line course. It is as if they are the only ones in the course. They come and go in terms of adding the required comments to questions posed, but there is no "place" where they can gather to relate to one another. It is like having a class where the students are seated outside the door in cubicles separating them from interaction. They never enter into the class place, but reside outside. They do not interact or become part of the class as a sharing community. They produce the assignments in a sterile space, not a communal place.

Eastmond studied students as they participated in an on-line class. In his ethnography, the overall theme that emerged was "alone, but together." Six students were involved in the class at various levels, and some contributed every day. They crafted long messages in response to reading materials and engaged each other in discussion. Others "lurked" and watched. The students experienced a sense of isolation as well as a relationship with the other students in the class. A couple of the students formed a close relationship and arranged to meet when the class was over.

It was interesting that the meeting never materialized and the relationships that were formed on-line in the class evaporated after the class was over. The glue for the class relationship was a common interest. After the class finished, there did not seem to be a reason to meet. Is this the same for classes that meet face-to-face? What is the nature of relationships? Why are they formed? Can relationships only be maintained because of common interest? Can I ever get to know someone on-line? How can I know a person I have never met physically— in-body? Are we invisible on-line? Is there a "line" drawn "between" while I am "on" line?

I logged into the computer conference and thought, "I wonder if anyone from my class is on-line?" How would I know? I read each student's introduction of themselves. They were words of this is what I do, this is my graduate program— full of "this is" rather than "I am." I wondered if anyone was there. There did not seem to be a person for me to connect with. Yet, when I wrote a response to a question posed in the conference, someone out there replied and commented. I was unable to connect the comments of the students with their introductions. They never took shape for me. I tried to imagine what this person would look like. I did not seem to have enough information to hook my imagination. They were image-less and person-less for me. It made me feel even more alone to realize the possibility of other, yet other was strangely beyond my grasp. How do we become a "we"? What level and what type of knowing is necessary for me to be able to imagine a "you"? What binds us in a computer matrix?

PEDAGOGICAL IMPLICATIONS

I think of being in an on-line course as a necessary evil . . . as something you've got to do. It's not something fun. It s not something interactive. It's just a tool. It is an impersonal tool. I use it and that's it. It's funny that now we are so computer literate we are dying to meet the person. I just want to meet the person. I feel like I need that. (Mary)

Clearly, for this single young mother, an on-line learning environment was missing a sense of other—someone to interact with. Do we, as educators, want to condemn our students who take Web-based courses to a learning environment that is a "necessary evil"? What can we do to make the on-line learning environment an experience that is rewarding for students? Necessary comes from the Latin word *necessarius*, which means unavoidable or inevitable (*Webster's* 1200). Would students take the courses if they did not feel that they were unavoidable in their set of circumstances? Are there other imaginative ways that classes can be arranged to leave students thinking they have choices? Are computer classrooms the inevitable future? If they are inevitable, is there a way to design them so that they are not "evil"? "Evil" comes from the Anglo-Saxon word *yfel*, having bad moral qualities, sinful, bad. It also means causing pain or trouble; harmful; injurious (*Webster's* 634). Clearly, the students with whom I had conversations did not prefer learning on-line. It is a space devoid of other—it is a mechanistic, impersonal tool. Rather than interaction there is only the barren transfer of text-object. How can other and community be built into a Web-based learning environment? How do we as educators get students involved and interacting on-line? If they do not come, will they learn anything from our classes?

We make meaning as a community (Kincheloe and Pinar). Meaning making is not the consumption of information, but taking the information and making it my own. I make meaning in conjunction with—it is not a solitary process. It is through the sharing of stories that we learn not only about one another, but also about how to be. It is the reflective process of the story that brings about transformation at the deepest levels. Story is rooted in a shared place. Can storytelling create shared place in on-line environments? Will stories gather students into a place?

The challenge for both faculty and students is to build a place, *chora*, filled with energy and senses, in an on-line course. It is each story that begins in a place—a classroom, a kitchen, a meadow full of flowers. The community hears each story and responds in a sensuous engagement with the details in the story. This process is used by Peter Reason in his classes where narrative is the language of the curriculum. Narrative builds a *chora* where the community sensuously understands itself. The community feels and knows itself in a public and existential way.

In Web-based learning environments, the navigational constructs form a space. There are pictures pointing where to go and how to enter text. However, these constructs are *topos* and do not address the existential public dimension of *chora*, place. It is the language of the narrative that offers a medium to build a sense of communal place, a place to come and be. Without a place, a place to sensuously reflect, the students will not enter into the class. They may type in an answer from the comfort of their home, but they are only represented by an answer to a question. The narrative can be a curriculum language to build a place for shared community in cyberspace.

How can students establish a sense of place? As I began to reflect on the connection between place and narrative in the process of social meaning making, I created a narrative technique that I use in an on-line bulletin board. It is designed to draw in my students to fashion a place to gather and share stories. First, I ask my students to tell a story about a personal experience that relates to the content of my course. They then decide, in pairs, the differences and similarities in their stories. They post their lists to the class bulletin board. The class then creates a list of themes that capture similarities and differences in the class. These themes are used to describe the qualities of the experience, and together we form a class theory of the experience. The class theory is then compared to theories found in research literature that relates to the experience described in their stories.

This technique accomplishes several things for my students. It empowers them to reflect on their own experiences with the experiences of others to theorize and make meaning. It reinforces the meaning they have made from their own experiences as they connect them with the experiences of others—both in the lived experiences of peers and reading research in the field. The personal narrative gives the students a glimpse into the other individuals in the class. It is not a list of what students do, but a description of their perceptions of a common experience. They not only have individual voices, but these voices combine to form a common song.

CONCLUSION

We orient ourselves in terms of spatiotemporal relationships with our bodies. That sense of orientation is shifting as we find ourselves interacting more and more in cyberspace. We confront at an experiential level basic ontological questions. Where am I? Where are you? Who are you? How do you know me? How do I know you? This disorientation in cyberspace—a hybrid that exists between actual and virtual—pushes us to orient ourselves bodily in place and time. We need to consider as educators how we can create learning places that facilitate the meaning-making process. We create and re-create our world within a sociocultural context—a complex series of relationships. On-line educators must ask themselves the question, "Where is every-body?" Without addressing the basic orientation issues this question suggests, we may doom our students to a learning experience that is "a necessary evil."

WORKS CITED

Betty. Personal interview, Oct. 1998.
Casey, Edward S. "How to Get from Space to Place in a Fairly Short Stretch of Time:

A Phenomenological Prolegomena." In *Senses of Place*. Ed. Steven Feld and Keith H. Basso. Sante Fe, NM: School of American Research Press, 1996. 13–52.

Eastmond, Daniel. *Alone, but Together: Adult Distance Study Through Computer Conferencing*. Cresskill, NJ: Hampton Press, 1995.

Hannah. Personal interview, Oct. 1998.

Heidegger, Martin. *Being in Time*. Trans. Joan Stambaugh. Albany: State University of New York Press, 1996.

James. Personal interview, Nov. 1998.

Kincheloe, Joe, and William Pinar, eds. *Curriculum as Social Analysis: The Significance of Place*. Albany: State University of New York Press, 1991.

Levy, Pierre. *Becoming Virtual: Reality in the Digital Age*. Trans. Robert Bononno. New York: Plenum Trade, 1998.

Mary. Personal interview, Apr. 1997.

McHoul, Alec. "Cyberbeing and ~space." *Postmodern Culture* 8:1 (1997).

Merleau-Ponty, Maurice. *The Phenomenology of Perception*. Trans. Colin Smith. Atlantic Highlands, NJ: Humanities Press, 1965.

Reason, Peter, ed. *Human Inquiry in Action: Developments in New Paradigm Research*. Thousand Oaks, CA: Sage Publications, 1989.

Robinson, Paulette. "Within the Matrix: A Hermeneutic Phenomenological Study of Student Experiences in Web-Based Computer Conferencing." Diss., University of Maryland, 1999.

Walter, Eugene. *Placeways: A Theory of the Human Environment*. Chapel Hill, NC: University of North Carolina Press, 1988.

Webster's New Twentieth Century Dictionary of the English Language, 2nd ed. New York: Simon & Schuster, 1979.

Chapter 10

Transforming Professionals via the Web: Promoting Social Justice in Web-Based Ethics Education for Counselors

Marvin J. McDonald

INTRODUCTION

Professional education in counseling, psychology, and mental health professions is undergoing major transformations. In North America many commentators are calling for broadened access to services, greater accountability for the quality of services offered, and increased social and cultural diversity in the professionals being trained. Many facets of the Internet revolution are magnifying these changes, yielding increasing demands for distance education, social and political activism on behalf of those receiving health care, and the development of on-line counseling services. Although these different trends have divergent roots, they are now coming together in a dynamic combination of opportunity, risk, and conflicting interests.

In this chapter, I trace several threads through the design of Web-based instruction for professional ethics for master's-level counselors and psychologists. I begin by highlighting several background issues for training in professional ethics. Then I introduce principles of emancipatory pedagogy as they pertain to professional education. Finally, I propose several design principles for guiding Web-based instruction in professional ethics.

PROFESSIONAL ETHICS IN PSYCHOLOGY AND COUNSELING

Professional ethical standards in the mental health professions directly echo trends in the larger society. The recent shortages in health care funding are reflected in concerns about fair access to services, accountability for the quality of services offered, and the appropriateness of available services for clients from diverse social and cultural backgrounds. In one recent example, psychologists serving in rural communities engaged the American Psychological Association to help formulate the principles about the ethical uses of bartering. In smaller communities, bartering had a more important place than was true in larger cities, and the standards were reworded to reflect that fact.

In the domain of human diversity, most professional organizations explicitly endorse human rights guidelines for the practice of their professions (American Association of Marriage and Family Therapy; American Counseling Association; American Psychological Association; Canadian Psychological Association). For example, many codes of ethics state the grounds for discrimination that are disallowed, such as gender, race, religion, and so on. In North America, these codes sometimes obtain legal force when they are adopted by credentialling bodies of the regional governments (Uhlemann and Turner). This incorporation of social justice principles into professional ethics reflects both the self-interests of the profession (public relations promotion in the public eye) and the public interest (protection of the public from oppression or discrimination by professionals). As Haney and Madaus point out, the processes behind the development and adoption of professional standards of conduct and practice are inherently political.

The politics of diverse interests shape many facets of psychology and counseling. The pressure for accountability of professional services often results in recommendations that therapy approaches be scientifically validated (e.g., Dineen). Disseminating the results of clinical research to students and practitioners has traditionally been difficult, although trends in scholarly publishing may increase the ease of access to some resources (for instance, see the AUCC/CARL report [Association of Universities and Colleges of Canada and the Canadian Association of Research Libraries]). Yet the changing research dissemination systems are laden with both promise and pitfalls, due in part to the same political and economic forces involved in standards of ethics. By reducing the reliance of scholars on centralized access to print media, new potentials are emerging for participation by scholars who reflect a greater diversity of social location, institutional background, and perspective. While this diversity can contribute to radicality and depth of critique in the academy, the dangers of a new elitism arise based on limitations to access to telecommunications. Although the local infrastructure for electronic systems is relatively inexpensive, wider social and technological infrastructure demands yield other constraints (language competencies, technological training, and resource requirements for telecommunications systems are often more demanding than are comparable demands of postal systems, for example). Moreover, once infrastructure is in place, the proliferation of participation in scholarship challenges traditional practices of quality control, search efficiency, and effective dissemination. The actual balance of risks and benefits for various stakeholders will undoubtedly vary across different implementations.

The Internet revolution magnifies some of these changes in counseling professions. The desire to increase the diversity in background of mental health professionals can be addressed partly through distance education. One key barrier to professional training for some underrepresented groups is the limited access those groups have to traditional university campuses and classrooms. To the extent that professional education can be more effectively delivered across geographic barriers with the aid of Web-based instruction, the profession will be able to more effectively meet its own standards of diversity. Additionally, social and political activism on behalf of people receiving health care has spawned a substantial self-help movement, and that movement has taken to the Internet with great intensity. Finally, movements toward on-line counseling are under way, generating responses from professional organizations and significant controversy along the way.

In short, the connections between professional ethics, pedagogy, and the Web emerge at several levels. First, *perception* provides a connection when the Internet becomes simply another context in which familiar human enigmas are expressed (e.g., disseminating information on ways to kill oneself, or addictive abuse of on-line pornography). Second, Web-based technologies can *enhance* practices by which professionals can discharge ethical responsibilities (e.g., disseminate legal and ethical information, make contact between geographically separate people, or decrease gaps between the "haves" and the "have-nots"). Third, the Internet is involved in *transforming* the practices of therapy and help-seeking by creating new forms of counseling activities (on-line counseling, on-line self-help and support resources, or changing the kinds of "peer consultation" available to the profession). These transformed or novel practices require ethical reflection as well. Web-based instruction in professional ethics should probably address each area, although the significance of any particular instance may be quite small. The ethical import in any specific instance may vary from simple identification of a familiar ethical concern to the actual creation of professional practices for embodying a particular vision of ethical practice (cf. Hacking; Idhe). Furthermore, these different levels of interaction can be evaluated for their contributions, or lack thereof, to a particular vision of social justice. To address that concern, I turn now to a discussion of principles behind pedagogy.

EMANCIPATORY PEDAGOGY

Within this larger context, Web-based instruction is well positioned to realize the opportunities of emancipatory pedagogies. Feminist pedagogy, community development training, and human rights education are among the many available models of social transformation through educational practice. From popular objectives such as critical thinking and experiential education to more radical pedagogies like consciousness raising and empowerment, a variety of strategies and practices are currently being promoted.

Traditional classroom systems for professional education in legal and ethical issues have often been constrained by several factors, including (a) the high speed of developments in professional and legal environments, making traditional texts obsolete in content; (b) the forms of ethical decision-making and accountability found in professional practice matching poorly with traditional codes of ethics and case studies (Rossiter, Walsh-Bowers, and Prilleltensky; Whitbeck); and (c) multiple, widely dispersed stakeholders who are engaged in legal and ethical facets of professional services offered by therapists.

Web-based instruction offers opportunities, at least, for addressing some of these concerns through (a) access to on-line news coverage, press releases, ethical documents of professional societies, and current legislation; (b) potential for participation in discussion groups and interrelay chat events which include practicing professionals, students, and academics with common interests; and (c) possibilities for exchanges among clients, family members, self-help groups, members of various mental health professions, members of the legal community, and government staff. Yet how can we evaluate these and other strategies for adequacy as education for social justice?

There is a vast literature promoting various facets of emancipatory pedagogy (see Adams, Bell, and Griffin; Joldersma; Ng, Staton, and Scane). For the present joint exploration of pedagogical ethics, professional socialization, and social responsibility in a Web-based instruction environment, I draw on Paul Ricoeur's work.

Ricoeur's critical hermeneutics is informed by two major strands of social theory in the twentieth century. He characterizes understanding in hermeneutic theory as "lived experience" grounded in belonging to a community and tradition. This grounding shapes our interpretations and enables us to transcend misunderstandings coming from backgrounds in different traditions. Cross-cultural communication often incorporates hermeneutic principles. Ricoeur also draws upon critical theory that identifies hidden interests sustaining oppressive social practices and a presumed neutrality behind those institutions sustaining the status quo of current social order. Familiar critical theories include Marxist critiques of capitalism, feminist critiques of patriarchy, and postmodern critiques of modernism, each promoting social justice and visions of emancipation from oppression. Moreover, Ricoeur traces an emphasis shared by critical theory and hermeneutics: situating and contextualizing a form of social science grounded in a detached objectivity modeled after natural science methods and the instrumental rationality of modern technology.

Ricoeur's own synthesis draws attention to concrete possibilities for rapprochement among the interests of emancipation, communication among different communities of discourse, and instrumental control. Promoting social justice, reconciling misunderstandings between different social groups, and promoting the benefits of science and technology can be dialectically engaged without reducing these interests to one another or requiring each position to violently co-opt the others. For the demands of professional ethics education, the vision proffered by Ricoeur's critical hermeneutics is invigorating. By drawing on traditions of social critique, emancipation can be incorporated into pedagogy.

By engaging a multiplicity of formative traditions shaping the helping professions, acknowledgment of human diversity can help transcend mistrust and differences in social location. And by promoting the critical appropriation of empirical research, public accountability for therapy practices can be nurtured at the very heart of professional identity.

By focusing on a dialect among all three interests, Ricoeur provides a rich orientation for elaborating an emancipatory pedagogy in professional education. Movement toward Web-based pedagogy merely intensifies the three-way dialectic, yielding a dynamic combination of risk and opportunity. The Internet as an educational medium embodies this risk-opportunity ambiguity by virtue of (a) being embedded in bureaucratic institutional forms, while (b) accentuating the negotiation of moral orders through presence of counter-institutional activities (cf. Idhe).

One the one hand, we have the strenuous efforts of business, educational, professional, and political institutions to gain some leverage on Web activity. On the other hand, there are effective, informally enforced norms (against "spamming," for example), counter-institutional activities (cheating sites for school essays, mirroring of illegal sites), and proactive advocacy and critique (promoting human rights, disseminating information on committing suicide, etc.). The combined potentials for risk and opportunity offered in Web-based professional education are best explored separately for each interest: instrumental control, communication, and emancipation. Of the three interests, emancipation may be the most difficult to realize.

THE WEB AS PEDAGOGICAL TOOL

Advocates of the Internet and Web-based pedagogy are quick to identify advantages in terms of educational activities difficult to replicate in the classroom. Flexible time scheduling, ease of geographic access, the immediate connections with diverse educational resources are all available. The key danger associated with the Web technological medium is the ideological potential for obscuring the normative order required for true dialogue and reducing it to bureaucratic rules and depersonalized interactions. In the instance of education in professional ethics, the danger and promise operate at two distinct levels.

First, the content of professional ethics and legal issues in the professions includes the laws, administrative rules, and professional standards used in institutional definitions of counseling. Educators frequently identify objectives in terms of moving students from rule-based strategies of ethical reflection to approaches incorporating dialogue among different stakeholders and sharing responsibilities for informed judgment and decision-making (Whitbeck). One difficulty encountered in professional education and practice is that moving beyond rule-based strategies to dialogical models is hindered by institutional constraints (e.g., some legal practices) and political interests (e.g., "turf" protection by professionals). Active promotion of bureaucratic, mechanical approaches is just as common on the Web as in any other educational medium (texts, class-rooms, degree programs). The objective of implementing dialogue-based professional education will have to be explicitly identified and actively promoted in Web-based instruction in the same way as in other educational systems.

At a second level of risk and opportunity, it requires intentional effort to resist the bureaucratization of professional responsibility in the technological medium of Web-based education. Professionals skilled and experienced in face-to-face interactions and small group activities can find the transition to chat or e-mail discussion artificial. Until skills in dialogue and expression can be adapted to the "new" medium and disseminated, the movement beyond rule-based ethical practice can be hindered. Specific attention to this transition can be handled with Web-specific enhancements such as including clients in chat sessions, incorporating client-generated Web resources, and following specific cases over time as events unfold.

The combination of risk and promise in the medium of Web-based interaction is unavoidable. Just as classroom activities cannot guarantee the successful implementation of a dialogical educational process, so the success of Web-specific designs will depend upon the cooperative activities of students, instructors, and their institutional contexts for each instance of a course.

THE WEB AS OPPORTUNITY FOR DIALOGUE

Professional mental health education is explicitly multicultural in North America, and one of the primary criteria of multicultural competence is familiarity with the practices of other cultures. This includes both experiential and cognitive familiarity. A key dialectic of danger and opportunity arises when the communication interest is pursued. How adequate are the understandings and skills obtained when the professional training is mediated through activities over the Internet?

One opportunity arises for Web-based dialogue with those from different backgrounds when professionals access the many personal stories of people who have struggled with various personal issues, psychological problems, and treatment modalities. In addition to accessing these stories via personal Web pages, many chat rooms are consistently available through, for example, the Mental Health Net. Besides bridging client-therapist distinctions, these chat opportunities promote contact between practitioners and researchers as well as between proponents of different sides in professional debates, and sharing of resources across boundaries of geography, professional discipline, and political jurisdictions.

In addition to dialogue through personal contact in chat media, the Internet has also become a major medium for ongoing contact of professionals with professional organizations, government organizations, the news media, and members of other professions. Web pages of many professional organizations are filled with press releases, public education brochures, support for political activities of the profession, training materials, continuing education materials, and so on. Moreover, it is relatively easy for professionals to maintain contact with members of other professions since some of the professional organization material is open to full public access, and it is relatively easy to locate mental health professionals with shared interests in the "public" medium of the Web. In addition, many political jurisdictions are placing government resources on-line, including electronic copies of legislation and court reports, access to government departments and some publications, and information about health care resources. Through the exploration and promotion of unique Web-based dialogue opportunities, professional education can likely broach new horizons of dialogue in professional practice.

There are important dangers and constraints to be recognized, of course. The diversity of backgrounds represented is constrained by the language of access and by the uneven distribution of Web access across different social classes, countries, or ages. The evaluation of the quality of resources on the Web is a tremendous concern requiring continual attention. The very ease of access and electronic publication also enhances possibilities for deception, misinformation, and distortion. In some instances, Internet activity may be more vulnerable to some of these dangers, but developments in cryptography and on-line security may help in some arenas.

In some ways, the communication interest is perhaps more fully addressed than the other interests by moving professional education to Web-based media.

THE WEB AS MEDIUM FOR EMANCIPATION

How can political interests of challenging institutions be served by professional education on the Internet? Here the risk-opportunity tension reaches a new level of intensity. On the one hand, the much-discussed decentralization and cross-jurisdictional extent of the Web has created difficulties for the institutions of government and law enforcement to control the system, especially when it comes to the flow of information. On the other hand, access to Internet resources requires significant resources: finances, skill, and time. Is the Internet a "new frontier" or is it more a plaything of privileged classes? Engaging the political structures shaping the Web and the professions represents a significant challenge for professional education guided by ideals of social justice. And though the structures of mental health professions in North America are deeply entrenched in dominant social institutions, a growing insistence on social accountability has leveraged significant attention by the professions. Small activist movements among mental health professionals have been strengthened by this social climate. The most widely influential critical perspectives in recent years have been feminism and advocacy for multicultural awareness. And though the "political correctness" debates continue, emancipation ideals are widely influential, both in practice and in the research base sustaining professional practice (see, e.g., Renner, Alksnis, and Park).

The pursuit of social justice engages Internet-based education in several ways. First, scholarship, the academy, and libraries are being profoundly transformed by the Internet. Second, social activists have a large presence on the Web. Third, Web-based resources for self-help and alternative forms of service delivery hold some potential for countering oppression. I consider each point in turn.

A recent report by the Association of Universities and Colleges of Canada and the Canadian Association of Research Libraries (AUCC/CARL) has examined the impact of electronic publication on the academy. On the one hand, the relative ease of access to journals promises a "democratization of scholarship." The transformation of public libraries and their integration with academic libraries via the Web holds the same promise for consumers of scholarship, including therapists and the clients of mental health services. A "leveling" effect through increasing access to specialized resources for professionals, their clients, family members of clients, and other stakeholders is already under way. On the other hand, the potential for creating new elites grows in connection with many Web features. Education and general experience with computers often make use of the Internet easier. And as Internet pages become more resource-intensive (movies, intensive graphics, need for quality printers, on-line phones and video, etc.) and as access to resources results in increasing expenses, Web access may remain one more distinction between the haves and the have nots. Language barriers, differential availability of Internet service in various communities, schools, and geographic areas, and education levels among people of different ages illustrate some of the additional social factors related to Web access.

The presence of social activism on the Web is also relevant to emancipatory professional education. Concern for social justice takes many forms, including disseminating information, public education, electronic publication of resources, and ongoing exchange, action coordination, and support of causes via e-mail and discussion groups. For example, the British Columbia Civil Liberties Association (BCCLA) has a long history of activism on behalf of mental health consumers in the province. In addition to offering public education and sophisticated analyses of human rights issues faced in therapy, the BCCLA actively intervenes in current political and legal activities to promote emancipation in people's lives. Joint action with other groups is common in their activities, and students training in the mental health professions can gain firsthand experience by becoming involved in current projects. In that regard, some social justice sites on the Web offer an alternative access to current events that focuses social justice issues more than is true of traditional media outlets.

Third, Web-based resources for self-help and alternative forms of service delivery hold some potential for countering oppression. As clients gain greater familiarity with Internet resources for self-help, those resources can empower clients to hold professionals accountable for the quality of care being offered. Strengthening the position of clients by providing them with opportunities to compare experiences with others in therapy can help counteract oppressive facets of professional power in health care institutions. For training purposes, then, ethical standards recommending that professionals offset the negative dimensions of power in therapy can be pursued by having professionals gain familiarity with Web-based self-help resources for clients. This example simply adds one more medium to a list that already includes self-help resources such as books, videos, and local support groups.

Finally, professionals can, when promoted with emancipation interests in a guiding role, encourage the development of alternative forms of service delivery. As discussed below, there is currently a debate among mental health professionals about the adequacy of providing counseling services over the Internet, via a private chat room or over e-mail. The emancipatory potential is evident when these alternatives, when delivered in adequate manners, can provide access to services for people who could not otherwise obtain service. Now, for example, some counselors provide counseling services over the telephone when geography separates would-be client from therapist. Historically, a parallel debate arose in the 1960s about the viability of offering crisis intervention services over the telephone. Crisis hotlines are now fairly common across North America, and some professional consensus has been developed about the strengths and limitations of such services. The transformation of service delivery to match more closely the ways people seek help can support social justice foundations for counseling.

In summary, the interests of communication across communities, emancipation, and instrumental control cannot be simply reduced to some monolithic system of rationality or political adequacy. Some legitimate tensions exist between social justice, bureaucratic effectiveness, and dialogue between communities. Moreover, current practices in the mental health professions and in use of the Internet demonstrate potentials in serving all of these interests. Given ethical standards, none of these concerns should be minimized. So the general potentials of Web-based pedagogy are rich enough to sustain the complexity required for adequate professional practice. And the close connections between risks and opportunities in Web-based education in professional ethics can be fruitfully addressed by maintaining a dialectical engagement among these interests. With Ricoeur as steersman, I now propose guidelines for practice. I formulate these principles in an invitational mode as aspirations and practices to imitate. A dialogical stance is required to maintain the dialectic of interests in pedagogy and professional practice.

DESIGN PRINCIPLES FOR WEB-BASED INSTRUCTION IN PROFESSIONAL ETHICS

To simplify the design process for the present purposes, I summarize course design issues in four categories. *Curriculum* is the content domain of professional ethics for therapists, *objectives* are the performance criteria defined for the curriculum, *activities* are the structure of assignments and course events scheduled for student involvement, and *evaluation* is the process of identifying students' degree of attainment of the course objectives. The examples selected for presentation here are used to highlight the value of directing our design process via Ricoeur's three interests (communication, emancipation, and instrumentality). Furthermore, these interests can help counseling students by drawing explicit parallels among the process of therapy, pedagogy, and the practices of ethical responsibility by professionals in today's society.

Curriculum

Reflexive coherence among pedagogy, therapy, and professional responsibility is especially clear in the professional ethics curriculum. Explicit parallels between sound pedagogical and therapeutic technique can be drawn, bridges must be constructed between communities of discourse in the classroom and the clinic, and advocacy for social justice is just as relevant to education as to therapy. Web-based instruction can move instructional activities even closer to participation in ongoing, actual events in the profession, enabling education to take on a mentoring atmosphere. The parallel in counseling is that clients' work in therapy must engage their daily lives. Coordinating professional ethics curriculum with internship and practicum placements is a promising focus, where students bring topics from their caseload to class for consultation with the group. Incorporating on-line material directly into internship consultation may require Internet access in clinic staff rooms and university classrooms.

Current debates about on-line counseling are a case in point. The Web page of the International Society for Mental Health On-line (ISMHO) presents papers outlining positions promoting on-line counseling and offers opportunities to become involved in discussion of the proposals. By joining the ISMHO mailing list or contributing to an interactive Web page, browsers engage other therapists from many different professional backgrounds. Incorporating this resource into professional education, students can become involved in the site by providing explicit analysis, critique, and feedback on various responses encountered in the original page and by following up with others' responses to their contributions. Here a joint project by several students could prove useful. Similarly, participation in mental health chat sessions ("Community") with other professionals and with clients can become curriculum. I propose that activities like these, in conjunction with course-based chat rooms and similar structures, are a part of the curriculum in professional ethics, not merely illustrations or "practice" in applying ethical principles. Interacting effectively with colleagues in the profession, including consultation and confrontation, is crucial to effective ethical practice.

All of our three primary interests can become the focus of these topics. For instance, explicit consideration of power structures, especially as they impact clients and individual professionals involved in on-line counseling, can serve emancipation interests while gaining technical competence in dialogue with adherents of other positions. Identifying and legitimating political interests as criteria for formulating actual positions in on-line discussion is much better professionally than armchair analysis of news reports or textbook examples. "Better," here, implies objectives to be met.

Objectives

The interests of emancipation, communication, and instrumental control all find their place in formulating objectives for competence in professional ethics. Procedural justice principles, well established in legal traditions, reflect instrumental rationality in the domains of politics and professional ethics. Social justice principles are directly incorporated into professional ethics codes and practices to promote benefit to society and protection of clients. Finally, the interest of communication between different traditions or social positions is embodied in the recognition of different stakeholders in professional ethics. By recognizing that the interests of professionals and clients are not always the same, and by acknowledging that clients are sometimes at odds with family members, work settings, or educational settings, attempts to resolve miscommunication can be motivated for professionals. Promoting the reflexive coherence of pedagogy and counseling practice again provides fruitful direction. In therapy, counseling goals are negotiated among client, therapist, and other relevant stakeholders. In professional education, professional standards and practices have a powerful institutional "voice" as well. A parallel here for examination is "What powerful institutions shape clients' lives and the goals they set for therapy?" Consider the following structure for a training dialogue.

Responsible Use of Formal Testing

It is relatively difficult in the on-line environment to maintain distinctions between professionally adequate psychological and educational tests on the one hand and "tests" designed for entertainment purposes on the other. The Web pages *Assessment & Evaluation on the Internet* (Drake and Rudner) and the *Test Junkie* illustrate professional and entertainment resources, respectively.

Mental health professionals should be able to distinguish Web resources that (a) can be responsibly assigned to clients for self-help purposes to replace professional services; (b) can be used as supplements to ongoing counseling; (c) effectively critique the political and technical inadequacies of professional testing; (d) provide recreational activity independent of any needs for therapy; and (e) can be discredited as potentially harmful to at least some people.

A student project of this kind incorporates professional principles of test evaluation ("Joint Committee on Testing Practices"), dialogue among different stakeholders in the testing enterprise, and examination of the power structures shaping professional standards and practices (e.g., see Haney and Madaus). In particular, examining the appropriateness of on-line testing offers the possibility of directly engaging all three primary interests via negotiation among students and instructors (shaping this activity), clients and counselors (in therapy), client advocates, and persons without counselors (self-selected), all with direct reference to institutionally defined standards and practices.

Activities

What activities are open to counseling students in Web-based courses? By involving students in course design, parallels and disanalogies between professional education, professional ethical practices, and therapy can be explored. Consider the process of monitoring student progress in Web-based professional ethics courses. Instructors using Web-based courses sometimes formulate monitoring student activities through the course site as an issue of informed consent: once students are made aware of the practice and its purpose, they have the choice to participate in the course under those conditions or go elsewhere. If, however, we join with O'Neill in formulating consent in therapy as a process of negotiation, of an ongoing give and take, then negotiating consent around the monitoring of student progress becomes curriculum for the study of professional ethics.

While exploring power relationships between students and instructors, professionals-in-training can engage the educational process in ways analogous to client engagement in therapy. For O'Neill, the practices of negotiation contribute to the benefits of therapy as well as the ethical value of the professional relationship. In professional ethics education exploration of parallel principles contributes to the formation of professional identity. In what ways are the interests of various stakeholders or the cultural background of students and clients influential in evaluating power relationships? Since some clients benefit from therapists taking an "expert" role in therapy, when does the parallel hold in professional education, and when do standards of professional autonomy and responsibility override the social background of the student? In my experience as an educator, I am trying to find ways to negotiate multiple forms of "balance" among the interests of negotiation, communication, and instrumentality. And since student progress tracking in Web-based instruction is often "hidden" to the student, this enables the class to explore the dynamic interplay between technological developments and ethical responsibility.

A good parallel to progress tracking is the promotion of privacy legislation in Canada ("National"). A spring 1999 press release from a national coalition addresses federally proposed legislation with direct application to health records, thus becoming an element in the curriculum for a course ˙ ɩ professional ethics. By drawing on the experience of a Web-based course with student progress tracking, the "hidden" impact of technological development can become more effectively visible to students, in both legitimate and questionable forms.

Evaluation

Building on previous points, evaluation of student, course, and instructor performance directly parallels contracting in therapy and professional responsibility.

Web-based course design as proposed here incorporates the entire Internet directly into course activities. The vast resources related to mental health, therapy, professional organizations, and legal contexts supersede textbooks while potentially incorporating classroom activities such as small group discussions and presentations. In overview, evaluation of student performance in Web-based professional ethics education should address four traditional domains used to assess competency in professional ethics: personal awareness, cognitive understanding, experiential understanding, and skilled performance.

Awareness of one's own personal values and ethical responsibilities is fundamental in ethics education. Web-based instruction supports this process. By enabling students to engage other professionals, diverse client groups, and people with different cultural backgrounds, personal awareness can be nurtured. This assertion assumes that students are able to engage the on-line medium with the same degree of personal involvement as small group discussion in a face-to-face situation. Personal awareness of emancipation issues may be more readily available than in the classroom due to the ease of access to diverse efforts at promoting social justice. Other facets of personal awareness, including consciousness raising about experiences of oppression or personal explorations of professional identity and aspirations, may be more difficult to sustain unless students are fully socialized into the full range of Web-based media. Experiential understanding of professional ethical responsibility, like personal awareness, may be addressed partially via Web-based instruction. Evaluation of these facets of ethical competence should be addressed through coordinated activity with active professional work. During graduate training, this could be accomplished in conjunction with supervised internship sites. The continuing education facet of professional education most easily incorporates personal awareness and experiential understanding into Web-based ethics instruction since the participants have concurrent professional activity to bring to the course.

Cognitive understanding of professional ethics issues can probably be addressed as adequately in Web-based instruction as in the classroom, with some advantages for bridging geography and the barriers of time schedules. Skill development depends specifically on the activities and projects engaged in the course. Skill in Internet usage has direct professional relevance for the curriculum topics mentioned above. However, involving students in negotiation over course content, activities, objectives, and evaluation is directly supportive of a central goal of professional ethics education: Professionals are responsible for continuing education over the long term. The resources available on the Internet are currently of such an extent that successful completion of a Web-based course directly imparts a set of useful skills for ongoing professional development. For example, student and instructor joint evaluation, the mobilization of Web-based participation of different stakeholder groups, and the skills used to evaluate on-line information are skills with lifelong relevance. Nonetheless, the active skills of ongoing negotiation in specific professional settings cannot be replaced with Web-based activities. Like traditional classroom instruction, Web-based education in professional ethics requires direct involvement with professional settings to meet the full range of professional requirements.

Overall, Web-based design for professional ethics courses compares favorably with the capacities of traditional classroom training. If the transition from face-to-face activities to Web-based interaction is successfully managed in course design, instructors have a number of advantages to incorporate into professional ethics education. In fact, the profile of potentials and pitfalls suggests that Web-based instruction may be superior to classroom or workshop formats for post-graduate continuing education in professional ethics.

CONCLUSION

The demands of ethical training for mental health professionals match well with the resources and technologies of Web-based instruction. In particular, emancipatory pedagogy is fundamental to implementing social justice principles in professional standards and entirely sustainable for Web-based study. Significant risks are also present, especially in the shift from face-to-face interaction to on-line interaction. The switch of medium from small group to Internet is important, with potentially profound implications. I suggest the following implications of this analysis.

First, Ricoeur's emphasis on an irreducible dialectic among the interests of emancipation, instrumentality, and communication provides key insights into implications of professional education on the Web. Although many parallels can be found, the balance of interests tends toward communication in face-to-face contexts and toward objective science and technology in the Web-based format. While both practices tend to constrain emancipation interests, emancipatory pedagogy can address that imbalance. The institutional weight of professional ethics codes, advocacy groups, and legislation helps keep social justice on the agenda when they are not co-opted by professional self-interest. Similar contributions can be obtained by engaging groups that promote social justice interests on the Internet, such as Electronic Frontier Canada. Given the power and status of institutional voices, the maintenance of a sound emancipatory pedagogy requires alliance and support with activist groups and others maintaining the effort to sustain social justice in the face of self-interest.

Second, the processes of negotiation are key practices for promoting the interest of justice in professional education, ethical responsibility, and therapy process. Full embodiment of negotiation activities into Web-based courses is crucial, and efforts are being made to build such capacities into available software (e.g., Goldberg). To adequately reflect and engage diverse interests, participants from different communities must be drawn into conversation. Professional standards stipulate the interests of the public and clients as primary, highlighting the importance of including the self-help community and other client groups. Professional organizations, human service agencies, and regulatory bodies all offer important voices, yet often they are mediated solely by course instructors, textbooks, and official publications of various sorts. The time-honored practice of inviting guests to graduate classes can now be mirrored via chat sessions, provided that proper infrastructure can be disseminated throughout the human service and regulatory systems. Unfortunately, the inclusion of voices from different cultural communities into professional education activities via the Web may be more difficult to attain given the uneven dissemination of Internet technology, experience, and resources.

Third, Web-based pedagogy for professional education is not an all-or-none proposition. The Internet component of a course can be complemented through the coordination of small group activities on a local basis, for instance. A major contribution of emancipatory pedagogy is the intentional critique and confrontation of implicit constraints on social justice. By identifying and directly addressing justice interests, emancipatory instruction can compensate for potential problems arising from Web-based format for professional education: constraints on the informal and spontaneous interaction among students often found in the classroom; "decontextualizing" of people in electronic media; reduction of negotiation to rule-based, bureaucratic action; or inhibition of creative, authentic engagement with the processes of constituting professional identity as accountable to others. Emancipatory educators must take direct responsibility for constituting the course medium.

Finally, the advantages of Web-based design for professional ethics education could be further enhanced through cooperation among training sites. Combining continuing education and courses for continuing graduate students, at least for some activities, is relatively simple if the training has been moved to a Web-based medium. Cross-disciplinary cooperation, rarely practiced in classroom-based professional education, becomes more possible in electronic form. In this instance, self-interest issues arise fairly easily given the competitive political stands taken by many mental health professions in relation to one another. Web courses offer a novel option that holds promise for serving emancipatory interests more directly than does traditional classroom instruction in these domains. Recognizing the resources each student brings to the process further supports Web-based strategies once a sufficient number of sites are on-line and ready to cooperate. In my estimation, these strategies are professionally viable, politically viable, and educationally promising.

WORKS CITED

Adams, Maurianne, Lee Ann Bell, and Pat Griffin. *Teaching for Diversity and Social Justice: A Sourcebook.* New York: Routledge, 1997.

American Association of Marriage and Family Therapy. "AAMFT Code of Ethics." *American Association of Marriage and Family Therapy.* 1 July 1998. 1 Aug. 1999 <http://www.aamft.org/about/ethics.htm>.

American Counseling Association. "ACA Code of Ethics and Standards of Practice." *American Counseling Association.* 1999. 1 Aug. 1999 <http://www.counseling. org/resources/codeofethics.htm>.

American Psychological Association. "Ethical Principles of Psychologists and the Code of Conduct." *American Psychological Association.* 1 Dec. 1992. 1 Aug. 1999 <http://www.apa.org/ethics/code.html>.

Association of Universities and Colleges of Canada and the Canadian Association of Research Libraries (AUCC/CARL). *The Changing World of Scholarly Communication: Challenges and Choices for Canada: Final Report of the AUCC-CARL/ABRC Task Force on Academic Libraries and Scholarly Communication.* Nov. 1996. 1 Aug. 1999 <http://www.aucc.ca/en/publications/carl_aucc/aucccarl.htm>.

British Columbia Civil Liberties Association. 1 Aug. 1999 <http://www.bccla.org/>.

Canadian Psychological Association. "Canadian Code of Ethics for Psychologists." *Canadian Psychological Association.* 1991. 1 Aug. 1999 <http://www.cpa.ca/ethics.html>.

"Community Chat Schedule." *Mental Health Net.* 1 Aug. 1999 <http://mentalhelp.net/about/chats.htm>.

Dineen, Tana. *Manufacturing Victims: What the Psychology Industry Is Doing to People.* Montréal: Robert Davies, 1996.

Drake, Liselle, and Lawrence Rudner. *Assessment and Evaluation on the Internet.* 1 Aug. 1999 <http://ericae.net/intbod.stm>.

Electronic Frontier Canada. 1 Aug. 1999 <http://www.efc.ca/>.

Goldberg, Murray. *Communication and Collaboration Tools in World Wide Web Course Tools (WebCT).* Proceedings of the Conference Enabling Network-Based Learning, 28–30 May 1997, Espoo, Finland. 1 Aug. 1999 <http://www.webct.com/webct/papers/enable/paper.html>.

Griffith, James L., and Mellisa Elliot Griffith. *The Body Speaks: Therapeutic Dialogues for Mind-Body Problems.* New York: Basic Books, 1994.

Hacking, Ian. *Rewriting the Soul: Multiple Personality and the Sciences of Memory.* Princeton, NJ: Princeton University Press, 1995.

Haney, W., and George Madaus. "The Evolution of Ethical and Technical Standards for Testing." In *Advances in Educational and Psychological Testing.* Ed. Ronald K. Hambleton and Jac N. Zaal. Boston: Kluwer, 1991. 395–425.

Idhe, Don. *Instrumental Realism: The Interface Between Philosophy of Science and Philosophy of Technology.* Bloomington: Indiana University Press, 1991.

International Society for Mental Health On-line. 1 Aug. 1999 <http://www.ismho.org/>.

"Joint Committee on Testing Practices." *American Psychological Association.* 1 Aug. 1999 <http://www.apa.org/science/jctpweb.html>.

Joldersma, Clarence. "The Tension between Justice and Freedom in Paulo Freire's Faith-Full Pedagogy." Paper presented at the With Heart and Mind. Trinity Western University, Langley, B.C., May 11. 1 Aug. 1999 <http://www.calvin.edu/~cjolders/WHAM99paper.html>.

Mental Health Net. 1 Aug. 1999 <http://mentalhelp.net/>.

"National Coalition Demands Effective Privacy Legislation." Press release. *Electronic Frontier Canada.* 22 Apr. 1999. 1 Aug. 1999 <http://www.efc.ca/pages/pr/efc-pr.22apr99.html.

Ng, Roxana, Patricia A. Stanton, and Joyce Scane. *Anti-Racism, Feminism, and Critical Approaches to Education.* Westport, CT: Bergin & Garvey, 1995.

O'Neill, Patrick. *Negotiating Consent in Psychotherapy*. New York: New York University Press, 1998.

Renner, K. Edward, Christine Alksnis, and Laura Park. "The Standard of Social Justice as a Research Process." *Canadian Psychology* 38 (1997): 91–102.

Ricoeur, Paul. "Hermeneutics and the Critique of Ideology." In *From Text to Action: Essays in Hermeneutics, II*. Trans. John B. Thompson. Evanston, IL: Northwestern University Press, 1991. 270–307.

Rossiter, A., Richard Walsh-Bowers, and Isaac Prilleltensky. "Learning from Broken Rules: Individualism, Bureaucracy, and Ethics." *Ethics and Behavior* 6 (1996): 307–20.

Test Junkie. 1 Aug. 1999 <http://www.queendom.com/test_frm.html>.

Uhlemann, Max R., and D. Turner. *A Legal Handbook for the Helping Professional*. 2nd ed. Victoria: The Law Foundation of BC and the Sedgewick Society for Consumer and Public Education, 1998.

Whitbeck, Caroline. "Problems and Cases: New Directions in Ethics 1980–1996." *Online Ethics*. 1 Aug. 1999 <http://onlineethics.org/essays/probcase.html>.

Chapter 11

The Roles and Interrelationships of Presence, Reflection, and Self-Directed Learning in Effective World Wide Web–Based Pedagogy

Sherry Wulff, Joan Hanor, and Robert J. Bulik

INTRODUCTION

In March 1999, the Nielsen/NetRatings service released their first report on Internet use in the United States. Defining the audience as "persons, ages 2 and above, who have access to the Internet from home" (2), the service estimated the U.S. Internet population at 97.1 million, which represents not only 36 percent of the total U.S. population, but a 43 percent increase when compared to the first quarter of 1998 (1). The rapidly growing U.S. Internet population has intriguing implications for Web-based pedagogy. We can reasonably assume that as the Internet population grows so will the demand for diverse Web-based commercial services and products, including preschool through postsecondary courses, seminars, and "camps" as well as educational products and resources.

Indeed, since the early 1990s the World Wide Web has proven to be a valuable tool and an important medium for education. When interacting with the Web, students, faculty, and staff have the unique potential for rapid, immediate, and synchronous (at the same time) or asynchronous (at a different time) connections to banks of information, displays and deliveries of various text-based and multimedia learning materials, and links to meeting places in cyberspace. As educators and students become accustomed to the value of the Web as an instructional tool and medium, they will search for appropriate educational resources (from data to courses and materials) for themselves as well as others. Constraining their search may well be the quantity of Web-based educational resources. Defining their search may well be the quest for quality in Web resources, such as proficiently designed distance education courses grounded in principles and strategies associated with effective Web-based pedagogy.

After briefly considering the relationship between Web-based pedagogy and distance education as well as raising several points of critique in a section on "Effects and Effectiveness," this chapter sharpens its focus on the concepts of presence, reflection, and self-directed learning. Using constructivism as a theoretical frame, we explore how the roles and interrelationships of these three concepts serve as significant pedagogical factors. They contribute not only to the development of engagement and connectedness between learner, instructor, other learners, and the learning environment, but they contribute to the development of learner initiative and responsibility. The design and development of presence, reflection, and self-directed learning directly and indirectly influence the effectiveness of learning and the degree of learner empowerment in Web-based educational environments. In particular, we argue that to be effective as a learning tool and medium, Web-based pedagogy must strive to integrate and support high degrees of presence, reflection, and self-directed learning.

SECTION I: WEB-BASED PEDAGOGY AND DISTANCE EDUCATION—SHARED CHARACTERISTICS AND DISTINGUISHING FEATURES

Web-based pedagogy fits neatly within the category of distance or distributed education. According to Marina McIsaac and Charlotte Gunawardena, in their on-line chapter "Distance Education," the traditional definition of distance education emphasized "instruction through print or electronic communications media to persons engaged in learning in a place or time different from that of the instructor or instructors" (History Section 1–2). To facilitate a fuller understanding of contemporary distance education, McIsaac and Gunawardena weave in the work of Desmon Keegan, who in 1980 further characterized distance education pedagogy. His characterization fleshed out these additional features: the "influence of an educational institution," the "use of media to link teacher and learner," a "two-way exchange of communication," and "learners as individuals rather than grouped," along with the concept of "educators as an industrialized form" (History Section 1).

The 1990s, due to technological innovations, witnessed a blurring and merging of boundaries between formats of distance education and traditional on-location or classroom education (Kurzweil; McIsaac and Nirmalani; Phipps and Merisotis; Institute for Higher Education Policy; and Panel on Educational Technology). Nevertheless, from its inception, the success of distance education has relied upon the independence of students in the absence of teacher-student physical presence. Indeed, independence and separation have been the definitive characteristics of distance education.

Historically, distance education students were nontraditional, that is, working adults typically twenty-two and older, with needs linked to time and place flexibility. The New Millennium Project on Higher Education Costs, Pricing, and Productivity sponsored by the Institute for Higher Education Policy, the Ford Foundation, and the Education Resources Institute forecasted "growing 'nontraditional' student populations" (3), populations inclined toward various forms of distance education, accommodating diverse learner needs by offering choice and independence, along with time and place flexibility. In fact, McIsaac and Gunawardena's research indicated that during the 1990s distance education has been steadily increasing its nontraditional student base, while establishing a traditional student base. At the same time, distance education formats such as Web-based courses have been achieving higher levels of social acceptance as viable learning modes (Summary and Recommendations Section 1).

Although Web-based pedagogy can be categorized as distance or distributed education, not all distance education is Web-based (e.g., print correspondence courses or video and teleconferencing courses). Nevertheless, Web-based pedagogy and distance education share fundamental features such as the expectation of learner independence and the physical separation of instructor and student by place, though not necessarily by time. On the Web, instructional communication no longer needs to be the asynchronous two-way exchange between the time- and place-separated teacher and independent learner of traditional distance education. Teacher-student mediated communication can be either time synchronous or asynchronous in Web-based instruction. Moreover, depending on technological factors and systems, a class of independent learners on the Web can achieve social presence, that is, "the degree to which a person feels 'socially present' in a mediated situation" (McIsaac and Gunawardena, Theory Section 3). They establish and develop social presence by interacting with one another and their instructor either in real time, with minimal delay, or at different times on a continuum of delay to accommodate conflicting schedules.

Over the past few years, the Web has gained broader recognition from educators for its potential to support pedagogy. The hypermedia format of the Web can facilitate a reasonably intuitive and efficient process for educators and students in their search for and retrieval of salient information (Dimitroff and Wolfram). It has the potential to encourage and sustain autonomous learning through critical actions, informed processes, and focused procedures. Purposeful browsing, planned searching, and evaluative data retrieval, that is, qualitative decisions about the value and relevance of data before mining it, can provide evidence of students' higher-order learning, particularly when coupled with self-motivated and self-controlled actions in a Web-based instructional context. Additionally, hypermedia formats have the potential to support nonlinear, interactive, and individualized instruction (Becker and Dwyer), which may, in turn, increase the potential for constructing and maintaining self-directed, motivating, and learner-centered Web-based pedagogy.

SECTION II: EFFECTS AND EFFECTIVENESS

The potential advantages of the Web and hypermedia as viable tools and formats for effective pedagogy have generated considerable enthusiasm among theorists and teachers. However, as with all instructional technologies, *potential* and *reality* are not always synonymous. *What's the Difference? A Review of Contemporary Research on the Effectiveness of Distance Learning in Higher Education*, which considered original research from the 1990s on the efficacy of distance learning and its technologies, found that the majority of studies came to a similar conclusion: "[R]egardless of the technology used, distance learning courses compare favorably with classroom based instruction and enjoy high student satisfaction" (Phipps and Merisotis 9). However, the *Review* also found significant gaps in the studies overall: "Many studies do not adequately control for feelings and attitudes of the students and faculty—what the education research refers to as 'reactive effects' " (Phipps and Merisotis 10).

These "reactive effects" are germane to the consideration of effective Web-based pedagogy as a form of distance education delivered and displayed by rapidly evolving communication technologies. Two key effects can be described as follows: The *novelty effect* suggests the highly positive influence of new or different technologies on teachers' and students' perceptions of and feelings about learning by "doing something different not better per se" (10). The *John Henry effect* suggests the positive influence of competition on teachers' and students' perceptions of and feelings about learning. They may feel "threatened or challenged by being in competition with a new program or approach and, as a result, outdoing themselves and performing well beyond what would normally be expected" (10–11). The *Review* went on to explicate several other shortcomings as well as formulating three broad implications for distance education linked to computer-based pedagogy and its potential for effectiveness. Of these, two implications are particularly well connected to the concerns of this chapter.

First, the *Review* addressed the broad implication of access to education, saying the issue of access remains ambiguous at best. Access can be viewed as the raison d'être of distance education and Web-based pedagogy. Yet the issue of access is closely tied to several significant categories of assumptions: (1) technology availability and compatibility, (2) prior technical knowledge and/or previously acquired specialized skills, (3) technical support structures, along with (4) the technology purchasing and maintenance costs for institutions, faculty/ staff, and students (13). A sophisticated and educationally sound piece of Web-based pedagogy may be in place, but if it cannot be used, for whatever reasons— for example, little or no availability of appropriate technological systems, no transferable technological experience, few if any support systems—then how effective can the proficiently designed Web-based pedagogy be?

A second implication addressed by the *Review* stood out as one of high concern for this chapter—*the human factor*. The *Review* stressed the critical relationship of human contact to pedagogical quality and effectiveness in technology-mediated learning environments (14). In this chapter, the human element is considered within a context and continuous cycle of interpersonal/ intrapersonal communications influenced by continuums and degrees of presence, reflection, and self-directedness. In turn, these are conducted through, as well as supported and influenced by, complex social, technical, and content systems. These systems include numerous categories and components. For example, in social systems associated with Web-based pedagogy there are numerous categories of people, such as faculty, staff, administrators, consultants, mentors, technicians, and so forth. In affiliated technical systems there is a broad range of technology categories and components, from software, hardware, and peripherals to various networks as well as all of their parts. Likewise, in content systems connected to Web-based pedagogy there are category layers and diverse components of curriculum, from those at the institutional level to those at the discipline and/or departmental and course levels. Certainly, each system produces effects and impacts effectiveness as it encounters and works through issues of quantity, quality, function, and structure (to name a few), along with systems theory principles such as equifinality, that is, quality in–quality out or garbage in–garbage out, and entropy–neg-entropy (chaos–order).

The concepts of presence, reflection, and self-directedness in Web-based pedagogy are deeply influenced by the systems in place and the systems being constructed during the teaching and learning experiences. They also rely not only on constructing and being present in social systems based on relationships stemming from ongoing interpersonal communications, but on constructing and being present in a continuous, reflective relationship with oneself and the action of learning through intrapersonal communications. The concepts and interrelationships of presence, reflection, and self-directedness, which occur in a variable cycle of interpersonal and intrapersonal communications, play crucial roles in creating effective pedagogy. However, before further consideration of these three concepts in Sections III–IV of this chapter, there are several key points to review regarding the effect and effectiveness of instruction delivered and displayed through technology.

The March 1997 *Report to the President on the Use of Technology to Strengthen K–12 Education in the United States* serves as another source for exploring the difference between the *potential* and the *reality* of Web-connected learning (Panel on Educational Technology). While the *Report* specifically referred to self-directed learning in conjunction with distance learning, it was in the context of using the Web to complete a self-directed project. This functional goal was linked in the *Report* with a student's ability to "quickly gain greater familiarity with the particular subject area in question than her teacher" (37–38). The emphasis centered on the rapid access and acquisition of information/ data other than content a teacher would in traditional paradigms be expected to give.

If self-directed learning and distance learning become connected in the literature *primarily* because of technologically functional issues, such as speed (in access and acquisition of information/data) and quantity (of information/data) rather than more educationally grounded issues, such as quality in the construction of knowledge and the role and responsibility of self in learning, then the field regresses to the kind of reform Ralph Tyler suggested in 1949. Tyler's work, which spawned the *efficiency movement,* has led to a linear perspective on classroom planning that supports technical implementation of curriculum over conceptual intentionality.

There exists a tendency to perceive the Web as a convenient, valuable, efficient, and inexpensive medium through which to conduct learning. Certainly, the Web can provide the means for learners to access, gather, and possibly interact with data. However, educators cannot presuppose that learners will actively process given information in ways that develop or exhibit critical and creative thinking. There is considerable doubt that the availability of information is always an advantage; simply accessing or acquiring data must only be a first step. Even educational technology tools for designing and implementing Web instruction, such as hypermedia software systems that provide format structure and integrate text with still and moving images, as well as link information or resource nodes, are not necessarily the answer.

In an article that examined findings from experimental studies of hypermedia technology, Dillon and Gabbard reported, "Clearly, the benefits gained from the use of hypermedia technology in learning scenarios appear to be very limited and not in keeping with the generally euphoric reaction to this technology in the professional arena" (345). In other words, the World Wide Web through Web-based resources and courses only has the *potential* to support and motivate effective pedagogy. Likewise, hypermedia technology used to construct, display, and deliver instruction and other educational resources only has the *potential* to develop and facilitate effective teaching and learning. Consequently, faculty who design Web-based courses must go beyond limited methods and tools. Providing access to educational resources and equating access to educational resources with effective pedagogy is insufficient. Designers, instructors, and administrators of Web-based courses must take the total "virtual" learning environment into account. They must critically consider and act on how the roles and interrelationships of such concepts as presence, reflection, and self-directed learning influence the learning effectiveness of Web-based pedagogy.

SECTION III: CONSTRUCTIVISM AND PRESENCE

Theoretical foundations for U.S. distance education have been consistently critiqued in the 1990s as tangled and lacking (McIsaac and Gunawardena). Distance education research intended to build theory suffered from various shortcomings and gaps. Overreliance on qualitative versus quantitative methods raised concerns and issues related to the reliability and viability of strategies and findings (Phipps and Merisotis; Dillon and Gabbard; Panel on Educational Technology). In the midst of these concerns constructivism emerged as one theoretical foundation for distance education and contemporary pedagogy (McIsaac and Gunawardena; Panel on Educational Technology). To consider a concept of presence (and reflection as well as self-directed learning) grounded by constructivism, it is important to establish our understanding of constructivism as a theoretical base for pedagogy in general and as a theoretical frame for this chapter more specifically.

Catherine Twomey Fosnot offers a sound discussion of constructivism as a "psychological theory of learning" in *Constructivism: Theory, Perspectives, and Practice*. With roots in the work of Lev Vygotsky and Jean Piaget, constructivism can be described as poststructuralist theory that regards "learning as an interpretive, recursive, building process by active learners interacting with the physical and social world" (30). Furthermore, constructivism "describes how structures and deeper conceptual understanding come about, rather than [a perspective] that simply characterizes the structures and stages of thought [maturation theory of learning] or [a perspective] that isolate[s] behaviors learned through reinforcement [behavioral theory of learning]" (30).

In describing how learning comes about, Fosnot outlines five key tenets of constructivism:

1. "Learning is development"(30). In other words, learning and development are synonymous in that development does not determine the depth and breadth of learning. Rather learners must experiment, imagine, and initiate, that is, be self-directed in structuring and managing these actions-interactions. They must be present with their selves and in presence of the process. Self-awareness and active-in-the-process learner behaviors suggest dimensions of psychological, physical, and social presence. To foster learning and development through presence in the design and implementation of Web-based pedagogy, educators must strive to integrate learning experiences that cultivate physical and social presence (e.g., presence in time and cyberspace of student with teacher, student with other students, and student with other support or resource people) and engage or motivate psychological presence with the content and actions of learning.

2. "Disequilibrium facilitates learning" (30). Mistakes, contradictions, ambiguities, diversities, and problems with perceived no-win solutions encourage learning by disrupting the flow of logical processes and by disturbing the mainstream of standards and norms. To learn from mistakes, contradictions, and so forth, students must experience them in a way that is worthwhile and purposeful. They (students and factors of disequilibrium) must be present, whether synchronously or asynchronously, through some mode of communication. Communication modes, mediums, and/or channels are tools, in a sense, facilitating the reality or perception of presence and the capacity for action-transaction-interaction.

To facilitate effective Web-based pedagogy, educators must think carefully about the role, balance, and presence of disequilibrium that on the one hand occurs spontaneously in the social, technical, and content systems of Web instruction and on the other hand is purposefully planned by the instructor and/or students. Two important questions for Web educators to consider and prepare for include, but are not limited to, these: How can spontaneous disequilibrium be, in a sense, planned for and utilized to maximize learning? How can/should students' perceptions of, experiences with, and responses to frustrations evoked by spontaneous or planned disequilibrium, whether in the social, technical, content or some combination of the three systems, be facilitated for optimal learning? Possible strategies may center on creating opportunities for ongoing public address of disequilibrium, such as making time and space to respect the mistakes and honor frustrations through display and interaction.

3. "Reflective abstraction is the driving force of learning" (30). Concrete expressions of intrapersonal reflection evoke a presence of self. This process and its products allow learners to direct and deepen the construction of knowledge prompted by learning experiences. In Section IV of this chapter we further discuss the role of reflection and strategies for its development in effective Web-based pedagogy.

4. "Dialogue within a community engenders further thinking" (30). When a Web course becomes a community of learners through social and personal presence facilitated by interaction and exchange, then insights and ideas are produced, revised, or refined, and learning increases. A critical factor, according to Fosnot, is the self-directedness of learners within a community: "The learners (rather than the teacher) are responsible for defending, proving, justifying, and communicating their ideas to the classroom community" (30). Web educators can redistribute learning control and power by supporting and/or developing interaction-exchange formats, such as synchronous and asynchronous chat sites and display rooms, to cultivate social and individual presence.

5. "Learning proceeds toward the development of structures" (30–31). Students engaged in the process of learning build, shape, and reshape learning experiences into patterns of meaning and arrangements of knowledge. Learning engagement indicates a presence of self, that is, the learner is psychologically and through one or more senses "physically" aware of and involved in the experiences of learning. Presence of self, in turn, suggests a concurrent action of reflection. Drawing from the work of Donald Schon (further discussed in Section IV), we are referring to either conscious or subconscious reflection on the actions of learning. Reflection, in this sense, can be viewed as the learners' awareness of and thinking about or mirroring to their self in an immediate manner the experiences of learning, then making meanings from those experiences, followed by organizing those meanings into knowledge and/or linking them to prior knowledge structures.

SECTION IV: REFLECTION

We have come to view reflection as a process central to the development of understanding within Web-based learning environments. Reflection can be seen as a capacity we possess both as individuals and as organizations to think about oneself, events, or circumstances with a view toward interpretation and understanding. We recognize the interdependent roles and synergetic relationship of reflection with dialogue. "Human culture and society have developed through the reflective process as people form and share their understandings with one another and take actions on these bases" (Evans 12). Positioning reflection in the light of rediscovery and discovery, our intent centers on the following: (1) to help convey an understanding of reflection, (2) to explore its relationship to presence and self-directed learning, (3) to consider its role in the development of learner initiative and responsibility, and (4) to inquire about its influence on the degree of learner interaction and empowerment within Web-based learning environments.

In professional and educational practice, whether Web-based or site-based, reflection is an important part of the teaching-learning process. For example, when students are having difficulty with an assignment, reflecting on the possible causes, like the level of difficulty or unclear expectations, may lead to practical actions, for example, chunking the assignment or clarifying the criteria. Not all reflection results in practical action; sometimes it leads to abstract action, such as coming to deeper understandings of the problems, issues, and concepts associated with what is being reflected upon.

Schon, an important scholar in the movement to establish the centrality of reflection to professional learning and practice, argues that a significant factor in how practitioners learn to "do" their profession stems from reflection on their practices (*Educating*). They learn not by an unthoughtful doing; rather they learn through a continuum of implicit-explicit reflection on their own actions. In other words, they develop knowledge in action. Schon's perspective of reflection as "knowing in action" (*Educating* 25) offers an interesting connection with Fosnot's tenet about constructivism and learning: "Reflective abstraction is the driving force of learning" (30). One purpose of reflection is to provide the necessary space for learning and for the development of knowledge at a deep level. Reflection honors the capacity of the individual for internal dialogue, a conscious presence with self. Critical self-reflection adds clarity and structure to the inner landscape, creating space for transformation. As reflection shapes and reshapes our internal landscape, it also alters the frame through which we view, experience, and come to know the world.

Perhaps the best way to convey this understanding of reflection is through a story from one of this chapter's authors, Joan. Not too long ago, she was working with technology and teaching art to sixth graders. Her students were clustered around a circular table and immersed in the initial stages of frog dissection. Their task was to closely observe the form and to draw it as accurately as possible. Glancing over their shoulders, she began to note a consistent pattern emerging from their sketches. Regardless of individual positioning in relationship to the frog, each student's drawing portrayed the same linear view of a stick-figure frog with head at top and legs straight out to the right side. For those interested in studying children's art, this might be interpreted as an example of how children draw what they understand, not what they see.

Joan wanted this activity to help them develop new understandings, not just confirm prior ones. Reaching for the video camera, she invited each student to walk around the table with it, pretending they were (tall) her, or short Rosa, or sitting down, or standing up. They looked at the monitor and guessed the position of the camera as the student projected a particular viewpoint. There was no need to record. They were doing it to better understand the process of viewpoint, not to create a video product. Afterwards they cut small frames from paper and purposefully framed their favorite view of the frog form, noting shapes and sizes, relationships of what was near to the front and what fell off into the distance, and points of intersection with the paper frame. Starting anew, the students' drawings were charged with energy and intent that was not previously visible.

We change the world by changing the ways we perceive the world. When those students thought about cause and effect and when they conceptualized the relationships among things in their viewer, the process of reflection helped them build deeper understandings. Did it take technology to allow that to happen? We think not. But the technology of the video camera provided a lens through which they could frame their thoughts, manipulate visual data, explore alternative frameworks, and develop new paths to effective action. The openness of the reflective and collective process of dialogue encouraged and enabled change to occur.

While this example draws from the lived experiences in an elementary classroom, when the use of reflection is transferred to a Web-based learning environment the use of technology is no longer an option, but a requirement. Understanding the consequences of creating these opportunities as well as how they are managed within the Web-based settings is a significant dimension in the design, production, implementation, evaluation, and refinement of effective Web-based pedagogy.

What capacity does reflection build within us and within the on-line community? Reflection, much like physical exercise, helps to build strength and endurance over time. Moreover, reflection is frequently associated with promoting change. For learners, reflection can support and prompt initiative and responsibility, leading to engagement and empowerment. Reflection can influence teachers to change their practice in a variety of directions (Dexter, Anderson, and Becker). If learners and teachers change because of experience and reflection upon that experience, then one might infer that their reflection was perhaps somehow influenced toward valuing certain actions and practices.

Suggestions for Starting Reflective On-line Teaching and Learning

How do we start reflective on-line practice and how do we sustain it? To answer these questions, Ragan suggests we examine the fundamental principles of what constitutes reflection within quality instructional interaction. He indicates that the guiding principles for reflection are less about distance education and more about what makes an effective educational experience, regardless of where and when it is implemented. With this in mind, our suggestions for the design of on-line learning environments include the following:

* Ecological design of on-line environments in which empty space invites the presence of reflections rather than filling an already crowded space with more concepts
* Creation of a setting that is calm, conducive to focus, and away from stimuli
* Selective on-line interactions through learning activities, e.g., problem-solving tasks, quiet tasks, selected readings
* Learner/participants' assurance of a sense of confidence and safety
* Instructor's communication through and about the on-line process that puts the learner/ participant in a frame of mind to slow down, back off, and reflect
* Valuing opportunities

What are some barriers to reflection? While Johnson suggests the collection of additional data, factors emerging from her research include the following:

* Lack of experience with reflection and teaching
* Lack of security—either through lack of confidence or through lack of environmental safety in which risk-taking is not promoted by other participants and/or instructors
* Fear of not being an expert
* Time

On-line learning requires the management of time, both the personal time of the participants and the overall time of the session or course. Sometimes the dynamics of on-line interactivity lead to a social cohesion that resembles sports or games where players are drawn along by interest in the next step in the action (Feenberg 27). The goal of furthering on-line reflective practice is to develop the capacity for "reflection in action," as indicated by Schon, in which learners consciously think about an action as it is occurring, make sense of what is happening, and modify actions as a result. Reflection is not as complicated as it may seem. It is a looking back at oneself, events, or circumstances with a view to interpreting and understanding those things (Evans). It is a process of rediscovery and discovery of insights, of identifying and examining closely the things that most matter, and of coming to new understandings. It is a time to draw upon and build those intuitive and abstract forms of knowledge that are not based within textual form.

The practice of reflection is not without its shadow. Through the process of reflection, one might develop powerful insight into personal or opposing factors of resistance. Reflection may enable understandings that are emotionally staggering without also providing the internal resources for handling them. Because reflection makes space for individuals to explore very difficult and challenging concepts, care must be taken to assure an ecological safety. Valuing is evidenced through the nurturing of reflective processes, honoring and respecting diversity, and recognizing the contribution of presence.

SECTION V: SELF-DIRECTED LEARNING

Self-directed learning (SDL) has become a central theme in adult education, as evidenced by the creation of a commission on self-directed learning, meta-analyses, critical reviews of research, and an annual international symposium devoted solely to research on SDL (Brookfield). With the adoption of SDL by various segments of the business community (Foucher; Zomorrodian) and by diverse professions such as law and medicine (Skeff et al.), this approach to learning is becoming a recommended curricular outcome and a major aspect of teaching across a broad spectrum of education.

Houle expressed the belief that self-direction in learning is and always has been the dominant means for learning. SDL is aligned with constructivism, a learning theory that emphasizes the importance of the knowledge, beliefs, and skills an individual brings to the educational experience. It relies on the belief that knowledge cannot be transferred intact from the head of a teacher to the heads of students; rather, students construct their own knowledge by combining new information with prior understanding and previous experience. Similarly, SDL has given rise to an approach to educational practice that places the locus of initiative and control primarily within the student.

The current emphasis on self-directed learning research grew out of Houle's research in the 1950s, Allen Tough's investigations in the 1960s, and Malcolm Knowles's work in the 1970s and 1980s. A definition of self-directed learning by Knowles has become the most accepted description of this process in which "individuals take the initiative, with or without the help of others, in diagnosing their learning needs, formulating learning goals, identifying human and material resources for learning, choosing and implementing appropriate learning strategies, and evaluating learning outcomes" (18).

Two major themes that appear to be embedded in the above definition, *inter-activity* and *learner control*, dispel the myth that SDL is necessarily an isolated, unconnected, self-sufficient, autonomous, or solitary approach to learning (Bulik and Hanor). *Interactivity* can be described as a process of initiating an engagement or dialogue with learning resources (human or text-based) that allows for an active role on the part of the student in constructing knowledge and participating in the evaluation of learning outcomes. *Learner control* (that is, the learner has the control versus others having control of the learner) can be understood as a process of reflecting on personal learning needs, formulating learning goals (in conjunction with expert faculty), and choosing and implementing appropriate and preferred learning strategies.

SDL and the Web

Interaction, through discussion and collaboration, has become an essential component of any Web-based course. The literature supports a common argument—social interaction (i.e., from our perspective, being present with others in a process of communication exchange) among distance learners plays an important part in learning outcomes (Berge). A dialogue, which can be considered an action of presence, that is, dialogue presupposes presence (whether actual or mediated physical and/or psychological), can occur in various ways—between the student and faculty, and between the student and other students, through chat rooms, threaded discussions, or e-mail. Further, a dialogue can also be created between the learner and the subject matter. However, students need to do more than simply access information. Creating opportunities for students to adapt the information on the Web site by adding to it, reflecting about it, or changing it creates a conversational framework with the content. Students must not only have access to the major concepts being explained or advanced, but must also be able to act on these explanations, to obtain feedback on their own thoughts on the same or different information, and to adapt the Web materials as a result of reflection (Laurillard).

Dialogue and structure are two elements of transactional distance, a term describing forms of communicative presence with others. These two elements have also been discussion points in relation to the student-teacher transaction in the traditional classroom and have been important themes in distance education since the early 1970s (Bischoff, Bisconer, Kooker, and Woods). More recently, the term "transactional distance" was defined by Bischoff et al. (5) for the electronic environment as "the perceived interpersonal closeness between the teacher and student, among students, and between students and the teacher, as perceived by the student respondents."

With respect to the traditional adult education classroom, the student-teacher transaction (or transactional distance) has taken on the status of a metaphor. Metaphors and slogans exist in use, and in the literature, as generalizations and implied comparisons. If a metaphor or slogan accurately represents a connection between an actual and a perceived similarity (or difference), its use will become widespread and accepted, and it will hold the status of "theory." The power of a metaphor or slogan resides in the process and product of thought, which in turn defines reality.

Metaphors have applicability to this discussion of dialogue and structure as these concepts are embedded within the definition of transactional distance. A "sage on the stage," for example, was an early metaphor that attempted to depict the function of faculty in their classrooms. The traditional classroom was high in structure and low in dialogue—a teacher-centered learning environment that tended to inhibit self-directed learning. Students sat in rows of chairs facing the front of the room where a faculty member lectured for fifty-five minutes. A lectern or desk was located a comfortable distance from the students and visually and spatially separated the faculty member from the students. Formal, faculty-created objectives and a linear approach to course content helped lead to a large transactional distance.

As constructivist dialogue entered the mainstream of educational discourse, the metaphor for the student-teacher transaction changed from the sage on the stage to a "guide by your side." Small group discussions and problem-based learning (PBL) began to decrease the structure of the student-teacher interaction, and to increase the dialogue. Faculty now sat with students in a roundtable discussion format, dialogue was initiated between and among students and faculty, and learning issues were developed from cases or real-world problems. This decreased structure and increased dialogue represents a close or small transactional distance. Additionally, the evolution to self-directed learning increased the intimacy of education by involving students directly in development and management of the learning experience.

In other words, the Web (through Web-based courses) only has the *potential* to support constructivist-oriented, self-directed learning. Faculty who design Web-based courses must take the total "virtual" learning environment into account, and not just provide access to educational resources; equating access to educational resources with self-directed learning is insufficient. It is faculty who are responsible for creating a self-directed learning environment, in the academic classroom, in a business training setting, or in the computer-assisted/Web-based "virtual" classroom. Specifically, faculty have the responsibility for creating Web-based learning environments that encourage, not inhibit, constructivist-oriented, self-directed learning.

CONCLUSION

To transpose the structure of Web-based pedagogy on the evolving concepts of presence, reflection, and self-directed learning is a challenge for instructional designers and distance educators, but certainly not an impossible task. The various social, technical, and content systems associated with any Web-based course present numerous problems, concerns, and opportunities. Yet thorough planning, realistic implementation, and ongoing evaluation can resolve many of the problems, ease concerns, and enhance the opportunities. Developing effective Web-based pedagogy relies on, we believe, at least two central guidelines: First, establish and sustain the smallest transactional distance possible. In other words, facilitate close, mediated feelings and perceptions of presence between students and faculty. Second, develop and maintain a nonlinear, interactive learning environment that features reflection and self-directed learning. To further support the potential for developing effective Web-based pedagogy we formulated four practical strategies to inform and enhance Web instruction. They are intended to be general and adaptable to multiple disciplines. We believe these strategies "cue" the design, production, implementation, evaluation, and refinement of effective Web-based pedagogy.

Strategic Cues for Effective Web-Based Teaching and Learning

Critical Responsibility

Build into Web-based instruction "responsible" opportunities for students to develop learning goals, objectives, criteria, or projects specific to their interests and relevant to the course and/or curricular program. Not all students will have the same interests, learning needs, or approach to studying. Again, course management software (or even e-mail) would allow for individualizing the learning environment. When students build a plan of action together with faculty (e.g., learning contracts) they develop processes for lifelong learning. Many students have not yet developed those resources that enable them to complete these tasks: (1) identify a learning issue, goal, or objective; (2) systematically plan activities or methods to meet a learning goal; and/or (3) identify assessment criteria.

Usability Flow and Choice

Build into Web-based instruction opportunities for learner control of the environment. At the same time, design for interactivity and intuitive use. Drawing from the work of Clement Mok, a highly regarded design architect of information, consider these issues and questions of usability and user-friendliness: Are there visible, cued paths for variable pace and flow through information and activities? Does the design accommodate experience diversity? How appropriate are the content, activities, and expectations of operation for the learners? Is there consistency and predictability in the design? What are the modes of learner operation? In other words, how will learners interact with the computer and content—should they command, manipulate, or record? Do students receive immediate, functional, and/or motivating feedback on their actions? For instance, when they click on a button that is linked to an improper answer, do they receive a raspberry sound or a sound that encourages them to think again? How does the design build visual impact through coherence of textual, visual, and audio elements? How does the design of content and activities along with their display create an "immersive experience" (127) that engages students in learning through self-directness and social transaction?

Cohort Social Transactions

Build into Web-based instruction opportunities for students to interact with cohort learners. Typically the reflection and exchange processes can be readily facilitated by course management software or other well-designed, that is, easily accessed, intuitively usable social transaction sites, such as a chat room. Providing multiple opportunities for students to share and assess their work, engage in discussion and informed debate, and reflect and give feedback is critical to the development of a community of learners. For example, where to browse for critical resources can be informed not only by individual reflection based on prior knowledge of the problem being addressed, but by group reflection and dialogue as well. Group interaction can prompt and sustain individual action. Developing, and then defending, an argument for a particular approach to solving a problem occurs routinely in the business/professional setting. Through threaded discussions cohorts of students can be given the opportunity for position-taking, well-reasoned argumentation, and investigation and defense of opposing perspectives, as well as the generation of possible solutions. When social presence, through diverse forms of dialogic interaction and community reflection, is encouraged and supported by the organizational structure of the content, learning tasks, the Web structure, and other instructional or communication technologies, then a close social transactional distance can be imbedded and developed in "distance" learning.

Critical Reflection

Finally, build into Web-based instruction opportunities for students to reflect critically on an individual and social (as a learning community or in subgroups) basis. For example, open-ended questions, to which students can respond by posting a reply through course management software such as WebCT or directly to faculty e-mail, can prompt and guide reflection on subject matter content in relation to specific learning objectives, relevancy, and prior knowledge. Students can be asked to reflect on what they already know or contribute to a discussion on a particular topic, prior to engaging in the course or modules. Based on specific standards or criteria (either instructor or student formulated), they can also be asked to judge their learning performances and their peers' learning performances as well as the outcomes of the course. Thus we come full circle. Critical reflection reinforces critical responsibility. Students become, in a sense, co-evaluators of learning, which enhances the interactivity of the learning process and contributes to the intimacy or personal connections to the course as well as to closing the transactional distance. Evidence of learning can be established in a number of ways, such as student-developed projects, papers, analysis, or research. Defending the evidence of their own learning places the responsibility back on the student and enhances the constructivist, self-directed learning approach.

The most effective learning environments, we believe, ensure that educational resources are used in a technical system of integrity, a content system of curriculum coherency, and a social system of community with learners working in groups, discussing the issues, reporting back, presenting findings, interviewing, and debating the issues. These learning actions provide students with opportunities to articulate, negotiate, and defend their knowledge. Intrapersonal and interpersonal communication through reflection, exchange, and transaction is fundamental to individual and social presence in learning, and to learning itself. We argue that it is the faculty's responsibility to cultivate and guide presence, reflection, and self-directed learning in educational environments, regardless of whether that setting is an adult academic classroom, a business-training site, or a Web-based "virtual" K–12 classroom. Said slightly differently, we feel it is necessary for faculty to focus on the principles and practices associated with constructivist-oriented concepts of presence, reflection, and self-directed learning to develop and sustain effective Web-based pedagogy.

WORKS CITED

Becker, D., and M. Dwyer. "Using Hypermedia to Provide Learner Control." *Journal of Educational Multimedia and Hypermedia* 3 (1994): 155–72.

Berge, Zane L. "Facilitating Computer Conferencing: Recommendations from the Field." *Educational Technology* 35.1 (1995): 22–30.

Bischoff, Whitney Rogers, Sarah W. Bisconer, Barbara M. Kooker, and Lanell C. Woods. "Transactional Distance and Interactive Television in the Distance Education of Health Professionals." *American Journal of Distance Education* 10.3 (1996): 4–19.

Brookfield, Steven. "Self-Directed Learning, Political Clarity and the Critical Practice of Adult Education." *Adult Education Quarterly* 43.4 (1993): 227–42.

Bulik, Robert J., and Joan Hanor. "Self-Directed Learning in a Digital Age: Where Next to Browse Is Informed by Reflection." In *Practice and Theory in Self-Directed Learning*. Ed. Huey B. Long and associates. Norman: College of Education, University of Oklahoma (in press).

Dexter, Stephen, Robert Anderson, and Henry Becker. "Teachers' Views of Computers as Catalysts for Changes in Their Teaching Practice." *Journal of Research on Computing in Education* 31 (1999): 221–39.

Dillon, A., and R. Gabbard. "Hypermedia as an Educational Technology: A Review of the Quantitative Research Literature on Learner Comprehension, Control, and Style." *Review of Educational Research* 68:3 (1998): 322–49.

Dimitroff, A., and D. Wolfram. "Searcher Response in a Hypertext-Based Bibliographic Information Retrieval System." *Journal of the American Society for Information Science* 46:1 (1995): 22–29.

Evans, Terrance. "An Epistemological Orientation to Critical Reflection in Distance Education." In *Beyond the Text: Contemporary Writing on Distance Education*. Ed. Terrance Evans and K. Bruce. Geelong, Victoria, Australia: Deakin University Press, 1991. 7–26.

Feenberg, Andrew. "The Written World: On the Theory and Practice of Computer Conferencing." In *Mindweave: Communication, Computers and Distance Education*. Ed. Robin Mason and Anthony Kaye. Oxford: Pergamon Press, 1989. 1 Aug. 1999 <http://www-icdl.open.ac.uk/mindweave/chap2.html>.

Fosnot, Catherine Twomey. "Constructivism: A Psychological Theory of Learning." In *Constructivism: Theory, Perspectives, and Practice*. Ed. C. T. Fosnot. New York: Teachers College Press, 1996. 8–33.

Foucher, Ronald. "Self-Directed Learning in the Workplace: Data on the Gap Between Individual and Organizational Practices." In *Developing Paradigms for Self-*

Directed Learning. Ed. Huey B. Long and associates. Norman: College of Education, University of Oklahoma, 1998. 169–77.

Houle, Cyril O. *Patterns of Learning: New Perspectives on Life-Span Education.* San Francisco: Jossey-Bass, 1984.

Institute for Higher Education Policy. "Reaping the Benefits: Defining the Public and Private Value of Going to College." In *The New Millennium Project on Higher Education Costs, Pricing, and Productivity.* Washington, DC: Institute for Higher Education Policy, 1998.

Johnson, Judith. "It Takes a (Global) Village to Prepare Teachers: Teaching/Technology/ Reflection." In *Selected Papers from the Eighth National Conference on College Teaching and Learning, 16–19 April 1997.* Ed. Jack Chambers. Jacksonville, FL: Florida Community College at Jacksonville, 1997.

Knowles, Malcolm S. *Self-Directed Learning.* New York: Association Press, 1975.

Kurzweil, Ray. *The Age of Spiritual Machines: When Computers Exceed Human Intelligence.* New York: Viking Press, 1999.

Laurillard, D. *Rethinking University Teaching: A Framework for the Effective Use of Educational Technology.* London: Routledge, 1993.

McIsaac, Marina Stock, and Charlotte Nirmalani Gunawardena. "Distance Education." 1 Aug. 1999 <http://earthvision.asu.edu/~laurie/mcisaac/distance.htm>.

Mok, Clement. *Designing Business: Multiple Media, Multiple Disciplines.* San Jose, CA: Adobe Press, 1996.

Nielsen Media Research. "Nielsen//Netratings Announces Top Web Site Properties and Advertisers for February 1999." News release. *Nielsen Media Research.* 1 Aug. 1999 <http://www.nielsenmedia.com/netratings2.html>.

Panel on Educational Technology, President's Committee of Advisors on Science and Technology. *Report to the President on the Use of Technology to Strengthen K–12 Education in the United States.* Washington, DC: Executive Office of the President of the United States, 1997.

Phipps, Ronald, and Jamie Merisotis. *What's the Difference? A Review of Contemporary Research on the Effectiveness of Distance Learning in Higher Education.* Washington, DC: Institute for Higher Education Policy, 1999.

Ragan, Lawrence. "Good Teaching Is Good Teaching: An Emerging Set of Guiding Principles and Practices for the Design and Development of Distance Education." *CAUSE/EFFECT Journal* 22.1. 22 May 1999 <http://www.educause.edu/ir/ library/html/ccm9915.htm>.

Schon, Donald. *Educating the Reflective Practitioner: Toward a New Design for Teaching and Learning in the Professions.* San Francisco: Jossey-Bass, 1987.

———. *The Reflective Practitioner: How Professionals Think in Action.* New York: Basic Books, 1983.

Skeff, Kelley M., Georette A. Stratos, William K. Mygdal, T. G. DeWitt, Lynn M. Manfred, Mark E. Quirk, Kenneth B. Roberts, and Larrie W. Greenberg. "Clinical Teaching Improvement: Past and Future for Faculty Development." *Family Medicine* 29.4 (1997): 252–57.

Zomorrodian, Ashgar. "Learning Organizations: Empowerment and Institutional Support." In *Contemporary Issues and Practices in Self-Directed Learning.* Ed. Huey B. Long and associates. Norman: College of Education, University of Oklahoma, 1999. 197–209.

Chapter 12

Using the Web to Create Student-Centered Curriculum

Bijan B. Gillani

THE PROBLEM

Three fundamental developments have rocked the foundations of education in recent years: information overload, student diversity, and explosion of the Web as a medium of instructional delivery. These three parameters provide a challenge to education that will significantly alter the educational process in the years to come.

Information overload has become an ordinary occurrence. A common anxiety I often perceive in the behavior of my graduate students is that they never have adequate time to learn what they need to know. I generally do not admit to it, but I suffer from the same type of anxiety. I spend twice as much time preparing for my classes as ten years ago. The fundamental reason for such devotion, in addition to my love of teaching, is the ever-increasing amount of information that I need to feel adequately prepared for my lectures.

I am not the first to be confronted with information anxiety. The phrase "information overload" was first popularized by Alvin Toffler. Furthermore, Saul Wurman expanded upon Toffler's concept by explaining that information overload leads to "information anxiety." What is interesting is that the explosion of information is not a haphazard phenomenon. It is growing and following a specific pattern. James Appleberry has provided a systematic explanation of information growth:

The sum total of humankind's knowledge doubled from 1750–1900. It doubled again from 1900–1950. Again from 1960–65. It has been estimated that the sum total of humankind's knowledge has doubled at least every five years since then. . . . It has been further projected that by the year 2020, knowledge will double every 73 days. (1)

If students are having information anxiety today, what shall we do when information is doubling every seventy-three days in the year 2020? One rational answer is to personalize curriculum where students can become adept to collaborate, find, analyze, organize, evaluate, and internalize new information in light of their own academic and cultural backgrounds.

The second parameter challenging the educational system today is that the social composition of our students has changed drastically from the traditional homogeneous group to heterogeneous groups. Not too long ago, students in our schools had essentially the same linguistic, cultural, and academic backgrounds. Diversity among the student population was an exception. Students were often evaluated based on their IQ scores without giving much consideration to their other personal attributes. The "slow" learners were placed in special schools or classes. The others attended traditional classes where "one curriculum" was adequate to deal with linguistically and culturally homogeneous groups of students.

Today, diversity is no longer an exception in our schools, but a norm. The concept of "one curriculum for all" is no longer acceptable or applicable in schools. Now schools are composed of minority, immigrant, honor, bright, passive, handicapped, exceptional, and academically challenged students. It would be a mistake to apply the traditional approach of one textbook, one curriculum to such diverse groups of students, each with its own special social characteristics, communication styles, personality, cognitive ability, linguistic style, and academic background. Such diversity demands a paradigm shift and the need for student-centered design that personalizes education.

The third parameter affecting our educational system is the explosion of the Web as an instructional delivery medium. Unfortunately, a great majority of educational Web sites are just a conversion of printed materials into HTML (hypertext markup language) pages. Such insistence to place text-based materials on the Web has been responsible for educational sites that are in essence ineffective. The failure is not due to the lack of effort put forth by educators and parents, or to lack of financial support. Rather, the failure of such an approach rests upon the lack of a clear understanding of the role the Web can play in our educational system. Fortunately, the Web, with its adaptive and flexible attributes, places educators in a unique position to face the challenges that recent developments in education have created.

The purpose of this chapter is to discuss how the Web can be used to develop student-centered design to serve as a personalized instructional tool that would satisfy both the demands of the information explosion and the diversity of the student population. To achieve this goal, I first present Lev Vygotsky's socio-cognitive theory and derive a social inquiry teaching model from it that would allow curriculum personalization. Second, I discuss the design for the Web, as an appropriate technological tool, to apply Vygotsky's sociocognitive theory (*Mind; Thought*) to create educational environments that are student-centered and responsive to the needs of students and their diverse backgrounds.

STUDENT-CENTERED DESIGN

The key to a successful education for all students is to place students' needs at the heart of the design process and to take their backgrounds into consideration. Comb et al. explain that the more relevant the education is to the individual, the more meaningful the learning and retention process. The farther the events are from the inner perceptions of the students, the less effect they have on the learning process. The closer the events are to the inner perceptions of the students, the more likely they will change behavior, learning, and retention. To make education meaningful, Comb and other humanistic psychologists (Abraham Maslow; Carl Roger) suggest personalization of curriculum or student-centered design. Student-centered design should account for students' social characteristics, communication styles, personality, cognitive ability, linguistic style, and academic background. These personal attributes are gained through developmental periods, and they form children's inner perception about themselves and the world in which they live.

The challenge of student-centered design is to develop curriculum that is flexible and adaptable to individual students' inner perceptions. Student-centered design is not an easy task. It requires enormous preparation time, appropriate teaching models, diverse tools, and an in-depth knowledge about the diverse personal backgrounds of all students. However, as technology advances, especially the Web with its uniquely flexible interactive and adaptive characteristics, curriculum personalization is becoming a reality.

One of the main objections to curriculum personalization is that it is impossible to personalize education for all students because there are too many unique characteristics. The issue of the infinite characteristics of all students can be considered from a psychological perspective called modal personality (Bock), or the most common traits within groups. Therefore, curriculum personalization concepts discussed in this chapter are based on modal personality rather than purely individual personality.

Before discussing the design ramifications that the Web offers curriculum personalization, we should understand how children acquire and develop their modal personality, which includes social characteristics, communication styles, personality, cognitive ability, linguistic style, and academic background. Such knowledge about development will provide the theoretical foundation for the design of the Web as a tool for curriculum personalization.

SOCIAL FORMATION OF THE MIND

One of the most robust and original social theories, with tremendous implications for education and the Web as a social tool, was postulated by Vygotsky

(*Mind; Thought*). A salient feature of Vygotsky's notion is that human development and learning (e.g., social characteristics, communication styles, personality, cognitive ability, linguistic style, and academic background) originate and develop out of social and cultural interaction within what he calls the "zone of proximal development." This zone will provide the theoretical framework for the proposed social inquiry teaching model in this chapter. A brief overview of four major themes found in Vygotsky's work is vital to understanding the zone of proximal development. These themes are:

• Internalization of external activities
• The role of language in cognitive development
• Knowledge formation within the zone of proximal development
• Activities within the zone of proximal development

Internalization of External Activities

Internal restructuring of external social patterns is what Vygotsky refers to as internalization. Vygotsky (*Mind; Thought*) has argued that a child's development cannot be understood by a study of the individual. One must also examine the external, social, and historical world in which the individual's life develops. Development is a collaborative enterprise between the members of the society and the child. Each member of the society assists the child by providing a learning environment that enables the child's cognitive development. This learning assistance is repeated many times during ontogenetic development and enables the child to master the cognitive, linguistic, and cultural patterns of his or her environment. This notion of socially based cognitive development by Vygotsky claims that all higher human functions develop at two levels, the social plane and the psychological plane:

Every function in the child's cultural development appears twice: first, on the social level, and later, on the individual level; first, between people (interpsychological), and then inside the child (intrapsychological). This applies equally to voluntary attention, to logical memory, and to the formation of concepts. All the higher functions originate as actual relations between human individuals. (*Mind* 57)

The process by which social patterns become psychological, called internalization, is not a passive transfer of external activities. Rather, children actively reorganize and restructure their internal knowledge as more external planes are introduced by parents or other adults or by more capable peers. When the process of social activities is repeated over time, children will internalize the social patterns at the psychological level, which becomes their inner perception of themselves and the world. As will be discussed in the process of Web design, any curriculum design in school must take into account these personal inner perceptions, which include social characteristics, communication styles, personality, cognitive ability, linguistic style, and academic background.

The Role of Language in Cognitive Development

In Vygotsky's view, internalization of inner perceptions does not occur in a vacuum. Rather, the transfer of perceptual patterns from the social to the individual level is mediated by tools of the mind. Language as a tool of the mind plays the most crucial role in transformation of social patterns to individual psychological functions. Just as technical tools play an essential role in shaping the physical environment, language as a symbolic tool plays a corresponding role in the internal construction of knowledge or cognition that is culturally and socially situated.

Human language develops during the early ages. Piaget refers to the early stages of language as "egocentric speech." At first egocentric speech is used by children to solve problems. Children often talk to themselves in trying to solve simple problems. The more complicated the problem, the more talking and planning.

Vygotsky argues that, as children mature, their "egocentric speech" transforms itself into two separate, yet related tools: external and internal speech. The external speech becomes a communicative tool (language) and the internal speech becomes a vehicle for thinking and planning (thoughts). Vygotsky has stated:

On the basis of these experiments my collaborators and I developed the hypothesis that children's egocentric speech should be regarded as the transitional form between external and internal speech. Functionally, egocentric speech is the basis for inner speech, while in its external form it is embedded in communicative speech. (*Mind* 27)

The construction of individual psychological functions has its origins in social life, and it is mediated by the combination of internal and external speech, which allows children to plan their activities prior to execution. During development, as children encounter social situations, internal speech becomes a vehicle for thinking and planning to deal with those situations. If they cannot analyze, organize, solve, or understand the situation on their own, then external speech becomes a communicative tool by means of which children are assisted in understanding social situations. As these social patterns are mastered by children through self-discovery (internal speech) or guided interactive discovery (external speech), their cognition develops.

Cognitive development, therefore, is the internalization of these social patterns as they are mediated by tools such as language. In the design of curriculum for education we should carefully consider the use of language as a tool to promote cognitive development and academic achievement. Exclusion of language as one of the essential tools in the design of curriculum results in inadequacies for both cognitive development and academic learning.

Knowledge Formation Within the Zone of Proximal Development

Internalization of social patterns into psychological learning occurs within the confines of what Vygotsky calls the zone of proximal development. It is within this zone, by the use of internal tools such as language, that social characteristics, communication styles, personality, cognitive ability, linguistic style, and academic knowledge are transmitted from external social activities into internal psychological knowledge.

Vygotsky believes that the relationship between learning and development is a dynamic process that begins from the moment of birth and continues during the school years and beyond. Such a dynamic process has at least two levels that relate to development. One level is what the child can do on her or his own; the second is what the child is capable of achieving if the appropriate environment and assistance are provided. In other words, the child has the potential of doing more if assisted.

Vygotsky introduced the zone of proximal development to explain the dynamic relationship between learning and development, defining it as "the distance between the actual developmental level as determined by individual problem solving and the level of potential development as determined through problem solving under adult guidance or in collaboration with more capable peers" (*Mind* 86).

Learning and development within the zone of proximal development is a recursive process where actual development is transformed into potential development with assistance from other members of the society. It is within this zone that instruction transforms social functions into psychological functions when they are repeated over time.

Activities Within the Zone of Proximal Development

Learning is often much more complex than simple interaction between one teacher and a group of students who passively participate in a classroom. For learning to occur effectively within the zone of proximal development, a theory of learning must also formulate a set of collaborative and interactive social activities in a context that includes the community whose members interact and collaborate with the students to achieve educational goals.

In order to make the progression through the zone of proximal development a social occurrence, Vygotsky (*Thought*) introduced a set of social and contextual activities in which collaboration and interaction for educational purposes occur. Leont'ev, one of Vygotsky's students, elaborated on Vygotsky's social activities and introduced a new theory that has come to be known as the activity theory.

Activity theory has become popular in recent years as the foundation of research in the discipline of human computer interaction (Nardi). In the field of education, Cole and Engestrom have posited a number of elements for the activity theory and a set of complex relationships among them. An activity, according to Cole and Engestrom, is goal driven where external and internal artifacts such as language, the Web, or the computer can mediate between the student (subject of the activity) and the student's purpose (the object of the activity). The outcome of such mediation is to allow progression through the zone of proximal development to achieve the educational goal of the activity.

In the model posited by Cole and Engestrom, activities are not limited just between two individuals. Rather, activities involve a community of mentors who would collaborate with the individual learner to achieve an educational goal. Such collaborative interaction is socially situated, and the activity is distributed between the members of the community and the individual learner. The relationship between the learner and each member of the community must be well coordinated so that their roles and their responsibilities can assist the learner to effectively progress through the zone of proximal development.

SOCIAL INQUIRY TEACHING MODEL FOR THE WEB

Vygotsky's notion of the zone of proximal development and its ramifications for the concept of the activity theory can provide an appropriate teaching model for the Web. As an educational tool, the Web is a flexible multimedia communication network that can combine content presentation, interactive and collaborative communication, and research for further learning, and be a production tool for students' hands-on activities.

Children progress through four phases of the zone of proximal development where there is a gradual internalization of social patterns to psychological patterns (Tharp and Gallimore; Gillani, "Application" and "Web"; Gillani and Relan). These phases are reliance on others, collaboration with others, self-reliance, and internalization. Figure 12.1 shows the four phases of learning as a scaffolding progression through the zone of proximal development.

The role of students in this dynamic learning environment changes from passive to collaborative to active as they progress through the zone of proximal development (Gillani, "Application"). During each phase the concept of scaffolding enables the learner to progress through the phases from total reliance on others to collaboration with others, to self-reliance, and finally to internalization of the goal of the educational activities. As I will discuss in the student-centered design process, the interface, the educational content, and the architecture of the Web site should be designed to be compatible with these four phases of learning by the students as they progress through the zone of proximal development.

These four phases can also provide the syntax (order of instruction) of a social inquiry learning model. Such a model is socially based, and learners subconsciously inquire to learn about social and academic activities. Figure 12.2 shows how such a teaching model can be applied to designing a Web site as a mediating tool that guides and scaffolds the activities of the learner through each phase of instruction. These activities are social and inquiry-based. Instruction

Figure 12.1
Progression Through the Four Phases of the Zone of Proximal Development

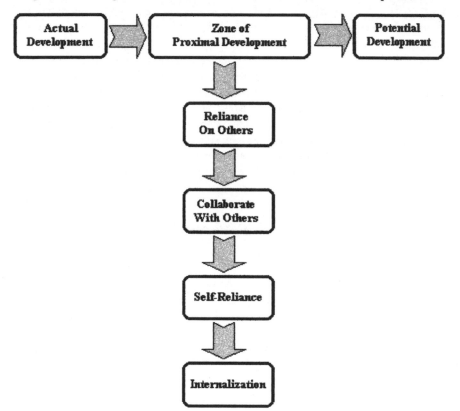

begins with an intellectual confrontation, and learners are then scaffolded through inquiry procedures to find, gather, evaluate, and organize information to hypothesize a possible answer to the intellectual confrontation.

In the first phase, *reliance on others*, the learners are passive as they rely on the modeling and presentation of the teacher. Instructional activities in this social inquiry teaching model begin at the first phase where all students enter a center on the Web site to receive content presentation. The content is in the form of an intellectual confrontation where students are challenged to find answers to an academic question. Strategies such as webbing and modeling are used to attract the students' attention, invoke their prior knowledge, and generate their interest in the content and the themes to be presented. Web use at this level should include multimedia components such as audio, video, text, and animation to focus students' attention on the theme, content, and intellectual confrontation of the educational unit.

During the second phase, *collaboration with others*, students become inter-

Figure 12.2
Social Inquiry Model of Teaching for the Web

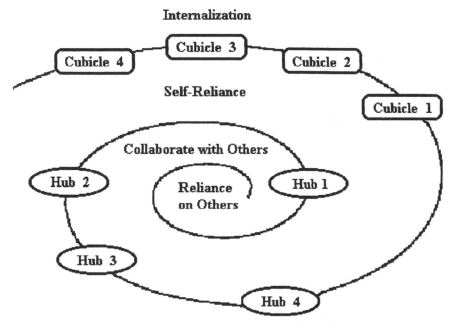

active by using both internal and external speech as well as other mediating tools like the Web to interact with mentors to construct their own potential development. In this phase, each student enters a personalized community of learning centers on the Web. I shall call these centers "hubs" because these centers are where students interact and collaborate with members of the community of mentors to gain more information about the intellectual confrontation. Collaboration, interaction, and communication with others are the key elements during development of this phase of learning. The Web is a wonderful tool to create communities of learning centers where the concept of division of labor in the activity theory can be applied. Hubs in Figure 12.2 represent centers where the roles of teachers, professors, mentors, parents, administrators, and more capable peers are well coordinated to provide assistance for the students to gain more information about the intellectual confrontation.

Depending on the nature of the educational goal, the activity in each hub should be a collaborative effort and well coordinated between the student and the individuals providing assistance. Such virtual learning communities would follow a specific set of rules. Discussion times, ethics, behavior of students, responsibility of information providers, and time for parents to be involved are just a few examples of such rules.

In the third phase, *self-reliance*, students become active and rely on their acquired knowledge to reflect on what they have learned and seek ways for further learning. In this phase of instruction learners enter research centers on the Web that I have called "cubicles" in Figure 12.2. These virtual cubicles are very similar to the research cubicles found in libraries. The virtual cubicles on the Web allow students to initiate their own search, gathering information for further learning. They gather, evaluate, and organize information and data related to the intellectual confrontation. Learning strategies and activities can be embedded in the design of the Web site to encourage students to seek out other related resources (e.g., libraries, learning centers, universities, on-line courses) to further their learning.

In the final phase, *internalization*, students internalize the concept underlying the original intellectual confrontation through repeated active application. It is within this phase that students become capable of using their newly acquired potential development, without much conscious effort, to be creative in generating solutions to the original intellectual confrontation. The Web can provide the proper environment where students can create their own Web sites to show what they have internalized. Or they can create on-line communities to generate new ideas about what they have internalized and become mentors to peers who are not as capable as they are.

STUDENT-CENTERED DESIGN PROCESS FOR THE WEB

With the explosion of the Web as an instructional delivery medium, educators are in a unique position to deliver student-centered curriculum that fits the personalized needs of the students. Because of the flexibility of the Web, it can be designed to satisfy both the demands of the information explosion and the diversity of the student population. Furthermore, the personal needs of students can be reflected in the interface design so that students with diverse backgrounds can feel at home, and therefore at ease. Moreover, the architecture of a Web site can be developed to serve as a collaborative tool between the learner and the community of mentors. Such design in terms of information presentation, interface design, and site architecture allows a socially situated educational setting that is responsive to the personalized needs of students.

Designing and developing effective educational Web sites should follow a systematic process. For example, IBM's guidelines for designing easy-to-use Web sites recommend a process approach for developing Web sites that includes planning, design, production, and maintenance. These categories can be modified for educational purposes as follows:

Planning

      Define educational purpose

      Students' needs analysis

Content organization for a student-centered design

Interface design

Content presentation

Site architecture

Development of student-centered Web site

Maintenance

Evaluation

Learners' feedback

Planning

In the planning stage, you gather valuable information about the educational goal and the needs of the students. This stage involves defining the purpose and students' needs analysis.

Define Educational Purpose

Every educational Web site should be designed to address a specific instructional need. The first step is to define the educational problem the Web site should solve. Without a clear idea of the educational problem(s) the site intends to solve, there is a good chance that the project will lose its focus and fail. Defining the educational goal will guide the developer throughout the whole process.

Four steps help define the educational purpose. First, determine the level of existing knowledge. Second, decide on what is to be learned. Third, identify the educational goal, which is the gap between existing knowledge and desired knowledge. Finally, develop an intellectual confrontation scenario that represents the educational goal.

Students' Needs Analysis

In the students' needs analysis step the modal personality needs of the targeted students are identified, which includes their social characteristics, communication styles, personality, cognitive ability, linguistic style, and academic background. Students' needs analysis is critical to designing an effective Web site. With the students' needs and characteristics established, you can thoughtfully structure the site to reflect their modal personality needs. The analysis also provides essential information for the next level of Web design, which is content organization. Learning about the personalized needs of the students involves (1) becoming involved, (2) seeking appropriate information about your students, and (3) recognizing design implications from your findings.

First, finding information about students' background requires becoming involved and assuming the role of a member in the community about which you are seeking information. There are numerous communities where you can assume an active role, such as churches, workplaces, art shows, ethnic festivals, social groups, support groups, and social services. Once you have become part of that group, read magazines and focus journals about that group to become acquainted with their patterns of thoughts and their preferences. Then, you should assume the role of an anthropologist and create surveys and interviews to gain information about your students' social characteristics, communication styles, personality, cognitive ability, linguistic style, and academic background.

Second, in seeking appropriate information about your students, you should interview the community members about their modal dimensions and plan the design of your Web site accordingly. For example, Shade et al. have provided the following guidelines for African American and Mexican American cultural characteristics that contribute to the design of classrooms (Table 12.1).

Similar types of information about students' social characteristics, communication styles, personality, cognitive ability, linguistic style, and academic background can be elicited from the members of a community by interviews and surveys for developing Web sites that are responsive to the personalized needs of the learner. These types of knowledge are vital to the design of the Web for student-centered purposes.

Third, during the students' needs analysis step you should recognize the design implications from your findings about the students' modal dimensions. This type of information forms the building blocks of student-centered Web sites. Based on the profiles of the students, you should consider the following questions to prepare for the next design phase:

- What interface design features will represent the students' modal dimensions?
- What instructional model should be implemented?
- How should the information be structured?
- How should students communicate?
- What activities should be included?
- What level of interactivity is needed?
- What linguistic style is appropriate?
- What kinds of graphics are appropriate?
- What kinds of media best represent the students' backgrounds?

Content Organization for Student-Centered Design

In the content organization level, you translate the results of the students' needs analysis into planning the look and feel, content, and relationship of educational materials and activities. This stage includes planning and organizing for interface design (look and feel to represent diversity), content presentation

Table 12.1
Cultural Characteristics

African American Cultural Style	Mexican American Cultural Style
• Aesthetic appreciation of bright colors, fashionable clothing, and hair styles as the need to express their self-identity	• Individuals should identify closely with their community, family, and ethnic group.
• A deep respect for spirituality and humanness that is often manifested through religion	• Individuals should be very sensitive to the feelings of others.
• A spontaneity and ability for improvisation and rhythmic orientations shown in dance, music, and verbal and non verbal communication	• Status and role definitions within the community and family are clearly defined and should be respected.
• Value system that incorporates not only the desire for success, but also group unity, freedom, and equality	• Achievement or success is highly dependent on the cooperative efforts of individuals rather than competitive individualism.
• Socialization experiences that develop a preference for cooperation and supportiveness, which manifest itself in group affiliation	
• A highly developed skill to understand and correctly perceive the affective dimensions of people and situations.	

(teaching model), and site architecture (activities) to account for the diversity of students and personalization of information.

Interface Design

Interface design refers to the look and feel of the Web site, including the screen design, navigational tools, and interactivity. The styles of graphic presentations, color selection, placement of audio, types of video, the menu system, the navigational elements, and other elements of interface design play essential roles in the design of student-centered Web sites.

One of the main objectives of student-centered design is to create a learning environment that fits the actual knowledge, background, and culture students bring to school with them. In other words, the Web site should adapt itself to the "diversity" of students. By choosing the right design for the interface, you can provide a look and feel to Web pages that reflect the diverse needs of students.

Students' needs analysis during the first stage provides essential information that will guide the design of the elements of the interface to appeal to different student groups. Once we gather information about the students' modal dimensions, the interface can be designed so that students see themselves in their own needs. In *Global Interface Design*, Fernandes provides three general areas that need particular attention: language, visual communication, and appropriateness of features.

There simply is no global language that students from different backgrounds understand. However, at the initial stage of student-centered curriculum, it is best for the language or the dialect of the Web site to reflect the linguistic background of the student. The same Web site can be designed so that different linguistic backgrounds present the same educational content. For example, the interface design of the first page of a student-centered Web site can provide buttons representing different dialectical backgrounds. These dialects can range from Black English to Hispanic, and in some cases totally different languages like Vietnamese or Spanish. Clicking on the appropriate button will navigate students to the pages where instruction is presented with the appropriate dialects that represent students' linguistic backgrounds.

Visual communication is the second area suggested by Fernandes for interface design to be responsive to the needs of students. Visual communication refers to different elements of interface design. When designing student-centered interfaces, consider using the following visual communication tools:

- Include video and audio as elements of interface design. These media can be designed to provide culture-specific interfaces that are appealing to students.
- Design cooperative centers: For example, certain indigenous groups enjoy cooperative work with different groups. Create shared areas including chat rooms and forums for cooperative work on the Web pages.
- Create lockers for long- and short-term projects. Most students like to have a storage area like lockers, backpacks, or briefcases. It gives them ownership of their work. In

a similar manner, lockers can be presented on the interface by icons, graphics, or buttons that are connected to an actual folder on the server. In this manner, the interface acts as a locker for students to save their work. The actual saving and transferring of students' work is done through the FTP capability of the Web.

• Using specific colors that different cultural groups prefer for the interface gives a feeling of being at home to students of different cultures. Color should be used in the background selection, artwork, artifact, and lesson presentation.

• Provide cultural centers as an element of interface where students of the same cultural background can share information.

Effort should be made to include appropriate features for interface design to make students feel at home. These features include pictures, maps, flags, artifacts, linguistically relevant signs, proverbs, cultural videos, cultural stories, audio, icons, metaphors, people, music, food, mythology, and other related features that are culturally appropriate. The results of your needs analysis during the first level of design should provide the appropriate features for different student backgrounds. Once these appropriate features are identified, then it is simply a matter of embedding them into the interface to make students feel at home.

Recall that it was previously recommended that the interface design of the first page of a student-centered Web site provide buttons representing different modal backgrounds. Clicking on the appropriate button will navigate students to the pages with the appropriate features for interface design to make each group of students feel at home. You should establish visual identity for different groups and consistently use these features. A consistent visual style representing appropriate features gives a site a sense of belonging and reinforces a feeling of ownership for the learner.

Content Presentation

Content presentation is the effective presentation of educational materials on the Web that adheres to the educational needs of the students. These educational needs should be supported by using appropriate learning theories, proper instructional models, and cognitive styles. There is no one specific theory, teaching model, or cognitive style that fits all students. However, we need to consider a general teaching model that would satisfy the demands of the information explosion and curriculum personalization using the Web.

Deciding which type of theory, instructional model, and cognitive style to use for a Web site is best done by considering the advantages the Web has to offer. As mentioned, the Web is a multimedia social tool that allows content presentation, interactive communication, and research for further learning, and becomes a production tool for hands-on activities. Because of these features, one of the most appropriate theories to use for content organization on the Web is a sociocognitive theory that allows social interaction for cognitive development and learning.

As noted, Vygotsky (*Thought; Mind*) postulated a sociocognitive theory that states that human development and learning originates and develops out of social and cultural interaction as mediated by tools. Vygotsky's zones of proximal development can become units of instruction on the Web where socially situated settings are created that allow students to use the presentation, communication, research, and production features of the Web to internalize educational materials.

Content presentation also relies on proper teaching models. In the previous section, I discussed in detail that we could derive a social inquiry teaching model from Vygotsky's theory. When a social inquiry teaching model is used, students follow specific steps:

- Students are presented with a situation where elements of an intellectual puzzlement are involved. (For example, a movie about lightning is shown and the intellectual confrontation is to find what causes lightning.)
- Teachers and students in groups rely on each other to interact, communicate, and react to the causes of the situation.
- Students search different resources to gather data, further their learning, and experiment. They isolate relevant information, hypothesize a possible answer to the intellectual confrontation, and test it.
- Teacher and student groups analyze their findings and apply their learning to new situations.

The proposed social inquiry model has a universal syntax (order of instruction). However, because the Web is a flexible and adaptive tool, both the types of information and the manner in which information is presented can be personalized to fit the needs of students. During the first phase of instruction all students receive the same intellectual confrontation scenario. However, as they progress to the next phase, the Web becomes a community of learning centers. The goal of this phase is for individual learners to go beyond the walls of the classroom, using the Web to interact, collaborate, communicate, and react with others to find the reasons and justification for the intellectual confrontation that was presented in the first phase. As such, each student has his or her own personal learning centers connected to specific people to gain more information. As students accumulate more information and develop their own power of evaluation as to the validity of resources, they progress to the third level of instruction where they carry out personal research to gather data and isolate and organize relevant information to further their personal learning experience. Finally, each learner applies his or her own learning in light of his or her cognitive structure to new situations.

The Web's presentation, communication, research, and production features fit appropriately with the four phases of the zone of proximal development as well as the syntax of the social inquiry teaching model. In the reliance on others phase, the learners are passive as they rely on the mentor to model and present the intellectual puzzlement. Considerable multimedia units for the Web should be used to invoke students' prior knowledge and to generate student interest in the concept. For example, if the educational goal of instruction is survival of animals, then a variety of graphics, video, animation, audio, and text about animals around the world are presented. Furthermore, stories and animation about endangered species and reproduction can also spark students' interest in the survival theme of the units. Finally, during this phase a clip of endangered species, as an intellectual confrontation, could be shown and students asked what they might do to save animals from extinction.

In the collaboration with others phase, each student enters a personalized community of learning centers on the Web—"hubs." In these "hubs" students are guided to interact and collaborate with members of the community who serve as mentors. The function of each mentor is to assist students to gain more information concerning the intellectual confrontation. Each hub would represent centers for different disciplines where teachers, professors, mentors, parents, administrators, and more capable peers provide assistance for the students to gain more information in regard to the original intellectual confrontation. These centers do not necessarily have to be academic. Some of these hubs can be learning centers where students can gain more information about cultural and personal attributes that would help them to achieve the educational goal as defined in the first phase.

Continuing with the same theme of animal survival as an example, five different areas can be designed to represent math, science, language, art, and social studies. Each of these centers could have chat rooms, forums, and video conferencing to create interactive centers where students can communicate with each other and the mentor about the survival of animals. Students are encouraged to move from one center to another to discuss animal survival from different perspectives of different disciplines. Such interdisciplinary interaction allows the mentor and the more capable peers to assist students to gain knowledge about animals and understand how different disciplines deal with the theme of survival. Note that these hubs are not limited to academic disciplines. There are hubs for parents, principals, peers, or anyone who can assist the learner to be scaffolded to the next level.

In the self-reliance phase, students become independent and no longer require extensive assistance from others. They search different resources on the Internet to gather data to further their learning experiences. They depend on their own knowledge to seek ways for further learning. Designers should embed learning strategies and research activities as elements of interface for the centers called "cubicles" in the previous section. These strategies should encourage students to seek out other related Web sites and resources (e.g., libraries, learning centers, universities, on-line courses) to further their learning. Furthermore, organizational and management software for the Web should be embedded in this phase of learning to allow students to evaluate, isolate, and organize relevant information and then hypothesize a possible answer to the original intellectual confrontation question.

Continuing with the animal survival example, links can be created to related Web sites around the globe for students to carry out research. Or students could be assigned to search different libraries or on-line courses to find books and related articles about animal survival. Or a mentoring partnership could be created with university professors in different disciplines for students to get first-hand research information. Once students have gathered information they can isolate relevant information and hypothesize a possible answer to the question of animal survival.

Finally, in the internalization phase students become comfortable implementing their newly acquired knowledge. They are now able, without much conscious effort, to be creative and to generate solutions to problems that are similar to the concept they have mastered. For example, students might create their own Web sites about what they have internalized. Or they could create on-line communities to generate new ideas about what they have internalized and become mentors to peers who have not yet mastered the concept. Or students can work on projects and write or deliver interactive reports on the Web about what they have learned.

Continuing with the theme of survival as an example, students might create an interactive Web site where the endangered species is placed in an environment with all the elements that would cause survival or extinction of the species. Then, based on the information they have gathered, they could make the Web site interactive, with negative elements being reduced and the positive elements being increased to allow survival of the species.

Site Architecture

Site architecture governs how the pages of a Web site are linked to one another. This relationship should be based on the syntax of a teaching model and the elements of the activity theory that supports the site. Depending on the students' needs, or the function of the Web site, the architecture of the site may be structured in a variety of forms. Horton has suggested four basic structures: sequential, hierarchical, grids, and web. The site architecture that is most appropriate for the proposed teaching model and the elements of the activity theory is a combination of sequential and hierarchical.

Before beginning any site development, a flow chart should be drawn to represent the syntax of the teaching model and the elements of the activity theory. Such a flow chart defines all pages of the site and the pathways linking each page.

Based on the site architecture, navigational elements can be designed. However, most large-scale Web sites have a very complex structure. IBM guidelines for Web site development suggest the following to inform users where they are in a site:

- Provide easy access to some form of table of contents, from where users can link to any other place (the table of contents may be the home page itself, or another separate page).
- Always provide an immediate way to return to the home page.
- Make the resident section heading clear.

Furthermore, testing the navigation design before it is placed on the server is absolutely essential. IBM guidelines also recommend asking the following questions:

- Do users know how to find the information they need?
- Does your navigation design connect all related information in a sequence that makes sense to users?
- Do users know where they are in the site structure?
- Do users know how to return to points they visited previously?
- Are there any unnecessary links that clutter the navigation design?

Development of a Student-Centered Web Site

Development of a student-centered Web site requires that you have some knowledge of new technologies (Internet tools, server abilities, HTML, scripting, database, and multimedia). Many Web projects miss the fact that Web development is an interdisciplinary effort. The goal of the student-centered design process is to ensure that the final product is educationally effective and satisfies the learners' needs. To achieve this goal, the first step is to follow an interdisciplinary approach to designing educational Web sites. Web development requires the skills of an interface designer, programmer, media specialist, content specialist, writer, secretary, marketing specialist, actors/actresses, and voice-over individuals.

It is most essential that at least one student be an integral part of the design team. Involving students at every step of the design process is a must that is often ignored by developers. Students can provide valuable information about problematic elements of the site. During the maintenance phase and other phases of development, student input can help to refine the Web site to be truly student-centered. The development of prototype Web sites should follow these steps:

- Develop flow charts based on the educational needs of the students.
- Review the flow chart as a team.
- Determine the media types to be used.
- Create a storyboard (a sketch of each page on paper).
- Determine the programming required (structure and special effects).
- Produce the first module (a prototype).
- Review with peers and revise the first module.
- Produce the remaining modules.
- Test on pilot students.
- Revise.
- Test on general students.

Maintenance

Finally, maintenance of the Web site involves evaluation and learners' feedback. The evaluation process determines the extent to which you have achieved the expected educational outcomes. Evaluation is a continuous process. It starts from the first step when the purpose of the site is being defined and continues even after the site has been developed and published. A student-centered Web site's effectiveness can be evaluated by answering the following questions:

• Are the elements of interface design representative of students' backgrounds?
• Are samples of art, music, and mythology that represent students' backgrounds present on the site?
• Is the site structured to allow the syntax of a social inquiry teaching model?
• Are there centers that encourage collaboration and discussion with other mentors?
• Does the site encourage interaction and communication with peers and teachers?
• Does the site represent elements of the activity theory?
• Does the site provide the means for students to help each other?
• Does the site promote further research?
• Is instruction interdisciplinary?
• Does the site provide the means for students to carry out independent research?
• Does the site provide the means for students to carry out hands-on activities?

The most effective way to evaluate and maintain an educational Web site is to give the learner a way to contact the site developers. This can be done with a form on the Web site or by e-mail. In a more elaborate feedback, learners can be surveyed or interviewed. In either case, to achieve student-centered curriculum learners should be kept involved as long as the Web site is functional.

ACKNOWLEDGMENTS

Special thanks go to my wife, Judy Gillani, for reviewing the first draft of this chapter and making wonderful suggestions.

WORKS CITED

Appleberry, James. "Changes in Our Future: How Will We Cope?" Faculty speech presented at the California State University, Long Beach, California, 1992.

Bock, Phillip. *Rethinking Psychological Anthropology: Continuity and Change in the Study of Human Action.* New York: W. H. Freeman, 1988.

Cole, Michael, and Yrjö Engestrom. "A Cultural-Historical Approach to Distributed Cognition." In *Distributed Cognition.* Ed. Gavriel Salomon. Cambridge: Cambridge University Press, 1991. 1–47.

Combs, W. Arthur, Donald Avila, and William W. Purkey. *Helping Relationships: Basic Concepts for the Helping Professions.* Boston: Allyn and Bacon, 1971.

Fernandes, Tony. *Global Interface Design*. Boston: AP Professional, 1995.

Gillani, Bijan. "Application of Vygotsky's Social Cognitive Theory to the Design of Instructional Materials." Diss., University of Southern California, 1994.

——. "The Web as a Delivery Medium to Enhance Instruction." *Journal of Educational Media International* 35 (1998): 197–202.

Gillani, Bijan, and Anju Relan. "Incorporating Interactivity and Multimedia into Web-Based Instruction." In *Web-Based Instruction*. Ed. Badrul Khan. Englewood Cliffs, NJ: Educational Technology Publication, 1997. 231–39.

Horton, William. *Designing and Writing Online Documentation*. New York: John Wiley and Sons, 1994.

IBM. "IBM's Ease of Use." *IBM*. 1 Aug 1999 <http://www.ibm.com/ibm/easy/design/lower/f060100.html>.

Leont'ev, A. Nikolaevich. "The Problem of Activity in Psychology." In *The Concept of Activity in Soviet Psychology*. Ed. James V. Wertsch. Armonk, NY: M. E. Sharpe, 1981. 37–71.

Nardi, A. Bonnie. *Context and Consciousness*. Cambridge, MA: MIT Press, 1996.

Piaget, Jean. *The Language and Thought of the Child*. London: Routledge & Kegan Paul, 1959.

Shade, Barbara J., Cynthia Kelly, and Mary Oberg. *Creating Culturally Responsive Classrooms*. Washington, DC: American Psychological Association, 1997.

Tharp, Roland G., and Ronald Gallimore. *Rousing Minds to Life: Teaching, Learning and Schooling in a Social Context*. New York: Cambridge University Press, 1988.

Toffler, Alvin. *Future Shock*. New York: Bantam Books, 1970.

Vygotsky, Lev Semyonovitch. *Mind in Society: The Development of Higher Psychological Processes*. Ed. and trans. Michael Cole, Vera John-Steiner, Sylvia Scribner, and Ellen Soubermann. Cambridge, MA: MIT Press, 1978.

——. *Thought and Language*. Ed. and trans. Alex Kozulin. Cambridge, MA: MIT Press, 1992.

Wurman, Saul. *Information Anxiety*. New York: Doubleday, 1989.

Chapter 13

The Scholarship of Web-Based Teaching

Martha Daugherty, Autumn Grubb, Jude Hirsch,
and H. L. "Lee" Gillis

In recent years, American institutions of higher education have begun to reexamine and redefine professorate scholarship. Reasons for this movement are varied. However, most concerns tend to focus on the need to realign faculty responsibilities with individual college missions and to improve teaching and learning as we enter the twenty-first century. Restructuring practices for promoting and rewarding faculty productivity are also at the center of this reform.

Not surprisingly, widespread interest and heated debate among university faculty have resulted. The use of the Internet for teaching has compounded the debate by challenging the whole notion of classroom for many academicians. Evident throughout university dialogue is a desire to extend rigid categories of scholarship to a more comprehensive, dynamic understanding of a professor's academic role and mandate. From this reconceptualization a renewed respect and recognition for the scholarship of teaching has emerged.

The concept of teaching as scholarly work was initiated in *Scholarship Reconsidered*, a 1990 report by former Carnegie Foundation president Ernest Boyer, and further extended in the 1997 follow-up publication, *Scholarship Assessed*, by Glassick, Huber, and Maeroff. These works present the scholarship of teaching as a clearly defined process, one that is inherently shared by all other forms of scholarly work produced at the higher education level. Subsequently, common dimensions for scholarship itself were established. The scholarship process is guided by qualitative standards and begins with an intellectual commitment to a subject, discipline, or issue. Those who teach must, above all, be well informed and widely read, consumed with the knowledge of their field. The bridge between a teacher's understanding and the student's learning then becomes a dynamic endeavor. Components of this venture include the development of specific goals, effective skills, methods, and communication, the ability to connect theory to practice, and reflective critique (Glassick, Huber, and Maeroff 25). Teaching, in the end, must also be judged by the significance of its results. Outcomes can be measured by the quality of student learning, the degree to which instructional goals have been met, and through the development of innovative models for teaching.

Critical evaluation for the scholarship of teaching lies within reflective critique and documentation of the instructional process (Glassick, Huber, and Maeroff 33). Reflective critique refers to thinking about one's work, participating in dialogue and conversations with peers and others about it, and applying what is learned from these activities to improve teaching and learning. Through individual reflection come insight and self-awareness, both of which encourage the development of new skills and knowledge. In addition, peer collaboration promotes intellectual scholarship and engagement. To move beyond the narrow confines of one's own teaching, multiple perspectives are necessary. In particular, conversations with colleagues engaged in similar pursuits stimulate creativity, refinement, and thoughtful evaluation of one's scholarly work. Teaching therefore becomes a craft, a professional endeavor, where the process of scholarship is supported and enhanced.

Evidence of scholarship in higher education is most often provided through documentation of a faculty member's work. Traditionally, evidence for an individual's teaching performance is comprised of student evaluations or ratings, syllabi, and, in some cases, samples of instructional materials. However, current work on scholarship suggests that documentation of the teaching process needs to be expanded and broadened. In essence, thoughtful documentation of one's work promotes critical review and, subsequently, reflective practice and improvement. Multiple data sources with more varied types of evidence are recommended to illustrate the richness and rigor of true teaching scholarship. One mode of evidence that is often mentioned within recent literature is a record of research that has been conducted on one's own teaching (Boyer 40).

The purpose of this chapter will be to share a record of research on teaching produced by four university faculty members. Through collective and individual narratives, conversations and dialogue, and critical reflections, we describe specific themes on teaching that have emerged from our experiences. We relate these themes to scholarship and its components. However, our case study does not address traditional forms of teaching. Rather, it takes teaching to a different plane and reflects upon a delivery system that is likely to become more and more common in the twenty-first century, that of Web-based instruction. We have called the chapter "The Scholarship of Web-Based Teaching" because the process of scholarship is seen and documented throughout our work. It is also our premise that scholarly work can and must be present in Web-based instruction to ensure that it is an effective, viable medium for teaching and learning.

METHOD

In this section, we provide a brief summary of our research design. Descriptions of the setting, participants, and method of data collection and analysis are presented.

Setting

Georgia College and State University is a senior comprehensive institution of the university system of Georgia with a liberal arts mission. The university is an established leader of technology among the university system institutions. Looking forward into the twenty-first century, the state of Georgia is strongly dedicated to distance learning. At the University of Georgia Gerontology Center Web home page, in an article entitled "Georgia Statewide Academic and Medical System GSAMS," Governor Zell Miller is quoted as stating, "No other state has invested as much in distance learning and telemedicine as has Georgia" (paragraph 1).

The technological infrastructure of Georgia College and State University reflects the technology focus of the Georgia university system. It includes a Distance Education Unit, an Office of Electronic Educational Services, and a dedicated coordinator of faculty training, all of which support a variety of distance learning initiatives in various schools and colleges. A Connecting Teachers and Technology Committee has overseen the technology training of 40 percent of the faculty through extended workshops. In addition, the university developed and houses a K–12 Educational Technology Center that provides technology training and support for the middle Georgia public school systems.

Georgia College and State University is also involved in some unique technology projects that have been reported and written about most recently in the *New York Times* on-line article "Distance Learning" (paragraphs 1–3). The university, in cooperation with GSAMS, the Georgia Statewide Academic and Medical System, was the first in the world to offer courses to a deployed ship, the USS *Carl Vinson*, as it traveled in the Pacific and the Persian Gulf. The Distance Education Unit and Department of Government and Sociology have been delivering graduate program courses via the teleconferencing system aboard the ship for over two years now. As a leading member of the GSAMS network, the largest two-way interactive video network in the world, the university further serves over 400 students a semester enrolled in higher education courses at fourteen different locations. In addition, the university is participating in a joint project to bring the Georgia Telemedicine network and the Georgia Distance Education Network together to serve rural health care needs through education and training.

The technological advancement of the university, coupled with its liberal arts mission, has several implications. The university recognizes that a true liberal arts education prepares students for the twenty-first century and is global in scope. It therefore becomes imperative that learning environments be structured to meet these educational goals and subsequent student needs. The university's commitment to technology reflects these educational standards. For example, learning and student development are not limited to the classroom when state-of-the-art technological tools are readily available. In addition, faculty trained in technology can competently integrate it into the curriculum. These illustrations mirror the university's vision to provide the most advanced scholarly and professional practices within a liberal arts academic setting.

Participants

We initially came together during an extensive faculty development workshop on technology sponsored by the university. This semester-long, weekly venture consisted of in-depth training in all areas of computer applications and multimedia technology, including designing instructional Web sites and teaching on-line courses. While three of us participated as students, the fourth member of our union was the instructor.

The workshop provided seeds for conversation about technology and its role in education. Although we were at different levels of competency, a bond was formed among the four of us because of our similar perspectives on instruction and student learning. We began to extend the setting for our conversations beyond the confines of the workshop to various social contexts. Within weeks, these sessions became regularly anticipated events and, as a result, we decided to record our thoughts, insights, and questions.

Much of the dialogue focused on experiential and contructivist theory and how best to integrate technological instruction with these educational philosophies. Connections to scholarship were made when we became involved with committee work related to scholarship in teaching and began attending conferences and workshops on the topic. Those connections are presented in this chapter.

The coauthors bring to this work unique backgrounds, perspectives, and technological experience:

Autumn Grubb is Distinguished Professor of Teaching and Learning and Coordinator of Professional Faculty Development at Georgia College and State University. "I teach undergraduate and graduate courses across the curriculum and collaborate with faculty members who desire to incorporate technology into their face-to-face instruction or develop on-line courses. I also serve as the lead trainer for the annual Faculty Development Workshop and have designed six Web-based core courses for the Master's in Education with an emphasis in Distance Learning."

Lee Gillis is a psychology professor who began using e-mail at 300 baud and who continues to look for more efficient ways to utilize technology in conjunction with face-to-face classroom encounters in courses that focus on interpersonal relations, personality, group dynamics, and group leadership. "I have been fascinated by the Web responses of introverts and extroverts who belong to the same cooperative learning group. I have begun to wonder if the Web-based work gives voice to those who choose not to have it in the traditional classroom. In the past I was the only one who saw the thoughts of the introverts when they turned in a paper or answered a discussion question on a test. With a Web-based forum, all in the group can 'see' the thoughts of those who otherwise would be silent. I am excited at how the Web-based environment in combination with a traditional environment levels the playing field for students."

Jude Hirsch teaches in and coordinates a B.S. and a M.Ed. in outdoor and environmental education. "I am an experiential educator who spends a good deal of my time teaching outdoors. The decision to develop computer-enhanced pedagogy for the outdoor education degree programs was a difficult one. Not only did it mean that my learning curve would take me a significant distance from my technological comfort zone, it meant that I would have to deal with the certain backlash from some students who firmly believe that mixing computers and outdoor education is an insult to the profession—and I was not sure I could disagree with them. I have long accepted the fact that as a writer and an administrator, my computer is an essential component of effective and informed communication. However, I prefer face-to-face interaction with my peers and with the participants I work with. Like many other decisions for which avoidance tactics work, if I wait long enough, someone else will make the decision for me. In this case, Georgia College and State University declared a strong commitment to technologically enhanced instruction, and the Association for Experiential Education called for submissions to an upcoming journal edition related to the theme of computers as experiential education. Risk and challenge come in many forms, so I took the plunge."

Martha Daugherty is a professor in the School of Education with a primary focus in educational research. "I received a faculty development grant in 1996 to develop a Web-based graduate research course, the first on-line class offered by the university. Although I've redesigned and taught the course successfully several times since, I still question the effectiveness of this medium for instruction. As a result, I am interested in evaluating Web-based teaching and learning."

Design

This investigation was a case study of four university faculty members' experiences with Web-based instruction. The primary focus of the study was to provide a detailed examination of one developmental process common to the group, that of incorporating technology into higher education. The process was then interwoven with the scholarship of teaching. Our intentions were to share common experiences of lessons learned and knowledge gained. It is thought that our perspectives may be common to most university faculty involved in similar pursuits. Therefore, the study is timely and important. It is offered as our contribution to the current conversation concerning the redefinition of university teaching in the twenty-first century.

Data for the project consisted of our individual and collective narrative reflections on a wide range of challenges in the development and delivery of Web-based instruction. Individual critical reflections provided data on processes, pedagogical strategies, and experiences. Group conversations and collective dialogues generated similar data. All data were recorded, transcribed, and coded. Common themes and patterns emerged from systematic analysis of the data. Themes were then related to the components of scholarship discussed in current literature.

FINDINGS AND DISCUSSION

In this section, we describe five themes related to our combined experiences with Web-based instruction. We also identify the components of scholarship that were apparent within each theme. Dialogues, experiences, and narratives are provided as examples to support thematic development.

Theme One: A Paradigm Shift

The overriding theme throughout all of our scholarly work has been the recognition that we operate from a similar set of values, beliefs, and assumptions about teaching and learning. Therefore, it is appropriate to begin with the primary perspective from which we operate in our Web-based teaching. Change is a fundamental human condition that defines education and the institutions that support it. Educators live with constant change as assumptions are challenged, new knowledge is created, innovations are implemented, and institutions realign themselves with societal values and beliefs. Fullan suggests that there will always be pressure for change in a pluralistic society (17). He states that the challenge of educational reform is not simply to master the implementation of a single innovation that improves the efficiency and effectiveness of what is currently done. Rather, it is to deal with second-order changes that affect the culture and structure of our institutions and necessitate restructuring roles and reorganizing responsibilities (Fullan 29). A paradigm shift is a second-order change that means redefining the values, beliefs, and assumptions that we hold about teaching and learning. Often accompanied by feelings of loss, anxiety, and struggle, a paradigm shift is necessary in order for real and enduring change to occur.

Kuhn offers a simple, but pervasive, account of a paradigm shift, suggesting that it must be sufficiently unprecedented to attract an enduring group of adherents away from competing modes of teaching and learning (10). Specialized journals, specialists' societies, the claim for a special place in the curriculum, and empirical work that is taken to articulate the paradigm are evidence that a shift is in progress with respect to Web-based instruction. The process is open-ended enough to leave all sorts of questions to be answered and problems for our redefined group of professionals to resolve. It is an exciting time for teachers and learners who are interested in the scholarship of teaching because we are at the edge. We have an opportunity to create an intertwined theoretical and methodological set of beliefs that permit us to select, evaluate, and critique what we do.

Paradigm shifts, in the sense we are speaking about, are ultimately about the values, beliefs, and assumptions we make about teaching and learning. Our paradigms influence the way we think and feel about, as well as act, in the situations in which we work. We engage, implicitly or explicitly, in the development of rules and standards to guide the use of new models and patterns for teaching and learning. Reflection helps us agree on problems to address, how to replicate by example and dissemination, and how to investigate the match between prediction and outcome. What is changing? Who will benefit? Is it achievable? What are the consequences for primary stakeholders? Who is learning what, where, when, how, and for what purpose? Why change anything? What will happen if we do not adopt the new paradigm? Describing a new, predominant paradigm for Web-based instruction, challenging old paradigms associated with teaching and learning, and answering these questions is important scholarly work.

Fullan reminds us that, in addition to understanding and managing the process of change, there is a subjective meaning of change that is the day-to-day reality of all who engage in it (33). Cini and Vilic comment on some of the difficulties many faculty members face as they adopt Web-based instruction (38). Their comments bring credence to many of the discussions we have had in our small group. Time and time again we have reflected on the need for administrators to understand that this change involves human, not merely technological, issues. Autumn frequently describes the impact of her willingness to go to a faculty person's office to coach him or her through a difficult endeavor. She explains that the time taken to do so is a necessary part of her work because, within the safety of that low-risk environment, she is able to offer technical support as well as address the subjective issues that are at the heart of real change.

Cini and Vilic suggest that many students and faculty expect on-line services and on-line learning (39). The authors go on to say that teachers and learners who perceive these expectations as a threat often express concerns about educational quality, faculty replacement by computers, cheating issues, course ownership, and misperceptions of what constitutes Web-based instruction. All of us have struggled with these issues and the time necessary to learn how to deal with them. Jude recalls enthusiastically making a plan for bringing Web-based instruction into her courses. However, she reflects, "I still didn't do it right and many of my greatest fears about the quality of my courses degenerating to the point of negative student feedback became a reality. Do I fix it, or go back to the way I used to teach because I know that worked?" Martha was overwhelmed with her perceived need to respond to every student about every question asked and comment written. Her search for ways to think about and implement Web-based instruction necessitated a new way of thinking about teaching and learning that better fit her day-to-day reality. Lee has often offered the rest of us suggestions about how to construct Web-based interactions to help ensure that learners are less likely to cheat and more likely to monitor the integrity of their work and the work of others. We agree that making a shift and viewing Web-based instruction as a challenge, rather than a risk, is underpinned by some basic tenets about teaching and learning.

The *Book in Progress* describes learning architecture in terms of a set of twenty-four key elements, or structural features, and their associated dimensions (Asian Development Bank Institute, paragraph 1). All of the elements imply a shift in values associated with teaching and learning. One element is essential to the paradigm shift associated with Web-based instruction. It relates to our fundamental beliefs about human capability, capacity, and the potential to learn. Moving from reception of knowledge to construction of knowledge, for many teachers and learners, means letting go of the traditional view of teacher as the provider of direct and systematic instruction. Marra suggests that the new paradigm focus is on context-dependent knowledge construction (61). In this sense, information in its context is authentic and has more meaning for the learner because multiple perspectives are engaged. Learners are challenged to actively use knowledge and skills to interpret experience, as learning grows out of the learner's physical and social constructs.

Teachers, as well, are challenged to bring together the learner, the teacher, and the thing to be learned. We must strive to be aware of our biases, judgments, and preconceptions of how we influence the learner. Our primary role is to select suitable experiences, pose problems, set boundaries, and support the learner by ensuring physical and emotional safety and facilitating the learning process. The presence of the teacher in this equation is described by the following paraphrase of the definition of experiential education and its guiding principles:

Experiential education is a process through which a learner constructs knowledge, skill, and value from direct experiences. It occurs when reflection, critical analysis, and synthesis support carefully chosen experiences. Learners are required to take initiative, make decisions, and be accountable for the results. The learner is actively engaged, intellectually, emotionally, soulfully, and/or physically. Learning forms the basis for future experience and learning, multiple relationships are developed and nurtured, outcomes cannot be totally predicted, values are examined, and the possibility to learn from natural consequences, mistakes, and successes is maximized. (*Experiential Education* 2)

These simplified descriptions of constructivism and experiential education have inspired our thinking about the sophisticated mental operations reflected in the semantic content of student presentations. One of Jude's students commented on the process, stating, "It's a cycle of taking knowledge that is outside of you, putting it inside you, making it relevant, being able to use it in situations where it is needed, and then being able to reflect on it to become better for further experiences." Another student commented on the match between learning goals and outcomes for a Web-based assignment:

To me it was very authentic. Any time that I facilitated, I would wait like a kid at Christmas for those pieces to come across the Web. Now I could have sat and waited for letters to come in the mail too, but. . . . And just putting it out in a public forum for everyone to read and everyone to keep, you had to be very sure of what you said, and there were consequences and you were held accountable. And that is one of the principles [experiential education], taking responsibility and being held accountable for your learning.

Jude, reflecting on a comment that Autumn made about students wanting her to tell them what, exactly, she wanted from them in a Web-based assignment, intimated, "It is a never ending source of amazement to me that students usually make more meaning from what I ask them to do than what I initially hope for. When I let go of my expectations and predefined concepts of learning outcomes and trust the process, I am excited by the possibilities. It is truly a learning experience for me."

Teachers and learners become partners. Martha's experience teaching a Web-based research methods course confirms the potential of the shift to a paradigm that places the learner in control of the process and the teacher as a guide. She states, "Without Web-based instruction, I couldn't hope to provide access to such a vast body of knowledge and then require students to synthesize and evaluate information related to particular units in the course. Furthermore, the technical support for collecting and analyzing a small amount of data that is meaningful to each student is immediately accessible."

Lee facilitates learning by intertwining face-to-face experience in base group initiative tasks and reflective discussion about the process, Web postings about the textbook and related articles, and face-to-face and Web-based discussions about major themes that define the course. Generally, there is no right or wrong answer; however, there must be evidence of a high level of engagement and intellectual processing. One of Jude's students stated, "It gave the recipient the ability to hear the words clearly and revisit the feedback for clarification, something that can't be done as thoroughly by verbal means. As well, feedback comes from several individuals via a sterile medium so that the recipient has the chance to look past being defensive and hear the entire message without interruption from debate or point fixation." This comment suggests these principles and the relationships between face-to-face and Web-based feedback.

Clearly, a paradigm shift to a more constructivist way of thinking is a challenge for teachers and learners. However, the shift is rich in opportunity for the teaching scholar. Web-based instruction provides significant amounts of qualitative and quantitative data about teaching and learning, and about the particular subject matter in which we claim expertise. Some of the standards suggested in *Scholarship Assessed* are particularly important for scholars to consider (Glassick, Huber, and Maeroff 36). As examples, how does a constructivist way of thinking impact the content and communication of course goals and objectives, and how are they enhanced by Web-based instruction? How does a teacher prepare to become an experiential educator, and what is the impact of preparation on the teaching and learning? Does our view of research significance need to be redefined for particular problems or settings? What are the benefits and consequences for professional advancement, scholarship, service, and teaching for those of us who take the time to invest in shifting our paradigms? How do teachers, learners, administrators, parents, and society view the paradigm shift? These questions bring credence to the earlier statement that a paradigm shift is open-ended enough to leave all sorts of questions to be answered and problems for our redefined group of professionals to resolve.

Theme Two: Levels of Use

Sharon Gray, in the book *Web-Based Instruction*, outlines a model for faculty development that mirrors the typical stages a faculty member experiences when developing skills and competencies for Web-based teaching (329). There are three stages or levels of use that most faculty experience: (1) the development of productivity skills with the computer; (2) the utilization of the computer as a delivery tool; and (3) the utilization of the computer as a cognitive tool. In the first stage, faculty members learn computer skills such as file management (so you don't lose your documents), copy and paste, using multiple windows at once, personalizing your desktop, efficiently using e-mail, using the applications in Microsoft Office, and so on. In the second stage, Gray notes that the faculty member incorporates skills learned in the previous stage and first attempts Web-based instruction. Typically, in this stage, a faculty member puts massive quantities of materials on-line, tends to communicate a great deal one-on-one with students via e-mail, and is often replicating the traditional face-to-face environment of learning where the faculty member is "the expert."

The third stage begins when the faculty member starts to actively incorporate collaborative activities, nurtures an on-line learning community, and begins to increase expectations of student participation in the on-line environment. Students are encouraged to help one another more, to share more, and to actively find, synthesize, and share content with the group. At this point the faculty member is much more of a guide and fellow learner.

Subsequently, the term "levels of use" refers to a need for preparation and reflection on the development and presentation of Web-based instruction prior to student involvement. In campus-wide faculty development workshops on technology, the instructor layers the training process so it is tied to competency building. We have seen that this process is also necessary for our students who participate in Web-based instruction. Students should be introduced to the necessary technology skills in phases, and those skills need to be intimately tied to course content so the students deem them to be important. However, in this section we will focus on our levels of use as faculty members.

We began developing computer productivity skills during our graduate studies. In 1982, Lee discovered he could take a floppy disk to the computer lab and "edit my psychological reports once they came back from the Prof. all marked in red—it beat re-typing!!!!" Martha, while writing her dissertation during the 1990–91 school year, realized, "I knew I had to develop some computer application skills to get through that phase of my doctorate, to become efficient." Jude, who began her doctoral program in 1983, realized, "I was spending too much money paying others to type my work." Autumn, in 1991, discovered she needed to learn how to make backup disks of her data when "my hard drive crashed and the department had to pay Tech Support to retrieve my files."

Each of us had a concrete reason to learn computer productivity skills. Based on our needs at a specific moment in time, we saw these skills as something worthwhile and important to learn. Over time, we learned the profound usefulness of these skills. Jude states, "As an administrative tool, technology freed me to do more important things—then I saw that it helped me to work better, write better, develop better teaching aids, etc. because I could pilot and change, write and edit, create and recreate much more easily!" Lee, through critical reflection about productivity skills, realized the "life skills that learning word processing, etc. would bring" to his students. Martha, after designing and delivering her first Web-based course in 1996–97, became very aware of the need for ongoing professional development in these skills. She states, "I've been in constant training, one way or another, ever since. I find I have to constantly upgrade my skills because of new technology being born every day."

As each of us moved into the second stage of technology-infused instruction, we again had concrete instructional reasons for attempting to use the computer as a delivery system. Autumn, who had been training faculty members in the use of technology for instructional purposes since 1995, realized that for training to be effective, faculty members must be immersed in technology to learn how to apply it in individual instructional moments. Her initial effort was using the computer as a delivery tool for the development of a training CD-ROM. The project was to serve as "a model for faculty members to see how instruction could be generated locally using a computer." Lee began with e-mail by "having students e-mail me their notes from counseling sessions and then e-mailing their notes of feedback to others." From e-mail, he moved on to using computer conferencing groupware and course management systems.

Jude first used the computer as a delivery system in an environmental education graduate course. She explains, "I wanted each person to read a pivotal book—Rachael Carson/*Silent Spring* type stuff—and everyone to benefit. I looked for a way to have a discussion over time that necessitated [that] everyone . . . write well, respond, compare, contrast. I tried it first by e-mail—group address—then I learned about Web-based tools and away I went." Martha began using the computer as a delivery tool because she received a faculty development grant in 1996 to design an educational research course on-line. She recalls, "It was the first content on-line course offered by the university. It was very difficult because I had very few skills myself and there were few instructors doing Web-based teaching on campus. I felt very alone and what I produced was extremely primitive by today's standards."

During this second phase of our development as Web-based instructors, we experienced a number of frustrations and learned a great deal about the process of designing and delivering on-line instruction. For example, Lee reflects on his first attempt to use e-mail as a delivery system by explaining, "[The students] didn't cc: well. I did not teach the basics well or assumed they knew what they were doing—my learning [from this experience was to] begin to assess knowledge first." Summing up her learning experience, Martha states, "I learned from the experience more efficient ways to communicate, to transfer information from one place to another more efficiently, that students need prerequisite skills in order to not just learn technology in a Web environment but also content, how to build a team and individual and group confidence to be successful, and that teaching on the Web was a viable form of instruction."

Before describing our experiences in the third stage of using the computer as a cognitive tool, some discussion needs to be provided about the Web as an instructional tool. William Winn, in an on-line article entitled "Learning in Hyperspace," states that

converting traditional university courses to Web pages, or worse, just putting lecture notes on a Web page, is a serious mistake. All the Web can do is bring information to students. To learn anything at all, students have to construct knowledge from that information. To do so, three things need to happen. First, processes need to become active that connect information with existing mental models and alter the mental models to accommodate the information. Second, often the context in which knowledge is constructed and applied has to be identified and brought into the picture. Third, the social nature of knowledge construction must be considered and opportunities provided for students to interact with other students, teachers or other members of the community.

Winn is suggesting that as instructors we must design Web-based content and activities so the students interact with the content and each other in order to develop knowledge about the content. Gray describes the third level or phase of technology-infused instruction as using the computer as a cognitive tool (329). In this phase the faculty member begins to incorporate more collaborative activities, requires more active participation by the students in the on-line learning environment, and encourages students to help each other (paragraph 50).

Our experiences of moving to the third phase of using the computer as a cognitive tool were again grounded in specific instructional goals. Lee wanted his psychology undergraduate students to connect concepts to day-to-day life, then connect those concepts to personality theories. His application of using the computer as a cognitive tool to meet this instructional need was to

ask students to find information on particular concepts etc. from the glossary or chapter we are studying and investigate them in the news—then explaining how they can tie the two together . . . with personality theory, I have sent them to particular Web sites to find information. They must then respond to the discussion forum with what they have discovered. Then I will ask students to respond to each other's work, describing how the student has employed the concept to life, and then to theory.

Martha, in her research methods course, wants students to be able to determine which type of statistical process should be employed with certain types of data. Her computer-based application to teach this skill is described as follows: "I give my statistics class a Web site where you can analyze data using whatever statistic is needed. But the students have to figure out what appropriate statistical procedure is needed for their activities and actually run the data and interpret their findings."

Jude, in a graduate outdoor education course, wanted her students to "learn how to do thematic analysis, and to become acquainted with current professional issues through an examination of the content of a set of electronic mail lists. Students joined an electronic mail list and posted a weekly analysis of the content of discussions on the list according to a set of instructions provided by the instructor."

In each example, the instructor, motivated by an instructional need, designed on-line activities which required the student to interact with content, respond to the instructor and other students about the content, and eventually internalize some knowledge about the content or reshape current mental models about the content.

The three stages of using the computer for instructional purposes are somewhat developmental in nature. In other words, faculty members must develop core competencies in computer productivity skills before they can use the computer as a delivery method or as a cognitive tool. However, the stages are not discreet. We learned more complex computer productivity skills through our experiences of using the computer as a delivery method. By using the computer as a cognitive tool, we learned more complex skills related to using the computer as a delivery method. For example, when asked, "How is your computer-based instruction different now from when you first started experimenting?," Lee responded by saying, "I try to assess and teach necessary skills first. I am way more patient with students, and I do not respond to every single posting by students." Martha described her growth and development as a Web-based instructor by stating:

My designs and delivery system are much more sophisticated now. I incorporate more advanced tools such as discussion boards and WebCT management systems and my course is more attractively presented and instructionally, I think, more sound. I also expect more from my students because they are more advanced (technologically) than my first ones. I find I worry more now about how best to present content, develop group skills, and other things teachers worry about to be more effective in any instructional environment. The technology supports the course now rather than driving it as it did when I first began.

Jude reflects on what she has learned by saying that her on-line instructional components have much more complexity, and her "instructional goal enhancement has far more depth, creativity, and attractiveness." Obviously, the practice and application of computer productivity skills, using the computer as a delivery tool and as a cognitive tool, have helped us to develop and shape our skills as Web-based instructors.

Levels of use as a concept is interconnected to the scholarship of teaching in three ways. First, from our discussion it is clear that levels of use is closely connected to defining clear goals. In order for us to be able to employ certain Web-based instructional strategies, we began by clearly defining the instructional goal we wanted to meet. This practice was revealed throughout our dialogue on our stages of level of use. In *Scholarship Assessed* it is suggested that having clear goals "means understanding the project's scope. Good guiding questions help the scholar to define a project, give it structure, recognize relevant material, identify exceptions, and see new possibilities" (25). Within our discussion of levels of use we repeatedly referred to specific instructional goals that we wanted to achieve by using Web-based instructional strategies.

Second, our levels of use discussion consistently referred to the importance of adequate preparation, another standard described in the scholarship of teaching. The whole notion of developing core computer productivity skills involves a process of learning that helps us to be adequately prepared to deliver quality Web-based instructional experiences for our students. As Winn points out, simply placing lectures on-line or transferring traditional courses to the Web is not sufficient to help our students develop knowledge about the content (paragraph 50). Sound professional development opportunities are critical to any institution attempting to develop a core group of faculty who can design and deliver quality Web-based instruction. Providing opportunities for faculty members to explore and experiment with Web-based tools is necessary in order to develop the ability to systematically employ appropriate Web-based instructional strategies.

Third, our levels of use discussion reveals the importance of using appropriate methods, which is another component to the scholarship of teaching. Our reflections on the levels of use in Web-based teaching suggest that to be able to select appropriate methods, we must be afforded the opportunity to develop the necessary core computer productivity skills and establish clear instructional goals. Through our discussion, it was revealed that over time, we have chosen Web-based methods or tools, tested them, and modified them judiciously as our projects evolved. We have actively become learners in our journey to become good Web-based instructors. As learners, we understand that our goal is to develop and establish sound methods for Web-based teaching and learning.

Theme Three: Curriculum Development

No matter the primary curriculum being taught, the use of the Web presents challenges to the student and faculty member if they do not consciously address secondary and tertiary curriculum needs. Primary, secondary, and tertiary curriculum definitions are most often course and instructor specific, depending on how one views curriculum. Primary curriculum is the cognitive, psycho-motor, and affective course content that relates to the primary area of study. Secondary curriculum, as it relates to this chapter, addresses the skills the student needs to be able to access the Web-based instruction. For some classes that skill may simply be the ability to send and receive e-mail. For other classes it may involve a wider variety of skills such as finding and filtering information about a specific subject from an Internet search engine or being able to maneuver through the Web-based software utilized for the class. This latter area, skills surrounding the Web-based software, is often neglected by many Web-based instructors. Students' unfamiliarity with and fear of the new software can be a substantial impediment to progressing through the initial phases of the course.

Tertiary curriculum often deals with the students' connection to their broader discipline or related academic skills. For example, in Lee's psychology class links to weekly e-zines or disciplinary based electronic mail lists help students see how the subjects they are studying are part of the larger discipline. Such a connection allows them to see how one class relates to another class within the discipline and how the class relates to the larger discipline or to other related disciplines. In another example, Lee's interpersonal relations class uses Web-based software to have students locate current news articles through the Web. These news articles must highlight concepts they are reading about in the primary curriculum. To do this, students use the secondary curriculum skills of finding and filtering information that they will eventually place in a discussion forum in the Web-based software. They are also staying abreast of current events (tertiary curriculum) by having to scan news-based Web sites for relevant material. Asking the students to reflect in a Web-based discussion forum upon the news article they have read by giving reference to the specific Universal Resource Locator (URL) of the article and connection to the content of the text or lecture material is one place all three curricula can be seen in operation at the same time.

Asking students to reflect upon material from a reading or from a classroom experience and to place this material in an e-mail or discussion folder requires them to synthesize their learning into a format that will be viewed by all members of their class or group within the class. Such reflective critique is not unique to Web-based teaching. Our experience has shown that sharing information with other class members requires an exposure of self that is more public than having students write a paper in the traditional classroom structure and share it with the faculty member—or even their fellow students. For example, in response to a question at the beginning of the semester focused on what each individual brings to the group, one student commented in a forum that her group members would later read:

A weakness is that I am very stubborn and do not like to be disturbed a lot while working. In a group I may not be the leader, but if there is something really wrong that I don't agree with, I will speak up. I tend to sit back and watch and judge, and then try to mediate, especially if there is a conflict. I will be pleased to do my share of the work, but if someone volunteers to do more than me, I will not stop them. A weakness would be that I don't like to really work in groups, but I will look at this as a challenge for myself.

This student is being very open in an initial posting, using a personality style instrument as her guide for outlining how she may be perceived in the group. In many uses of the Web for teaching, students are able to read those who post first, and are able to build upon the thoughts of others.

Plagiarism issues are practically nonexistent in students' documentation of their work since repetitious writing by students or "stealing of ideas" can be seen by all who participate in the e-mail list or discussion group. The secondary curriculum of learning skills in Web-based courseware allows students to "see" who has posted ahead of them or behind them in time. They often have to refine their postings if someone else has posted on the same idea ahead of them. By encouraging students to build on the ideas of others, they are also encouraged to read the postings that go before theirs in order to expand, clarify, or even correct points made by others. Thus, the skills of the secondary curriculum (Web-based courseware) have helped further the students understanding of the primary curriculum. Experience has shown that students are able to stand on the shoulders of others and build on points made or offer more in-depth analysis. A question in the Web forum during Lee's group dynamics class generated the following dialogue:

Teacher Instructions: Look over your group's postings in Reflection #2 and find at least 5 examples of feedback that was specific to a situation, based on observations, and focused on behavior of the individual being mentioned. Cut and paste those feedback examples here giving credit to the author. Do not take all the examples from the same person. Do summarize why these are examples of good feedback making use of material in your text to support your claim.

In the survival task Monday he (S) did sit back and let everyone say what they thought but he was not afraid to step up and tell the group what he thought was most important and why. (Student "W")

Take the winter survival exercise we did on Monday night he had difference of opinion on what the priority of survival [*sic*]. "S" shared his opinion, and then listen [*sic*] to another group member's ideas. He wasn't . . . totally in agreement, but he went alone [*sic*] with the ideas because of the majority. (Student "S")

You [J] have opened up more as the group has formed and have offered valuable opinions to help us make our decisions especially during our plane crash project. (Student "A")

These are examples of good feedback for several reasons. First of all, they allow each of us to see how other group members perceive our individual behavior and its consequences. They also tell us how others are reacting to our behaviors. We now have some insight into how our peers individually perceive each of us. These examples provide us with the opportunity to compare our behaviors to the "accepted" or "expected" behaviors that have been standardized over time. This feedback will help to increase our self-awareness and also our self-esteem. Some of us are trying out new behavior for us personally, and these feedback sessions help us to see how effective our new behaviors are in the group.

The secondary curriculum that is developed in many Web-based classes is the computer skills required to access the Internet. While students come to the class with a range of computer skills, all tend to exit having developed basic skills in e-mail access, Internet searching, and backing up material to a secondary source. In addition, students are able to navigate the Web environment (multiple layers) of the courseware, as well as other components of the WWW and the Internet. For example, the current courseware being supported by our university requires students to manipulate through several layers of discussion forums in order to find the correct place to post their reflections. Such navigation is generally easy to learn once the student has an overview of how the discussion forums are set up. Once students understand this structure they are better able to understand where their information should go. In addition, teaching students the necessity to back up their Web postings by typing information out in a word processing program prior to placing it into the Web-based courseware is part of the learning in the secondary curriculum. Students learn to utilize the technology available in order to manage their time and resources. If a spontaneously typed posting is not accepted into the software due to hardware, software or human error, the backup method can be a time, life, and computer saver! Despite instruction and warning on the use of backups, most students discover the utility of the backup experientially—by not having one when they need it!

Faculty members who do not attend to secondary and tertiary skills may find themselves frustrated with student inability to follow through on assignments. All of us recall that the development of a curriculum that requires students to critique classroom experiences has led to the need to be very explicit and specific with questions to be answered. Development of a timetable for posting the reflective critiques and asking for a minimal number of words in the posting were structures learned over time. The instructions given above to the students ask for a specific number of examples and ask them to cut and paste the actual comments from the Web forum in their answer. This posting, as with others of its kind, gives specific deadline times ("by midnight on Tuesday the 29th") and specific consequences for being late ("no posting will be accepted that is more than 24 hours late"). In addition, taking class time to have students demonstrate computer skills related to getting onto the Internet and sending e-mail or posting answers proved to be time well spent in building the foundational skills of the class. Jude uses a skill checklist that is submitted to her when each student demonstrates competency. Martha requires students to attend an orientation in the computer lab before beginning the Web-based course. Her first unit includes activities such as joining an electronic mailing list and completing a Web search. We have observed that as students develop a comfort level with the foundational skills of accessing the Web, their abilities to respond to questions in a public forum increase.

The theme of curriculum development is related to the scholarship of teaching through presentation, skills and methods, and reflective critique. The instructor must effectively employ these components of scholarship to develop primary, secondary, and tertiary curriculum in Web-based teaching and learning. Having clear goals for the use of Web-based instruction is by far the most important aspect of curriculum development. However, we have yet to answer many questions related to the process of developing Web-based curriculum and instructional technique. What are the specific advantages of various Web-based instructional tools? Our experience has been that unless instructors have clear ideas about what they would like to achieve by using the Web for classroom instruction, why they wish to utilize a particular software to enhance their primary curriculum, and how they can ensure that students have the necessary skills to engage Web-based instruction, they may find themselves and their students frustrated, both in the classroom and late at night when sitting in front of the computer screen.

Theme Four: Filtering Versus Finding

The theme filtering versus finding refers to the skill Dede argues students and faculty must now learn to be successful in twenty-first century society. Dede best explains this process when he states: "The core skill of today's workplace is not foraging for data, but filtering a plethora of incoming information. The emerging literacy we all must master requires diving into a sea of information, immersing ourselves in data to harvest patterns of knowledge just as fish extract oxygen from water via their gills" (6). To develop this competency, educators must learn to create immersion-based activities for students which will help develop competencies in filtering and interactivity with large amounts of information.

The first time faculty members or students are faced with wading through a Web search they are so overwhelmed they usually go running from the computer, claiming, "It is all garbage out there!" or "There was nothing usable that I could find." Those claims tend to be based on being unable to filter out the important information in an environment that is foreign to them. They do not understand the presentation, the structure, and the hierarchy of conducting a search on the Web. Once you learn to filter the on-line format, you are able to successfully find what you are looking for. Filtering refers to being able to sift out the unnecessary information and focus in on what is useful.

Our discussions about filtering revealed three different levels or meanings for the activity, all of which involve learning how to electronically negotiate the Web-based environment. First, we describe filtering as learning how to understand and use the Web-based environment. Second, we explore filtering in terms of searching on the Web. Finally, we discuss filtering in terms of validity and reliability of Web sites.

Three of us indicated feelings of being overwhelmed when we were first exposed to the Web-based environment. Jude states, "Initially, I was so confused, I wanted to cry. I knew the potential, but it rattled me and frustrated me so that I couldn't make sense of things others seemed to understand so easily." Martha echoes Jude's first experiences with the Web: "My early experiences with the Web were overwhelming. I used one search engine, I think Yahoo, and cutting through all the trivia on the Web was very time consuming." Autumn also had experiences of being overwhelmed when she first began using the Web. She reports, "I felt like I had to read everything so as not to miss what I was looking for. I've developed stronger filtering skills, in that the Web environment is familiar now and I do not have to scan so closely. In other words, I've learned what the redundant images and areas of the Web are, and areas of the screen I need to focus in on to find information." These experiences all refer to the process of learning to filter and respond to the Web environment. As we learned we had to hit Enter on the keyboard after entering a URL into the location line in Netscape, or hit Reload sometimes when we realized we were not getting the most updated version of a Web page, we were developing skills of how to make sense of, and filter, the Web-based visual environment.

The second level of filtering that surfaced in our discussions was that of searching on the Web. Describing her evolving search skills, Martha states: "I've learned to do preparation before I start to search. Before I search, I think about what, specifically, do I need, what search tool would best lead me to it, and what key words would best find it. A lot of times it is still trial and error though, especially if you're searching for information that is not common. I still have difficulty finding true research studies on the Web." Jude feels that searching on the Web is one of her strong points: "I am very good at asking the right question, choosing the right category or term, so I am less frustrated by this piece."

Lee describes the third level of the activity of filtering by suggesting that "filtering is a matter for me of knowing 'from whence it came' and being able to value the credibility of what is being found, so a filter for me is to understand the reliability and validity of the information." Good filtering skills in determining validity and reliability help the faculty member locate critical Web-based material for students to use in course activities. Describing how she has employed filtering to help her students be more successful in specific Web-based activities, Martha explains, "I have found some sites that offer information on evaluating Web-sites and I have my students read them before we begin work on the Web. I also give the students specific information to look for at a site— who developed the site, does the site have this or that, etc. I also provide specific sites for them to use." Lee also uses this technique when requiring students to define a psychological concept, then discover that concept in some example of a news story. Rather than requiring students to search for on-line news Web sites, he has spent time filtering through these sites and provides links to them at the course site. He has also used filtering skills to locate quality Web sites that describe and explore personality theories and makes those available as links to students as well.

Jude and Autumn use filtering skills to locate professional, discipline-specific electronic mail lists for class projects in their graduate courses. Students must monitor one or more electronic mail lists and report on key concepts and issues discussed over a period of time.

In all the examples we've discussed so far, the faculty member is actively filtering information for students so that they can focus on a particular instructional activity. This work is done to save time on the student's part and allows the student to focus on applying the information to particular course activities. We also use this strategy to assure that students are accessing valid information. But what about activities that require students to do the initial filtering?

Autumn describes an example of an activity where students must do the searching and validity filtering to find information on the Web:

I require students to do Web searches to find information, such as definitions for key terms, or [to] assess the current status of something, such as the existence of virtual public schools, or current funding trends in distance learning. From these immersion activities, students not only report in the discussion forum on the information they gathered, but also their experience of searching. By getting the students to talk about their process, frustrations, successes, and questions, I am then able to redirect, suggest, provide hints and tips, etc. Through these searching experiences and my evaluative comments, I think the students begin to develop some initial filtering skills.

Students also report feeling overwhelmed when they initially begin to develop filtering skills. A student in one of Autumn's graduate education courses summed up this feeling by saying, "I have been overwhelmed with the amount of knowledge floating in space. Trying to decipher what I need and want almost leads me to turn off my computer!" Although students do seem to experience feelings of frustration, Jude comments on the importance of developing filtering skills in students by stating, "Filtering, in order to find information, is a basic synthesis intellectual skill. Our students can benefit from the process big time!"

When employing on-line filtering and finding strategies, the instructor significantly changes the traditional way of delivering and experiencing education. That is, rather than feeding students information and then testing them on their retention of that information, filtering activities often require students to become quite active in their learning, to employ critical thinking skills, and to attempt to use the course content in a context that encourages growth or change in their current mental model about the course content. Lee reports that one student responded in class to the computer activities by saying, "I just want to come to class, have you tell me what I need to know and then test me on what you told me; I don't want all this computer stuff." This student's response to the computer activities indicates a need for faculty members to explain why the assigned computer activities are so important to surviving in twenty-first century society. Although filtering is perceived by all of us as an important skill to develop, students may need help in understanding why this skill would be of value to them.

The filtering theme is interconnected with the scholarship of teaching in two ways. First, the skill of filtering is intimately tied to clear goal setting. If we are not clear about our instructional goals and expected outcomes, it becomes difficult to clearly understand the filtering that must take place by the faculty member to provide the necessary instruction and on-line resources, as well as what must be provided to the student about the art of filtering Web-based information. Second, the act of systematic filtering suggests an effort by the faculty member of trying to employ appropriate methods. Whether we are filtering Web sites for the students, or requiring students to develop filtering skills through immersion-based activities, we are attempting to provide quality instruction grounded in sound methods.

Theme Five: Evaluation of Instruction and Student Learning

At the heart of all evaluation is purpose. We find that Web-based evaluation strategies center around three major goals: the assessment of our students' ability to internalize and apply course content; the determination of their development and application of technology competencies; and the gathering of feedback on the Internet as a teaching and learning tool. Evaluation of these goals is both a dynamic and a developmental process. For example, our work indicates that evaluation of any Web-based activity begins prior to the teaching strategy, is especially crucial at the onset of the experience, is fluid throughout the activity, and will continue even after that experience has concluded. Much of initial evaluation centers on making sure students have necessary skills and competencies to complete Web activities and access to appropriate equipment. During this stage, we spend a great deal of time monitoring and directing "start-up" processes and problems. As students become more comfortable with the Web environment, evaluation changes focus to individual and group dynamics; students' abilities to locate, apply, and understand course content and information; and the subsequent production of student work. Student work is often posted, published, or shared, and then evaluated accordingly by the instructor, and sometimes by fellow students.

We have found a number of effective tools and procedures to measure student learning. For example, traditional evaluation tools can be utilized quite readily on the Web. As Jude states, "Most of the techniques I use are based in traditional evaluation. I select from a set of evaluation alternatives—tests, essays, case studies—and create an approach on the Web that satisfies my evaluation goals." Other traditional measures are reflected when Lee has students develop and contribute multiple choice test items for exams and when Autumn employs on-line quizzes "not as a formal evaluation tool but rather as a way for students to self-evaluate their learning." Martha also has students complete and electronically submit a traditional paper and/or project for her course.

However, we often prefer nontraditional assessment techniques and strategies due to the nature of the Web learning environment. Discussion forums are a favorite tool because of the unique evaluation features they offer. This activity requires students to post on-line their applications of content-related material and is usually accomplished through electronic mail lists, chat rooms, or forums provided within course management systems. Student presentation of information is conveyed through written dialogue or narratives. The use of language and written expression therefore becomes central to communicate that learning has occurred. We find that the art of synthesizing and presenting semantic information requires sophisticated mental processes of our students. When those processes are consistently used throughout a course, students often mention that they are more reflective and thoughtful about course content and that more substantive learning has taken place. Autumn summarizes our group viewpoint on discussion forums with these comments:

The strategy of using on-line discussion forums to determine students' understanding and application of course content has worked very well. I am also able to monitor and evaluate students' development of technology skills, as well as determine when serious problems exist that are hindering a student from moving forward. After several weeks, I have the documentation of a student's work over a period of time. This allows me to really get a good impression of the student's development.

Discussion forums can also be organized a variety of ways, from individual to group activities, to students responding to each other's postings. For example, both Jude and Autumn incorporate on-line peer review projects where students critique and edit each other's work before it is posted for a final grade. Students learn "technology editing tools as well as having opportunities for peer teaching, revisiting specific content, and clarifying processes, theory, or method for the writer of the final product." In addition, Lee and Martha organize their classes into small groups for either private discussions on sensitive issues or debates on relevant course topics. During each of these activities the instructor is free to monitor student interactions or interject comments, suggestions, and questions to encourage and expand student thinking on issues.

Private e-mails between instructor and individual students are another non-traditional mode of evaluation. Martha requires her students to complete "e-mail journal responses" periodically throughout her Web-based course. Via e-mail, students answer specific questions related to navigating through a Web-based environment or on a content topic that has been addressed in a unit. Autumn also asks her students to submit a private e-mail after each reading assignment. These e-mails provide information on student understanding of course material and oftentimes indicate how the student is progressing both technologically and cognitively.

Students receive individual or group grades for their work. Criteria for discussion forums and private e-mail narratives are specifically stated at the onset of the activity. For example, Lee uses a four-point scale when assessing his student postings, where to receive full credit students must provide a reference Web site in HTML format related to the content being addressed in their discussions. Students appreciate this specificity and very seldom will complain about grades when they know what is expected beforehand.

Evaluative feedback from instructor to students is also supplied for each of the activities mentioned above. Feedback is generally delivered through on-line summaries of student work that are presented to the entire class. The narrative usually consists of an overall evaluation of the class's progress with comments on individuals' exceptional work and directions that need to be considered for future work. Feedback to each individual student via private e-mail is another alternative strategy that we have utilized. This technique is extremely time-consuming but does provide more individual attention to students. The important point, however, is that feedback should be provided throughout the Web experience. According to Autumn, "Students have consistently responded that they really appreciate this feedback because they are able to get a feeling for how I see the class progressing or problems we need to work on."

Summative evaluation is another crucial component for assessing Web-based instruction. We have developed a variety of student surveys designed to gather student feedback on learning via the Web. Similar to traditional teaching, these data provide excellent feedback for future modifications of course presentation, completion, and requirements. Through our student surveys, we have gleaned specific evaluative information. Students mention most often the benefits of Web instruction as being (a) meaningful learning of technology through the integration of course content and computer applications; (b) increased access to current and global content information; (c) increased motivation; and (d) convenience. It is interesting to note too that students consistently identify technological skills as being one of the strongest learning experiences during Web-based instruction (Daugherty and Funke 21).

Our surveys also assess other criteria that we feel are essential to evaluate in Web-based instruction. These criteria tend to focus on vital issues of communication and support for on-line learning environments where face-to-face contact is minimal or completely absent. For example, Autumn queries students on the presence of supportive interactions and transformative communication in her on-line courses. These indicators determine the degree to which students collaborate in learning processes, forming supportive networks and guiding much of their own learning, and if the instructor's communication style enhanced and nurtured these interactions. In addition, survey items evaluate the development of student initiative for solving technological and content problems, and the interactivity of sharing those solutions with other students and the instructor. We have noticed that students tend to move from individual to cooperative ventures for a Web experience to be successful. For example, students will network to form supportive systems as they negotiate acquiring technological skills. Evaluative feedback provides the instructor with insights on these individual and group dynamics. It also helps the instructor mold and tailor her role in a Web-based learning environment so that those dynamics can be mutually supportive of all class members.

Evaluation is a critical, and, perhaps, the major component of the scholarship of Web-based teaching. As with any new innovative instructional model, the Web-based medium must demonstrate its merit in higher education. Rigorous assessment strategies that document effective goal setting, content presentation, and learning strategies are crucial for establishing its potential value and worth. The significance of student results, and the processes by which they were obtained, should also be documented and shared within our educational communities. And, most important, faculty engaged in Web-based instruction must participate in reflective critiquing of their experiences. It is through critical reflection and discussion that we learn. Autumn put it best when she said:

Many times meeting with you three and talking through method, presentation, or evaluation issues, I see how as a group we all have pieces to the puzzle we are trying to put together to help us be high-quality Web-based instructors. Often, a new perspective from one of you will unlock the door to helping me see a solution to a specific problem in my Web-based teaching. This suggests that as a group, we are able to be much more powerful in our ability to fashion Web-based environments.

CONCLUSIONS AND IMPLICATIONS

We conclude with a reminder of our purpose. Our goal was to share reflective critiques on Web-based instruction and tie those reflections to established standards of scholarly work. Five themes were generated, commonly experienced among us. We acknowledged and recognized that scholarly processes, such as clear instructional goals, appropriate methods, significant results, and effective presentation, were very much interwoven throughout these themes. We hope our comments and questions at the end of each theme lead the reader to explore scholarly activity about Web-based teaching and learning.

However, thoughtful reflection has left us with more unanswered questions than solutions. We see that our conversations and inquiry have just begun. We realize that we must continue to support the notion that scholarship is the cornerstone to effective Web-based instruction. We also recognize that our project was a small quest within a larger intellectual expedition. There is much left to explore, to understand, and to share.

WORKS CITED

Asian Development Bank Institute. *Book in Progress*. 1998. 1 Aug. 1999. <http://www.adbi.org/bookinprogress/home.htm/>.Lkd.<http://www.adbi.org/bookinprogress/concept.htm/> <http://www.adbi.org/bookinprogress/shift02.htm/>.

Boyer, Ernest. *Scholarship Reconsidered: Priorities for the Professoriate*. Princeton: Carnegie Foundation for the Advancement of Teaching, 1990.

Cini, Marie A., and Boris Vilic. "On-line Teaching: Moving from Risk to Challenge." *Syllabus* 12.10 (1999): 38–40.

Daugherty, Martha, and Barbara Funke. "University Faculty and Student Perceptions of Web-Based Instruction." *Journal of Distance Education* 13 (1998): 21–39.

Dede, Chris. "The Evolution of Distance Education: Emerging Technologies and Distributed Learning." *American Journal of Distance Education* 10.2 (1996): 4–36.

"Distance Learning Even Reaches Ships at Sea." *The New York Times on the Web*. Jan. 1999. 1 Aug. 1999 <http://www.nytimes.com/library/tech/99/01/cyber/education/20education.html>.

Experiential Education: Definitions and Principles. Pamphlet. Boulder: Association for Experiential Education, nd.

Fullan, Michael G. *The New Meaning of Educational Change*. New York: Teachers College, 1991.

"Georgia Statewide Academic and Medical System GSAMS." *UGA Gerontology Center Homepage*. 1 Aug. 1999 <http://distance.geron.uga.edu/gsams.html>.

Glassick, Charles, Mary Taylor Huber, and Gene I. Maeroff. *Scholarship Assessed: Evaluation of the Professoriate*. San Francisco: Jossey-Bass, 1997.

Gray, Sharon. "Training Teachers, Faculty, and Staff." In *Web-Based Instruction*. Ed. B. Khan. Englewood Cliffs, NJ: Educational Technology Publications, 1997. 329–32.

Kuhn, Thomas. *The Structure of Scientific Revolutions*. London: University of Chicago Press, 1970.

Marra, Rose M. "Whither Constructivism." *Educational Media and Technology Yearbook* 19 (1993): 56–77.

Winn, William. "Learning in Hyperspace." *Healthlinks*. June 1999. 1 Aug. 1999 <http://healthlinks.washington.edu/iaims/ideal/webpaper.html>.

PART II

EMPIRICAL AND PRACTICAL CONSIDERATIONS

Chapter 14

Creating an Environment for Successful Technology Integration

Kay S. Dennis

INTRODUCTION

This chapter describes the swift progression of events at one school of nursing to the point of recognition at the university level and beyond as a forerunner in technology applications, including but not limited to distance education. The background of this metamorphosis is presented, with a particular focus on the participation of faculty in an interinstitutional graduate curriculum, offered totally on-line. This success story is analyzed for the administrative strategies that helped to create an environment that fostered and enabled technology integration. The strategies are compared with the findings of recent research and other literature. Finally, I present specific action steps within a context of transformational leadership, which can be adapted elsewhere to encourage faculty participation in technology-oriented initiatives.

THE SETTING

This case study takes place at the school of nursing at a mid-size, Doctoral II university, as classified by the Carnegie Foundation for the Advancement of Teaching, in the southeastern United States. For several years, particularly since the completion in 1995 of an $18 million campus-wide fiberoptic system, the administration at the school had encouraged faculty to embrace and integrate computer technology into their teaching and research activities. To address infrastructure problems, an aging amphitheater classroom was transformed into a multimedia classroom. Substantial school and university funds were allocated to equip all faculty members with computers, printers, and Internet access. In addition, the Learning Resource Center at the school was successful in obtaining considerable external and internal funding for technology equipment, software, and furnishings.

Faculty needed knowledge, skills, and experience in using technology. Faculty development retreats on technology were held, and software and computer training workshops were conveniently offered on the premises. The Learning Resource Center sponsored brown-bag lunch forums on topics such as "Instructional Design Principles" and "Fostering Analytical and Problem-Solving Skills in Students." These measures proved very successful in energizing a small number of faculty who quickly began to implement a number of creative uses of technology in their classes. However, these strategies did not incite a culture change. Instructional strategies remained largely the same, as faculty persisted in teaching as they were taught—primarily with lectures. When I surveyed the faculty in late 1997 concerning their computer skills, 65 percent reported using e-mail on a regular basis. About 50 percent reported using the Internet for purposes other than e-mail once a month or more. No personal Web pages of faculty existed at the time.

As part of a focused, comprehensive effort to add options for graduate study, applications were made for three federal grants. To everyone's delight, all three were funded, resulting in an unprecedented amount of funds to support program development, including technology applications. Of particular importance to the school's growth in use of technology was a four-year training grant that focused on the preparation of physician assistants, nurse midwives, and family nurse practitioners for a remote, rural, sparsely populated region. This project, funded by the Robert Wood Johnson Foundation (RWJ), provided the impetus to integrate technology, for it committed the school to developing and offering two entirely on-line curricula in partnership with another university school of nursing. This formalized impetus, replete with deadlines and quality standards, accomplished what no amount of infrastructure, planning, faculty development workshops, and cajoling could do. It helped to crystallize the vision of the school. It demonstrated clearly the school's commitment to on-line education, resulting in allocation of a 0.5 full-time equivalent instructional design consultant from the faculty development center at the university. Moreover, it enabled the hiring of technical support personnel and an external computer technology consultant to collaborate with faculty on course design, development, and implementation. The grant also led to the acquisition and renovation of additional physical space for a multimedia production laboratory, and provided the necessary fiscal support to compensate faculty for developing courses over the summer.

THE IMPACT OF POSITIVE TESTIMONIAL

Even with the approaching deadlines mandated by the project, on-line course development proceeded very slowly. The risk of grant default prompted the administration to put acceleration strategies in place. A spring workshop was held in 1998 for faculty who had expressed willingness to develop an on-line course for the fall. The workshop was billed as "A Primer for Faculty—On-line Course Development." Its purpose was to (1) set the context for development of a new way of offering courses, (2) give faculty an opportunity to understand more about the commitment and what is involved, and (3) develop strategies for course development teamwork over the summer.

At the workshop, a member of the technical staff at the Center for Health Sciences Communications on campus demonstrated a range of Internet and multimedia capabilities. He suggested potential applications to fit various types of nursing course content. For most of these nursing faculty this was their first exposure to streaming video, animated graphics, and synchronous and asynchronous forums. The faculty recognized the value of the technology for conveying very complex subject matter and for preparing lessons on stable content in a form that would not decay over time.

Additional presenters discussed instructional design principles, course management strategies, copyright issues, and the importance of student orientation to Web-based courses. An extensive bibliography was provided along with a list of useful Web sites. Administrators present spoke in support of and appreciation for the time-consuming, challenging, and important work the faculty members were undertaking.

The greatest impact on the workshop participants was made by the eloquent account of Web-based course development and implementation provided by a faculty member from another school on campus. She recounted her experiences of the past several years—the early struggles and challenges of producing and offering quality on-line courses—and the rewards, mostly unexpected. She described the climate for innovation at her school, and the results, as follows:

[We have] a real spirit of teamwork here, an atmosphere of trust and encouragement. I was never afraid to try, never afraid to fail. Our dean and department chair didn't expect perfection. That knowledge gave me the freedom to try these new approaches without worrying about my evaluation. Collaboration was critical for me. With one course, we had the department chair and three of us meeting an hour every week—the result was pretty amazing. It was mentoring at its best. Another time we planned a syllabus and then volunteered to teach individual units. Again, there is no way that the quality of my individual campus class matched what happened in that on-line learning environment. *The key to making it work for faculty* is generating excitement about a new way to learn, and removing the fear of failure. They have to know that it won't work smoothly the first time. (Reaves 28 June 1999)

This presenter, who (not surprisingly) has won university teaching awards, held the nursing faculty spellbound as she described the deep engagement and rich relationships that developed for administrators, faculty, and students. Her commitment and her appreciation of the rewards of Web-based teaching greatly impressed the nursing faculty as she read course evaluation comments by students whose lives and careers had been transformed by the educational opportunities made possible through this technology. One student stated that Web-based instruction offered a way to pursue an educational dream that had been dashed "many responsibilities ago." Another reported that an on-line degree program had forced him to dig deep for solutions to real problems. Still another student said that she had new hope for her future and restored confidence in her abilities that had been lost following a stroke, so that she now plans on "doing great things" (Reaves 8 April 1998).

IMPLEMENTING THE CURRICULA

"Reproductive Physiology," a core course in the midwifery curriculum, includes subject matter that is highly complex. Learners typically find it quite challenging to master the content using traditional methods and instructional media. For these reasons and because "Reproductive Physiology" content remains stable over time, the course was selected for redesign using the full range of technical and multimedia capabilities. The on-line production of this course was so involved that initially it was developed in a "just-in-time" manner, presented live to on-campus students on Monday, and mounted for Web-based delivery on Tuesday each week. The technology-enhanced course has been extremely popular with students because they can review portions of the streaming video, graphics, and animation as often as necessary. The Web version of the course has been shown at several conferences and received the Information Resources Technology Award from Sigma Theta Tau International Nursing Honor Society, Region 7, in the spring of 1999.

Less graphic-intensive courses, such as "Nursing Theories" and "Pharmacology," underwent much simpler redesign for the midwifery and family nurse practitioner curricula. At the beginning of the training grant period, Domino by Lotus Notes was the course development and delivery system that was adopted by the two schools of nursing. The learning curve for faculty and students with this product was considerable. The synchronous chat was unreliable during inclement weather, as well as less effective and less popular with students as a learning strategy, than was the asynchronous forum.

At the time the school did not own a dedicated server but instead used as many as four different university Web servers for the nurse midwifery and family nurse practitioner courses. This situation created much confusion and inconvenience for the faculty and administration, as servers frequently were down. In addition, timely and competent service for the servers proved to be a significant problem. Therefore in late 1998 the school purchased its own server specifically to support on-line courses and related administrative functions, including development of an Intranet. The administration also took additional steps to clarify roles and responsibilities of faculty and staff and to improve the technology infrastructure. Classrooms and conference rooms in the school were wired for Internet access. New laptop computers and projectors were acquired for classroom use by faculty.

SYSTEMS AND INFRASTRUCTURE

By the summer of 1998, faculty activities and energies were moving at such a rapid pace that the school's infrastructure proved to be inadequate to keep pace. That fall, as the university steadily increased its focus on distance education initiatives and established a Virtual University Task Force, the dean introduced a new Technology Integration Oversight Committee, which was to operate on these assumptions:

1. Information literacy is now a requirement in the workplace; therefore curricula must provide mechanisms for learners to become marketable in their profession.
2. The increasing needs of remote site learners necessitate the exploration of multimodal systems for providing instruction.
3. Courses identified as appropriate for offering on-line are prioritized, designed, developed, implemented, evaluated, and revised using a systematic and coordinated approach.
4. Ongoing faculty development is vital to the continued success of courses and programs and is dependent upon administrative support.
5. Appropriate infrastructure as well as technical and secretarial support will be necessary for a smoothly operating system of on-line course delivery.
6. The overriding goal is to deliver curricula in a reliable, robust, and research-substantiated method.

The Technology Integration Oversight Committee was charged with (1) creating a prioritized list of courses for development in Web-based format, (2) pacing the integration of technology in the school, (3) encouraging, motivating, and training faculty to incorporate technology in teaching, and (4) prioritizing faculty requests for technology assistance. Committee membership included both faculty and administrators.

Two groups support this committee. One group is the On-line Delivery Team, which is charged with coordinating all functions of course production for faculty assigned to develop an on-line course. The On-line Delivery Team establishes production timelines and assures course delivery in a timely manner. The other support group is the Technical Service Team, which provides assistance with hardware and software problems encountered by faculty and staff.

Beyond the courses in the RWJ project, decisions on which courses were to be targeted for Web-based delivery were based chiefly on the strategic plan of the school and the needs of learners in the region. The course selections in turn determined which faculty members would be involved. As it happened, most of the faculty members teaching these courses were quite receptive to Web-based course development. Where resistance was encountered, faculty members met with the Technology Integration Oversight Committee to express their concerns and receive detailed information about the technical support and pedagogical guidance that would be forthcoming.

In January 1999, the administration introduced the following vision statement for technology integration: "Design and develop the technical infrastructure to support achievement of educational, research and outreach goals." Also introduced was a plan for an Information Systems Infrastructure for the school that would provide innovative resource management, quality technical support, rapid response and issue resolution, and Web-based course delivery support. The plan differentiated Instructional Information Systems from Administrative Information Systems and incorporated a new position for a chairperson of Instructional Information Systems, whose role included responsibility for leadership and oversight of integration of technology into instructional programs.

The school selected CourseInfo by Blackboard, Inc., as its course development and delivery system. This product offers a flexible, open architecture and incorporation of numerous features that enhance Web-based courses considerably. It was selected on the recommendation of a faculty member who discovered it during an Internet search for a user-friendly course development program. She had been assigned to teach "Primary Health Care" on-line the next semester as part of the RWJ project; and over a weekend she was able to design and develop her course almost completely (on their public server). The intuitive, user-friendly features of CourseInfo impressed other faculty members and the administrators. Subsequently, the school and the Virtual University Task Force selected CourseInfo as the standard development and delivery system for all Web-based courses. Since its introduction, faculty have recognized that developing a Web-based course is far less time- and labor-intensive than they had anticipated.

Services provided to the faculty by the On-line Course Delivery Team include consultation on pedagogical issues for Web-based instruction, software training, and assistance with audiovisual aids. The external consultant provides general oversight and guidance to the administration in the areas of technology planning and purchasing.

Two markedly different approaches to Web-based instruction have been described. One faculty member collaborated with as many as four technical staff members almost on a daily basis to design and develop a highly complex, interactive multimedia course on reproductive physiology. In contrast, another faculty member constructed a Web-based version of her course over a weekend. Each model has been successful, with the second scenario exemplifying a course development and delivery model that is much more likely to appeal to faculty for its simplicity and to administrators for its cost-effectiveness. However, when the fiscal, human, physical, and technical resources are available, and complex course material is stable over time, it makes sense to consider the approach taken with "Reproductive Physiology."

SUCCESS FACTORS

The success enjoyed at this school in integrating technology can be attributed to several factors and conditions, all carefully set in place by an administration that moved to the cadence of unmistakable trends in education and technology. In this section, these factors and conditions are presented as a prescription for similar success at other institutions.

Supportive Infrastructure

A supportive infrastructure is critical to the success of a cultural transformation as described here. Faculty need to know there is a structure in place to enable them to develop and offer Web-based courses (Core). Infrastructure includes hardware, software, Internet access, physical workspace, technical training and support, and staff support. Faculty benefit from other types of support besides those directly related to their courses. At the suggestion of the external technical consultant, the school established an Intranet to facilitate administrative tasks. For example, a template repository for syllabi, schedules, conference travel reimbursements, and the like offers faculty additional support in the form of convenient access to materials they use on a regular basis.

Openness to Change and Learning

Even more important than the technical dimension, which everyone anticipates, is the human dimension of this infrastructure. Faculty, although they may not acknowledge or accept it at first, need to undergo acculturation to the learner-centric paradigm which characterizes quality instruction. This paradigm requires a shift from the teacher-centric model of traditional higher education. Faculty need access to persons with expertise in teaching and learning to help them translate principles into action steps. Many faculty are unaware of or do not utilize research findings on learning and cognition. Technology-driven courses enable learning facilitation and instructional strategies that are very different from the usual lecture format. The acculturation process for faculty should include demonstrations of Web-based courses and discussion of quality indicators. In particular, faculty must have a basic grasp of the technology, so they can take advantage of its capabilities.

Nonthreatening Environment

Faculty need a nonthreatening environment in which to acknowledge their learning needs and obtain training. Ongoing training and support are absolutely essential to a successful endeavor. We have found that when faculty work in pairs or trios in a training setting they express their uneasiness and lack of familiarity with high-tech media. Once they do so, and enter the transition stage of recasting and retooling themselves, resistance diminishes. Technology-infused teaching then becomes tangible, real, and doable, and a path worth taking, rather than nebulous, overwhelming, and a road to avoid. Most faculty, once they develop even basic skills at revising a course for the Web, are pleased to show-case it to others and lose their fear of placing it on display for the world to see.

Incentives and Rewards

Faculty need protected release time, preferably one semester prior to offering a Web-based course, to develop a course. Teaching assignments at our school are made with the understanding that a Web-based course may involve more faculty time the first semester it is offered. Having a designated secretary is convenient; however, if this is not possible, other staff members must be assigned duties in support of the Web-based curriculum. Pay subsidies are provided only when the students enrolled exceed a predetermined number. For example, if the typical enrollment for a course is fifteen students, and twenty students register for the on-line version of the course, the faculty would receive additional compensation.

Skilled Secretarial Support

Secretaries who are to be involved with on-line courses from design stages through implementation should be informed in advance and given training as necessary in order for them to provide the faculty with assistance when needed. For example, permission to use copyrighted materials may be required, or print material may need to be scanned prior to being included in course materials.

Standards for Student Preparation

Curriculum-wide standards are needed concerning appropriate hardware, software, browser, and audiovisual components such as sound card and speakers. Students must be informed of these standards well in advance, in order to allow adequate time for purchase, installation, and training. They need to be competent if not proficient at using their operating system (Microsoft Windows, Macintosh, or UNIX) and a mouse, e-mail, and the Internet in general—in addition to word processing. Using class time during the semester to work through these issues and enable students to develop basic abilities should not be an option. Faculty should not have to shoulder the responsibility for these preliminary and critical details. A designated technology "guru" is needed to render decisions on which hardware, software, and specific knowledge and skills students will need to be able to participate in a Web-based curriculum.

Course Gatekeeper

Students, staff, and faculty require different levels of access to the courses. For example, faculty and staff need editing privileges, while students would not be granted this level of use. Upon completion of the term, students need to be unenrolled. These tasks should be anticipated, monitored, and included in the duties of a designated person.

Other Supports

As students require the services of the library and learning center, these facilities need to be willing to provide service and send books and other materials to students by mail. It is helpful if other departments, such as the English department or the writing center, are agreeable to working with students via online writing workshops (Bergstrom 25 May 1998).

THE LITERATURE

As noted previously, the insights and conclusions reached by administrators at this school of nursing are generally consistent with recent research and other current literature on the topic. In this section I present some recent literature on faculty participation in Web-based course development. Issues of incentive, rewards, and benefits to faculty are included. This is followed by citations on the benefits for learners. Lastly, issues of transition management and transformational leadership are addressed within the context of facilitating change, growth, and development. The chapter concludes with a list of conditions and factors that proved successful in the integration of technology at our school of nursing.

Faculty Participation

Betts reported a study conducted at the George Washington University which sought to determine why faculty participate in distance education. Out of a sample of 1,001 faculty and deans, 539 respondents provided their views. This study found that intrinsic rewards such as personal motivation to utilize technology, intellectual challenge, ability to reach additional students, and opportunity to pursue new ideas exerted a positive influence on faculty participation. Negative influences were exerted by factors such as lack of release time, lack of technical support, absence of funding, and concerns about work assignments. No significant influence was exerted by extrinsic factors such as additional pay, royalties, awards and recognition, or credit toward promotion and tenure.

The research also revealed that deans and faculty held different perceptions of what factors inhibit faculty participation. The deans in general did not recognize the concerns faculty had over lack of release time, lack of technical support, and overall workload issues. Moreover, many respondents, including some deans, were unsure how to become involved in distance education, what the institutional policies on distance education were, or where to obtain information. The author suggests that faculty participation in distance education might increase if information were made available, inhibitory factors were acknowledged and remedied, and positive aspects of participation were given more attention.

Once faculty agree to participate, they need reassurance that their involvement with a Web-based course will not require around-the-clock vigilance at the computer, according to Serow and Brawner. These researchers explored the implications of technology-rich instructional innovation for faculty evaluation and development. They investigated the potential advantages and disadvantages for faculty in relation to expectations of students, course outcome measures, resource allocations, and institutional policies on promotion and tenure decisions. Their findings summon attention to the tensions among technological innovation, institutional conventions, and faculty well-being, especially that of junior faculty. They suggest the need for (1) criteria for evaluating learner outcomes of technology-driven courses in addition to mastery of course content, (2) socialization of students to the realities of technology-based courses, and (3) use of productivity and effectiveness measures that correspond to faculty effort.

Incentive and Reward

Every campus has a contingent of faculty members who become the champions of technology, who are motivated by the same intellectual curiosity that induced them to become educators in the first place (Short). For them the rewards of innovation and of teaching in general are largely intrinsic. They derive gratification from the success of their work, which takes various forms—positive relationships with students, good evaluations, and peer recognition, as well as knowing they are making a difference in the lives of their students. For these faculty, extrinsic rewards assume less importance than the satisfaction they derive from doing a good job (Theall). Nonetheless, according to one dean, "faculty like to showcase their work once they have mastered something" (Sheerer).

Benefits to Faculty

In addition to various forms of intrinsic and extrinsic reward, faculty may participate in technology integration based on perceived benefits or advantages. Web-based courses are easy to revise; new information can be added and outdated material removed in a few minutes' time. An additional advantage for faculty teaching Web-based courses is the acquisition of new technical and information literacy skills along with relevant and current resources (Brahler, Peterson, and Nils). Bazillion and Braun suggest that Web-based courses enable faculty to combine the best features of electronic access to information with the social dimensions of face-to-face interaction with their students.

Benefits to Learners

For some faculty, the knowledge that their effort to use technology in their teaching benefits their students serves as a powerful reason for making that effort. These faculty typically are known for their outgoing manner toward students, their continuous efforts to enliven their courses, and their desire to "maybe do it a little differently this year." Administrators hoping to engage faculty in teaching Web-based courses can succeed by pointing out the importance of preparing learners for the society and workplace of the future and using the most appropriate instructional methods and strategies to do so. In future decades, essential skills will include critical thinking, reasoning through abstract and symbolic codes, using inference and synthesis in thought, effective group process skills, and constructing and negotiating meaning (Privateer). Faculty must help prepare students for their future roles as well as provide them with discipline-specific knowledge and skills. Students who are successful in Web-based courses will leave with important knowledge and skills in computer literacy and information management. They will become critical judges of the merits of the information they encounter on the Web (Herron).

Developing Expert Learners

What faculty member would not appreciate learners who approach a course from a results-oriented, systematic, and strategic perspective? Who would not welcome learners who are fully engaged, responsible self-starters—expert learners? While most faculty go to considerable lengths to prepare subject matter that is current, logical, and relevant, it is equally important that they integrate what is known about expert learners into the overall design and implementation of a course that stimulates and enables learners to strengthen their learning skills.

In contrast to novice or less skillful learners, expert learners possess knowledge that is better organized and integrated; employ superior strategies and methods for accessing their knowledge, applying it, and integrating it; have different motivations; and tend to monitor and regulate themselves (Ertmer and Newby). Moreover, expert learners are more aware of themselves as learners, reflective, and flexible in their work. These metacognitive tendencies enable expert learners to discern what is important, and how, where, when, and why to apply their knowledge. They are capable of detecting when they are not learning or problem solving effectively. Expert learners possess the desire as well as the ability to learn and to evaluate the efficacy of their learning processes on an ongoing basis.

Students who are offered Web-based courses encounter unique opportunities to improve learning skills that are uncommon to the typical traditional classroom. In order to be successful, on-line learners must motivate and regulate themselves. No one rings the class bell or determines how many pages are to be read by a specified date. No one is at hand to assist the learner in choosing the sequence of learning tasks. As Privateer asserts, "Our students, like our institutions, should be prepared for a different path, a road that provides the opportunity of enhancing their intelligence by using information technologies deployed in strategic ways that as of yet have not been articulated" (77).

Transition Management

The strategies that proved successful at this school of nursing are supported by the writings of Bridges, who offers these recommendations to leaders and managers seeking to overcome resistance to change in their organizations:

1. Introduce change in a coherent package, with as much detail as possible.
2. At all times make expectations very clear.
3. Provide information repeatedly and consistently so there can be no mistaking it.
4. Consider the need to create temporary policies, reporting patterns, and roles to facilitate moving through a chaotic period.
5. Convince followers of the existence and urgency of the issue/problem that requires the change/solution.
6. Recognize that people need to undergo a psychological transition before altering their behavior.
7. Examine reward systems carefully; people need to perceive that they are in a better position for having changed their behavior.
8. Celebrate successes.
9. Reiterate the mission and vision.
10. Create a sense that "change is the norm" and couch it in positive terms.

Transformational Leadership

A review of the achievements at this school of nursing over a two-year period establishes that such positive results for students, faculty, a sparsely served region, and the institution as a whole could not have been achieved without appropriate leadership. As noted earlier, an aggressive campaign to attract external funding resulted in the awarding of three federal grants in addition to two private foundation grants and several one-time university allocations. Adequate fiscal resources enabled the hiring of highly competent technical experts and faculty as well as the procurement of state-of-the-art technology resources and facilities. Faculty were offered summer salary for course development, and work schedules were adjusted to support on-line teaching. Key faculty and administrative staff members were included in planning the design of an effective infrastructure to meet the needs of this major initiative for the school.

A systematic approach was taken to curriculum development, faculty development, technical and staff support, and communications. As a result, all faculty and staff members acquired a cohesive, solid understanding of the magnitude of technology integration, its value to the school, and the action steps necessary for its successful implementation. Yukl describes this type of leadership as transformational, and notes:

The extent to which a leader is transformational is measured primarily in terms of the leader's effect on followers. Followers of a transformational leader feel trust, loyalty, and respect toward the leader, and they are motivated to do more than they originally expected to do. The leader transforms and motivates followers by: (1) making them more aware of the importance of task outcomes, (2) inducing them to transcend their own self-interest for the sake of the organization or team, and (3) activating their higher-order needs. (351)

Yukl adds that a primary requirement for transformational leaders is to appreciate the need for change. Particularly when a change runs counter to the existing culture, leaders find it more challenging to implement than if the change is consistent with existing values. In this instance, the necessity for faculty to change their teaching so dramatically sparked an initial reaction of discomfort, fear, and concern. The second element of transformation involves managing transition by helping followers retain their self-confidence and optimism about making a shift. Faculty development activities signaled a desire to support faculty growth. The third element requires that a new vision be created in order that participants may internalize the new values and methods. According to Yukl, to be motivating the vision must establish a common purpose and an appealing view of the future. Institutionalizing the changes may involve changes in organizational structure, roles, policies, or strategic initiatives. To this end, transformational leaders have been characterized as viewing themselves as change agents, able to articulate a set of core priorities and values which undergird their behavior, and willing to take risks prudently. They believe in their people, are sensitive to their needs, and are flexible. Moreover, transformational leaders possess cognitive skills, are willing to learn from experience, and are inclined toward disciplined thinking and analysis of problems. They are visionaries who believe in themselves.

CONCLUSION

What Gould and Gould term a new "cultural cohort" (9) has emerged from the Information Age and the World Wide Web. According to them, the experience of today's students with digital technology has molded them into a more reflective, collaborative, and openly curious group of young people. They are caught in an evolving culture of nonlinear, interactive communication systems that foster dependence on self, critical thinking, discovery, and a responsiveness to the issues, diversity, and challenges of a fast-moving global community. The impact of digital technology has engendered a kind of mental flexibility that matches the team-oriented, lifelong learning–based, constantly changing workplace of the new millennium. It is only just, therefore, that the learning environments provided by institutions of higher education coexist with, or at least be compatible with, cultural environments.

The mainstays of a learning environment are the subject matter and the faculty who design, develop, implement, and evaluate courses. Technology offers a powerful set of tools with which to deliver instruction and facilitate learning—but technology is no more than a set of tools. It is unlikely to completely replace the human dimension of the learning environment. Those who remain unconvinced of the urgency with which Web-based technology must be integrated into the educational mainstream are reminded that technology "provides some great tools, but . . . technology by itself cannot organise lessons, communicate enthusiasm, or discern what best meets the needs or encourages the intellectual growth of students" (Tripathi).

To summarize, an environment that fosters successful technology integration includes the following elements:

1. A clear and focused vision is articulated and enacted by the administration.
2. Infrastructure and systems are established to support the realization of the vision.
3. Adequate fiscal resources are available.
4. Individuals at all levels are willing to fail, to learn, to collaborate, and to persist despite impediments.
5. A strong commitment to high-quality programs exists in the academic culture.
6. Faculty and staff development are ongoing and included in work schedules.
7. Incentives and rewards reflect respect for faculty time and their need for recognition.
8. The needs of students for standards, orientation, and training are accommodated.
9. For each essential task, someone is designated as accountable for ensuring its timely completion according to standards.
10. Communication is ongoing in all directions as necessary for purposes of feedback, monitoring, and evaluation.

NOTE

I would like to thank Drs. Phyllis Horns, Lou Everett, Phyllis Turner, Rita Reaves, and Linda Bergstrom, Mr. John Core, and Mr. Johnnie Dennis for their useful comments and support.

WORKS CITED

Bazillion, Richard, and Connie Braun. "Teaching on the Web and in the Studio Classroom." *Syllabus* 11.9 (1998): 22 pars. 1 Aug. 1999 <http://www.syllabus.com>.
Bergstrom, L. Personal communication, 25 May 1998.
Betts, Kristen. "Why Do Faculty Participate in Distance Education?" In *Case Studies.*

Technology Source. On the Horizon. Ed. James Morrison. October 1998. 13 pars. 1 Aug. 1999 <http://www.horizon.unc.edu/TS/cases/1998–10.asp>.

Blackboard.com. *Blackboard, Inc.* 1 Aug. 1999 <www.blackboard.com>.

Brahler, C. Jayne, Nils Peterson, and Emily Nils. "Developing On-line Learning Materials for Higher Education: An Overview of Current Issues." *Educational Technology and Society* 2.2 (April 1999). 1 Aug. 1999 <http://ifets.gmd.de/periodical/vol_2_99/jayne_brahler.html>.

Bridges, William. *Managing Transitions—Making the Most of Change.* Reading, MA: Perseus Books, 1998.

Core, J. Personal communication, 3 June 1999.

"Domino by Lotus Notes." Software. *Lotus Development Corporation.* 1 Aug. 1999 <http://www.lotus.com>.

Ertmer, Peggy, and Timothy Newby. "The Expert Learner: Strategic, Self-Regulated, and Reflective." *Instructional Science* 24.1 (1996): 4–24.

Gould, Larry, and Stacey Gould. "Education and the Net Generation: Lead, Follow, or Get Out of the Way?" *On the Horizon* 6.3 (1998): 9–10.

Herron, Terri. "Teaching with the Internet." *The Internet and Higher Education* 1.3 (1998): 217–22.

Privateer, Paul. "Academic Technology and the Future of Higher Education." *Journal of Higher Education* 70.1 (1999): 60–79.

Reaves, R. Personal communication, 8 Apr. 1998.

———. Personal communication, 28 June 1999.

Serow, Robert, and Catherine Brawner. "Implications of High-Tech Instructional Innovation for Faculty Evaluation and Development." Paper presented at the Annual Meeting of the American Educational Research Association, San Diego, April 1998.

Sheerer, M. Personal communication, 16 Apr. 1999.

Short, Doug. "Enhancing Instructional Effectiveness: A Strategic Approach—Thirteen Steps to Creating an Initiative." 2 Oct. 1996. 1 Aug. 1999 <http://ike.engr/washington.edu/news/whitep/eie.txt>.

Theall, M. Personal communication, 18 Feb. 1999.

Tripathi, A. Personal communication, 29 June 1999.

Yukl, Gary. *Leadership in Organizations.* 3rd ed. Englewood Cliffs, NJ: Prentice-Hall, 1994.

Chapter 15

The "Time" Factor in On-line Teaching: Implications for Faculty and Their Universities

Claudine SchWeber

"How much time does it take to teach an on-line course?" This question has been asked by senior administrators, concerned about the cost of faculty release time; by faculty, wondering how much is really involved in this new venture; by department heads, besieged by faculty concerned about what the on-line environment really means in terms of other commitments. In order to respond from the perspective of hard data and to deal with the many rumors (which in several cases exceeded the number of hours in a week!) and individual stories implying valor and bravery, it was clear that a systematic study was necessary (Hiltz).

The Graduate School of Management and Technology at the University of Maryland University College undertook an investigation in the fall and spring 1997–98 and fall 1998 to discover (1) how long it took, on a weekly basis, to teach on-line; (2) the activities involved (i.e., preparing lectures, providing resources, designing the course, developing and grading exams, conducting individual communications, etc.); and (3) how the on-line data compared with face-to-face classes.

BACKGROUND OF GSMT/UMUC

The history and context of the University of Maryland University College (UMUC) and its Graduate School of Management and Technology are critical in understanding the implications of the data that were collected. UMUC was established in 1947 as an institution devoted to the education of adult learners, particularly those in the United States armed forces throughout the world. It offered only baccalaureate specialties until 1978, when the Graduate School was established, offering one master's degree in general administration. At present the GSMT offers eight master's degrees in varied fields of management. UMUC serves primarily working adults who attend school part-time. In fiscal year 1998, GSMT had about 3,600 students.

The faculty are also part-time, with a unique asset: they are "scholarly practitioners" who have the doctorate (88%) plus at least five–ten years experience in the field in which they teach. Many are senior government, corporate, or nonprofit leaders whose interest in teaching has been prompted and retained by the adults in the classroom. GSMT faculty typically teach one course per semester. These faculty, a pool of approximately 250, are supported by a small staff of administrative personnel including approximately 30 full-time program directors who manage the degree programs, design the master syllabi, supervise and hire faculty, advise students, and teach two courses per year. There are no tenured faculty at UMUC (*GSMT Catalog*).

Almost two decades after its founding, the Graduate School initiated on-line distance education activities via computer-mediated instruction in the spring of 1996. This was a course in technology management, offered via a Windows-based proprietary software program called Tycho. Eighteen months later, the GSMT (and the rest of the university) moved to a Web-based conferencing system, WebTycho. By fall 1998, GSMT offered 59 sections (51 different courses: 46 credit, 5 noncredit) totally on-line via the Web. Of the eight degree programs, five could be completed on-line without any residency: the Master of Science (M.S.) in Management; M.S. in Technology Management/basic program; M.S. in Computer Systems Management/Information Resources Track; Master of International Management; and M.S. in Environmental Management. Beginning in fall 1999, all eight master's degree programs will be offered on-line, plus a new On-line MBA (*Graduate Distant Education*).

The on-line degree programs are all offered asynchronously in a semester mode. Students are expected to work in teams as well as individually, to be actively involved in the class, and to provide a variety of graded deliverables. It should be noted that UMUC also offers distance education using interactive video (two-way video, two-way audio) throughout the state of Maryland. This latter program is much smaller than the on-line programs, and is outside the scope of the "time" study.

Finally, the GSMT was very careful about training its faculty for the on-line experience, since the pedagogy and practices of on-line teaching and learning are quite different from the traditional face-to-face classroom. The Faculty Training Plan (FTP) involved two components conducted at least one semester before teaching which resulted in a training certificate. Part 1 involved initial training plus homework assignments, which move the instructor from the student's perspective to the faculty perspective. Part 2 involved "shadowing" an existing on-line class, plus using a practice class to develop and lay out the course for the future. Guidelines for the shadowing experience were given to the observers and a memo was submitted to the distance education director. GSMT faculty received payment for completing the training when they taught their first course, and received an additional stipend for teaching an on-line course (*Continuous Learning Program*).

THE "TIME" STUDY

How critical is the amount of time involved in on-line teaching—in recruiting faculty, in budgeting for remuneration, in the teaching experience, in maintaining a teacher-student relationship? Before we could explore these kinds of questions, we needed to develop baseline data which told us how much time was involved on a weekly basis, what elements made up the teaching experience, and how these data compared with classes taught face-to-face.

A survey was sent to all the Web instructors in fall 1997, spring 1998, and fall 1998 (n=90) and to face-to-face instructors teaching the same courses as the Web ones (n=158). Sixty Web faculty (67%) and 88 face-to-face faculty (56%) responded. Given the small number of respondents, the data were analyzed as medians (not means) to avoid data skewed by a few extreme responses. The survey was originally designed with significant input from on-line faculty with respect to the main activities involved in teaching; a similar survey was adapted for the face-to-face faculty.

The survey asked for weekly time estimates (in half-hour blocks) on several variables that might impact the amount of time involved in teaching. The variables were lecture preparation, on-line conferencing, involvement in group work, individual contact with students (such as e-mail), telephone contact, exam preparation and grading, finding additional resources, use of alternative delivery mechanisms such as fax, and pre-course development time. Some of these variables were collapsed to provide summary data (see Table 15.1). We also obtained background data such as class size, how often the faculty had taught the course in this medium (on-line or face-to-face), and how often they had taught on-line to see how these variables might impact the amount of time spent teaching. We were interested in the frequency variables for longitudinal purposes: we wanted to see what happens when the same course is taught over several semesters or years. To assure confidentiality of responses, a telephone survey was conducted by research assistants who entered the data on the survey forms; a check mark was then entered into our logbooks.

Several caveats are necessary with respect to these data. First, these are self-reported data and thus depend on the memories and perceptions of the respondents. Second, the surveys were distributed at the end of the semester and are thus subject to a possible "recency" effect. Third, the number of respondents so

Table 15.1
Time Spent Teaching On-line and Face-to-Face: Composite Summary.
Course Load: 1 per semester (Median data; hours *per week*)

Category	Web (N=60)	Face-to-Face (N=88)
Overall Time	18	17
On-line Conferencing/ FTF Class Meeting (meeting time, group work)	3	3
Student Contact (individual contact, office hours, telephone calls, e-mail contact, personal meeting)	4	1.5
Lecture Work (preparation, additional resources)	5	5
Exam Activity (preparation and grading)	4	4

far is too small for statistically significant conclusions (except in the course development area). Nonetheless, the data indicate patterns that bear watching and issues that need attention.

FINDINGS

Please keep in mind that faculty at the Graduate School usually teach one course per semester, since they are part-time instructors. If they are program directors (full-time staff), they have a two course per year teaching load. Thus, the data are a reflection of this reality.

Overall Graduate School Results

The results indicate that Web faculty spent about one hour more per week teaching on the Web (18 hours total) than those in an on-site classroom (17 hours total). While this difference is negligible, the amount of time the instructors spent on individual student contacts is not. As Table 15.1 shows, *on-line faculty spent more than twice as many hours per week (4) with students than those involved in face-to-face instruction (1.5).* While the number of respondents is too small for statistically significant conclusions now, the amount of time spent on individual contact with students is a variable of great interest. It is one to which we will be paying close attention in the longitudinal study; preliminary remarks are presented later in the chapter.

Table 15.2

Pre-course Development Time for One Course (Median data: hours *per semester*)

	Web Faculty	Face-to-face Faculty
Course Development	40	15

In the other areas—exam activities, lecture work, on-line conferencing/class meeting—the weekly time was quite similar for both teaching modes. The time for on-line conferencing/class meeting was the same for both types of instruction (3 hours), as was the time for lecture work (5 hours) and exam activities (4 hours). The three hours for face-to-face class meetings is logical, since these classes are scheduled for three hours each week. (Note: The exam data were a great surprise to this author, who spent, she felt, much more time grading on-line papers than those from her face-to-face classes.)

While the above differences were not statistically significant, the amount of pre-course development time per semester was: On-line faculty reported they took almost three times longer to prepare for a Web course as for one taught face-to-face. (See Table 15.2).

This finding may be due to the substantial amount of time it takes to convert notes, charts, discussion questions, weekly assignments, assessment tools, and so on to the on-line environment, plus the need to be extremely well organized in advance. Our experience with on-line courses is that the entire semester must be laid out in substantial detail before the semester begins. Although the way in which each class discusses and applies the material varies, and new resources—particularly from the Web—continually appear, the on-line course itself must be complete on the first day. At UMUC, for example, on-line courses are opened two weeks before the semester formally begins so that students can familiarize themselves with the materials.

The 25-hour difference in course development time may also be due to the lesser experience of Web faculty with their on-line courses than that of face-to-face faculty with theirs. As Table 15.3 indicates, most Web faculty had taught their course on-line only once before, whereas face-to-face faculty had taught their course, on average, six times. It is certainly not due to class size, since Web classes are smaller (median, 23) than face-to-face classes (median, 30). (See Table 15.3.) This size is due to a university policy of capping on-line courses at 25 students, while face-to-face classes may be in the low thirties.

Discipline-Focused Results

While the summary data give us a picture of the graduate faculty as a whole, closer examination by discipline offers some insights into patterns of faculty according to their academic specialties. Two departments with very different

Table 15.3
Background of Web and Face-to-Face Faculty (Median data)

	Web Faculty	Face-to-Face Faculty
Class Size	23	30
How Often Taught Course in This Medium	1	6
How Often Taught Any On-line Course	2	0

Table 15.4
Computer Systems Management Faculty Time Spent Teaching On-line and
Face-to-Face (Median data; hours *per week*)

	Web (N=12)	Face-to-Face (N=7)
Overall Time	19	18. 5
On-line Conferencing/FTF Class meeting time	3	3
Student Contact	6	2
Lecture work	6	6
Exam activity	3	3.5

subject matter were selected for closer observation: Master of Science in Computer Systems Management (CSMN) and Master of Science in Management (MSM).

The CSMN faculty time factors reflected the patterns of the entire graduate faculty: similar overall weekly time for Web faculty (19 hours) and face-to-face instructors (18.5), as well as for the exam activities, lecture preparation, and class meeting/on-line conferencing time. (See Table 15.4). The major difference was in the amount of time involved in student contact: 6 hours per week for Web faculty and 2 hours per week for face-to-face faculty. The small number of respondents reinforces that this is a pattern worth watching over time, rather than a definitive statement.

MSM faculty reported that they spent 5 hours more per week in the on-line environment (21.5 hours) than did the face-to-face instructors. A closer look indicates that, once again, the greatest difference was in the amount of student contact time: 4 hours per week for Web faculty and 1.5 hours for face-to-face faculty. (See Table 15.5).

Table 15.5
Master of Science in Management Faculty Time Spent Teaching On-line and
Face-to-Face (Median data; hours *per week*)

	Web (N=23)	Face-to-Face (N=60)
Overall Time	21.5	16.5
On-line conferencing/FTF class meeting	3.5	3
Student Contact	4	1.5
Lecture work	4	4
Exam activity	4.5	5

Table 15.6
Student-Faculty Interaction: Contact Hours and Conferencing/Class Time by
Discipline, and Overall (Median data; hours *per week*)

	Web contact + conferencing hours	Face-to-Face contact + class time
Computer Systems Management	6 + 3 = 9	2 + 3 hours = 5
Master of Science in Management	4 + 3.5 = 7.5	1.5 + 3 = 4.5
All Graduate Faculty	4 + 3 = 7	1.5 + 3 = 4.5

The importance of the student contact variable is that this appears to be the factor that most differentiates the on-line teaching environment from the face-to-face (FTF) classroom. That is, the ability to have ongoing access—increased interaction—to instructors by students, beyond the "formal" class time (conferencing or FTF classroom), is often noted as one of the benefits of the on-line experience. These data suggest that this increased interaction is indeed occurring. As Table 15.6 shows, if we combine the "formal" class time with student contact to see the amount of time devoted to student-faculty interaction, on-line faculty spent almost twice as much time weekly as their face-to-face colleagues.

When we explored the time it took to develop these courses, the significant difference that appeared for the entire graduate faculty is also reflected in these two departments. Both CSMN and MSM faculty required two and a half to five times the hours to prepare an on-line course, in total, in comparison with the face-to-face classes. (See Table 15.7).

This pattern is likely due, in part, to the fact that face-to-face faculty had

Table 15.7
Pre-Course Development Time by Discipline, Total Time for One Course
(Median data; hours *per semester*)

	Web	Face-to-Face
Computer Systems Management	50	20
Master of Science in Management	50	10
All GSMT faculty	40	15

taught their course more often, as shown by the MSM faculty: on-line faculty had taught their course once, whereas face-to-face faculty had taught their course ten times. This was not the case for the CSMN faculty—both groups reported having taught the course twice.

COMMENT: PATTERNS AND ISSUES

This research on faculty "time" in teaching on-line courses indicates several areas that need continuing observation. First, the area of student contact time—which is a composite of individual contact such as e-mail, telephone calls, office hours, and personal meetings—needs annual tracking. We noted earlier that this variable most differentiates the on-line class from the face-to-face one: on-line classes involve almost three times more student contact (4 hours per week) than face-to-face courses (1.5 hours per week). When these data are combined with the time spent in the "formal" class environment (see Table 15.6), we can see more clearly how much faculty-student interaction there is in the two types of classes.

Interaction is the essence of the on-line learning process—the ability to shift to a learner-centered environment from the instructor-dominated one typically associated with traditional classrooms. Thus, how much time is spent in this aspect of the on-line class, and whether it changes over time, may be an indicator of this pedagogical shift. If the above pattern continues, then it will be important to see whether one element in the composite is responsible for the disparity. A closer look at the data revealed, for example, that for on-line faculty, e-mail accounted for the largest amount of student contact (2.5 hours), as opposed to telephone calls (1 hour) for face-to-face faculty.

One possible reason for this development is that e-mail queries are sequential, (asynchronous), so responses, clarifications, and conclusions to a point occur over a series of back-and-forth interactions. Telephone questions are simultaneous (synchronous), so that the clarification and elaboration are immediate. If this pattern continues, how might faculty deal with this situation? Furthermore, will the "formal" class time remain as it is now, about the same for both me-diums, or will the need to continually update content in keeping with the infor-mation explosion result in an increase in this area, as well as in the lecture preparation category?

Second, the finding that pre-course development time is significantly greater for Web courses than for face-to-face ones needs watching to see if this changes over time as faculty become more experienced with Web teaching. Web faculty, like their face-to-face counterparts, often teach the same course. With the advent of new technological options, such as audio, video, and multimedia, which must be included in continually revised courses, will the course development time increase? What kinds of support must faculty receive from their departments and from the university to assist in course development? At the Graduate School, faculty typically teach one course each semester. What is the impact of the course development time on instructors who teach a typical load of three or four courses a term?

Third, how is academic discipline impacted in the matter of time? Continual observation of two different fields—Computer Systems Management and Master of Science in Management—will indicate whether the overall time difference in the MSM continues and whether student contact remains the distinguishing fea-ture of on-line coursework. What similarities and differences will these two departments present as they continue to offer courses in both mediums? Will course development time change more in one than another as a result of changes in their fields?

Finally, what might be the effect of how often faculty have taught their courses on-line? At present, most reported that they taught the course once before. Will the time to teach decrease as faculty teach the same courses, or even similar ones (in one discipline, for example) over several semesters? Or will the need to be continually current, and the high amount of student contact time, result in no overall change or in increases?

Once we have some longitudinal data on these points, we will be in a better position to answer related questions about appropriate faculty remuneration, re-cruitment strategies, release time, teaching-learning strategies that use the best of the on-line environment without overwhelming the faculty, and eventually, about the teacher-student relationship in the brave new world of cyber learning.

WORKS CITED

Continuous Learning Program for Distance Faculty. Graduate School of Management and Technology, Distance Learning and Instructional Technology Office. College Park, MD: University of Maryland University College, May 1998.

Graduate Distant Education. University of Maryland University College. 1 Aug. 1999 <http://www.umuc.edu/gsmt/gsmtdist>.

Graduate School of Management and Technology. University of Maryland University College. 1 Aug. 1999 <htttp://www.umuc.edu/gsmt>.

Graduate School of Management and Technology Catalog. College Park, MD: University of Maryland University College, 1999–98.

Hiltz, Star Roxanne, Nancy Coppola, and N. Rotter. "Preliminary Results of Semi-Structured Interviews on 'Becoming a Virtual Professor.' " New York: International Conference on Asynchronous Learning Networks, November 1998.

Chapter 16

Seven Principles for Good Practice in Teaching and Technology

Alec M. Testa

Many higher education institutions have made a commitment to introduce Internet and computing technologies to their campuses (Green). Following the commitment and expenditures, administrators and faculty have begun to ask, "What effect has this change had on the campus? Is the equipment being used? Is the equipment being used effectively? Have teaching and learning been improved?"

This chapter describes the results of the Teaching and Technology Questionnaire (TTQ) at Eastern New Mexico University. Eastern, as its constituencies know it, has made a concerted effort to infuse Internet and computing technologies into its curriculum. The results of the TTQ describe how the faculty use the technologies made available to them. Eastern is also very committed to outcomes assessment and describes itself as a "teaching/learning" institution. With expertise in assessment, explicit expectations for student learning, and a commitment to technology, it was only a matter of time before technology and assessment questions were asked. Eastern's commitment to technology and teaching, outcomes assessment, and organization around student learning were critical reasons the university was named a recipient of the 1997 Pew Leadership Award for Revitalizing Undergraduate Education.

THE STUDY

Chickering and Gamson's *Seven Principles for Good Practice in Undergraduate Education*, first published in March 1987 in the *AAHE Bulletin*, distilled findings from decades of research on factors that effectively promote undergraduate learning and development. On the TTQ, faculty were asked how their use of Internet and instructional technologies promoted each of the seven principles. Respondents also were asked to what extent they agreed (on a four point Likert-type scale) that emerging and Internet technologies promoted each principle, and to provide examples. Faculty were also asked the extent to which they used common computing software and which technologies they used in their teaching. Demographic data on discipline, rank, and tenure were not collected, to ensure anonymity due to small sample size. All 130 full-time tenured, tenure-track, and full-time temporary faculty at Eastern were asked to complete the TTQ. Sixty-eight surveys were returned. Survey distribution and collection were handled at the college level, and only one TTQ was distributed to each faculty member.

The results provide an important look at how emerging technologies are changing the way that faculty teach. When compared to what is known about effective teaching (for which there is no shortage of research literature), evidence of the value of emerging technologies can be seen.

THE RESPONSES

1. Good Practice Encourages Student-Faculty Contact

Frequent student-faculty contact in and out of class is a most important factor in student motivation and involvement. Faculty concern helps students get through rough times and keep on working. Knowing a few faculty members well enhances students' intellectual commitment and encourages them to think about their own values and plans. (Chickering and Gamson)

No other technological application since the office hour has promoted student faculty contact more than electronic mail (e-mail). Where Chickering and Ehrmann pointed out its potential uses, faculty are now finding that e-mail is evidence of technology's ability to enhance this vital faculty and student interaction. By enhancing communication and making asynchronous communication and learning possible, e-mail demonstrates the potential of other World Wide Web (WWW) applications such as Web-delivered instruction and on-line advising services. At Eastern the WWW has demonstrated that barriers of location and time can be overcome.

Emerging technologies have had another profound effect on the way that faculty teach, not just what content they cover. As faculty wrestle with emerging technologies, they have involved students, resulting in side by side instruction in place of the traditional lecture or seminars. In addition, Web technologies such as chat facilities and listservs have been implemented to promote communication in traditional lecture type classes. More than 90 percent of the respondents indicated that they used e-mail to communicate with students, and a similar number indicated they felt that Internet and instructional technologies promoted faculty and student contact.

Anonymous sample comments provided by the faculty illustrate this phenomenon:

- "Much more frequent student-teacher contact and student-student contact. Easier and more thorough communication of assignments and addressing of questions."
- "Working with students one-on-one to help them learn/use new technologies."
- "Email makes communication and contact very easy; it extends office hours to 'virtual office hours' and allows for contact that is personal, but not 'face-to-face' (which sometimes inhibits students). It also expands the classroom!"
- "Our students are exposed to Sun computers used for GIS [Geographic Information System] archaeological mapping and other analysis. Undergrads who ask faculty can receive 'follow up' from class introductions of this technology."

2. Good Practice Encourages Cooperation Among Students

Learning is enhanced when it is more like a team effort than a solo race. Good learning, like good work, is collaborative and social, not competitive and isolated. Working with others often increases involvement in learning. Sharing one's ideas and responding to others' improves thinking and deepens understanding. (Chickering and Gamson)

The use of emerging and Internet technologies enhances students' collaboration and cooperation. Frequently this takes place because students are trying to learn how to use new technologies together. In "Implementing the Seven Principles: Technology as Lever," Chickering and Ehrmann refer to these events as "spontaneous student collaboration." Perhaps such collaborations are evidence of students succeeding in spite of the best intentions of faculty. It will be interesting to see if, when computer and technological sophistication increases, such collaboration continues.

Students are also more often able to work with one another because of enhanced communication. Barriers of time, place, and distance between and among students are more easily overcome or eliminated. This is true not only at a small rural university, but also at a large urban community college or an elite liberal arts institution.

New technologies also allow students to increasingly work together with simulations and "real life" projects. Therefore, learning activities become increasingly real. When asked if they agreed if emerging and Internet technologies promoted this good practice, 84 percent of the faculty surveyed agreed, as these sample comments reveal:

- "Internet annotated bibliographies encourage interaction; 'I found this site you may need,' etc. Simply helping one another is enriching."

- "I have seen students that do not know each other get together to learn how to use computers to solve problems and to surf the Net for more information."
- "For example, we use the Web to find pedagogical resource information on Hispanic culture, etc., and then students share these resources with each other. We compile or distribute lists of interesting sources of information."
- "Teaching collaborative writing skills with group-writing software. In each group of three or four students, each student works at a screen on a document that also appears on each other member's screen. Enhances awareness of the conscious process of putting ideas on paper."

3. Good Practice Encourages Active Learning

Learning is not a spectator sport. Students do not learn much just sitting in classes listening to teachers, memorizing prepackaged assignments, and spitting out answers. They must talk about what they are learning, write reflectively about it, relate it to past experiences, and apply it to their daily lives. They must make what they learn part of themselves. (Chickering and Gamson)

Chickering and Ehrmann point out that the communication improvements made possible by Internet and instructional technologies that enhance the previous two principles also positively influence this third principle. They go on to categorize additional benefits that include apprentice-like activities such as learning the necessary computer applications for a discipline, simulation techniques that do not require a computer but a manipulative that is used for practicing a behavior, and computer simulations.

Through the TTQ, it was observed that active learning was enhanced through communication, but mostly because, as discussed previously, students had more ready access to faculty and each other through e-mail, listservs, and chat facilities. Also, students work together on simulations and other interactive learning activities, sometimes simply to learn the technology in order to complete the assignment. Interestingly, students are more likely to seek out new information through the Web.

More than 90 percent of the faculty agreed that Internet and instructional technologies promoted active learning techniques. The examples they provided include the following:

- "Students assist each other in locating sources for papers from the web. One student found sign information [for the deaf] on some Australian web pages. She brought the material to class, shared, explained how she accessed it, encouraged and helped others."
- "The combination of independent research brought back to a team setting is a much more realistic model than solitary study, research, and reporting. Technology enhances this."
- "Use of language-learning software allows students to become more active and 'interactive' (all of our programs are 'inter-active'). Visits to the Web are basis for reflective journal assignments, and this is very productive."

- "Students are able to relate to real world situations in real time—makes discussions more meaningful."

4. Good Practice Gives Prompt Feedback

Knowing what you know and don't know focuses your learning. In getting started, students need help in assessing their existing knowledge and competence. Then, in classes, students need frequent opportunities to perform and receive feedback on their performance. At various points during college, and at its end, students need chances to reflect on what they have learned, what they still need to know, and how they might assess themselves. (Chickering and Gamson)

Enhanced communication and lowered barriers of time and place are two previously discussed examples of how Internet and instructional technologies promote prompt feedback. Chickering and Ehrmann rightly point out that technology provides opportunity for storing and evaluating larger and larger amounts of information—students' portfolios, for example. The TTQ respondents provided further examples of how emerging technologies and the Internet can be useful tools.

Not only can instructors notify students of their homework or exam marks outside of class time, but instructional time is also saved because it need not be used to collect and redistribute assignments. Web pages not only deliver course content, but in many ways give students feedback in either static or interactive manners. More vigorous and sophisticated Web tools such as Java and Common Gateway Interface (CGI) scripts make scoring of exams, for instance, instantaneous. Some networking applications, for example, allow students to speak to one another, with video, over the Internet. Students can also share common "worldware" (commonly available software not purposely intended for educational use) applications such as word processing and spreadsheets.

Again, more than 90 percent of the TTQ respondents believed that Internet and instructional technologies promoted this principle, and they supplied several examples.

- "Response by e-mail is quick and personalized. Follow-up is private and supportive."
- "Homework solutions are available on the Web—all students may check their current knowledge by comparing what they obtain in answer to homework questions with the correct answers."
- "In astronomy class, the students use a CD which came with the text to quiz themselves. I encourage this with the publicized practice of putting some of these same questions on the major tests."

5. Good Practice Emphasizes Time on Task

Time plus energy equals learning. Learning to use one's time well is critical for students and professionals alike. Allocating realistic amounts of time means effective learning for students and effective teaching for faculty. (Chickering and Gamson)

Chickering and Ehrmann allude to the benefits of asynchronous learning. Internet and instructional technologies can also improve student learning by helping students to learn more efficiently (simulations and similar learning activities). In addition, students are able to use their time better. The current generation of students may have never typed on a manual typewriter or used correction fluid or carbon paper. They certainly have not had to punch computer cards or send commands to a system operator in order to pick up printouts from a central computer facility. Therefore contemporary students are able to focus on more important learning activities.

The TTQ respondents pointed out that students have new freedom in how they organize and use their time. They can be freed from lectures, checking out reserved books, or meeting a faculty member during office hours. They can have more and more communication with fellow students and faculty. And, as described by Ehrmann, worldware is becoming increasingly sophisticated. Word processors help students be more organized and efficient, as does presentation software that creates slides, outlines, and handouts.

TTQ respondents overwhelmingly agreed that this "time on task" principle was enhanced through Internet and instructional technology (more than 90 percent). Some of their specific examples include:

- "I think word processing, spreadsheets, and data from CD roms and web are saving students time and allowing them more time to think, write, rewrite than pre-computers. Quality of research papers has improved."

- "Technology is often fun. Fun always enhances learning."

- "PowerPoint presentations' efficiency and computer word processing solves necessity of rewriting whole pages or documents."

6. Good Practice Communicates High Expectations

Expect more and you will get it. High expectations are important for everyone—for the poorly prepared, for those unwilling to exert themselves, and for the bright and well motivated. Expecting students to perform well becomes a self-fulfilling prophecy. (Chickering and Gamson)

Chickering and Ehrmann point out that Web publishing of students' work and using Web pages to show examples of exemplary work are two strategies for communicating high expectations. The TTQ participants indicated that, relieved from some of the burden of revising, students can be expected to prepare papers and projects free from errors. When students make classroom presentations, they can be expected to do professional quality work with worldware applications such as Microsoft PowerPoint.

TTQ respondents were less clear on how the Internet and instructional technologies promoted this principle. Only 82 percent of respondents with an opinion agreed. These are some of the specific examples they provided:

- "When students complete exercises on the computer, especially involving data analysis, they tend to be very concerned with making the output look its very best—much more so than if done by 'hand.' "
- "Especially with word processing I see a real change. Again, the time not spent on typing and retyping can be spent on rewrites, find[ing] new ideas, examples etc."
- "Near perfect reports and graphics (generated by word processors and drawing packages) are expected from students."
- "Integration of graphics, scanned images, and stringent composition mechanics are expected by students submitting term papers. They rise to the level of higher expectations."

7. Good Practice Respects Diverse Talents and Ways of Learning

Many roads lead to learning. Different students bring different talents and styles to college. Brilliant students in a seminar might be all thumbs in a lab or studio; students rich in hands-on experience may not do so well with theory. Students need opportunities to show their talents and learn in ways that work for them. Then they can be pushed to learn in new ways that do not come so easily. (Chickering and Gamson)

Internet and instructional technologies not only help students learn at their own pace at different times of the day, but can change *how* students choose to have information presented. Students can choose from text, audio, video, animation, simulation, and interactive discussion (again with text, audio, video, and graphics). Students can also choose to explore background or related material with ease.

More than 90 percent of Eastern New Mexico University faculty who completed the TTQ agreed that Internet and instructional technologies promoted diverse talents and ways of learning. Examples include:

- "Students use different approaches to search for information on the Internet and using the computer."
- "I strongly agree that the WWW offers possibilities we've not yet even considered for active and challenging learning outside the confines of the classroom."
- "The traditional classroom forces one style of interactive behavior. Technology allows the student to provide input according to their style of interaction (e.g., e-mail versus talking in class)."
- "PowerPoint for visual learners, interactive software and audiocassettes for auditory learners, etc. As many forms/formats as technology allows us to approach students from a different perspective, that's how many more opportunities we have to reach diverse students."

DISCUSSION

The Teaching and Technology Questionnaire was designed to determine if, and how, new Internet and instructional technologies were being used to enhance teaching and learning. The TTQ was an attempt to answer the question, "Is the investment in computers and other technology improving teaching and learning?" A secondary question was, "How are faculty using these new resources to improve teaching and learning?"

The results were qualitative and subjective, but organized against a rubric of agreed upon principles of effective teaching and learning. Based on the responses, it appears that the teaching and learning at Eastern New Mexico University has been improved through the infusion of new computers, enhanced Internet access, and the availability of other technology resources. Several specific examples were found for each principle, and it is likely to be only a matter of time and experience until newer and more exciting pedagogical and curriculur changes occur. More interestingly, the examples provided by the TTQ show how faculty can use the Internet and emerging instructional technologies. Further studies will shed more light on how to improve teaching and learning in higher education.

This research is investigative in nature, and may not add to the theory of how students learn. It only tells us what experienced higher education practitioners can do with new tools. Meanwhile, the Flashlight Project, directed by Steve Ehrmann at the TLTGroup, will collect quantifiable data, thereby allowing statistical investigations of how technology does and does not promote each of the seven principles. Further studies like the TTQ can be a good addition to this line of research, sharpening the focus of the Flashlight Project even more.

Replication with a national audience will instruct us more on how the Internet and instructional technologies are being used in American higher education. The results will be useful in developing new initiatives in classrooms, whether they be in traditional buildings or cyberspace. Chickering and Ehrmann's seven principles are useful in determining which technologies to employ and when to use them, and a myriad of existing assessment techniques exists to help understand in what ways they were useful.

WORKS CITED

Chickering, Arthur, and Steve Ehrmann. (1996) "Implementing the Seven Principles: Technology as Lever." *AAHE Bulletin*, Oct. 1996. 1 Aug. 1999. <http://www.aahe.org/technology/ehrmann.htm>.

Chickering, Arthur, and Zelda Gamson. *Seven Principles for Good Practice in Undergraduate Education*. Winona, MN: Winona State University, Seven Principles Resource Center, 1987.

Ehrmann, Steve. "The Flashlight Project: Spotting the Elephant in the Dark." *Assessment Update* 9.4 (1997): 10+.

Flashlight Project. *TLTGroup*. 1 Aug. 1999 <http://www.tltgroup.org>.

Green, Kenneth C. "The 1996 National Survey of Desktop Computing in Higher Education: Instructional Integration and User Support Present Continuing Technology Challenges." *Campus Computing Project*. 1997. 1 Aug. 1999 <http://www.campuscomputing.net/>.

Chapter 17

Copyright and Web-Based Education: What All Faculty Should Know

David W. Throne

BACKGROUND

Many higher education instructors and professors in the United States are creating Web sites to deliver their courses at a distance. They spend hundreds of hours creating new material or revising old materials for distance delivery. Sometimes they are paid by their respective institutions for this design and development; other times they are not. However, problems concerning copyright and ownership of materials on faculty-created Web sites are surfacing as evidenced by chat on listservs such as DEOS-L—The Distance Education Online Symposium and Indiana University Online Copyright Tutorial (Copyright Management Center).

These listservs are run exclusively as higher education discussion forums. They provide educators and administrators with places to discuss and learn about contemporary issues and evolving problems concerning distance education and copyright. Intellectual ownership, in particular, has become an extremely sensitive issue for administrators and educators with wide-ranging opinions. When adjunct faculty and work made for hire are added, it becomes confusing, and litigation is occasionally necessary. Cyrs states, "Distance education is the most discussed, least understood, and fastest growing area of technological change in higher education today" (387).

The Internet, as used for Web-based courses, provides a unique situation and medium where complex copyright issues arise. Many authors have written about this, but few have addressed adjunct educators developing Web-based courses for schools and retaining the copyright of their courses when dismissed or moving to another work situation. This chapter is directed toward adjunct faculty (who are usually nontenured faculty) developing instructional Web sites for institutional employers; it offers suggestions to help them avoid problems associated with the process.

THE PROBLEM

Initially, issues of who owns what are not brought up. On the one hand, many educators assume they own what they created. On the other hand, administrators, citing institutional policies, assume they own what their employees created. Adjunct faculty are particularly affected because they are not afforded the same rights as tenured faculty at many institutions.

Professional organizations are urging their members to help one another understand these sensitive issues. For instance, the Association for Educational Communications and Technology (AECT) writes in its Code of Ethics: "In fulfilling obligations to the profession, members shall inform users of the stipulations and the interpretations of the copyright law and other laws affecting the profession and encourage compliance" (on-line posting).

Suggestion One: Carefully Read and Understand Contracts

Adjuncts should read their contracts and understand their legal rights before giving institutions Web sites they have created. They should look for ownership policies in particular. Kurtz, a copyright attorney at Pennsylvania State University, says, "It is deceiving to the employee for the contractor to not specify up front who will own the finished product. The contractor usually has already been advised by legal counsel and is intentionally ambiguous in the contract, because absent a specific written assignment to the creator (employee), the law grants ownership to the employer or to the contractor" ("Intellectual").

Adjunct faculty should understand their contracts and employment status before they allow their time, work, words, and ideas to be taken.

- First, they should understand their legal position as adjunct faculty and the term "work made for hire."
- Second, they should understand their rights as owners of words and ideas, which fall under copyright, intellectual property, and fair use.
- Third, they should understand the difference between creating under contract and bringing in developed material prior to contract. If they have developed material prior to contract, they should document it, and, even better, they should note it in their contract.
- Fourth, they should know what can happen if they do not protect themselves and understand certain court cases that may be relevant to their situation.

• Finally, they should be aware of sensible remedies in situations where infringements have taken place in relation to their work on Web sites.

Suggestion Two: Know Institutional Policies Concerning Adjuncts

Adjuncts should know their position at institutions. That is, they should understand their legal rights as nontenured employees. For instance, in Colorado, the Colorado Community College and Occupational Educational System (CCCOES) policy, which governs fourteen state system community colleges and oversees district community colleges, states that "exempt employees are those who fill positions which are exempt from the State Personnel System" (*Administration*). This basically means that adjunct faculty have been hired on an as-needed basis; are subject to terms of employment written in their contract at the time of hire; and have no benefits except those provided by law (CCCOES, for example, allows adjuncts to contribute to the Public Employees Retirement Association).

Arguably, adjuncts are independent contractors, although classified as exempt employees or nontenured faculty. They have *fewer rights* compared to those of tenured faculty, which may include appeal processes if terminated. Also, many institutions are not legally required to give adjuncts reasons for ending employment. Different institutions have different policies concerning adjuncts' status, so adjuncts should check with their personnel departments. However, these policies concerning non–tenure track faculty members are slowly changing as "bills of rights" are now being considered at many institutions, such as the University of Colorado at Boulder.

Consequently, adjuncts should understand their rights and responsibilities before they sign institutional contracts, and be aware that they are expendable and that their contracts can be terminated without reason at any time.

Suggestion Three: Know Institutional Policies Concerning Work Produced and Encourage Institutions to Be Forthright about Including Ownership Clauses in Contracts

Before adjuncts agree to sign contracts to design or develop on-line courses and supporting materials, they should understand institutional policies concerning work produced. Smedinghoff states, "Copyright [ownership] is an issue that is frequently not even discussed between the parties" (147). Adjuncts and their institutional administrators should agree on who owns the course and its contents; how much they will be paid; and what percentage of royalties, if any, they will be afforded for future sales.

In most cases, since adjuncts are exempt employees, institutions will have them sign a contract that will most likely be a "work made for hire" document and falls under the Copyright Act of 1976 (17 U.S.C.A., Section 101). The act states that a work made for hire document is

(1) A work prepared by an employee within the scope of his or her employment; or (2) a work specifically ordered or commissioned for use as a contribution to a collective work, as a part of a motion picture or other audiovisual work, as a translation, as a supplementary work, as a compilation, as an instructional text, as a test, as answer material for a test, or as an atlas, if the parties expressly agree in a written instrument signed by them that the work shall be considered a work made for hire. (*Electronic Frontier Foundation*)

In other words, if you as adjunct faculty are under contract with an institutional employer to develop a course for the Internet, you do not own that course: the institution does, unless otherwise stipulated within the contract between you and them.

Institutional employers should provide information on copyright procedures because the policies concerning copyright and intellectual property can vary greatly from institution to institution. For instance, the policy at the University of Northern Colorado states:

It is the policy of the University of Northern Colorado not to interfere with the longstanding and traditional rights of the faculty and staff, on their own initiative, to write, create, produce or otherwise generate works or products which are copyrightable, patentable, or of commercial value. Any such materials written, created, produced or otherwise generated by a member of the faculty or staff shall remain the exclusive property of the faculty or staff member and that person shall have the sole right of ownership and disposition, unless the materials are written, created, produced or otherwise generated as "works-for-hire" or through significant use of University facilities, as specified in section 3.

In contrast, the policy of the CCCOES, the governing body for Colorado's community colleges, states:

Employees who develop or plan to develop materials which may be copyrightable or patentable shall submit a disclosure statement to the president when such materials are developed or will be developed, in whole or in part, with college/system assistance. The disclosure statement will include the specifics of any contract, grant, or assignment by the college or outside agency; the extent of utilization of college/system facilities and personnel; the names, titles, and roles of personnel to be involved; brief descriptions of the materials produced or to be produced and of the anticipated use of produced materials; and the calendar of development and utilization of the produced materials. . . . Failure to submit a timely disclosure statement of any such project may result in the project's being deemed the property of the Board. (*Copyrights*)

There is quite a contrast between the policies. The point here is that many educational institutions do not have their copyright and intellectual property policies stated within contracts when adjuncts sign them. Institutions should be encouraged to do so. If adjuncts want to retain the rights to their work, they should encourage ownership clause inclusions in all contractual agreements with institutions before beginning work. However, even if this has not been done, a fairly recent federal court decision favors independent contractors and possibly adjuncts.

Kaplin and Lee state that the Copyright Act's work made for hire doctrine seldom has been applied in higher education. Since the work made for hire doctrine is an exception to the Copyright Act of 1976's presumption that authors of works hold the copyright and that copyrights are owned by employers because of this doctrine, it is necessary for both parties to enter an agreement for authors to retain their copyright. However, a recent Supreme Court decision clarified this further. In *Community for Creative Non-Violence (CCNV) v. Reid*, 490 U.S. 104 (1989), the Court was asked to decide who owned a statue commissioned by CCNV since both parties (the sculptor and the employer) had competing copyright registrations. The Court ruled that the work made for hire doctrine did not apply to Reid because he was an independent contractor, not an employee of CCNV, listing factors that were relevant to this determination.

The case is considered quite significant because it rejected approaches to the Copyright Act's interpretation used by federal appellate courts, which ruled that a work was made for hire if an employer exercised production control, with the controlling issue being whether the author is an employee (Maggs, Soma, and Sprowl). While the Court ruled that Reid was an independent contractor, it did not further define the phrase "within the scope of employment." The Court felt that it was not clear whether the institution could, if it wished to, assert copyright ownership of books, articles, and so forth (Maggs, Soma, and Sprowl). However, the Court did rule that the institution could be a co-author, but remanded that decision and argument to a lower court for a retrial.

Kurz, an intellectual property litigation expert, states:

This traditional employer/employee relationship is to be distinguished from the relationship which arises when a party hires another as an independent contractor. The independent contractor may be specifically hired, paid and directed to perform a particular task, e.g., write computer software or create artwork. However, under the copyright laws, this situation does not necessarily give rise to a work being considered a "work made for hire." Instead (unless very specific conditions can be met), the independent contractor who created the software or artwork will be the copyright owner, rather than the party who hires the independent contractor. (9)

Kurz explains which conditions are to be considered or met that seem to favor independent contractors who do supplemental work for their institutions. He states that "there are many companies who . . . are not the copyright owners in various computer programs and other works which were created by independent contractors" and believes this could have "dire consequences should the independent contractor seek to enforce his or her copyright" (9).

In academia, several cases have upheld higher education professors' ownership of their published work: *Williams v. Weisser, Hays v. Sony*, and *Weinstein v. University of Illinois*. Other cases, such as *Colorado Foundation v. American*

Cyanamid, have not (Sinofsky, "Copyright" 13). Usually, a copyright owner's first goal is to stop the infringement (Smedinghoff). To recover monetary losses, a damage suit must be brought, incurring greater expenditure in time and money.

Copyright protection vests automatically to original works that are fixed in a tangible medium, so can an institution own the copyright to work that adjunct faculty created prior to the signing of a contract? Is this fair use? Carter says, "Work you do while moonlighting, or that is not part of your duties, is not work made for hire" (175). For example, adjuncts who create work during their schooling, and put this work on Web sites where they are exempt employees, own the copyright of the work. Such situations are now covered in the latest revision of the Digital Millennium Copyright Act (DMCA), which was enacted into law on October 28, 1998. This revision covers property rights over written material, audio recordings, and software in cyberspace. Smedinghoff states: "Only works created by the employees within the scope of their employment will be governed by the 'work made for hire' doctrine. Work done outside the normal scope of employment will not be normally covered" (147).

It makes sense, then, that adjuncts should look at their school's policies *first* concerning copyrightable material and intellectual property, understand them, and take appropriate action to protect their work. Otherwise, the old adage, "Ownership is 99 percent possession," threatens to become reality.

Suggestion Four: Thoroughly Read and Understand the U.S. Copyright Act of 1976 and Its Revisions and Request the Institution's Policies Concerning Copyright, Intellectual Property, and Fair Use

Since copyright is a form of protection provided by the laws of the United States to the authors of original materials, including literary, dramatic, musical, and other intellectual works, adjuncts should know their institution's position on both copyright and intellectual property—policies often written in faculty handbooks. These policies should be made available to all adjuncts. All institutions have their own policies favoring/not favoring employees, adjunct or otherwise; consequently, adjuncts should request these written policies in writing from the institution if they are not readily available.

After reading and understanding these institutional policies, adjuncts should understand the Copyright Act and its revisions, especially the recently passed DCMA, which addresses computer and Internet issues. Cavazos and Morin state:

Few computer communication issues have received more attention and caused more confusion than those dealing with questions of intellectual property. Copyright law . . . can seem especially difficult. Some legal issues in cyberspace require a great deal of attention because of the novel problems they present. With copyright law, however, the issues raised in cyberspace are readily addressed by well-established principles. (47)

These principles come from the act and its revisions. Usually, the policy as passed by our lawmakers and the policy at educational institutions are similar, but adjuncts should read the act or synopses of it. Excellent places to start are past issues of *Tech Trends'* copyright columns, the Electronic Frontier Foundation Intellectual Property Archive, and *Copyright Basics* (United States Copyright Office).

Adjuncts should read Title 17, United States Code, Chapters 1 through 8 to fully understand the stipulations/limitations of federal copyright law and its applicability. Adjuncts should also be aware that laws may not always favor them implicitly, especially since institutions will point out that they are exempt employees and declare that they signed "work made for hire" contracts. Adjuncts can fight this, but this should be their first warning that if they end up in litigation concerning ownership, it is going to cost a significant amount of money to retain lawyers to argue their copyright case, although monetary compensation is written within the law.

Another contested issue is fair use, a privilege that permits one other than the copyright owner to reproduce, distribute, adapt, perform, or display a work. Dalziel ("Fair Use Guidelines for Distance") states, "Due to the confusing nature of the Act with regard to distance education, many colleges and universities have very different notions of what constitutes fair use" (7). However, discussing fair use in detail is beyond the scope of this chapter. Thus, for an easy-to-understand report on fair use and recent legislative actions, see James. Dalziel also provides an overview of fair use ("Fair Use Guidelines for Educational").

Suggestion Five: Understand and Use the Copyright Symbol

Most Web site creators think that the copyright symbol and notice, if properly placed, will protect them per federal law. However, this is a misconception of the copyright notice itself. Since the United States became the eighteenth member of the Berne Convention, and Berne signatories do not require the copyright notice, Sinofsky ("Water's Not Safe") notes that this formal copyright notice is no longer required in the United States, which means that works copyrighted before March 1, 1989, require a copyright notice, and those after do not.

Although the misconceptions of protection begin here, there are fundamentals to the "copyright notice" that all Web site creators should follow, as it is still customary to attach a copyright notice on copyrighted works to be eligible for damages and to strengthen copyright claims in the event of litigation. There are four parts to a copyright notice (O'Mahoney): (1) the word "Copyright" and the symbol "©"—it helps to use both to avoid any problems in case of litigation in the United States and in foreign countries; (2) year of publication; (3) name of the copyright owner; and (4) reservation of rights, which is optional and used if you want to secure rights in Bolivia and Honduras. Thus, a full copyright notice would look like this:

Copyright © 1999 by David W. Throne. All Rights Reserved.

Suggestion Six: Register Web Site with U.S. Copyright Office

"To secure copyright protection . . . an original work must be registered with the Copyright Office" (Botterbusch 8). If adjuncts want to register their work, it is fairly simple and costs $20. An excellent self-help book is *How to Register a U.S. Copyright* by Warda, but other guides are available to walk adjuncts through the process. The fastest and easiest way is to go directly to the U.S. Copyright Office's Web site and download the forms. There are two reasons why adjuncts should pay this money and spend time filing a copyright: ability to sue and statutory damages. You cannot sue someone for infringing on your copyrighted work until you have registered your work with the U.S. Copyright Office even though copyright attaches upon fixation. Furthermore, if you register your work within three months from the date of publication or prior to the infringement date, you can collect statutory damages from the infringer; otherwise, as O'Mahoney notes, "you are stuck with actual damages, which depending upon the situation, may be only nominal."

Suggestion Seven: Understand Monetary Damages

In Chapter 5 of the Copyright Act, legal actions are spelled out succinctly to infringers of adjuncts' creative works. Statutory damages can range from $500 to $20,000 per work infringed, plus attorneys' fees, actual damages, and so forth. Court awards can run higher. If the plaintiff can prove that the infringement was committed willfully, the presiding judge may award damages up to $100,000 per infringement (Cavazos and Morin). Although Chapter 5 stipulates that employees of nonprofit educational institutions may not be liable for statutory damages if they believed that they were acting within the scope of their employment per fair use guidelines, the president of the institution and its governing body can be held responsible at least monetarily.

Infringement evidence must be collected for comparison if adjuncts copyright their Web sites with dates shown. This precedent was set in *Williams Electronic, Inc. v. Artic International, Inc.* when the Third Circuit Court noted:

There is overwhelming evidence in the present case that the [plaintiff's] computer program has been copied in some form. The following facts, among others, manifest the similarities between the [plaintiff's] program and that stored in the [defendant's] memory devices . . . other, miscellaneous evidence of copying abounds. (Quoted in Maggs, Soma, and Sprowl 147)

Adjuncts are advised to gather Web site snapshots weekly to show that the institutions were guilty of copying and using their work for profit. Adjuncts may try to sue the institution for damages within the ethical section of the act as it provides for compensable damages (lost profits). Where the infringement is blatant, punitive damages are set to the limits in the statute. Again, Congress has shown that it is willing to become even tougher on infringers with the recent passage of the DMCA. The questions raised with the passage of this revision are noteworthy to all educators and administrators: Does a higher education institution really want to put its nonexempt or tenured employees at risk for criminal charges for violating this revision? Is this ethical to employees who carry out orders from administrators who think they can interpret copyright laws? Are copyright policies made by institutions current with Congress's recent revisions of copyright laws? The following excerpt exemplifies the importance of such questions.

Traditionally, universities cared very little about copyrights as faculty mostly wrote and published in academic journals read primarily by other faculty and students conducting research, and there was little or no market value. Even the occasional text book which generated some royalties was not significant enough for the university to claim ownership. Those attitudes have drastically changed with the copyright of computer software and distance education. . . . Universities now see a new potential source of revenue. The course that will be presented over the Web, for credit, will bear the university's name and the university will have the final decision over whether the course is of sufficient quality to be placed on the Web. The university has a significant investment in its resources and a legitimate claim to ownership. . . . The faculty member has an equally strong claim for ownership as he/she has essentially created the content of the course and how it will be delivered, with little or no direct supervision from the university administration. (Kurtz "Course")

Suggestion Eight: Work with the Institution and Appeal to the President

Copyright and intellectual property questions that educators and administrators are facing today elude the existing legal provisions. What do adjuncts do if their Web sites are taken? Carter believes that there is a "disturbing poverty of ethics in the digital age" (163). To intelligently remedy copyright and intellectual ownership problems, go directly to the president of the institution and explain the facts. Sometimes these leaders are not fully attuned to the situation. Badaracco and Ellsworth state, "A leader must be exemplar to the organization, demanding the highest standards of integrity, and be doggedly consistent in word and deed in all matters affecting the company's values" (174). If leaders are not aware of unethical conduct such as copyright violations on Web sites, who is to blame for distance education programs that take adjuncts' copyrighted works? Can it be the dean of instruction, the distance education coordinator, or teachers? The task is to find the administrative level that can fairly resolve the issue. In a study done by Grace, the results clearly indicate that the majority of media directors across the United States do not have proficient knowledge of copyright law and related guidelines.

Leaders at institutions should want to avoid litigation. As Mills and Paul note: "A total quality programmme must start at the top. It must be more than the latest device to motivate staff to provide better service, but a fundamental value which is both espoused and exemplified by senior management" (117). Adjuncts should talk with the highest authorities at institutions and relate their concerns before starting litigation. Show these leaders the problems in the hope that they have integrity.

FINAL THOUGHTS

Ely states, "Advocacy for the use of educational technology has increased among policy groups" (25). He points out that the National Education Administration believes "training should be provided for educating employees in the use of technologies and their applications," including an understanding of copyright laws (28). Other authors have advocated these same thoughts and carried them to logical fruition. Talab says, "In a capitalistic society, it is necessary to maintain the concept of individual intellectual property . . . campuses should explore ways for faculty to retain rights to texts and images created by professors for use in classroom multimedia programs" (9).

Adjuncts may be declared independent contractors in the courts, although this depends, of course, on the nature of the contract they sign. What they have creatively produced for any higher education institution is owned by them, including the copyright, wholly or partially. Consequently, higher education institutions should seek adjuncts' permission to use these materials if adjuncts leave or are terminated. Institutional administrators should take responsibility to see that copyright concerns are current, proper, and follow federal law. They should make sure distance education policies are thoroughly intact before giving employees permission to develop sites and should make sure ownership policies are included on all contracts. They should also provide educational opportunities such as in-service meetings for their community of distance education administrators/educators to help them understand the institution's copyright policies.

Essential administrative personnel in distance education programs should also maintain high ethical standards concerning original author's ownership and keep current with the Copyright Act and its revisions. Willis states:

Effective distance education administrators are more than idea people. They are consensus builders, decision-makers, and facilitators. They maintain control of technical managers, ensuring that technological resources are effectively deployed to further the institution's academic mission. At the same time, they lead and inspire faculty and staff in overcoming obstacles that arise. (34)

Some people emphasize the importance of Web site and on-line ethics and point out that communities (or higher education institutions) with solid ethical standards work better and should not have to lean on legal standards (Carter).

Why would employees who worked for many years want to sue schools where they grew as educators? Why would institutional presidents risk litigation? In short, administrators should provide the modeling behavior that demonstrates integrity and trust to their students (Chase).

Stansbury states: "The future of distance learning is in the balance—the copyright balance. With distance learning guidelines, we can: balance an author's rights; provide access for teaching and learning; establish clarity for financial ambiguities; institute multiple use options; instill trust; and acknowledge ethical concerns" (11). However, if copyrights are to work in the era of digitization, Carter believes that ethical consideration will have to be woven into the Internet. Institutional presidents will have to make ethical choices. Quality distance learning programs start at the top. All administrators and employees should be held accountable for their jobs and responsibilities to make these programs successful.

NOTE

The contents of this chapter do not represent legal advice.

WORKS CITED

Association for Educational Communications and Technology. *Code of Ethics.* 1 Aug. 1999 <http://204.252.76.75:80/About AECT/Ethics.html>.

Badaracco, Joseph, and Richard Ellsworth. *Leadership and the Quest for Integrity.* Boston: Harvard Business School Press, 1989.

Botterbusch, Hope. "More Copyright Q&A." *Tech Trends* 41.2 (1996): 8.

Carter, Mary. *Electronic Highway Robbery: An Artist's Guide to Copyrights in the Digital Era.* Berkeley, CA: Peachpit Press, 1996.

Cavazos, Edward, and Gavino Morin. *Cyberspace and the Law: Your Rights and Duties in the On-line World.* Cambridge, MA: MIT Press, 1994.

Chase, Mark E. "An Evaluation of the Interpretation of the Fair-Use Doctrine with Respect to Videotaping in Pennsylvania State System of Higher Education and Selected State Related Schools." Master's thesis, Slippery Rock University, 1989.

Colorado Community College and Occupational Educational System. *Administration of Personnel.* 14 Dec. 1995. 1 Aug. 1999 <http://www.cccoes.edu/cccoes/SBCCOE/policies/bp3–10.htm>.

———. *Copyrights and Patents.* 16 May 1991. 1 Aug. 1999<http://www.cccoes.edu/cccoes/SBCCOE/policies/bp3–90.htm>.

Colorado Foundation v. American Cyanamid. 974 Federal Supplement 1339. Colorado District 1995.

Community for Creative Non-Violence (CCNV) v. Reid. 490 U.S. Reports 730. 1989.

Copyright Act of 1976. 17 U.S.C.A. Section 101–810. 1976.

Copyright Management Center. *Distance Education.* Indiana University-Purdue University Indianapolis Copyright Management Center. 1 Aug. 1999 <http://www.iupui.edu/~copyinfo/disted.html>.

Cyrs, Thomas E. *Teaching at a Distance with the Merging Technologies: An Instruc-*

tional Systems Approach. Las Cruces, NM: New Mexico State University, Center for Educational Development, 1996.

Dalziel, Chris. "Fair Use Guidelines for Distance Education." *Tech Trends* 40.5 (1995): 6–8.

———. "Fair Use Guidelines for Educational Multimedia." 1998. 1 Aug. 1999 <http://www.libraries.psu.edu/mtss/fairuse/dalziel.html>.

Digital Millennium Copyright Act (DMCA) of 1998. H.R. 2281 P.L. No. 105–304, 112 Statute 2860. Oct. 28, 1998.

Distance Education Online Symposium. Listserv. 1 Aug. 1999 <LISTSERV@LISTS. PSU.EDU; SUBSCRIBE DEOSNEWS Your Full Name>.

Electronic Frontier Foundation Intellectual Property Archive. Home page. 1 Aug. 1999 <http://www.eff.org/pub/Intellectual_property/cni_copyright_act_1976>.

Ely, Donald P. *Trends in Educational Technology*. Syracuse, NY: Syracuse University, Informational Resources Publications, 1996.

Grace, Mark. "An Analysis of the Knowledge of Media Directors Concerning Relevant Copyright Issues in Education." ERIC Document Reproduction Service No. ED 383 290, 1995.

Hays v. Sony Corp. of America. 847 Federal Report F2d 412, 416. 7th Circuit 1988.

Indiana University Online Copyright Tutorial. Listserv. 1 Aug. 1999 <listserv@http://www.iupui.edu/it/copyinfo/Online_Tutorial.html>.

James, Ferrel. "Understanding Fair Use and Fair Use Guidelines." *Tech Trends* 42.6 (1997): 11–13.

Kaplin, William A., and Barbara A. Lee. *The Law of Higher Education*. San Francisco: Jossey-Bass, 1995.

Kurtz, Cary. "Course Ownership." Online listserv posting. *DEOS-L@lists.psu.edu*. 10 Mar. 1998.

———. "Intellectual Rights." Online listserv posting. *DEOS-L@lists.pus.edu*. 17 Apr. 1998.

Kurz, Raymond. *Internet and the Law: Legal Fundamentals for the Internet User*. Rockville, MD: Government Institutes, 1996.

Maggs, Peter, John T. Soma, and James A. Sprowl. *Computer Law: Cases—Comments— Questions*. St. Paul, MN: West Publishing, 1992.

Mills, R., and R. Paul. "Putting the Student First: Management for Quality in Distance Education." In *Reforming Open and Distance Education: Critical Reflections from Practice*. Ed. Terry Evans and Daryl Nation. New York: St. Martin's Press, 1995. 113–29.

O'Mahoney, Benedict. *The Copyright Website*. 1999. 1 Aug. 1999 <http://www.benedict.com/basic/register/register.htm>.

Sinofsky, Esther. "Copyright and You." *Tech Trends* 42.4 (1997): 9–10.

———. "Copyright: The Water's Not Safe Yet." *Tech Trends* 40.6 (1995): 12–14.

Smedinghoff, Thomas J., ed. *Online Law: The SPA's Legal Guide to Doing Business on the Internet*. Reading, MA: Addison-Wesley Developers Press, 1996.

Stansbury, Ray. "Copyright and Distance Learning: A Balancing Act." *Tech Trends* 41.6 (1996): 9–11.

Talab, Rosemary. "Copyright and Multimedia, Part Two: Higher Education." *Tech Trends* 40.1 (1995): 8–10.

United States Copyright Office. *Copyright Basics*. 1 Aug. 1999 <http://lcweb.loc.gov/copyright/>.

United States Copyright Office. Home page. 1 Aug. 1999 <http://lcweb.loc.gov/copy
    right/>.

University of Northern Colorado, Board of Trustees. *3.0 Chapter 3: Faculty.* 19 Dec.
    1997. 1 Aug. 1999 <http://www.unco.edu/trustees/chptr3.htm>.

Warda, Mark. *How to Register a U.S. Copyright.* Clearwater, FL: Sphinx Publishing,
    1995.

Weinstein v. University of Illinois. 811 Federal Report F2d 1091. 7th Circuit 1987.

Williams Electronic, Inc. v. Artic International, Inc. 685 Federal Report F2d, pp. 870,
    876. 3rd Circuit 1982.

Willis, Barry. *Distance Education: A Practical Guide.* Englewood Cliffs, NJ: Educational
    Technology, 1993.

Chapter 18

Using the Web in Live Lectures: Examples and Issues

Graeme Lang

INTRODUCTION

Will Web-based courses replace lectures? Will the Web replace the library? Will lecture halls be converted into multiple workstations? Will professors and teachers become educational technicians? Yes, inevitably. But teachers are also integrating the Web into more traditional classroom teaching. The results are exciting.

Lectures will not become obsolete. In fact, the Web can be used to make live lectures more lively in the new high-tech "master classrooms" (Hannah). The Web can also be used during live lectures to help instructors demonstrate critical exploration and inquiry. In this chapter, I offer some examples of such uses of the Web and analyze issues raised by use of the Web in lectures.

WHY LECTURES?

What is different about using the Web in a live lecture, as compared to putting the Web links into lecture notes on a course Web site? I do not want to go into an extensive defense of lecturing here, since that is not the purpose of this chapter. But it is important to indicate how a lecture using Web material can be different, and better, than merely putting the links and some comments on a course Web page. I would like to discuss some techniques in using Web pages in lectures.

First, *the challenging question*. Nothing rivets the attention of a class quicker than presenting some striking graph or picture or table or finding, and then asking them a question that they should be able to answer *if* they are clever. University students all think they are clever. This presents an irresistible challenge to any group of students. Even those who believe that they "know it all" become focused and thoughtful. This technique, of course, can work in any lecture, but it seems to be particularly effective with Web-based material because the material has already attracted their attention, and seems to be clear. But— says the lecturer—it is not as clear as it seems. This is not "show and tell," but "show and challenge." I will provide some examples below.

Second, the lecturer can create *competitive problem-oriented attention* among students, which cannot easily be evoked through a course Web site. When students are challenged by the lecturer's question, they are aware of whether others in the class have found the answer (hands up, or knowing smiles and nods). The pressure is on. They think harder, and feel chagrined if someone finds an answer that they had missed. This "intensity" is one of the elements of a successful lecture that can be cultivated by many methods, but which can be enhanced through use of graphical Web material in focusing their attention and posing the problem. Of course, no lecturer can create this kind of challenge continuously throughout a lecture. But doing so at least three or four times in an hour, with the requisite build-up and space for silence while they reflect, is sufficient to create the right atmosphere for the lecture.

Third, the lecturer can demonstrate the process of inquiry, exploration, and surprise, using a selection of Web sites as illustrations. The lecturer is not merely pointing to available resources (which can be done through a course Web page). The lecturer is not merely saying, these are the important Web sites for relevant information. The lecturer is saying, *if* you want to explore this topic, *here are several interesting recent sites: let's explore them together*. The lecturer can show poor as well as good sites for particular topics, provide lively critical commentary while exploring partisan sites, and amuse the students with the praise or criticism that each site may deserve.

Of course, students should also be challenged to find partisanship or bias in the lecturer's assessment of each site. For example, the lecturer could appear to accept the material at a partisan site without critical evaluation, and then ask why students did not notice the lack of critical evaluation. Or the lecturer could ask the students to offer critical assessments of the site, and then proceed to such an assessment if the students do not see any problems with the material. This kind of exercise may require jumping back and forth in a site, and between sites, and would be much more difficult to do by simply putting links and comments into a course Web page, where the links are optional and the comments can be ignored. In the lecture, however, I can lead students through a sequence that I control, and yet still give them a vivid experience in critical exploration. To illustrate, I offer some examples from my courses on Science,

Technology, and Society (taught to about 200 students each year) and from another course on Selected Southeast Asian Societies.

POLITICS AND THE WEB

When discussing political uses of the Internet, I try to get the students to think about possibilities, not just current political uses. During elections, citizens could use the Web to pursue information about the backgrounds and legislative records of candidates, which would be much more difficult for most citizens to uncover otherwise. Political parties or candidates contesting elections place some of this kind of material on the Web. It is particularly interesting for many students to see what is happening in other societies that are now experimenting with democracy, or have recently experienced political upheavals. In my course on Southeast Asian Societies, in 1999, we were discussing the political changes in Indonesia after the forced resignation of General Soeharto. To get closer to these parties during the lecture, we go to the Web sites of some Indonesian political parties and their leaders.

One site was operated by supporters of Megawati Soekarnoputri, the daugher of Indonesia's first president, and a candidate in the June 1999 elections (*Megawati for President*). The site lists the main goals of her party, and switches the page regularly between Indonesian and English versions of the text. Students can see the Indonesian terms for her party's principles—*Pancasila, Demokrasi, Nasionlisme*, and *Hak Asasi*—and they discover, when the page switches to the English version, that the latter term is translated as "Human Rights." The page provides pictures of Megawati, texts of her speeches, and political comments. Thus, in the lecture we "drop in" on an election campaign in a distant country and look at local imagery and symbols. The lecturer has much to explain. What is *pancasila*? (Indonesian government sites are used to explain this term.) Why is Soekarno's daughter running for president? Why does Megawati's site switch periodically between English and Indonesian, while the sites of other parties do not? This last question prompts further discussion about the world press and international institutions, and their importance for some Indonesian politicians.

Whatever Indonesian sites are visited (and we can do the same exercise for most other countries in the region during elections), the effect of using a major candidate's Web site is to add immediacy and a feeling of "being there" to discussions of the political affairs of that country. However, this kind of material is not so accessible or interesting outside of election years. For another political use of the Internet, I illustrate with the example of sites that provide a point of access for citizens to government leaders, to ask questions, express opinions, and seek information.

E-mail access through a government Web site is a recent development. One possible benefit of using e-mail rather than writing letters to politicians is that e-mail messages can be much more easily categorized and processed using a filtering and categorizing system. Potentially, it could be an important method of interacting with citizens in the future in many societies. Should Hong Kong have such a system? What about other cities in China?

To focus students' attention on this question and give them a concrete example, I bring up the White House Web page (United States Government), which includes a facility for sending e-mail messages to the president or the vice-president. I ask the students how the system might work, how students think such messages would be processed (for example, messages agreeing or disagreeing with a policy), and so on. Then I show them the response-options provided in the e-mail form. For example, the form asks, "What is your purpose or reason for writing this message?" Clickable options include: ask a question about Administration policy, express agreement, express disagreement, ask for assistance from the White House, extend an invitation to visit or speak, offer neutral commentary or advice, and so on. The question "What is the general topic domain of your message?" provides options such as education, energy, environment, foreign affairs, and so on. The form also includes the question "In what capacity are you writing to the White House?" with options such as civil servant or armed forces member, foreign citizen, political advocate, private citizen, professional, young person (under 18 years of age). These categories provide some clues to the criteria used in processing messages.

I also display for the students (from a file on a floppy disk) the "autoresponder" message that comes back from the White House, acknowledging receipt of the message. It begins, "Dear friend, thank you for writing to Vice-President Gore. . . . Although the volume of mail prevents the Vice-President from personally reviewing each message, be assured that your concerns, ideas, and suggestions have been read carefully, and a detailed report of the mail is provided to the Vice-President on a regular basis."

After one class, a student came up to me and said that she had already tried the Hong Kong government's Web site and found no such facility, but thought we should have something like it in Hong Kong. She departed thinking about the possibilities and problems. I have observed that Hong Kong students pay keen attention to this demonstration. It appears to be a vivid experience for them to see the site on-screen, along with the e-mail form at the site. I ask them, "Well, shall we send a message to the White House?" They laugh, but they are intrigued.

The next step is important, and would be equally valuable for students in the United States or overseas: ask the students to discuss the uses and problems with this kind of system. Students can try to construct a method for the processing of such e-mail messages, the representativeness of this method of getting feedback from citizens, the categories used to classify respondents (Are they fair? What do they tell us about the way messages are processed?), possible abuses of the system, potential legal issues, and so on. Students can pursue these issues in a term paper, in a tutorial, or in the classroom. They can also be asked to imagine what this system might look like in five or ten years. In short, this demonstration provides a vivid and immediate "real-life" experience during a lecture that can be used to stimulate further reflection and analysis.

Of course, this demonstration could also be used as an exercise, with the appropriate Web links, in Web-based courses on politics, science and technology, or communications studies. However, it is more efficient and less bandwidth-intensive for me to demonstrate the sites in a class, rather than ask 160 students to explore the sites separately. The analysis of the issues raised by these sites, and the search for comparable sites in other countries, remains as a task for later work and discussions among those students who wish to pursue such topics for assignments or tutorial presentations.

As the Internet is increasingly used for political purposes such as discussion forums, activist organizing and collective action, and interest-group information sharing, the number of sites that could be used in lectures on technology and politics will proliferate. Lecturers will make use of the growing literature on such uses of the Internet to provide material for classroom discussions and assignments (e.g., Hill and Hughes; Tsagarousianou, Tambini, and Bryan). Some of the research results from these publications can be presented using transparencies or scanned images of tables and graphs (see, for example, Hill and Hughes). Thus, the lecturer can alternate between visiting and exploring sites, and presenting some of the academic research on such sites using more traditional methods.

HEALTH CARE AND THE INTERNET

Vivid examples from the Web are excellent for starting a discussion in a lecture. For teaching about the potential medical uses of the Internet, a good case study for which a large amount of documentation is available on-line involves the Beijing university student Zhu Ling, who fell into a coma in 1995. After the Beijing doctors were unable to diagnose the cause of her condition, two of her friends sent out a now famous appeal for help over the Internet, accompanied by a description of her symptoms and the treatments attempted by her doctors. A Chinese graduate student at UCLA picked up the appeal for help and posted it to various medical discussion groups. A large number of scientists and specialists around the world sent back the same provisional diagnosis, which was passed along to her friends in Beijing, and which turned out to be correct (thallium poisoning). The Internet response led to treatments that saved her life. The case is chronicled at a UCLA "telemedicine" Web site devoted to it (UCLA Telemedicine). The site includes a list of some of the scientists and doctors in various countries who provided the correct diagnosis. Also included are pictures of Zhu Ling before she became ill, CAT scans, X-rays, other medical data from her treatment, and pictures of Zhu Ling convalescing, along with a letter from her mother thanking the overseas researchers who had helped her daughter. This case, with its poignant pictures, international rescue, and vivid on-line medical imagery, is intensely interesting for students in Hong Kong.

The lecturer, however, can raise questions which are *not* answered by the material at the site: Why did so many doctors, researchers, and scientists overseas take time from their busy lives to provide a medical diagnosis for a sick student in a distant country? (This is my first "challenging question" to students when I present this case, and the answers are not self-evident.) What does this case tell us about some of the uses and functions of the Internet, and about online specialist discussion groups? What are the possibilities and constraints for this kind of international medical consultation in the future? What arrangements could be worked out with developing countries to take advantage of some of these possibilities? What legal and ethical issues are raised by such cases? In short, this striking case and its graphic on-line images can provide an intense focus for students during a lecture, from which to expand into a critical analysis and exploration of the issues. More in-depth analysis of uses of the Internet in healthcare systems is of course important for further reading and assignments (e.g., Nicholson), but use of such a case in the lecture provides an excellent introduction. I expect that there will be many such on-line cases in the future, and that lecturers will use them to explore many different kinds of issues.

ENVIRONMENT AND THE WEB

For teaching about the environment, the Web provides rich and vivid resources that cannot be matched by library-based material. For live lectures, there are some exceptional graphs and images. However, it is necessary to use this material critically, and to present it along with challenging questions.

For example, when discussing global warming and various projections into the middle of the twenty-first century, I use a site from the United Kingdom's Hadley Centre that includes images of the earth at ten-year intervals from the early twentieth to the mid-twenty-first century, with colors changing each decade to show estimated warming or cooling at various latitudes (Hadley Centre). The warming areas are shown in orange and red, while the cooling regions are shown in blue. It is very dramatic for students to see the world grow steadily more orange through the late twentieth century, and increasingly redder through the first half of the twenty-first century. My guess is that the images are intended to be shocking.

However, the series of images uses real data only up to the 1990s. Thereafter, the images are derived from projections. The students must then be challenged to think about the reasons why such projections may be inaccurate. What about the possible feedback effects resulting from human responses to these trends? What about climatic feedback effects, which are not yet well understood? Why does the Web site that contains these images not include some analysis of the problems with such projections? And why does the series use such shocking red colors for temperature increases of a couple of degrees? Is this propaganda? If so, is such propaganda justified?

The images are exceptionally useful in focusing students' attention on the apparent global warming trends (I admit that I use them to shock the students). But the images are also useful for starting discussion of issues that would immediately be raised by scientists aware of the problems with such projections. One must be reasonably well informed about these issues. So, it is valuable to make the students think about apparent trends in human-forced global climate change, but it is important to demonstrate a critical perspective about such projections and to emphasize their provisional nature. Some research both on and off the Web is necessary to do this with confidence. For teachers who have already done some of the research, the graphic images available for lectures are very good, and are likely to be astoundingly good in the future.

THE USES OF PARTISAN SITES

Teachers and researchers use the Web selectively, seeking useful data from universities and research institutions, assisted by both print and Web directories (Butler). However, good teachers may use material from a range of sites outside of the universities in covering various kinds of topics. To explore the resources on the Web intelligently, it is useful to conceptualize it. A "conceptual map" of the Web will help students and teachers assess Web-based resources and take an appropriately critical approach to material on these sites. I am not referring to a map of the categories used by "Web-masters" to organize sites, although analysis of these categories is also important (Blau), but rather to a conceptualization of the types of sites found on the Web on the basis of the resources, interests, and motives that underlie them.

The Internet originally reflected a small proportion of society: highly educated scientists, programmers, and engineers in the universities. Internet sites gained credibility from their locations in universities. Now, the Internet reflects virtually all aspects of industrial and postindustrial societies. Nearly every interest and activity can be found on the Web. Thus, in addition to universities and research institutes, the Web now also includes sites operated by governments and nongovernmental organizations, ruling political parties and opposition groups, partisan and nonpartisan associations, companies and consumer groups, religious cults and anti-cult groups, and innumerable individuals.

Some education packages now include Web-based assignments and exercises that go beyond the university sites for material. Some of these exercises, however, do not include critical attention to the nature of the sites included in the exercises.

For example, a sociology text now in its sixth edition includes Web-based assignments on environmental issues that require students to go to the environmental sites of an organization that argues for a free-market approach to most issues, including protecting the environment (*Competitive Enterprise Institute*). The text, however, does not identify the organization as a conservative free-enterprise institute funded substantially by corporations and dedicated to minimal government regulation. The environmental arguments at the site are certainly within the realm of respectable public debate. However, the text appears to take an uncritical approach to the material and does not ask students to think about the ideological links or agenda of the site's sponsors. A more analytical approach would help students develop a critical perspective on such material, while still making use of the site to promote debate on environmental issues.

Highly partisan sites can include very useful information. For example, in discussing computer crime and "hacking" in lectures to computer studies students, I refer to the case of the famous/infamous hacker Kevin Mitnick (who is mentioned briefly in the course text). There is a Web site set up by his supporters that is devoted to his legal tribulations and to criticisms of the government's treatment of his case (*Free Kevin*). Although the site is highly partisan (with banners such as "click here to see how to add a Free Kevin clock to your website"), it also includes a repository of scanned legal documents from his court cases. This material provides extensive documentation of his crimes, and a walk through the documents in the lecture overwhelmingly illustrates how much he has cost the system in investigations and trials. For computer science students who may be tempted to admire the man, the site is sobering. Thus, a partisan site, carefully explored, provides useful information even for those critical of some of the positions of the site's creators. This example is not intended to suggest that all partisan sites contain such material, but only that sites do not need to be resolutely nonpartisan, or to derive credibility from a university affiliation, in order to be usable for teaching purposes.

One way to promote a more critical analysis is to clarify the particular biases of sites by finding out about the creators of the site and their sponsors. In Web sites set up by corporations to market products or report results, the interests or bias of the sponsor are obvious, and can become the basis for critical classroom analysis in marketing or business courses (Phillips and Horton). Critical analysis of such sites, published in journals for educators (e.g., Amernic), will feed back into teaching.

In other kinds of sites, such as those set up by institutes, non-governmental organizations (NGOs), and political or scientific organizations, the biases may not be so transparent. A good Web site should include information about the institutional affiliations and backgrounds of the creators of the site, their partisan interests (if these are not obvious), and their sponsors. Many sites include such material, along with links to the organization's home page and to sponsoring organizations. It can be very interesting to pursue these links. The lecturer should do this before using a site in a lecture, to ensure that there are no surprises (for the lecturer) during the class.

Another way to assess sites would be to classify them according to the sources of their information. Can the information be checked through independent sites or sources that have high credibility? If the site reports scientific conclusions, how much of the material is supported by or cites independent and publicly available research carried out by other scholars or researchers?

CLASSIFYING AND RATING WEB SITES

It would be useful to classify or rate sites on the basis of the origins and reliability of the information, as an aid to critical analysis. What would such a conceptualization look like? Some educational packages that use Web-based exercises have already begun to classify sites. An example is the WebQuester system available from McGraw-Hill, which classifies Web sites included in its exercises as

- Scientific/Academic: the site is research oriented; it may use references and citations. The sponsor of the site is a university or governmental agency.
- Promotional: the site was established to promote a non-profit organization.
- Commercial: the site exists as advertising for a commercial enterprise yet may have information pertinent to topics in the social sciences. (McGraw-Hill)

The merit of this type of system is that it alerts students that there are indeed different types of sites, and that these differences in sponsorship may be important for an understanding of the material at the sites. The disadvantage is that the categories are crude, and do not provide much help in taking a critical approach to the material at any particular site.

RATING SCIENCE-RELATED SITES

The importance of assessing the information on science-related sites is widely recognized. One method is regular site-reviews by credible reviewers. Such a review function will become increasingly important for both scientists and educators. We are still in the early stages of the development of this function. Books on the Web for scientists or science students often include brief reviews of relevant Web resources (e.g., O'Donnell and Winger; Leshin), but the focus is usually on recommended sites that can be used without much critical reflection. However, many sites involve the partisan uses of science, and these require more careful treatment. Since scientific work and relevant Web sites must be updated, reviews in books may become obsolete rather quickly. Critical and continually updated reviews are just beginning to appear.

A current example of an early form of "Web-review" appears in *Science*, the journal of the American Association for the Advancement of Science. The journal includes a regular feature, "Netwatch," which highlights science-related sites. In a recent issue, the column reviewed two pollution-information sites, one of which was judged to be credible, while the other was considered dubious, at least by some authorities. The more credible site, called "Scorecard," provides data on pollutants for cities and towns in the United States. It is clearly intended to support environmental activism, with search-features such as "enter your zip [residential area code] and find out what pollutants are being released into your community, and who is responsible." Although the data were considered credible by a scientist contacted by *Science*, the reviewer noted that the site did not necessarily provide sufficient context to allow nonscientists to evaluate the extent of risk. Hence, such sites require careful use in lectures. The information and graphics are valuable, but some knowledge and experience are required to provide a critical perspective on the meaning of the data at the site. A critical perspective is *not* provided within the site itself. The lecturer can use the site to illustrate the data available on pollution, and to show the environmental activism of scientists and organizations. At the same time, the lecturer can model critical analysis of such material and such sites. For critical thinking, the modeling is as important as the data.

CONCLUSIONS: THE FUTURE OF LIVE LECTURES

Live lectures can make good use of the Web to enhance a lecture with vivid images and to engage in exploration and critical inquiry that can be exciting for both the lecturer and the students. The experience cannot be duplicated by course Web pages or in archived on-line lectures. In short, the Web will not replace lectures, but instead will invigorate them.

In the future, I expect that there will be increasing resources available for educators who use the Web in this way. In the realm of software and Web-based sources, I expect to see the development of programs for using the Web in lectures (current Web browsers are not ideal for this purpose), search engines that include indexes of reliable sites for educators and students, and expanding permanent archives of indexed material that is useful for educational purposes and that has been saved from sites that may be less permanent. At the same time, there will be a rapid growth in the critical analysis of Web-based material in journals both on and off the Web. Use of the Web in lectures will grow with the expansion of these kinds of resources.

Hardware developments may eventually allow live lectures to migrate onto Web sites, and may yet make some live lectures unnecessary. High bandwidth connections, compression, and faster computers may eventually allow high-quality streaming videos of lectures to students in some remote locations, along with the lecturer's use of Web sites for illustrations. However, as of 1999 we are not even close to affordable methods of providing TV-quality lectures through the Internet (Owen).

Even if the technological problems could be solved, most lectures would still have to be rerecorded periodically because of the rapid development of knowledge and the frequent changes in the Web world. Most teachers will only put printed material, graphics, assignments, and interactive facilities on their course Web sites. Students will still attend live classes for the challenging questions, the critical explorations, and the intellectual visions that can be generated, most vividly, by teachers who really know how to make students sit up and think.

WORKS CITED

Amernic, Joel H. " 'Close Readings' of Internet Corporate Financial Reporting: Towards a More Critical Pedagogy on the Information Highway." *The Internet and Higher Education* 1.2 (1998): 87–114.

Blau, Judith R. "Classifying Books and Knowledge—In the Stores and on the Web." *Contemporary Sociology: A Journal of Reviews* 28.2 (1999): 138–41.

Butler, John A. *CyberSearch: Research Techniques in the Electronic Age*. New York: Penguin, 1998.

Competitive Enterprise Institute. Home page. 1 Aug. 1999 <http://www.cei.org/>.

Free Kevin. Home page. 1 Aug. 1999 <http://www.kevinmitnick.com/home.html>.

Hadley Centre. *Research and Development*. The Met Office. 1 Aug. 1999 <http://www.meto.gov.uk/sec5/CR_div/ImgGlbl0/sul.html>.

Hannah, Richard L. "Merging the Intellectual and Technical Infrastructures in Higher Education: The Internet Example." *The Internet and Higher Education* 1.1 (1998): 7–20.

Hill, Kevin A., and John E. Hughes. *Cyberpolitics: Citizen Activism in the Age of the Internet*. New York: Rowman and Littlefield, 1998.

Leshin, Cynthia B. *Internet Investigations in Environmental Technology*. Upper Saddle River, NJ: Prentice-Hall, 1997.

McGraw-Hill. *WebQuester*. 1 Aug. 1999 <http://www.dushkin.com/webquester/>.

Megawati for President. Home page. 1 Aug. 1999 <http:/megawati.forpresident.com>.

"Netwatch." *Science*, 284 (1999): 551.

Nicholson, Louis, ed. *The Internet and Healthcare*. Chicago: Health Administration Press, 1997.

O'Donnell, Kevin, and Larry Winger. *The Internet for Scientists*. Amsterdam: Harwood Academic Publishers, 1997.

Owen, Bruce M. *The Internet Challenge to Television*. Cambridge, MA: Harvard University Press, 1999.

Phillips, Melodie R., and Veronica Horton. "Incorporating the Internet into the Marketing Classroom: Problems, Opportunities and Thoughts." *The Internet and Higher Education* 1.3 (1998): 223–30.

Tsagarousianou, Roza, Damian Tambini, and Cathy Bryan. *Cyberdemocracy: Technology, Cities, and Civic Networks*. London: Routledge, 1998.

UCLA Telemedicine. *The First Large-Scale International Telemedicine Trial to China: Zhu Ling's Case*. 1 Aug. 1999 <htttp://www.radsci.ucla.edu/telemed/zhuling/>.

United States Government. *Welcome to the Whitehouse*. 1 Aug. 1999 <http://www.whitehouse.gov/>.

Chapter 19

Untangling the Web: Developing Web-Enhanced Instruction for Political Science

Donald L. Goff

OVERVIEW

Hardly anyone is unaware of the effect the Internet is having in the classroom. The proliferation of cheap access, the ease of use, and the value of global information sources make the Internet an appealing medium for instruction. Advocates have promised much for it, but little actual research has been done to determine whether its use is proving beneficial at the classroom and individual user level. Enough experience is being gained to try to benchmark these early efforts, identify some lessons learned, determine user preferences, and support the migration of successful approaches to a less technical group of users. This chapter reports on a study of Web-enhanced instruction in support of traditional classes and its implications for courses in government, public affairs, and political science, for which information technology is a secondary learning area, the practitioner likely a hobbyist, and the instructor having little or no formal training or experience.

The pedagogical reasons for using Web technologies in support of classroom teaching seem obvious. Extending the class beyond its scheduled hours, facilitating communication between and among teacher and students, making supplemental materials available, collaboration among students on projects, and better time use are some of the obvious pedagogical objectives. The specific technological features of the Internet that support these objectives include e-mail, Web sites, chat rooms, collaborative computing, and file transfers. Use by faculty may take the form of posting syllabi and readings on a Web page, using e-mail and list serves to communicate with students outside of class, or posting assignments or tests by e-mail or on a Web site. Use by students may include communication with faculty or classmates by e-mail or chat, conducting research, reading posted documents, posting completed assignments, or collaborating on group documents.

For the past two years, I have used a proprietary Web-based instructional platform created by the University of Maryland University College (UMUC) to support teaching in the adult master's programs in information technology. My experience suggests a great deal of detail about the opportunities and risks associated with Web-enhanced instruction and, more important, a few things about how to manage the medium. Currently, I am attempting to migrate the best practices from that experience to the political science and government program at American University (AU). The results of a student survey conducted in December 1998 with the UMUC students are providing the focus for specific technologies, techniques, and services for the AU government classes.

STUDENT PREFERENCES

UMUC uses a proprietary platform known as Webtycho for Web-based and Web-enhanced instruction. This platform combines several electronic features, including e-mail, collaborative workspace, a chat room, and stored documents in one location accessible by students and instructors. This platform is on a Lotus Domino server. While the platform itself is proprietary, the features it contains should be readily available to any instructor seeking to use the World Wide Web or Internet to support the classroom.

Webtycho was developed over a period of years for use as a distance learning tool. Its primary use is for conducting courses taught completely on-line. Such courses are often called "Web-based instruction" in the instructional technology literature. Many of Webtycho's features, however, work in support of traditional classroom teaching. When Web-based methods are used in this support role for a traditional standup class, the term "Web-enhanced instruction" is more appropriate. The two terms will be so used throughout this chapter.

Webtycho's useful tools include space to post

- the syllabus
- the university's writing and grading standards
- the course outline
- the professor's resume
- required readings (once appropriate copyright clearances have been obtained through library services)

Other features include the following:

- connection to the Help Desk
- a roster of student e-mail addresses, which students must post and maintain
- an area for posting class announcements
- an area for posting assignments
- an area for submitting assignments
- a chat room
- an area for collaborative writing and asynchronous communication

The platform is password protected so only students and faculty registered for the course may see items placed on the site. Further, the faculty member may create secure workspaces for a subset of students, as, for example, in a group project, where other students may not see the filings. Students are also denied access to other students' work posted in the assignment section. The faculty member may, however, access all parts of the site.

Early impressions from casual conversation with students suggested that this platform provided a useful set of tools for them and facilitated communication and learning, was easy to use, and added significant value to the course. Students commuting a long distance to the class or stymied by evening rush hour traffic particularly seemed to like Web-enhanced classes, especially when the Web enhancement was conducted in lieu of a physical meeting.

However, a careful survey and further evidence reveal that a significant number of students harbor a reluctance to place too great a reliance on Web enhancement, do not use the available technology to its limits, and do not place a great value on its use. This was particularly surprising in light of the fact that they were in courses in computer systems and telecommunications management—the very disciplines that had spawned the Internet itself—and that most of the students are practicing adult professionals in information technology.

Students at UMUC are generally adults in the work force, with a median age of 36, and a great deal of diversity. A large percentage of them are employed as computer systems or telecommunication systems engineers for the federal government. A larger percentage work for information technology vendors and support contractors. Overall, they use information technology daily and are facile in its use; few, if any, are technophobes or computer illiterate. Before they came to these Web-enhanced classes, they had completed, on average, 27 hours of graduate work (nine or more classes) in information resource management, software development, telecommunications, Web commerce, and other technical courses.

Since September 1998, all students enrolling at UMUC have been required to have Internet access. The university uses the Internet to support a variety of administrative functions, including registration, snow closing and emergency announcements, billing inquiries, and so on. Each student is responsible for maintaining current e-mail information in the university database; this process, too, is Internet-accessible. In short, these students are highly technical, experienced, and facile at using the Internet.

In December 1998, survey questions were sent on-line to 143 students who had used the Web-enhanced format. In April 1999, this survey was replicated with an additional 43 students with no measurable statistical differences. Three messages were returned as undeliverable; 78 students completed all or part of the questionnaire, for a response rate of 56 percent, very high for survey research. Questions were designed to solicit students' preference and availability of various software capabilities, use of the features built into Webtycho, an evaluation of specific features, and an evaluation of the platform overall. In addition, questions were asked testing the students' experience with hypertext markup language (HTML) and Web site creation for a quick test of their experience with the Web itself, other than for e-mail use.

About one-third of the students completed their on-line assignments from home; nearly two-thirds did so at both home and the office, while only six (8 percent) depended upon their employers for computer access to the World Wide Web. A general discussion in class had previously revealed that no student was denied access to the Internet for educational purposes under his or her employer's acceptable use policy.

IBM compatible personal computers (PCs) remain the machine of choice; only one student reported owning and using a Macintosh. (Technically, most of these PCs are networked workstations rather than stand-alone personal computers, but for the purpose here, the distinction seemed irrelevant because of its transparency to the end user.) Five (6 percent) used Windows 3.× as their operating system. The rest used Windows 95, 98, or NT. The Macintosh owner used the variant for Macintosh. The preferred browsers for these students were Netscape (51 percent) and Explorer (18 percent), with the balance expressing no preference of one over the other. Only 9 percent reported delays in downloading the page onto their screen, that is, slow transfer of the graphic files. Ninety-one percent reported that Webtycho is easy to learn, while 6 percent had difficulty. Significant numbers of students reported the availability of Adobe Acrobat Reader (87 percent) and Real Media (65 percent), and their ability to open files in PowerPoint (94 percent). While 87 percent can save files in HTML, using their existing software, only a minority, 41 percent, has ever published a Web site.

Use of the site and its contents varied little, with 8 percent reporting little or no use, and 90 percent reporting usage of one to four times per week. Use included reading the syllabus (which in most cases included hypertext linked articles) occasionally (64 percent) or frequently (24 percent), while 8 percent used the paper version. Professors had posted reserve readings in full text upon the site, which were read by nearly three-quarters of the students (73 percent).

The chat room feature was the least used and the least liked by students. Only 38 percent had used the feature at all; 41 percent declared it "not very useful" and 28 percent found it "difficult to use." Other functions had both more utility and more supporters. The "assignments" section had been used by 92 percent of the students, while 88 percent found that feature "easy to use." Three quarters used e-mail and the embedded e-mail roster to communicate with classmates or the professor. Of those, 35 percent reported using the feature "occasionally," while 60 percent used it one to four times per week.

The discussion group area designed for collaborative documents is the feature that I had anticipated would be most used. Since the courses call for group projects, the ability to develop a collaborative document or to be able to conduct an asynchronous, private collaboration seemed to me to be a highly desired feature. Collaboration would obviate the need for one student to become the document handler, merging inputs from multiple sources and collating them into a cohesive whole. Personal experience in the corporate sector with such on-line "staff meetings" also had shown the potential value of this feature. But the students disagreed significantly. Less than one-third (27 percent) used the feature frequently, while a larger number did not use the feature at all or only occasionally (32 percent). The rest used the feature incidentally.

Overall, students rated the Web-enhanced format as a positive thing, with 63 percent evaluating it as "pretty good" or "great." But 14 percent either "didn't like it" or felt that it "didn't do much for me." An additional 22 percent "wouldn't miss it." Thus more than a third, 36 percent, were tepid in their attitude about using the Web-enhanced instructional technology.

DISCUSSION

The primary findings in the survey are that students have distinct preferences and, overall, are willing and frequent users of Web-enhanced methods. In migrating to another discipline, the values placed by the technical students suggest the need to optimize the formats for popular Web browsers like Netscape or Internet Explorer, and to take advantage of such software as Real Media and Adobe Acrobat to facilitate ease of use and add value to the course. If the instructor takes the time and trouble to post reserve readings and syllabi to a Web site, the students are likely to use them. Further, the technology supports communication between faculty and student and among students quite comfortably; there will be continuity of thought, explanation, and communication between class meetings. But synchronous "chat" is an unnecessary enhancement, at least at this point. The students accept asynchronous communication as satisfactory.

The expectation that technically trained adult commuting students, with distances to drive, tight schedules, and existing Internet skills, would think this online capability useful was not supported as strongly as expected. Despite overall support, there was clearly a hard nubbin of opponents who were critical of the technology or indifferent to its presence. I queried several of these students to find out why. The answers were insightful.

Several stated that they had specifically avoided on-line classes because they wanted human interaction with the professor and students. Others found the technology lacking in capability or robustness, compared to alternative technologies which they were using in their work and which represented something more of a cutting edge. Others reported that the software itself was too difficult to navigate, too rigidly hierarchical, or otherwise user-unfriendly.

Many said that, although training was conducted and that the system was easy to learn to use, they really didn't know how to employ it to advantage. When trying to work on substance, they had bogged down and were spending too much time in learning how to use the system rather than learning the content of the course. The technology had become a distraction rather than a learning enhancer.

A few just did not get it. One complained of the need to reload Netscape each time access to Webtycho was wanted; at the time, the program would not support Internet Explorer. When asked if the Netscape program was properly installed, the response was "Oops, I didn't install it." This person is a computer system professional at a large government agency, but had made a very basic computing error.

These responses suggest that training or trial exercises at the beginning of the course would be useful, so the technology becomes truly an enhancer and not a detractor. When beginning to use Webtycho, the first expectation was that students would already know how to use Internet technologies easily and well; they did not. Students need specific training for the features used in the course, and organized tasks to work through the problems and frustrations of learning a new system. While the students identified Webtycho as "easy to learn to use," they nonetheless had to go through a learning process.

The instructor goes through a learning process, too. The need to plan and execute in advance and to think through the process was greater than I anticipated. In setting up the course, I had to anticipate the way my use of language could accidentally create confusion. A reference, for example to "the book" for a given session, even if it was obvious to me that the reference was to the one in the readings for that session, would elicit several e-mails asking "which book?" So now I always refer to "the book" by author or title, rather than as a general or casual reference.

Asking the students to post assignments engendered a great deal of confusion until the detailed mechanics were clarified: Save in HTML, post to the assignments section instead of the discussion group, make sure it is the way you want it the first time, because you can't edit once posted, and so on. What may seem intuitive is not. Since few students and faculty have substantial experience in using on-line tools in class, each session becomes a challenge to communicate clearly and well. Students, having no repository of knowledge or experience on which to judge the instructor's expectations, justly warrant clarification or they will avoid using the on-line tool in favor of a clearer medium of communication. But the instructor should also be aware of the need to demand a certain level of technical skill in using the new medium.

The "Help Desk" remains the students' source for technical solutions. The instructor can support students in debugging their problems to an extent, but the instructor's focus must remain on the substance of the course. The mechanics of the platform are technical skills students must gain, and problems associated with those mechanics must be solved elsewhere. This distinction compares with writing skills and library research; the instructor can hold students accountable for those skills and help them somewhat to enhance those skills, but should send them to remedial training when the skills are inadequate.

VOLUME, VIRUSES, AND VIOLATIONS

Receiving a couple dozen take-home tests or papers on-line may cause home e-mail to crash. The file size of a paper may run half a megabyte, without graphics. Charts and graphics grow the file exponentially. So the loading time for each file may run several minutes or more; the cumulative effect can shut the instructor down for hours. Of course, a university network connection is often faster, but usually is not available at home, where one depends on standard telephone wires and a modem speed of less than 56 kilobits per second. The university server also contains more adequate file storage space than the typical home computer.

Furthermore, viruses have become a major problem. For example, the *New York Times* recently described the Class "B" virus as a global problem (Raney). This virus is transmitted by Word documents attached to e-mail. Once in a new computer or system, it proliferates among all word files. It manifests itself with a popup screen that states "(user name) is a big, stupid jerk." Most virus detection software cannot spot and correct for it, except in the latest versions. This virus came through the university like a common cold during a recent finals week. It was invisible to most anti-virus software installed on student and faculty machines, and took time to scrub.

Simple risk reduction strategies include not accepting and opening attachments and disabling macros in your word processing software under "preferences." Students should convert their papers to a text document before sending them by e-mail. This conversion also has the salutary effect of not having problems opening a document written in another program.

Finally, instructors need to become knowledgeable about the emerging complexities of intellectual property rights on the Internet. The posting of material on an Internet site constitutes "publishing," and instructors need to be aware of the consequences of seemingly casual acts both by themselves and by their students which can violate intellectual property rights. Authors have absolute ownership of their intellectual property, whether registered or not. This means that the habit of "lifting" text and graphics from Web sites, while technically easy, is a violation of intellectual property rules unless appropriate attribution is given. The copying of art, diagrams, comic strips, and the like from Internet sites is a common tactic, especially for harried instructors or students facing a deadline. But unless the document is cited and is in the public domain or qualifies as educational "fair use," permission may be required before it can be used.

For most published articles in scholarly or professional journals, a hyperlink is often available to the article itself or to an abstract of it. Posting a hyperlink is nearly always acceptable. But, of course, the article may only be posted for a short time. A more reliable method is to get the author's permission to copy the article into the class site under a "reserved readings" heading.

Intellectual property issues are arcane and complex. More information can be obtained at the Stanford University Fair Use page ("Copyright"). The University of Maryland University College library provides support services to our instructors for creating electronic reserves and help in obtaining copyright clearance, and most university libraries are probably equipped to provide similar services.

INFERENCES

The findings here suggest that for a less technical audience, less trained and experienced in computing and the Internet, the problems will be greater. The prevalence of relatively minor problems among students with substantial skills suggests that students with less formal training and experience are likely to wrestle with the technology even more. The need for greater preliminary training, clearer instructions on use, and practice are strongly indicated. The challenge will be to develop platforms that students will like and use.

WORKS CITED

"Copyright and Fair Use." *Stanford University Libraries*. 1 Aug. 1999 <http://fair use.stanford.edu>.

Raney, Rebecca Fairley. "New Virus Infects Microsoft Word Files." *The New York Times on the Web*. 21 Dec. 1998. 1 Aug. 1999 <http://nytimes.com/library/tech/98/12/biztech/articles/21virus.html>.

Chapter 20

The Promise—and Potential Pitfalls—of Cyberlearning

Peter Navarro

INTRODUCTION

The fiercest critics of cyberlearning see it as a dangerous catalyst for replacing professors with "digital diploma mills." They see in this on-line revolution the depersonalization of the learning process and an empty pedagogy that stresses memorization rather than synthesis and analysis. They also argue that "long-distance learning" tends to emphasize technology over course content even while it leaves large portions of the student population—the poor and disadvantaged—out in the cyber cold.

Proponents, however, counter that cyberlearning provides students with far greater access to information and other education resources. They see it as a cost-effective way to provide more individualized instructions and more accommodation for different learning styles, and argue that on-line education can teach our students as well or better than the traditional classroom. Some further suggest that students like their cyber classes better.

Unfortunately, amid this raging debate, there is equal disagreement about whether the weight of empirical evidence supports either side. On the one hand, proponents of cyberlearning cite literally hundreds of research articles that support its effectiveness (e.g., Russell). On the other hand, cyberlearning critics such as Phipps and Merisotis consistently dismiss the bulk of these articles on the grounds that "the overall quality of the original research is questionable and thereby renders many of the findings inconclusive" (3).

In a series of research articles (with Judith Shoemaker of the University of California-Irvine), I have attempted to add some additional empirical content to this raging debate. Some of the specific questions examined include: Can introductory economics be taught effectively in cyberspace? What kinds of students—by gender, level of computer skills, ethnicity, or other characteristics—might learn better in cyberspace? Why do some students prefer a cyberlearning environment over the traditional classroom? What kind of attitudes are students likely to have with regard to different instructional technologies such as CD-ROM–based lectures and on-line discussion rooms, how easy are these technologies to use, and what kinds of new instructional technologies are most essential—and enjoyable—to students? What kinds of technical problems are students likely to encounter in a cyber course? Can there be an acceptably high degree of "customer"—that is, student—satisfaction with a cyber course? And what do students see as the primary advantages and disadvantages of learning in cyberspace?

In this chapter, the empirical results of the two studies are reviewed from the perspective of what steps school administrators and instructors might take to design and implement an effective cyberlearning curriculum. Some reflections on the future of cyberlearning from the perspective of a hands-on practitioner are also offered. The overarching purpose of this chapter is to provide a framework for addressing key pedagogical issues in the cyberlearning revolution.

A SUMMARY OF ON-LINE EDUCATION CRITICISMS

The working assumption of this chapter is that a successful cyberlearning course must both recognize and address a set of criticisms—and potential pitfalls—that have now become a well-understood part of the on-line debate. Most generally, these criticisms revolve around six clusters of issues.

First, there are *student-related* issues such as performance, satisfaction, and interactions. Major concerns include the following: On-line students may not perform as well as traditional students. There may be a higher dropout rate among on-line students. Many students may prefer the traditional classroom. There may not be adequate professor-to-student and student-to-student interactions. Moreover, because of the lack of sufficient interactions, on-line learning may not allow a community of learners to fully develop.

The second cluster of issues revolves around *the problems of discrimination and access*. On-line learning may discriminate against women because computing is a more male-dominated environment. On-line learning may also discriminate against the poor and minorities because of the lack of adequate access to the necessary technologies, that is, computers and the Web.

The third cluster of issues revolves around *the pedagogical effectiveness of various instructional technologies*. In this regard, the criticism has often been made that many on-line teaching materials offer nothing more than digitized textbooks in cyberspace, providing more "sizzle" than steak. They therefore are not serious pedagogical instruments.

The fourth cluster revolves around *computer compatibility and technology-failure issues.* A fundamental concern is that too many incompatibility problems may arise because of the use of different types of computers, operating systems, and Web browsers. In addition, the technology, for example, the host computer or Web server, may break down too frequently.

The fifth cluster focuses on *course content and development-related issues* such as the lack of adequate equipment and instructor training for course development. A key concern here is that most instructors are ill equipped and untrained to design and implement an on-line course. In this regard, it is also asserted that instructors should not have to use their valuable time to engage in such activities. In addition, a key, but often overlooked, issue in this cluster is this: To the extent that on-line courses are textbook-based, many attempts to develop on-line courseware run the serious risk of violating copyright laws.

The sixth cluster includes *political economy–related issues* such as the expropriation of faculty property rights and potential job losses. A key concern here is that college administrators may be adopting on-line education more for economic reasons than educational purposes. In addition, professors and instructors may see their property rights to the intellectual content of their courses unfairly expropriated at the same time that on-line education may diminish the role of faculty and reduce job opportunities.

To set the stage for a discussion of these issues, I first briefly describe the two research experiments conducted with Dr. Shoemaker. These two studies compared "Traditional Learners" and "Cyberlearners" on academic background, entering demographic characteristics, exam performance, and attitudinal items from an exit survey administered to the students. Both chi-square tests and factorial analyses were used to examine the data, which were collected in the forms of student exit surveys and quiz and exam scores.

THE RESEARCH EXPERIMENTS

The first study was conducted in the Spring Quarter of 1998 at the Graduate School of Management at the University of California, Irvine (UCI). The sample consisted of 63 students enrolled in an introductory macroeconomics, core course in the MBA curriculum.

The MBA Group

In this study, the "MBA Group" was asked on the first day of class to sort themselves into Traditional Learners or Cyberlearners. By self-selection, the students separated themselves into two groups of roughly equal size.

As part of this selection process, students were informed that Traditional

Learners would be expected to attend each of the classes, listen to the lectures presented in class by the professor, and participate in policy discussions based on daily newspaper readings. In contrast, Cyberlearners would not be required to attend class. Instead, these students would be expected to use multimedia CD-ROMs containing similar lectures by the same professor, and to conduct their policy discussions on-line with the help of a threaded electronic bulletin board.

In addition, the Traditional Learners took weekly quizzes in class, while the Cyberlearners took the same quizzes outside of class using an on-line testing center. However, both groups were required to take their mid-term and final exams in class. There was also a weekly scheduled "chat room" for student discussions available to both groups.

To ensure that the two groups were equivalent at the beginning of the exploratory study, they were compared on background variables and entering academic ability. Results of the statistical tests comparing the two groups indicated that there were no statistically significant differences between the two groups on any of their entering characteristics. That is, the two groups were found to be comparable in terms of gender, ethnicity, first language, age, distance between home and campus, undergraduate grade point average (GPA), and GMAT scores.

The Undergraduate Group

The second study was conducted in the Fall Quarter of 1998. It involved 200 undergraduates enrolled in introductory macroeconomics. Eighty-seven percent of these students were non-economics majors; 65% were either freshmen or sophomores, while 9% were seniors.

At the beginning of the quarter, the "Undergraduate Group" was given the option of taking the class in cyberspace or in the traditional classroom. One hundred fifty-one students chose the traditional format, while 49 chose the cyber option. As with the MBA group, statistical tests indicated that students in the Undergraduate Group were very similar in terms of gender, ethnicity, class level, major, school, and average SAT scores for both math and verbal skills.

Regarding teaching format, Cyberlearners in the Undergraduate Group had requirements very similar to those in the MBA group. Class lectures were administered asynchronously by CD-ROM, students took weekly electronic quizzes outside of class on the electronic testing center, there was a weekly scheduled chat room for student discussions, and students were expected to participate in weekly threaded bulletin board discussions based on assigned readings. In this regard, the only face-to-face interaction Cyberlearners had with the instructor came at the start of the course, since students were not required to attend class.

The Traditional Learners in the Undergraduate Group did, however, have a much more traditional experience than those in the MBA group. In particular, they were expected to attend three one-hour lectures a week in a large lecture hall, and this was supplemented by a one-hour discussion group per week.

STUDENT-RELATED ISSUES

With this brief overview of the two research experiments, let us turn now to systematically addressing the criticisms listed above. I begin with one of the most important facets of the on-line debate, that of student-related issues.

Student Performance

While there is a myriad of questions about on-line learners, the central one has been, and perhaps always will be: Can students learn as well—or perhaps even better—in a cyberspace environment as they can in a traditional classroom environment?

On the one hand, there is a wealth of studies dating back to the early days of correspondence courses in the 1920s that appear to indicate that the answer to this question is yes. That is, as Russell's annotated bibliography of 355 sources indicates, there appears to be "no significant difference" between traditional classroom teaching and long-distance learning.

On the other hand, as Phipps and Merisotis have argued, relatively few empirical studies in this wealth of material provide a comprehensive test of the effectiveness of long-distance learning. In fact, a review of the research literature indicates that most of the published literature is devoted to case studies, that is, detailed descriptions of personal experiences using instructional technology in a particular classroom. Even rarer are studies that compare traditional and cyberlearning students. A major goal of the two research studies discussed in this chapter was to help fill the large empirical gap in the on-line performance literature.

MBA Group Performance

In the MBA Group, Cyberlearners and Traditional Learners were compared on the basis of performance on eight academic variables involving multiple choice and essay questions in a weekly quiz, mid-term exam, and final exam format. Results from the t-tests indicated there were no significant differences on six of the eight academic variables, including final exam performance, while significant differences were found only on average quiz scores and total score on the mid-term exam. Thus, in terms of student learning, the two groups achieved at approximately the same level. It was also found that regardless of gender, ethnicity, first language, GPA, and age, there likewise was no significant difference in amount learned under the two learning options.

Undergraduate Group Performance

In the Undergraduate Group, both Cyberlearners and Traditional Learners were administered 15 common exam questions. These questions were all of a

Table 20.1
Final Exam Results (Maximum Score = 15)

Group	Traditional Learners	Cyberlearners	Statistical Test Results
Mean	9.8	11.3	t-test = 3.70
SD	2.5	2.6	df = 191, p < .01

short essay nature and required some application of macroeconomic principles. Table 20.1 presents the final exam results.

From the table, we see that the Cyberlearners performed significantly better than the Traditional Learners. Mean score for the Cyberlearners was 11.3, while the mean score for the Traditional Learners was 9.8. With a t-test statistic of 3.70, this result was statistically significant at the 99% level. Cyberlearners also performed better on the final exam items, regardless of which subgroup they belonged to, when results were analyzed by gender, ethnicity, or class level.

These results clearly suggest that Cyberlearners can perform as well or better than students in the traditional classroom. Coupled with the results for the MBA Group, these results also suggest that such performance holds at both the graduate and undergraduate level.

Student and Professor Interactions

Of all the criticisms of cyberlearning, one of the most serious is that cyber education lacks crucial personal interactions not only between students and professors but among students as well. As a result, it is said to depersonalize education even as it does not allow a community of learners to fully develop.

At least in our studies, there did not appear to be a lack of professor-to-student interaction in a cyber environment. In exit surveys administered to both research groups, students indicated by a wide margin that they were satisfied with the degree of professor-to-student interactions.

We did not find this result to be surprising. In a cyber environment, there are numerous ways for such interactions to take place. They can occur synchronously in a chat room or videoconferencing environment. They can also occur asynchronously in an e-mail and threaded bulletin board environment. In fact, when compared to the large lecture hall format where professors deliver lectures to hundreds of students at a time with few if any questions, an argument can be made that cyberlearning offers *more* of a personal experience.

That is the good news. The bad news is that, at least with the teaching format we used, a majority of students in the Undergraduate Group (55%) expressed concerns about adequate student-to-student interactions, while some students in the MBA Group complained about feeling "disconnected" from the class and being unable to "share ideas" with other students.

On this point, I remain optimistic that this issue can be adequately addressed. One obvious fix is to establish formal student discussion groups and have these groups meet at regular intervals in cyberspace in a designated chat room. A second alternative might be to have students network by telephone or e-mail. My broader observation is that this is an issue that should be taken very seriously at both the instructor and school administrator ends.

Student Satisfaction and the Dropout Rate

Both groups of Cyberlearners reported a high degree of "customer satisfaction" with the cyber approach. With the MBA Group, over 90% agreed that their cyberlearning experiences provided advantages over presentation of the same material in the traditional classroom form. Perhaps the most interesting result was that 90% of the Cyberlearners believed they learned as much or more than they would have in a traditional classroom.

With the Undergraduate Group, almost 90% of the Cyberlearners responded "yes" when asked whether the university should offer more Web-based courses. In addition, when asked to rate the overall quality of the course, Traditional Learners provided a mean response of 3.80 on a scale of 1 (Poor) to 5 (Excellent) as compared to a mean score of 4.09 for the Cyberlearners.

As for the issue of student dropout, it was not a significant problem in either of our research studies. All students in the MBA Group completed the course, while all students enrolled in the undergraduate course after the registration "drop" period also completed the course. Based on conversations we had with the few students who dropped the undergraduate course, we believe the causes were unrelated to on-line learning, being instead a normal part of the "shopping for courses" process that undergraduates typically engage in.

More broadly, my sense is that dropout problems are potentially serious but can be successfully addressed in a number of ways. Perhaps the most obvious is to provide a quality, interactive course.

A more subtle solution is to design courses that provide students with frequent and regular "hurdles" to jump. For example, in my classes, I "lockstep" the students into a ten-week sequence in which they are tested weekly on both the textbook and CD-ROM materials. This approach requires students to stay engaged in the course. It also provides instructors with an early warning system in case any students have failed to engage.

ACCESS AND DISCRIMINATION

The issue of differential access to cyberlearning is a serious one; and it is more than fair criticism that cyberlearning as a general proposition runs the risk of leaving a large segment of the student population out in the cyber cold. After all, both computers and Web access are expensive propositions; and we, as a society, are nowhere near achieving a cyber-utopia of universal wiring and access such as has been envisioned by some of our political and business leaders. In this regard, it is equally clear that it will likely once again be the poor and minorities who will bear the brunt of any cyber-discrimination.

Having acknowledged this, it nonetheless seems unreasonable to use the thwarting of the development of on-line learning as the first best defense against such discrimination. Clearly, this is more a "supply side" problem that is better addressed by ensuring the access of the disadvantaged than by denying the access of the more advantaged.

In this regard, it is perhaps also worth pointing out that one of the advantages of cyberlearning is that while it may deny access to some disadvantaged groups, it can *increase* the access of other such groups. These groups range from less mobile senior citizens and disabled persons to individuals living in remote rural locations far from campus nodes.

Study Results on Access and Discrimination

As regards the specific issue of gender discrimination, no statistical evidence was found that men are more likely to self-select on a cyber teaching environment than women in either research group. Nor were any statistically discernible differences in performance or attitudes based on gender found.

However, it is much more difficult to evaluate the issue of access by the poor and disadvantaged minorities. This is because much of the discrimination that affects these groups has far more to do with a lesser ability of these groups to gain entrance into institutions of higher learning such as the University of California than it does with taking technology-based courses once entrance is achieved. (With the recent elimination of affirmative action programs on UC campuses by a statewide initiative vote, this issue has taken on a new importance as black and Latino applications and admissions have both suffered.)

Perhaps the only thing that I can say in this regard is that great pains were taken to ensure that no one was denied access into the Undergraduate Group because of the lack of access to adequate technology. In doing so, an important lesson in resource management was learned. Some background is in order.

When I first proposed the idea of an experimental on-line economics course, several department administrators expressed concerns about the possible lack of student access to adequate computing and Web resources. As a precaution, we made the very strong assumption for scheduling purposes that *none* of the students would have their own computers and no student without a computer could be excluded.

Under these assumptions, the "fail-safe" solution to this problem was to schedule the class at a time when it was possible to reserve sufficient computer lab space to accommodate all enrollees. That meant that even though students did not have to come to class, they were always guaranteed a seat in the computer lab at a particular class time if they did.

What is perhaps most interesting about this requirement from a resource management point of view is that it was totally unnecessary. On average, less than 5% of the students ever attended the lab sessions. This was for two reasons. The first is that 91% of the Undergraduate Group had their own computers, while 80% had home access to the Web. (Interestingly, these percentages were even higher for the Traditional Learners, so lack of the technology clearly did not drive the self-selection process.)

The second reason, as indicated by our survey data, is that the students without access to their own computers or the Web preferred to use the school labs at times more convenient to their schedules. The broader point here for school administrators is that available campus lab space can likely accommodate a much higher enrollment in cyber classes than the number of seats might suggest.

EFFECTIVENESS OF INSTRUCTIONAL TECHNOLOGIES

Let's turn now to the instructional technologies themselves. In this area, two major criticisms are that (1) most on-line teaching materials offer nothing more than digitized textbooks in cyberspace, and (2) many on-line teaching tools provide more "sizzle" than "steak" and are not serious pedagogical instruments.

Regarding these issues, my own content analysis of cyber course materials in the field of economics did, indeed, reveal that many on-line courses offer no satisfactory multimedia substitute for the traditional classroom lecture (Navarro; Navarro and Shoemaker "Economics," "Power"). Instead, course content is often limited to assigned readings in a traditional textbook and/or posted lecture notes with little real visual or audio stimulation offered in cyberspace. Accordingly, many of the courses I surveyed lacked the visual and audio stimulation that has been determined to be an important part of enhancing the learning process.

Based on my experiences, it is my view that a pedagogically sound cyber approach should have, at a minimum, the following features: (1) multimedia lectures that simulate the classroom experience; (2) asynchronous interactive communication opportunities that incorporate feedback loops and student interactions; (3) electronic testing of important course content with instant feedback; and (4) synchronous on-line discussions. (For a fuller discussion in a case study context, see Navarro.)

In the two research studies discussed in this chapter, this obligation was met by employing a set of interactive CD-ROM lectures, a highly interactive, threaded electronic bulletin board with rapid response e-mail, an electronic testing center, and an Internet discussion room. Because of the critical role these instructional technologies play in cyberlearning, it is useful to first briefly describe those technologies used in our research studies, state their primary pedagogical purpose, and then report on how students evaluated each technology.

The CD-ROM

The CD-ROM employed was *The Power of Macroeconomics* (Navarro and Kahr). This CD-ROM uses the visual graphic software Microsoft PowerPoint and features a digitally mastered audio soundtrack. It was specifically designed to simulate the lecture experience and includes eleven separate lectures on topics such as fiscal policy, monetary policy, and the international monetary system. (The CD lectures are also available in a Web-streaming format.)

A typical presentation includes roughly 100 slides, and each slide includes an audio portion of the lecture. Students are able to experience each lecture at their own pace, while each lecture usually takes from one to one-and-one-half hours to view.

As a means of providing stimulating visual feedback, the slides in each lecture include bulleted material from the audio track, dynamically constructed graphs such as the Keynesian or AS-AD model, animated charts and figures, historical photos or illustrations of people such as John Maynard Keynes and Alan Greenspan, or some combination thereof. Interactions are also built into many of the slides so that students are prompted to answer questions along the way, the pedagogical purpose of which is to engage the student in the lecture in an active rather than passive manner.

The Threaded Electronic Bulletin Board

The threaded electronic bulletin board employed a beta test version of Cyber Prof software. From an administrative perspective, the board was used to post the class syllabus, reading list, computer lab and exam schedules, and other administrative notices. It was also used to post important announcements throughout the course.

From a pedagogical perspective, a primary function of the board was to promote asynchronous policy discussions between the professor and students as well as among students. This was accomplished in the following manner.

Each week, several questions were posted based on articles taken from the on-line editions of publications such as *Business Week*. Students seeking to answer the questions were automatically linked to these articles through the bulletin board. Typically, these articles directly related to the lecture topic of the week or, as the course progressed, some articles allowed for a synthesis of ideas presented in previous weeks.

Students were required to post at least two responses per week to these questions. Alternatively, students could respond to the postings of their fellow students. These responses appeared on the board in a threaded style typical of such Internet boards and were designed to promote professor-to-student interactions as well as student-to-student interactions.

This group activity was supplemented by a rapid response e-mail system in which students had e-mail access to the professor, teaching assistant, and technical support staff. They were guaranteed a 24-hour reply, with a reply typically given the same day.

The Electronic Testing Center

Each week, students were expected to pass a 20-question multiple choice quiz based on the assigned textbook reading. A name and password were required to access the testing center, and it was accessible 24 hours a day. Upon submitting their answers, students were immediately provided with their results (percent correct on the quiz) as well as with helpful feedback on any wrong answers—in my view, an absolutely critical component of effective learning.

In this regard, the primary pedagogical purpose of the testing center was not evaluation per se but rather to motivate a careful reading of the textbook. As noted above, such weekly testing is likewise an excellent way to monitor student participation and help prevent dropout problems. In fact, with both student groups, we were able to make an early identification of a few students who were not doing the work. Prompt e-mail messages to these students in all cases helped them get quickly back on track.

The On-line Discussion Room

The on-line discussion room was accessed through a link in the Electronic Bulletin Board. The Chatspace software provides a "lobby" in which students can enter 24 hours a day to talk among themselves on-line. This lobby was used for regularly scheduled weekly discussion sessions conducted by either the professor or the teaching assistant. In addition, there were two special review sessions before the mid-term and final; and these sessions were very well attended.

Note, however, that we did not establish any formal groups of students to encourage their own group on-line discussions. In light of our findings above on student-to-student interactions, this is an issue that is well worth rethinking in the context of ensuring adequate student-to-student interactions in cyberspace.

Study Results

In exit surveys, students from both study groups were asked to rank each of the major instructional technologies according to how "essential" and how "enjoyable" each technology was. Here, I report the survey results from the Undergraduate Group, which closely track those of the MBA Group.

Eighty-three percent of the undergraduate students regarded the CD-ROM lectures as the most essential, while only 15% cited the textbook. However, the highest percentage of students (44%) cited the textbook as the second most essential element, while the electronic testing center featuring the on-line weekly quizzes was the clear winner at 50% for the third most essential component of the course.

In the category of "most enjoyable" learning component, the CD-ROM likewise finished first at 68%. It was followed by the electronic bulletin board at 14%, the on-line discussions at 11%, the electronic testing center at 9%, and the textbook with a meager 2%.

One interpretation of these results is that both a threaded bulletin board and on-line discussion room can be valuable components of any on-line course, at least when it comes to maintaining student interest. At the same time, it would appear that *well-executed cyber lectures can serve as an acceptable surrogate for traditional classroom lectures*, with these lectures "winning" both the essential and enjoyable categories.

COMPUTER COMPATIBILITY AND TECHNOLOGY FAILURE

No serious discussion of on-line learning should ignore the potential pitfalls involved in the failure of one or more of the technologies being used—although this is an issue that is rarely discussed. Conceptually, it is useful to separate the kinds of potential technical failures into two broad categories: (1) student computer and software problems, and (2) host computer or server problems.

Student Computer and Compatibility Problems

The initial hurdle with students is to ensure access to a computer that has a sufficiently fast coprocessor and sufficient memory to handle the requirements of the software employed. A related issue is ensuring an Internet connection with reasonable speed. In both research groups, we encountered little difficulty with any of these issues.

More vexing student computer problems involve compatibility issues that can arise over the use of different operating platforms (Apple vs. PC), different Web browsers (Netscape Communications Corporation's Netscape Navigator vs. Microsoft's Internet Explorer), and different vintages of software (e.g., PowerPoint 4.0 vs. 5.0). We did not encounter any of these compatibility problems with the MBA Group because this group all used a uniform laptop machine with uniform software. However, a number of problems did arise with the Undergraduate Group.

For example, the CD-ROMs were engineered for students with PC-based systems, so a few Apple users in the class had to rely on the school's computer lab to view the CDs. Note, however, that this will likely be a transitory problem with the availability of Web-streaming versions of the lectures.

In addition, we encountered a number of totally unexpected problems with a few students using older versions of Netscape. The net result was that students with this software simply could not log into the electronic bulletin board.

The broader points to be learned here are several. First, there should be a statement in the course catalogue that clearly identifies the minimum hardware and software computer requirements. Second, adequate technical support should be available to assist students who encounter problems. Third, on-line courses and software selection should be designed with these compatibility issues in mind.

Host Computer Problems

The host computer or "server" typically acts as the main engine that runs many of the on-line technologies. In our case, the three main technologies run off the server were the threaded electronic bulletin board, the electronic testing center, and the chat room. In order for a server to perform well, it must have adequate storage capacity and a fast enough processor. Ideally, all on-line materials should also be linked to a backup server in case the main server fails.

In the research studies, the most common technical problems experienced were server congestion or server failure associated with the use of the electronic testing center and electronic bulletin board. At least a fifth of all students in both groups complained of server problems at some time during the course.

With the electronic testing center, the root of the problem was the complex algorithm the testing center uses to prepare individualized tests for each student taking a quiz. In completing this task, the testing center must search through several thousand questions in the data bank and select a number of them based on certain criteria. In most cases, this task can be completed without incident. However, as an example of an unexpected practical problem that arose, at the beginning of the undergraduate course, many students would wait until an hour or two before the weekly deadline to complete the quiz. The resultant surge of users created significant congestion. This technical issue was resolved by ensuring adequate server memory during these peak times and by encouraging students to take their quizzes earlier.

More broadly, the possibility of server congestion or server failure highlights the importance not only of having a secure, high quality server but also having adequate technical support to rapidly respond to problems. It is not an overstatement to say, at least in our experience, that frequent server failure is the quickest way to alienate on-line students.

COURSE CONTENT AND DEVELOPMENT

Turning to the issues of course content and course development, two important nonnormative or descriptive criticisms are that (1) most instructors are not equipped with the technology to design and implement an on-line course, and (2) most instructors are not trained to develop on-line courses. A normative variation on this issue that spills over into the political economy of on-line learning is that instructors *should not* have to take their valuable time to engage in such activities. Finally, perhaps the most overlooked issue in course content and development is that of copyright infringement. That is, to the extent that on-line courses are textbook-based, many attempts to develop on-line course-ware are running the serious risk of violating copyright laws.

My own view is that the marketplace will render all of these observations unimportant. This is because on-line course content will likely evolve in the following manner. Most professors and instructors will *not* develop their own set of on-line lectures. Nor will they be expected to. Rather, they will rely on courseware ultimately developed or co-developed by the very same publishers who now produce major textbooks. This will happen for several reasons.

First, it is both very expensive and time-consuming to produce high quality, multimedia lectures. For example, I estimate the cost of producing *The Power of Economics CD-ROM* series to be well over $100,000. This cost includes not only expenditures for sophisticated recording and computing equipment but the cost of labor associated with the effort.

Second, the voicing, scripting, and multimedia production skills required to produce a set of cyber lectures are not the same as those required to *teach* the material. Besides the time and cost involved, it is for this same skill-related reason that every instructor does not write his or her own textbooks.

Third, and perhaps most interesting, *it is very difficult to write a set of lectures without consciously or accidentally violating copyright laws.* The obvious problem is that the vast majority of professors base their lectures on a particular textbook. Thus, while it may be perfectly acceptable now—indeed, publishers encourage this behavior—to reproduce textbook material in a classroom setting, it will not be acceptable for such material to become part of a revenue-generating on-line offering.

My own view again is that this is how it should be. That is, most professors and instructors should rely on commercial lectures in an on-line world just as they have relied on the use of commercial textbooks in a traditional classroom world. And the sooner publishers produce exciting courseware based on their textbooks, the sooner this revolution will occur.

POLITICAL ECONOMY

While the positive results of the research studies reported here appear to suggest that there might be a bright pedagogical future for learning in cyber-space, it is, however, equally true that the on-line revolution raises thorny issues in political economy that threaten its rapid diffusion. These issues range from the alleged sacrifice of good pedagogy for the sake of economic convenience and the potential expropriation of intellectual property rights from instructors to a potentially diminished role of, and reduced wages and job opportunities for, faculty and instructors.

An entire essay, indeed an entire book, could be written on the subject of the political economy of cyberlearning; and it is not really my place here—nor do I have the space—to comment extensively on these issues. Nonetheless, there are several observations I can make within the context of my research studies that may prove useful.

First, based again on my own experiences, I do not share the view that cyber courses will in any way diminish the role of the instructor. The cyberlearning option will simply change that role—in many ways, for the better.

In this regard, the communications between the instructor and individual students tend to be of a much more individualized and customized nature in cyberspace; and, in my view, this is all to the good. More broadly, instructors should perhaps welcome the liberation from what for many becomes the tedious chore of delivering the same lecture for the nth time over the course of a career. Instead, they will be able to use their talents to customize the instruction.

Second, based on my use of the available technologies, I do not see on-line education as a blanket substitute for a comprehensive, traditional classroom education, thereby rendering the traditional university technologically obsolete. Rather, I see on-line offerings as a complement that most successfully will focus on certain types of subjects.

My own view is that large, lecture hall courses that teach the elementary principles of a subject are best suited for the on-line approach. Examples of such courses might include introductory mathematics and science courses as well as introductory courses in economics and accounting. By contrast, courses in which the subject matter is more interpretive and subjective or complex may be less suited for a cyber approach—unless that approach includes substantial synchronous communications through vehicles such as on-line conferencing and videoconferencing. In this later case, instructors will continue to play their traditional synchronous roles but merely do so in a virtual classroom setting.

Third, the criticism that college administrators are adopting on-line education more for economic reasons than educational purposes may be well founded. However, it is equally true that these same administrators may be very surprised when the total costs of on-line courses are tallied up.

The use of on-line courses reduces the need for capital expenditures on physical classroom space. However, as noted above, it in no way reduces—and may actually increase—the time that instructors spend teaching a course, so salary issues are likely to emerge as a problem.

Perhaps even more to the point, effective on-line teaching requires other kinds of extensive expenditures, principally on ensuring that adequate computing and network facilities are available and operating with a high degree of efficiency. Such expenditures may more than offset any savings on providing physical plant. Nor should the need for significant expenditures on labor for technical support be underestimated.

Fourth, regarding the expropriation of property rights, this issue likewise is a significant one. My only observation in this area is based on my earlier observation that in an on-line world, the traditional individual classroom lecture for "principles courses" is likely going to be supplanted by commercial multimedia lectures available from major publishers.

As a final concluding comment, regardless of the many virtues of cyberlearning, those instructors and administrators who advocate its broader use will likely encounter significant resistance within the academy. In my own view, the best way to address such problems is to approach the on-line experience not only as a teaching venture but also as a research obligation.

In this regard, I recommend that any new cyberlearning venture launched on any college or university campus be conducted first as a research experiment, with the full cooperation and assistance of an independent research team. In my own case, I was fortunate to be assisted in my efforts by UC-Irvine's Division of Undergraduate Research. Through the help of this unit, and specifically through the help of Judith Shoemaker (co-author of the two research studies cited in this chapter), we were able to closely monitor the effectiveness of the on-line offerings. The resultant feedback has been enormously helpful not only in building a better cyber mousetrap but also in addressing the very legitimate concerns and criticisms of those skeptical of cyberlearning.

WORKS CITED

Internet Explorer. Software. *Microsoft Windows Technologies.* 1 Aug. 1999 <http://www.microsoft.com/windows/ie/default.htm>.

Navarro, Peter. "Notes from the Electronic Classroom." *Journal of Policy Analysis and Management* 17 (1998): 106–15.

Navarro, Peter, and Ron Kahr. *The Power of Macroeconomics.* Boston: Irwin/McGraw-Hill, 1998.

Navarro, Peter, and Judith Shoemaker. "Economics in Cyberspace: An Empirical Study." Working Paper. University of California Graduate School of Management, May 1999.

———. "The Power of Cyberlearning: An Empirical Test." *Journal of Computing in Higher Education* 11 (1999): 29–54.

Netscape Navigator. Software. *Netscape Netcenter.* 1 Aug. 1999 <http://home.netscape.com/computing/download/index.html?cp=hom08tdow>.

Phipps, Ronald, and Jamie Merisotis. *What's the Difference? A Review of Contemporary Research on the Effectiveness of Distance Learning in Higher Education.* Washington, DC: Institute for Higher Education Policy, 1999.

PowerPoint. Software. *Microsoft Office.* 1 Aug. 1999 <http://www.microsoft.com/office/>.

Russell, Thomas L. *The "No Significant Difference" Phenomenon.* 4th ed. Raleigh: North Carolina State University, 1998.

Chapter 21

Preparing Higher Education Learners for Success on the Web

*May Lowry, Christine Thornam, and
Cason T. White*

INTRODUCTION

Margaret, a thirty-year-old woman seeking a degree in an innovative university program, was very comfortable as a traditional classroom learner for the first sixteen years of her education. Now enrolled in a required on-line course, she reports her first reaction as "Where have they taken my classroom?" Her vague mental picture of an on-line course was that, at the designated time, she would log on and have a synchronous chat, discussing the required readings with the rest of her cyber-classmates and instructor. However, when she logged on, "nobody else showed up for class."

Describing herself as a "big picture" type of person, Margaret found herself paging through the on-line course, screen after screen, until she had no idea where she was, clicking away and hoping she wasn't missing something critical. In the past, Margaret counted on meeting with the instructor, and on informal social contacts with classmates in the hallway, to verify her understanding of course assignments and to coordinate group projects. This familiar structure was gone.

She reported that one of the most aggravating aspects of the course was the rush to be one of the first people to post comments on the topic under discussion. Margaret feared being the sixth or seventh person to contribute because the only thing left to say might be "I agree"—not a very satisfying contribution. As in many classes, it was not uncommon for some learners to dominate the on-line dialogue, while shy learners mustered every bit of courage to click the send button for the obligatory x-times-per-semester posts to get their participation grade.

By the end of the class, Margaret discovered that she held herself more accountable for her own learning in the on-line course. Required readings didn't fall through the cracks, because it was made clear that the on-line discussion was set to begin and end on specified dates. She found herself preparing more thoroughly for the on-line discussion, where there was no way to conceal a less than well-thought-out opinion: posted comments required defensible arguments. Her overall impression was that on-line learning had a lot to recommend it, but that it took all semester to become a full participant.

The Role of Learner Preparation

Our interview with Margaret illustrated for us the importance of preparing learners to be successful participants in the Web environment. Learner preparation has become a special area of emphasis in our work in the Technology and Learning Team at the University of Colorado at Denver. Our mission is to support learning on our urban commuter campus by providing instructional design consultation to faculty and administration (*Technology and Learning Team*).

We argue that, just as we would equip new drivers with what they need to be successful—a fully functioning vehicle, clear rules of the road, patient instruction in safety and effectiveness, encouragement and modeling in positive driving attitudes, an easily followed map, and coaching as necessary—so new learners in the Web environment need tools and preparation in order to travel successfully. In neither instance does the preparation happen automatically and without effort. In both instances, the journey itself has the power to transform the driver's beliefs about mobility, freedom, and responsibility (Jonassen, Peck, and Wilson 7–10). This is what, for us, makes participation in the Web environment intriguing.

In this chapter, we first give examples of strategies to prepare higher education learners for the Web environment at a variety of levels—at the individual class level, the program level, and the institutional level. Then we describe a learner preparation checklist that we review with our faculty and administrative clients. The list, a work in progress derived from literature and praxis, is for consideration during the creation of learning environments on the Web.

Content and Process

Perelman argues that time-travel visitors from nineteenth-century America would be completely disoriented by what they observed in a twentieth-century hospital, but completely at home in a twentieth-century classroom. It appears that change in higher education has accelerated more in the past ten years than it has the past ten decades, fueled in part by the use of the Web as a featured tool.

What has not changed is that good pedagogy attends to both the content and process of teaching and learning (Institute for Research in Learning; Cyrs 10). We are defining the *content* as that which is to be learned, the topic or subject matter of the instruction. The *process* addresses at least two aspects of learning: first, how the subject matter is taught, that is, the teaching strategies that are used to encourage learning (lecture, discussion, demonstration, symposia, reading, writing, group projects, simulations, and so on, in person or at a distance); and second, the social and cultural aspects of the learning community. Groups, including groups of learners, need to establish a degree of psychological safety and rapport in order to function and proceed to learn the content (Repman and Logan 35; Wolcott 23–24).

In the traditional classroom, this establishment of psychological safety and rapport is usually a result of meeting and becoming more familiar with colleagues, expectations, procedures, and the norms of the group. Traditional face-to-face courses typically include some kind of introduction of the participants and the instructor, and review of the syllabus and expectations for behavior. Activities like these begin to establish safety among group members and establishment of norms so that the group can proceed more efficiently and effectively (Wolcott 24). Learners can literally look to colleagues for the socialization and direction they need to participate successfully.

One of the jobs of the educator is to function as a skillful guide through the process and content of learning. Because instructors and learners have traditionally been synchronously and geographically face to face, this process has more or less been taken for granted (Wolcott 23). Lecture with some demonstration and discussion has often been the strategy of choice and, since all participants have been in the same room at the same time, the group development issues have been left to work themselves out.

However, distributed environments push us to reexamine the process of learning, including both instructional strategy and development of group cohesion among learners. For this reason, we have focused on preparing learners to be successful in the process of learning in the Web environment. What follows are examples of deliberate attempts to prepare learners for success on the Web at a variety of levels—the individual class, the program, and the institution.

INDIVIDUAL CLASS LEVEL: COGNITION AND INSTRUCTION

The first example of learner preparation is at the level of the individual class. Cognition and Instruction is a required course in many of the graduate programs of the University of Colorado at Denver School of Education. Instructors responsible for the course have been experimenting with on-line discussion groups as a supplemental forum to their in-class discussions for several semesters, with increasingly satisfactory results; plans are to offer the class entirely on-line in the near future. In preparation, they have made a concerted effort to work with the learners on the process as well as the content of the course.

Preparing learners can be a formative function, provided throughout the class, as well as an advance function provided only in the beginning of the class (Willis and Dickinson 81). In order to take a closer look at learner preparation on the scale of the individual class, we conducted an evaluation of the strategies used to prepare learners for on-line discussions in this cognition course. Every week, the learners were given two to four reading assignments that served as the basis for discussion. Beginning with the second week of class, every other class period was held on-line, with learners logging on synchronously and participating in threaded discussions on the given topics for that week. At first, the instructor for this particular semester led the discussion, then she asked class members to take turns in the leadership role. We periodically monitored on-line discussions and, at the end of the course, administered a Likert scale questionnaire to the learners. The instrument surveyed them on their perceptions of the discussion groups and asked them to identify techniques the instructor used to help them get ready to participate in the on-line discussions.

Evaluation Responses

Out of a total of twenty-five learners in the class, fourteen responded to the end-of-semester survey. The survey was voluntary; we do not have data on the perceptions of the nonrespondents. Overall, the learners recognized the strategies to prepare them for the on-line discussions and, with some reservations, reported feeling prepared and successful as participants and facilitators.

Consistent with the literature (Moore and Kearsley 164–67; Weinstein 24), learners recognized and appreciated certain benefits of the on-line portions of this class, such as the convenience of working from home and the ability to carefully consider their answers before posting. However, similar to Kilian's characterization of the computer as an "information desert" (31), they found that the on-line discussions lacked some important qualities of the in-class exchanges, such as the ability to use nonverbal communication and to have direct access to the instructor. In addition, they commented on the overwhelming number of messages in the discussion.

Respondents indicated six strategies they felt the instructor used to prepare them for the on-line discussions:

1. provided guidelines for on-line behavior;
2. set specific deadlines for contributions;
3. provided topics for each discussion;
4. provided appropriate feedback to learners' comments and questions;

5. modeled appropriate behavior for learners to follow;

6. assigned learners to facilitator roles.

The first five strategies can be important in on-line discussions because they provide rules of the road and a road map to learners who are traveling in a foreign environment in which they have not yet become comfortable. The sixth strategy, encouraging learners to take turns leading the on-line discussions, was identified by the learners as particularly effective. It allowed them to become more metacognitively aware of successful techniques, and gave them a format to practice the modeled behaviors.

The majority of the respondents indicated that the following strategies were not used by the instructor:

1. did not enforce a maximum length of messages posted to the on-line discussions;

2. did not provide more specific guidelines and organization for discussions;

3. did not show how to read and respond in the threaded discussions;

4. did not provide review or instructions for managing the discussion format.

Respondents reported that the instructor did not enforce a maximum length of messages, which they ranked as low in importance: none of the learners complained about messages being too long, only that there were too many of them. Furthermore, a review of the class conference revealed that most contributions to the discussion were rather short, only one or two screens worth of words. The last three strategies were more significant. Although they had been a part of on-line discussions in the past, respondents to the survey agreed that they wanted specific review and tutoring of the software application at the beginning of the course. Because learners in the CU-Denver School of Education are encouraged to use computer-mediated communication, they are sometimes assumed to be comfortable with its use and conversant with its features. Among the learners we surveyed, this proved to be an incorrect assumption.

Over the evolution of the course, the instructors have chosen to be proactive in preparing learners, using a combination of instructional design strategies and modeling of behavior in the on-line discussion. The learners surveyed recognized and acknowledged the preparation strategies, and commented on their effectiveness. However, they also wanted more direct instruction in the logistics of participation, especially in the beginning of the course. This was a surprise to the instructors, who have made note of this lesson: assume that learners want and need to be prepared for on-line discussions, and check with learners on the specifics and extent of their needs.

In this example, the instructors were responsible for designing an individual course. When a variety of courses share similar instructional strategies and software applications, learner preparation can efficiently occur at the program level.

This economy of scale is illustrated in our next example, a computer competency course at the program level.

PROGRAM LEVEL: THE CU SCHOOL OF NURSING

The University of Colorado School of Nursing has pursued an ambitious schedule of converting programs and classes to a combination of Web and tele-conference delivery systems. Because of this rapid change, many learners find themselves in situations in which their program has shifted from face-to-face classes to exclusively on-line classes in mid-stream. Learners first stumble on the realities of on-line learning when they log on to their class. For them, academic survival depends on rapid adaptability to new ways of learning.

In support of the School of Nursing learners, the Master of Science Program developed a mandatory computer skills competency course. The rationale for the computer competency course was to prevent having learners on steep learning curves in both content and process at the same time. Some of the learners' concerns that prompted the program to develop the computer skills competency course were apprehension about technology, fear of falling behind due to lack of critical skills, worry about embarrassment in front of more technically proficient colleagues, and questions about the penalty for turning in a less technically sophisticated course project. The faculty and administration were convinced that the cumulative effect of these factors could result in a compromised program of study for many learners. The plan was to fortify learners by giving them a chance to develop minimum standards of performance in relevant computer-based tasks in advance of the courses.

Debate on policy issues ensued. The decision was to make the course mandatory but ungraded (some instructors gave extra credit for completion of the course). Instead of trying to enforce minimum computer system requirements, the program made strong recommendations, with descriptions of the harrowing problems anticipated in taking an on-line course with less than the recommended minimum.

The preparation course was designed in three stages. First, a letter was mailed to all students in the Master of Science Program to inform them of the course. The letter included instructions for accessing the on-line computer skills competency course and passwords, along with words of encouragement explaining the necessity for completing the course. Participants were given several dates for optional on-campus orientations in preparation for the on-line course.

In stage two, the program held multiple on-campus orientation sessions of the computer competency course. These orientation sessions were important for the true technophobes who had always counted on their children to turn on the computer. Many learners who were fearful of the technology attended these sessions, and seemed to benefit from the personal attention they received. Low attendance at the sessions several weeks in advance of the start of the semester was balanced by high attendance at the session only hours before the first day of class.

Stage three launched the on-line course itself, which was taught concurrently with the multiple on-campus orientation sessions. In order to give learners an introduction to the software they would encounter in class, the computer competency course was designed using the same application used to support the other on-line Master of Science courses. Five topics were included in the competency course: becoming familiar with the hardware and software components of the computer system; sending and receiving e-mail and attachments; using the Web to search for resources; practicing on some of the most common collaborative and student-centered learning techniques used in the courses (for example, threaded discussions and public posting of work); and completing a self-assessment of computer skills and identification of areas that need to be strengthened.

All aspects of the computer skills competency course were designed to provide a realistic sense of participating in a School of Nursing on-line course. The course coordinator kept up communication by private e-mail with all learners, arranged for technical and instructional support as needed, and encouraged participants to coach peers who had difficulty with various aspects of the course.

Reluctant Learners

The course designers anticipated that a percentage of learners would be reluctant to take the computer skills competency course (Rogers 263). The policy was to discourage students from opting out of the course, though many of them presented rationales for their exemption. For example, learners who had prior experience with on-line courses felt that they did not need it. However, many members of this group either did not have the opportunity to use many of the features of the courseware, or they did not display the expected level of technical competency for on-line learning that the designers required. Some previous courses relied heavily on on-line conferencing, but had never formed private forums for collaborative project building. In other courses the instructors, although they expected learners to post written assignments, sometimes allowed people who hit technological snags to submit a hard copy of the assignment instead. Thus even after the experience of taking an entire course on-line, some learners were still not fully prepared in the technology.

Other learners, anxious about the program changes in general, tended to believe rumors that the competency course would take twenty or more hours to complete (in reality the course averaged about six to eight hours). The thought of this daunting task, coupled with uncertainty about becoming an on-line learner, put some in a state of paralysis. Some simply procrastinated and put off meeting the inevitable necessity of either buying into—or out of—on-line learning. A majority of the learners initiated the on-line course the week before classes started and completed it during the first few weeks of the semester.

Yet another group of learners had heard negative things about the Web environment. Frequently voiced fears were that they wouldn't get to know the course instructor or their classmates, wouldn't get the same quality of experience, and that somehow on-line courses would fall short of "real" courses. It became a goal of the course designers to demonstrate that seeing and feeling the physical presence of an instructor is not the only test of a course's quality. Learner perception of a quality learning experience has long been rooted in the physical presence of the instructor and in the positivist view that instructors are the holders and dispensers of expert knowledge (Seamons 199; Jonassen, Peck, and Wilson 13; Cyrs viii). The computer competency course attempted to help learners make the shift to a more constructivist epistemology (Wilson 3–8), which was more in line with that of the program.

Instructor Preparation

To prepare learners, the course designers also anticipated the need to prepare instructors, some of whom found themselves at a loss when facing their first on-line teaching experience. A sample course for instructors to participate as learners was designed and offered several months in advance of the majority of on-line courses, along with a training session for instructors to demonstrate and practice the course management features of the courseware. This just-in-time session was well received. While many of the instructors had actually taught an on-line course, most had not recognized the number and depth of course tools available to manage and create an on-line learning environment. Many found they had the same difficulties that learners experienced in the area of technical skills.

Lessons

After two semesters of experience in the program, developers have concluded that the course does need to be mandatory. They observed that learners were routinely unable to assess their actual skills level in the required tasks, either over- or underestimating their abilities.

Ideally, the program designers would prefer to reach learners well before the first on-line course and carefully plan to assist their gradual adjustment to taking courses on-line. The planners were struck by how potentially disruptive it is to have learners suddenly immersed in new instructional technologies and strategies. Web environments often prompt a dramatic alteration of the role of both instructor and learner (Shotsberger 101–6), and they felt that all participants need to be alerted.

Finally, the course designers noted the importance of simultaneously preparing instructors and learners for the Web environment. Their analogy was that moving from a traditional classroom to an on-line environment was like many cross-cultural experiences—you can easily lose something critical in the translation.

INSTITUTIONAL LEVEL: THE VIRTUAL UNIVERSITY

The third example of learner preparation for the Web environment is at the level of the institution. Both nationally and internationally, higher education has a long history of teaching at a distance. Among the pioneers are the British Open University, the University of Wisconsin, and the University of Maryland, who have for years offered distance education primarily through correspondence, broadcast, and audio tapes (Brand 42). In the past decade, many other institutions of higher education have begun to offer on-line classes as an adjunct to their on-campus classes. Popular use of the Web and its enhancing technologies, together with a growing market for distance learning, has ushered in the era of the virtual university, in which the primary platform for learning is distributed. *Peterson's Guide to Distance Learning* lists more than 2,000 degree and certificate programs from almost 900 institutions (*Peterson's Guide*). Some examples of this kind of modern virtual institution are Magellan University, the Western Governors University, Athabasca University, City University, Regents University, and Walden University.

Learner Preparation and Ethics

Reports and recommendations on distributed learning generally mention learner support as a priority consideration for institutional policies and procedures, along with planning, curriculum, quality assurance, faculty issues, tuition and funding, and technical standards (Oregon State System of Higher Education 2–3; Nunan and Calvert 10; Manitoba Minister of Education 10–11). Learner support encompasses a number of aspects of administrative and academic functions (such as records management and library services) and classic advising functions (like course selection), as well as what we have labeled learner preparation.

When addressed at the institutional level, the issue of learner support and preparation takes on a greater sense of urgency: because institutions operate at a more encompassing scale, they are in a position to effect deeper, more systemic change in teaching and learning (Levy 10). In contrast to the level of the individual class and the level of the program, institutions create policies and procedures that affect many people, that set benchmarks for the field, and that influence the international dialogue on learning in the Web environment (Raggatt and Harry 2; Nunan and Calvert 108; van Schoor 1–2).

Educational institutions are businesses, and even publicly supported businesses must account for a reasonable balance of income and expenditures. Sewart ("Teaching" 8–9), in his role as Director of Regional Academic Services for the British Open University, argues that educational institutions can choose to make decisions based on a *service model* or an *industrial model*. In a service model, the primary objective is to serve learners by direct contribution to their success; in an industrial model, the primary objective is to serve learners by maintaining a thriving institution through strategic allocation of resources. That strategic allocation may or may not include an investment in learner preparation. "For those responsible for creating student support systems, there is an overall decision to be made concerning an 'acceptable' rate of dropout and this will be arrived at in terms of the overall philosophy of education but also through an analysis of the overall costs of the institution" (9).

If, in response to the cost/benefit analysis, an institution declines to allocate resources for learner preparation in Web-based courses, some categories of learners might be especially at risk for disenfranchisement. For example, learners from technology-poor backgrounds may lack prior experience with the Web, and rural learners may lack access to equipment or the necessary infrastructure. These constraints can translate into systematic exclusion from an increasing number of higher education courses (Manitoba Minister of Education 5–6; Sewart, "Student" 9). Another example is surfaced by studies on gender differences and the Web, which look at the frequency and nature of women's on-line participation—emerging data question the compatibility with female learning and communication styles (Hipp 41–49; Yates 289–90; Wojahn 750–52).

Time will tell whether the Web environment will widen educational opportunity or exacerbate a system of inequity, will increase access or tighten restrictions. We argue that careful attention to learner preparation can be one strategy for recruitment, retention, and overall support for opportunity in the Web environment. Optimistically, these ethical and philosophical concerns will converge with good business practice: in virtual universities, where all learners are required to perform in the Web environment, the institution rightly has a strong incentive to help prepare its customers to succeed at the task.

Institutional Strategies

A survey of student preparation activities in virtual universities demonstrates a range of learner preparation strategies. The most common initial strategy is to direct learners to a self-assessment survey to help them determine if they have the technical aptitude, access to adequate equipment, and preferred learning styles that might presage their success as on-line learners. Typical self-assessment inventories that we previewed question learners on included:

- technical factors like the learners' access to appropriate hardware with Internet connectivity and familiarity with software applications;
- experience in the management of electronic communication functions;
- learning style considerations like preference for written discussions versus in-person class discussions;
- motivational issues like self-directedness, willingness to try new things, and tolerance for ambiguity;
- issues of time management and tendencies toward procrastination.

A good example of this type of on-line self-assessment is one offered by the Western Governors University. On this self-scoring assessment, the respondents receive a standard paragraph interpreting their answers. The assessment describes certain profiles of learners as good candidates for the Web environment (motivated, disciplined, technologically proficient, etc.). Those without these characteristics are encouraged to think twice before plunging into the on-line world. All respondents are advised, but not mandated, to use the information to consider their potential for success. Once learners are admitted, the institution typically assigns an academic advisor whose role is to guide course selection and use of resources.

An extensive site for on-line learner preparation is offered by Edmonds Community College. They provide a six-week On-line Internet Course, with the accompanying advice, "Do plan to spend at least three to five hours each week reading and practicing." In addition, they offer a sample class with links to technical support offered by the course design software.

Another good example of on-line learner preparation is provided by the University of Central Florida (UCF), which provides detailed information on hardware and software requirements, as well as discussion on the process of learning in an on-line orientation session. The format is inviting and friendly, offering advice to both learners and instructors—"The Ten Commandments for Learning On-line" and "The Ten Commandments for Teaching On-line."

Magellan University takes the approach of explaining what on-line learners might expect from their class experience, and provides an extensive series of links, both commercial and noncommercial, to other helpful sites—HTML resources, Internet culture and netiquette, Web search tutorials, and so on. A number of advanced degrees are awarded by Walden University, whose learner preparation strategy seems to place an emphasis on personal contact with mentor/advisors at each step on the learner's advancement toward a degree.

The British Open University pioneered the use of tutors and regional study centers. Tutors are assigned to each learner and provide a variety of learner support services. Study centers are locations that help learners bridge the gap between traditional face-to-face classes and on-line classes.

Institutional Issues

This sampling of institutional learner preparation strategies is based on publicly available information. It does not include information on proprietary services available only to registered learners, nor can it capture the role individual programs, instructors, or advisors play in assisting Web learners. However, it does point out two important issues in learner preparation. First, preparing learners is currently seen as a standard quality indicator and a recommended priority for distributed learning (Oregon State System of Higher Education 10–12; Nunan and Calvert 10; Manitoba Minister of Education 10–11). Second, there is an especially compelling policy dimension at the institutional level that has implications for educational equity and inclusion (Sewart, "Student" 9–10). We believe that, as higher education becomes more immersed in the Web environment, this implies a special responsibility on the part of institutions for careful consideration of the role of learner preparation.

CHECKLIST FOR LEARNER PREPARATION

In the examples described at the class, program, and institutional level, the adage "pay now or pay later" comes to mind. Emerging use of the Web environments challenges some preconceptions about learners and the extent of the support they may need to progress and succeed. It is safe to assume that for many learners, Web instruction introduces new concerns and needs; the question is how and when to address those needs, and the cost of neglecting to address them.

From research in instructional technology, systems theory, sociology, and cognitive psychology, and from experiences like those chronicled above, we have developed a seven-item checklist that the University of Colorado at Denver's Technology and Learning Team reviews with instructors and administrators as they design and promote instruction for the Web. The items are meant to prompt educators to consider the issue of what it takes to prepare learners to be successful in the Web environment. Addressing these items demands time and attention, resources that are always at a premium. Our experience is that this effort is rewarded by more effective implementation of instruction.

Because this checklist covers a lot of theoretical and practical ground, we have chosen to simply highlight items for consideration, citing their roots in theories and models. We provide references to resources to encourage further exploration. For now, our goal is to contribute to the evolving discussion about preparing learners for Web-based instruction.

Assumptions

The list is based on several assumptions. First, the best use of the Web is as an *interactive* tool in support of learning. Research in contemporary learning argues convincingly that there are more substantial gains in learning when learners are actively involved (Scardamelia and Bereiter 265–68; Honebein, Duffy, and Fishman 90). All of the items in the list are intended to lead learners away from passivity and toward active engagement.

A second assumption is that the use of the Web as a learning environment is relatively new. Especially in light of evolving technologies and strategies, this educational adventure is in the chaotic and creative period of development (Gleick 43). For this reason, it will likely be an innovation for most of us, instructor and learner alike. It is prudent to assume that participants are novices at either or both the technology and the instructional strategies until we have evidence of their proficiency.

As systems theorists like to remind us, never underestimate the tendency of human systems (and open systems in general) to seek homeostasis (Bateson 431). Literature on innovations can be a useful lens through which to view the use of the Web as an instructional tool because it reminds us of typical human behavior in the face of innovation (see especially Rogers; Havelock and Zlotolow). According to Rogers, in any given system for any given innovation, approximately 16 percent of those in the system will be eager and early participants, based on their favorable perception of the advantages of the technology, its compatibility with their own history and experience and self-image, the support they enjoy in using the technology, how complex it appears to them, and whether they have had an opportunity to observe it in action and try it out (Rogers 262). In that same system, the majority (approximately 68 percent will typically have mixed feelings about the innovation based on their own perceptions of these same factors. It is to be expected that the remaining approximately 16 percent, based on their perceptions of the innovation, may be strongly reluctant or unwilling to participate.

Another assumption is that, for our purposes, the phrase "preparing learners" does not imply that preparation activities are done only in advance of the class. Preparation of learners is, like any learning, an ongoing process and requires attention, review, and evaluation.

The final assumption is that the job of the educator is to create an environment in which it becomes more and more likely that learning will occur. Just as nothing can compel learning, nothing can compel learners to be prepared to learn. The feedback we have received from learners is that too much intervention from the instructor can be frustrating. The irony would be if, in expending too much time and effort to prepare learners, we deprived them of the responsibility and self-direction we espouse. We are looking to strike a happy balance between process and content.

USING THE CHECKLIST

Not all of the checklist items must be addressed at once. Fortunately, change in one part of a system will likely trigger change in other parts of the system (Kauffman 2). Focusing on one item will likely have an effect on the behavior of both instructor and learner. For example, gathering information on how familiar the learners are with the technology can begin to provide instructors with additional information about the learners, can contribute to the formation of the learning community, and can give instructors an opportunity to model good learning behavior. Because of their broad nature, the items overlap, and are designed to be applicable at the level of the individual class, the program, or the institution. In general, our approach is to keep relevant items like these in mind, strive to address them all at some point, and begin to experiment, balancing action and analysis to avoid paralysis (Fullan 31).

1. Find Out How Familiar the Learners Are with the Technology.

Determining the familiarity of the learners with the technology is a primary concern. Learners must first have access to the necessary technology, and must develop a level of proficiency with its functions in order to participate. Although it seems obvious, it is hard to overestimate the importance of this item. It may be an issue of knowing the hardware and software, or it may be an issue of availability and convenience. In rural areas, for example, inadequate infrastructure may delay participation to a frustrating crawl, or may not be able to accommodate full access to files and functions.

One standard strategy used by on-line programs in preparing learners is the self-assessment inventory (see the section on "Institutional Strategies" for samples). Having learners catalogue their access to technology and rate themselves on scales of proficiency as well as learning styles and motivation serves as a way to organize and highlight the issues that they will face, and encourages them to evaluate their likelihood of success.

This information can be invaluable to instructors and administrators in assisting learners and in systemic planning. In response, some instructors, programs, or institutions require specific technology; others offer or mandate training during an orientation period, update the training when new software is introduced, and review procedures at the beginning of a class.

Once a group of learners is generally up and running, it is tempting to assume that because most of the class is demonstrating proficiency, then all must be proficient. As noted above, it is typical for approximately 16 percent of any particular group or system, for any given innovation, to be unable or unwilling to use the technology (Rogers 262). In a class of twenty-five learners, for example, we might predict that four or five would require extra attention in order to remain and function; some may choose never to participate. Discovering more about learners' access and proficiency in technology leads to the next item: Find out more about the learners.

2. Find Out More about the Learners.

"Start with where the learner is." This classic educational advice is rooted in the recognition that learners differ not only in technological proficiency, but also along a variety of dimensions, for example, learning styles (Kolb 246), gender differences (Hipp 41–49; Yates 289–90; Wojahn 750–52), physiological barriers to the use of the equipment (*Trace Research and Development Center*), and stages of cognitive development (Perry 3). This is no different than any group of learners. An advantage is that in cyberspace, these differences can lose their ability to stigmatize and limit. Conversely, differences can also become magnified in the Web environment when preferences, capabilities, and technologies are mismatched.

Generally, instructional design principles would suggest that courses employ a wide range of strategies, both individual and group, to accommodate the range of learner differences (Siegel and Kirkley 267–68). Instructors may need to ask the learners explicitly what they perceive would support their success, and what might get in the way.

More than any other item, this one prompts a pedagogical sorting out of the balance between the responsibility of the instructor and the responsibility of the learner. Web learners need to be aware of their own needs and able to keep themselves focused, productive, and persistent in the face of process and content obstacles they may not have previously encountered (Schuemer 40). At the same time, instructors and administrators have a stake and a role in learner success. This item engenders interesting discussions among our clients: What are the boundaries of learner responsibility? In introducing Web instruction, how much preparation is desirable, and who is responsible for arranging it?

3. Articulate What the Learners Are Expected to Learn.

Learning is the centerpiece of educational activity (Fullan 8). This item encourages an instructional shift from "What do I need to cover in class?" to "What do people need and want to learn, and what are the best strategies and tools at our disposal to support that?" (Grasha 207–8; Cyrs 9–16). The difference between these two approaches becomes dramatic with the introduction of the fascinating array of Web affordances. All too often, we observe that the sophisticated and compelling Web technology wags the dog. The Web in higher education is sometimes adopted in response to a variety of professional pressures (van Schoor 2–10): perhaps it is adopted because it is novel, the competition is using it, resources and funding are newly available, it is intriguing, it is mandated, or the instructor is an enthusiastic Web user. Because we acknowledge the power of these realities, we advocate returning frequently to this question of what the learners are expected to learn in order to redirect attention to the centrality of this goal.

4. Consider the Nature of the Content Domain.

Like any textbook, the Web can be used to dispense information. Unlike a textbook, the Web is an example of "an open, ever changing, and ever-expanding information architecture" (Siegel and Kirkley 265). As such, it affords learners the opportunity to use it to explore more ill-structured domains (Jonassen, Peck, and Wilson 152). Sometimes structures like advance organizers, outlines, summaries, calendars and schedules, rubrics, and archives of excellent class projects can provide learners with the bridges they need; sometimes more flexible knowledge management tools serve best (Wilson). Being aware of the ill-structured or well-structured nature of the content is a good first step in providing learners with the scaffolding they need.

5. Identify and Model Effective Learning Behaviors.

Modeling behaviors that are expected of the learners is a powerful form of teaching (Bandura). Modeling and scaffolding to prepare learners can occur before the actual instruction begins, or can be woven into the content of the course. Jacobson and Spiro (326–29) suggest that learners who are given substantial modeling and scaffolding are significantly more likely to transfer their knowledge to related domains than are those who are not given any guidance.

One element that is important to the success of learning in the Web environment is the confidence and enthusiasm that the instructor has for the specific software and for the learning strategy in general. Saye (5–10) argues that learners can be highly influenced by the opinions and attitude of their instructors. A respected teacher who is willing to try novel learning environments will be more likely to succeed than one who appears to be intimidated by or skeptical of the benefits of the new technology. Instructors improve their chances of success in a Web environment by persuasive arguments for the use of the novel domain, selective use of the strategy, and a refusal to give up in the face of initial difficulties. Once they see instructional strategies working, at least some of the learners will begin to appreciate the benefits of the Web environment. Conversely, the fears and skepticism that learners may have can play a major role in how successful they are with the program (DeJoy 37).

6. Help Develop a Learning Community.

Contemporary distributed learning theorists and researchers make a compelling argument that it is critically important for on-line learners to become a part of a community of practice, and that instructors are the key to promoting the community (Lave and Wenger; Gunawardena 147). Specific design advice is offered by Wolcott (27), including encouraging informal communication, establishing study groups, and posting pictures and bios of everyone. A model by Schrage (151–63) builds on thirteen features of an on-line community of learning, including mutual respect and trust, shared goals, and communication guidelines.

7. Encourage Time Management.

This mundane item is one of the biggest challenges for everyone in the Web environment. In the absence of a scheduled and synchronous class period, all participants become responsible for the allocation of time. Course participation competes in the marketplace of life, work, play, and all manner of interesting choices. Some classic interventions include providing structure and pacing of projects, modeling by the instructor of on-time achievements, and reinforcement of the same when learners manage their time well. Web environments can also provide helpful links for explicit review of tried-and-true time management techniques (Mind Tools).

CONCLUSION

Preparing higher education learners for the Web environment is an evolving area of pedagogy. In some very fundamental ways, deciding how best to support learning is an old, familiar quest in education (Dewey 45–46). We are encouraged by the fresh look it is receiving as Web-based teaching strategies become more pervasive. It is tempting to become enthralled by the kaleidoscope of Web technologies, and neglect the realities of learners and instructors trying to survive and thrive in a Web environment. In "Things that Make Us Smart," Norman calls for technology that fits human social and cognitive needs, rather than insisting that human beings change to fit the technology (xi). Our hope is that, by maintaining a persistent focus on the best interests of learners, the Web will become both an effective and inclusive vehicle for learning.

WORKS CITED

Bandura, Albert. *Social Foundations of Thought and Action: A Social Cognitive Theory.* Englewood Cliffs, NJ: Prentice-Hall, 1986.

Bateson, Gregory M. *Steps to an Ecology of Mind.* New York: Ballantine Books, 1972.

Brand, Myles. "The Wise Use of Technology." *Educational Record* 76.4 (1995): 39–45.

British Open University. *Open University.* 1999. 1 Aug. 1999 <http://www.open.ac.uk>.

Crawford, Chris. "Lessons from Computer Games Design." In *The Art of Human-Computer Interface Design.* Ed. Brenda Laurel. Reading, MA: Addison-Wesley, 1990.

Cyrs, Thomas E. *Teaching at a Distance with the Merging Technologies.* Las Cruces, NM: New Mexico State University Center for Educational Development, 1997.

DeJoy, Judith K. "Incorporating Microcomputer Technology into Adult Learning Environments." *New Directions for Adult and Continuing Education* 50 (1991): 33–40.

Dewey, John. *How We Think: Restatement of the Relation of Reflective Thinking to the Educative Process.* Boston: Heath, 1933.

Edmonds Community College. *On-line Student Reference Manual.* 5 May 1999. 1 Aug. 1999 <http://www.cce.edcc.edu/online/manual.html).

Fullan, Michael. *Change Forces: Probing the Depths of Educational Reform.* London: Falmer Press, 1993.

Gleick, James. *Chaos: Making a New Science.* New York: Penguin Books, 1987.

Grasha, Tony. *Teaching with Style.* Pittsburgh: Alliance Publishers, 1996.

Gunawardena, Charlotte. "Social Presence Theory and Implications for Interaction and Collaborative Learning in Computer Conferences." *International Journal of Educational Telecommunications* 1.2 (1995): 147–66.

Havelock, Ronald, and Steve Zlotolow. *The Change Agent's Guide to Innovation in Education.* 2nd ed. Englewood Cliffs, NJ: Educational Technology, 1995.

Hipp, Helene. "Women Studying at a Distance: What Do They Need to Succeed?" *Open Learning* 12.2 (1997): 41–49.

Honebein, Peter, Thomas M. Duffy, and Barry J. Fishman. "Constructivism and the Design of Learning Communities: Constructivism in Practice." In *Designing Environments for Constructive Learning*. Ed. Thomas Duffy, Jost Lowyck, and David Jonassen. Berlin: Springer-Verlag, 1991.

Institute for Research in Learning. *IRL's Seven Principles About Learning*. 1999. 1 Aug. 1999 <http://www.irl.org/info/sevenprinciples.html>.

Jacobson, Michael, and Rand Spiro. "Hypertext Learning Environments, Cognitive Flexibility, and the Transfer of Complex Knowledge: An Empirical Investigation." *Journal of Educational Computing Research* 12.4 (1995): 301–33.

Jonassen, David H. "Instructional Design Models for Well-Structured and Ill-Structured Problem-Solving Learning Outcomes." *Educational Technology Research and Development* 45.1 (1997): 65–94.

———, ed. *Instructional Designs for Microcomputer Courseware*. Hillsdale, NJ: Lawrence Erlbaum, 1988.

Jonassen, David H., and Heinz Mandl, eds. *Designing Hypermedia for Learning*. New York: Springer-Verlag, 1990.

Jonassen, David H., Kyle L. Peck, and Brent G. Wilson. *Learning with Technology*. Englewood Cliffs, NJ: Prentice-Hall, 1999.

Kauffman, Draper L. *Systems One: An Introduction to Systems Thinking*. Minneapolis: S. A. Carlton, 1980.

Kilian, Crawford. "Why Teach Online." *Educom Review* 32.4 (1997): 31–34.

Kolb, David A. "Learning Styles and Disciplinary Differences." In *The Modern American College*. Ed. Arthur Chickering. San Francisco: Jossey-Bass, 1981.

Lave, Jean, and Etienne Wenger. *Situated Learning: Legitimate Peripheral Participation*. Cambridge, England: Cambridge University Press, 1991.

Levy, Amir. "Second-Order Planned Change: Definition and Conceptualization." *Organizational Dynamics* 15 (Summer 1986): 5–20.

Magellan University. *Web Hints*. 19 June 1999. 25 June 1999 <http://www.magellan.edu/webhints.htm>.

Manitoba Minister of Education. *Task Force on Distance Education and Technology: Final Report*. Winnipeg: Manitoba Department of Education and Training, 1993.

Mind Tools. *How to Get the Most Out of Your Time*. 1995. 1 Aug. 1999 <http://www.mindtools.com/page5.html>.

Moore, Michael G. "Purpose and Practice of Home Study in the Nineties." Paper presented at the National Home Study Council Conference, Notre Dame, Indiana, October 1986.

Moore, Michael G., and Greg Kearsley. *Distance Education: A Systems View*. Belmont, CA: Wadsworth Publishing, 1996.

Norman, Donald A. *Things that Make Us Smart*. Reading, MA: Addison-Wesley, 1993.

Nunan, Ted, and Jocelyn Calvert. *Quality and Standards in Distance Education*. Victoria: University of South Australia, Underdale, 1992.

Oregon State System of Higher Education. *Distance Education Policy Framework*. Portland: State of Oregon, 1995.

Perelman, Lewis J. *School's Out: Hyperlearning, the New Technology, and the End of Education*. New York: William Morrow, 1992.

Perry, William. "Different Worlds in the Same Classroom: Students' Evolution in Their

Vision of Knowledge and Their Expectations of Teachers." *On Teaching and Learning* 1 (May 1985): 1–17.

Peterson's Guide to Distance Learning. 1999. 1 Aug. 1999 <http://www.petersons.com>.

Raggatt, Peter, and Keith Harry, eds. *Trends in Distance Higher Education.* Buckingham, United Kingdom: The Open University, 1984.

Repman, Judi, and Suzanne Logan. "Interactions at a Distance: Possible Barriers and Collaborative Solutions." *TechTrends* 41.6 (1996): 35–38.

Rogers, Everett M. *Diffusion of Innovations.* New York: The Free Press, 1995.

Saye, John. "Technology and Educational Empowerment: Students' Perspectives." *Educational Technology Research and Development* 45.2 (1997): 5–25.

Scardamelia, Marlene, and Carl Bereiter. "Computer Support for Knowledge Building Communities." *Journal of the Learning Sciences* 3.3 (1994): 265–84.

Schrage, Michael. *Shared Minds: The New Technologies of Collaboration.* New York: Random House, 1991.

Schuemer, Rudolf. *Some Psychological Aspects of Distance Education.* Hagen, Germany: Institute for Research into Distance Education, 1993.

Seamons, R. Alan. "The Influence of Teaching Style and Instructional Device Use on Student Satisfaction and Student Preference in Electronic Distance Educational Methods." *Proceedings from the Third Annual Conference on Distance Teaching and Learning.* Madison, WI: University of Wisconsin–Madison August 1987. 198–200.

Sewart, David. "Student Support Systems in Distance Education." Paper presented at the World Conference of the International Council for Distance Education, Bangkok, Thailand, November 1992.

————. "Teaching: A Contradiction in Terms?" *Teaching at a Distance* 19 (1981): 8–18.

Shotsberger, Paul G. "Emerging Roles for Instructors and Learners in the Web-Based Instruction Classroom." In *Web-Based Instruction.* Ed. Badrul H. Kahn. Englewood Cliffs, NJ: Educational Technology Publications, 1997. 101–6.

Siegel, Martin A., and Sonny Kirkley. "Moving Toward the Digital Learning Environment." In *Web-Based Instruction.* Ed. Badrul H. Kahn. Englewood Cliffs, NJ: Educational Technology Publications, 1997. 263–70.

Technology and Learning Team. University of Colorado at Denver. June 1999. 1 Aug. 1999 <http://tlt.cudenver.edu>.

Trace Research and Development Center. University of Wisconsin-Madison. 1999. 1 Aug. 1999 <http://trace.wisc.edu>.

University of Central Florida. *Course Development and Web Services.* 7 June 1999. 1 Aug. 1999 <http://reach.ucf.edu>.

van Schoor, W. A. "Institutional Relevance in Distance Education: The Role of Strategic Planning." Paper presented at the World Conference of the International Council for Distance Education, Bangkok, Thailand, November 1992.

Vigotsky, Lev S. *Thought and Language.* Trans. A. Kozulin. Cambridge, MA: MIT Press, 1986.

Walden University. *Academic Counseling.* 1999. 1 Aug. <http://waldenu.edu/stud-srvcs/academic-counseling>.

Weinstein, Paul. "Education Goes the Distance." *Technology and Learning* 17.8 (1997): 24–25.

Western Governors University. *Self-Assessment for Distance Learning.* 1999. 1 Aug. 1999 <http://www.wgu.edu/wgu/self_assessment.asp>.

Willis, Barry, and John Dickinson. "Distance Education and the World Wide Web." In *Web-Based Instruction.* Ed. Badrul H. Kahn. Englewood Cliffs, NJ: Educational Technology Publications, 1997. 81–84.

Wilson, Brent G. "Introduction: What Is a Constructivist Learning Environment?" In *Constructivist Learning Environments.* Ed. Brent G. Wilson. Englewood Cliffs, NJ: Educational Technology Publications, 1996. 3–8.

Wojahn, Patricia G. "Computer-Mediated Communication: The Great Equalizer Between Men and Women?" *Technical Communication: Journal of the Society for Technical Communication* 41.4 (1994): 747–52.

Wolcott, Linda L. "Distant but Not Distanced: A Learner-Centered Approach to Distance Education." *TechTrends* 41.4 (1996): 23–27.

Yates, Simeon J. (1997). "Gender, Identity, and CMC." *Journal of Computer Assisted Learning* 13.4 (1997): 281–90.

Chapter 22

A Hierarchy of Access Issues Affecting On-line Participation by Community College Students

Allan Craig Lauzon, Tricia Bertram Gallant, and Susan Rimkus

INTRODUCTION

Distance education and other forms of mediated education have grown exponentially over the last decade. This is a direct response to developments in communication and computer technology and their subsequent convergence. Mason and Kaye argue that these developments and their application constitute a new paradigm of education. Lauzon ("Postmodernism") has argued that these developments correspond to changes in our understanding of the nature of knowledge and its relationship to learning. Subsequently we are seeing an increasing emphasis in education on learner-centeredness, interactivity, and collaborative learning. Gaines et al. have characterized these changes as the emergence of the *learning web*, while de Kerckhove describes these developments within the context of *webness*.

The purpose of this chapter is to offer our reflections on the various dimensions that seem to be important when using this type of learning environment. We will begin by reflecting on our experience of teaching an on-line course in interpersonal communications offered by the Department of Rural Extension Studies, University of Guelph. This will be followed by a reporting of the findings of a study conducted by Tricia Bertram Gallant and our collective reflections on the less than promising outcomes of Tricia's experience.

TEN YEARS OF TEACHING COMMUNICATION PROCESS ON-LINE

Communication Process was first developed as an on-line course in 1989. At this time it was offered in two formats: face-to-face and as a correspondence course. The motivation for developing the on-line course arose as a result of the discrepancy between the performance of face-to-face students and the correspondence students, with the face-to-face students having a class average that was one full grade higher than the correspondence students. At that time we speculated that the difference in performance might be accounted for by the lack of interaction the correspondence students had with the instructor and/or other students, making it more difficult for them to integrate and synthesize the course material. We then examined alternative ways of providing the distance student with learning opportunities that were interactive and decided that this was best accomplished through the use of computer conferencing.

The Course

The content of the course focuses, for the most part, on patterns of miscommunication and how miscommunication can be prevented or corrected. In addition, there is some motivation theory, perception theory, and management theory. The course is divided into five modules, each module covering four to five chapters of the text (approximately 85–150 pages). The course lasts twelve weeks. Students are required to participate in each module, and it is suggested that they log into class at least twice a week. In addition, students participate in two group assignments that are completed on-line and write a final examination. In order for students to complete the on-line group assignments they need to log on at certain periods of the semester more frequently than the two times requested for the general discussion. Students are then graded on the assignments, the final examination, and their participation. It should be noted that participation in the general discussion is graded according to frequency and the quality of the students' comments. The attempt here is to replicate the typical classroom discussion. Thus the instructor is likely to pose questions as a stimulus for discussion and then facilitate that discussion as necessary.

The structure of the class typically consists of 5 general discussion groups of 20–30 students and 26 smaller groups consisting of 4–7 students for the group projects. Therefore each student would belong to one large discussion group and one small "working" group.

The Students

The prerequisite for this course is 20 credits, which means students enrolled are either in their third or fourth year of university. This is, in general, a service course; students come from different disciplines ranging from the humanities and social sciences to sciences and professional schools. They are usually full-time students who also work full or part time and are involved with other time-consuming activities such as sports and family responsibilities. For the most part, these students appear highly motivated, and there is a great deal of on-line discussion.

Outcomes

This course has been, from our perspective, very successful. When the performance of on-line students was compared with face-to-face students, we found that the on-line students performed slightly better than the face-to-face students (although it was not significant statistically). Thus the on-line student class average had risen a full grade from that of the more traditional correspondence course. The department was so pleased with these results that they now offer this course only in an on-line format.[1]

SUPPORTING COOPERATIVE WORKPLACE LEARNING THROUGH ON-LINE FORMATS

The success at the University of Guelph in using CMC (Computer-Mediated Communication)-supported distance learning inspired Tricia, who is Coordinator of Cooperative Education at the University of Guelph, to explore ways in which technology could be used to support workplace learning. The need stemmed from the isolation of the cooperative students, often as a result of the geographical distance of their placement, and complaints about the absence of meaningful "learning assignments" during their cooperative work term. Typically, students would be asked to write a report which the faculty advisor would then use as the basis for passing or failing the student in the placement. The students received little feedback, nor did they receive any degree of real support from the university while they were in their work placement. Furthermore, their previous classroom learning was not integrated into their work experience in any meaningful ways. Thus there continued to be a separation between "book learning" and "doing." Tricia believed that there had to be a way of fostering higher level learning in the workplace and a means of providing support for the learners when they were in their placement. Furthermore, she felt that the university had a responsibility to search for ways of accomplishing these goals. Her answer—technology.

Initially Tricia contemplated using University of Guelph cooperative students and the cooperative program here for a pilot test. However, there was little support in place, and consequently, at this stage, the obstacles and logistics of running a pilot project seemed insurmountable. Fortunately, Tricia happened to meet a colleague at a conference who was very interested in her ideas and suggested that she might test a pilot project at a community college in New York that is well known for its cooperative program. It was ideal, as the students' current cooperative work terms were designed so that the actual work experience was complemented by a mandatory class at the college. The logistics were easily overcome since the on-line component to support the workplace learning would simply replace the face-to-face classroom component of the course. The following information, as it relates to the CMC-supported cooperative work term, comes from a study conducted by Bertram Gallant.

The College

The American community college used in the study has a diverse student population. Like many community colleges in the United States, it operates an "open door policy" that offers postsecondary education to all, especially the economically disadvantaged (Robertshaw and Wolfle). At this particular college, the student population represents over 100 countries, and collectively they speak 50 different languages. English as a Second Language (ESL) students represent 25 percent of the incoming class, and the majority of these students need remedial reading (more than 50 percent) and remedial math (nearly 75 percent) upgrading. Even in the overall student body, 42 percent of the student population requires remedial reading work. The major ethnic groups represented are Hispanic, African American, Caucasian, and Asian. With regard to gender and age, 65 percent of the student population is female, while 58 percent of the student population is under the age of 26.

Description of the On-line Class

The class offered on-line to cooperative education students ran for six weeks during the summer session (July 25–August 10, 1998). The intent of the designers—Tricia and Susan—was to develop a supportive learning environment that helped students explore the learning materials and interact with one another in a supportive environment. There, students could view their work experience in the context of curricular materials, sharing their insights and questions with their peers. The hope was that this would help students integrate and synthesize the curricular materials with their workplace experiences. Computer conferencing was chosen as the technology to support this because the research literature suggests that it is an effective medium for fostering interaction and active exchanges (Burge); it is a place for conversation much like a classroom. Both Kaye ("Computer") and Crook would support Burge's conclusions, with Crook stating that "participation in these computer conferences may come to resemble the experience of a seminar or workshop interaction" (195). In addition, computer conferencing allows students flexibility because it is time and place independent. Therefore, students may log on and participate at their convenience and may also reflect and formulate comments before making a contribution. This is quite different from the traditional classroom and is thought to create a more democratic learning environment (Harasim, "Teaching," "On-line"; Kaye,

"Computer"; Rice and Love). Because everyone is on an equal footing (Fey), shy students participate more readily (Kinner and Coombs) and contributions are judged more by the thoughts and ideas conveyed and less by the person doing the contributing.

In this particular study, the computer conferencing software used was the Virtual University (VU) developed by the Telelearning Network Centres of Excellence (Simon Fraser University, British Columbia). This system is currently in use by the Office of Open Learning, University of Guelph as part of a Beta test. The strength of the computer conferencing component of the VU is that it allows the structuring of various topics into conferences and subconferences. In addition, the messages can be sorted in a variety of ways. A learner may choose to read messages by date or author, or to follow a particular discussion thread. The appeal of the latter option is that a learner can follow the logic of a discussion without having to read messages that may have been posted in between the messages of a thread of discussion. The reader can also choose to list "all" or only "unread" messages in the conference or search all messages for keywords. These features, it is believed, allow students to "manage" the discussion in the manner that best meets their unique needs.

The curricular material was organized into six modules, one per week for each of the six weeks, and this corresponded directly to the material that was covered in the accompanying text. The first module, however, was covered in a two-hour section of the face-to-face training session provided by Tricia. The intent of this was to ensure that students could orient themselves to the on-line environment and to help them get started. If they needed help, then it would be available. The remaining five modules were run in the five subsequent weeks, and students were only allowed to participate in the module during the week that the module was specified. Thus very clear boundaries were established between modules. This was in keeping with the suggestions from the literature that maintaining clear directions and guidelines is necessary (Berge; Davie; Kearsley; Paulsen). In addition to submitting homework assignments, students were also instructed to log on to the conference three to four times per week, and they had to make at least two entries per week (one in response to the assignment and one in response to another's entry). The students received marks for weekly conference entries and submission of homework assignments.

The Students

The prerequisites for the cooperative education internship, and the accompanying seminar, are completion of basic skills courses as needed by each particular student; completion of the first co-op seminar (before internships); at least a 2.0 cumulative grade point average the term prior to the internship; and completion of appropriate courses in the student's major. The Co-op Faculty Advisor decides whether or not a student is ready for her or his first internship. Since co-op is required of all disciplines in the college, the students came from a variety of disciplines including computing science, liberal arts, paralegal studies, telecommunications, and travel. They were full-time students who were working full-time on their co-op internship as well as having additional time-consuming commitments such as sports and family activities. The age range was 19 to 24, and for 73 percent, English was their second language.

The Results

The twelve students who self-selected and registered for the on-line section of the course constituted 4.6 percent of the 259 students registered in thirteen sections of this course for the summer of 1999. However, there was a high percentage of dropouts and "lurkers." Of the twelve original participants, two transferred to a face-to-face section of the class the following week. While the numbers for this study are small, this does constitute an attrition rate of 17 percent, which is notably higher than the attrition rate of the face-to-face version of this course, which is 7 percent.

Of the remaining students, four regularly participated both in the conference and by submitting assignments, three participated irregularly in the conference and by submitting assignments, and three never participated after the initial session. While two contributions per student per week were required, the average number of conference entries was just over one entry per week per student. In actuality, the majority of the entries were made by two particular students and the facilitator. There was little dialogue between the students, and most of the contributions were in direct response to the assignment; a virtual, active classroom was not realized. Since students received marks for contributing, five of the ten students failed the class. This again is much higher than in the face-to-face version, which has an average failure rate of only 3.5 percent.

REFLECTIONS

Contemplating the outcomes of this pilot project in technologically supported cooperative learning, we have asked ourselves, "What went wrong?" All three of us had given careful consideration to the issues. We have had over a decade of success in other on-line ventures, and yet this one did not turn out as we anticipated or hoped.

Accessibility

The first issue we need to consider is accessibility. Figure 22.1 shows our perspective on issues of accessibility as expressed through their conceptualization as a hierarchy of accessibility issues for on-line education.[2]

Figure 22.1
Hierarchy of Access for On-line Education

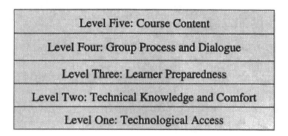

Level Five: Course Content
Level Four: Group Process and Dialogue
Level Three: Learner Preparedness
Level Two: Technical Knowledge and Comfort
Level One: Technological Access

Level One: Technological Access

The first step for successful on-line learning is for the learners to have access to the necessary hardware—computer, modem, Internet server, and Internet software—before they can begin participating. Often this will be available on campus, or in some cases students may have to gain access from home, through friends, or through their place of work.

When we compare courses and institutions there are some differences that may account for differences in success. On the one hand, the University of Guelph has a history of technological innovation. For example, the CoSy computer conferencing system was first developed here and the library has had electronic card catalogues since the early 1980s, which are now available over the Internet. Students are automatically assigned an e-mail account when they enroll at the university, and courses frequently require computer-generated papers and reports. There are Internet hookups in each residence room, and numerous computer and multimedia laboratories across campus. Thus, at the University of Guelph there is a culture that supports the application of computers and communication technology in education. The resources available and policies in place communicate to students that these technologies will play a significant role in their education.

The community college, on the other hand, has few computer resources on campus, and those that are available are associated with the computer science department. Furthermore, students do not automatically receive an e-mail account. These items, like those cited above, communicate a message to students: these resources are for *special* purposes and will not be a regular part of your academic life at the college.

The student populations are also very different. The community college student population is much more diverse than the student population at the University of Guelph. This is significant as research points to the fact that minority and low socioeconomic status (SES) students are less likely to have access to computers than are majority students (Resta; Schwalm). A survey of over 2,100 U.S. schools (Becker) suggests that "major inequalities in access and use of computers still exist across racial and economic groups" (Resta 121). Cole and

Griffin and Edwards also found that more computers are being placed in schools with a lower percentage of poor and minority students. And, as Edwards notes, the average income of black and Hispanic families in the United States is much lower ($16,000–$18,000) than the average income of home computer purchasers. Therefore, these students are not likely to have access to computers at home or in their previous public schools.

The context of the learning experience might also be a factor. The University of Guelph students were, for the most part, campus-based students taking advantage of the flexible scheduling of on-line learning. This meant that most of the students had access to the various computer pools on a regular basis and did not necessarily have to make a special trip to campus to log into class. The students at the community college, however, were on 'a work placement, and if they were to use the campus computers they would have to make the often lengthy trip to campus in the evening or at night after work in order to participate. While it is true that those in the other sections had to make a trip to campus to participate face-to-face, this was a scheduled trip, whereas it is much easier to procrastinate when one does not have a commitment to be at a certain place at a certain time. Therefore, while the qualities of time and place independence are often cited as advantages, they may have posed a disadvantage for this population.

Level Two: Technology Knowledge and Comfort

Once students have secured physical access, they need to become comfortable with the technology. If we consider the University of Guelph students, we can see that they are part of an institutional culture that actively promotes the use of these tools. Furthermore, recall that the University of Guelph students are either third or fourth year students and have had, therefore, a minimum of two years of using these tools in various capacities in their academic career. This is not the case for the community college students, and, as Schwalm notes, students need time to build expertise through regular use of these tools in the context of their education. Resta argues that physical access is not enough and that to fully master these tools students need to use them in engaging and sophisticated ways that foster cognitive development. Martin and Hearne explain that this is not the experience for many minority students, and if they do have access through their school these technologies are most likely to be used for drill and practice. Hence students do not develop the necessary skills to use these technologies in ways that would support the development of sufficient knowledge, comfort, and skills to engage in on-line learning.

It should be noted that some of the issues novices encounter can be ameliorated through appropriate training and support. At the University of Guelph there are extensive opportunities for training and access to support. For example, Computer and Communication Services operates a variety of free training workshops for students and provides extensive documentation for various applications upon request. Many of the computer laboratories are staffed with assistants, and there is a help number that can be called for assistance. The community college offers few if any formal supports. In an attempt to provide some support, Tricia made a trip to New York, where she conducted a hands-on training session for students enrolled in the course. While moderately successful, novice trainees are often anxious, and while they may be eager, they may suffer from "information overload." This may have been the case with the college students, as we had one student who was using her sister's computer and could not find the "right" icon on it. While we had no definitive proof, we suspect that she did not have the appropriate software, nor did she have a modem. As experienced users we often take some things for granted as we enter these training sessions. For example, Al recently participated in a training session for novices where approximately two hours had to be devoted to helping the learners simply develop the coordination to use a mouse effectively.

One of the essential elements to complement training is ongoing support. For example, in the early days of the communications course the instructor had a technical assistant assigned to the course whom students could contact for help. For the community college students we did try to provide support. First, students could e-mail for help, but this presupposed that they could in fact use e-mail and that they had access to a computer. As we have already seen, this appeared to be problematic for this population. We also offered support through the phone; however, this required that students make a long-distance call from New York to Guelph, Ontario. Given the economic profile of this student population, this may have been viewed as an extravagance rather than as a need. Support must be convenient and easy to access.

Level Three: Learner Preparedness

One of the unique dimensions of on-line learning is that, for the most part, it is a text-based learning environment requiring a high degree of literacy. Turoff has noted this, arguing that the research demonstrates that those students who experience difficulties with reading and writing are likely to be less successful in on-line learning environments. Davie and Wells attribute some of this to the fact that these students are likely to be less confident and hence have more difficulty on-line because of the elimination of visual cues or immediate feedback. Thus, even access to the hardware and comfort with the technology do not guarantee success. Students must also have the necessary cognitive skills/ tools (reading and writing) to participate effectively in a text-based environment. Shedletsky suggests that for the cognitively ill-prepared learner this is even more problematic, as "our understanding of written and spoken discourse is challenged by CMC; our understanding of interpersonal relationships is jarred; our ways of behaving are out of line with our expectations" (6).

If the University of Guelph students are compared with the community college students, we can again see why there might be some differences in performance. We can assume that the University of Guelph students have average or above average reading and writing competencies because they were able to gain entry to the university through a highly competitive process based on prior academic achievement. Furthermore, that they are in their third or fourth year implies that they have continued to be successful, and such success would not have occurred had they not been cognitively prepared. However, the community college students are another matter. First, while we support the open door policy of the community college, it may mean that the students admitted to the program are not cognitively prepared to participate in on-line learning. If they cannot function comfortably within a text-based environment, then they may encounter serious problems. Furthermore, since we know that this student population, particularly the ESL students, needs significant academic remedial work, it can be assumed that the students in the course may have been less assured and confident not only operating the computers but functioning in a text-based environment.

Other characteristics of computer conferencing could also have contributed to this problem. For example, on-line learning presupposes active, involved learners (Kaye, "Learning"); they must be willing to ask questions, state opinions, and challenge both the instructor and their peers. On-line environments can support the development of active learning skills in students who are ready to rise to the challenge of succeeding in the new environment. For college students used to passively taking notes in a lecture, the demands of the environment may have been too much. Furthermore, this is tantamount to changing the "rules," which means the learners are unsure of what is expected and appropriate. The tendency under these circumstances is to do nothing and "wait and see." Unfortunately, if all students are engaged in the game of wait and see, it undermines participation, and, as McCabe has noted, this becomes a self-fulfilling prophecy: low participation breeds low participation. It is worth noting that most of the community college students began the course, as evidenced in the face-to-face training session, with enthusiasm and excitement. What happened to that excitement and enthusiasm? We suspect that it is much like planning an exotic vacation: while the prospect of going is exciting, the strangeness of the territory is terrifying and can lead to withdrawal and a form of culture shock.

Level Four: Group Process and Dialogue

On-line education that utilizes CMC is premised on the idea of dialogue and cooperative approaches to learning. It is significant to remember that a great many of the studies examining the effectiveness and utility of on-line education have been conducted on a very privileged population, namely, graduate students. The nature of graduate education is very different from that of undergraduate education and community college education. Dialogue as a means of knowledge construction is taken as a given, whereas undergraduate education and community college education are more didactic in nature.

Looking at the University of Guelph students, we can see that they are more likely to share similarities with graduate student populations given that they were third and fourth year students. Therefore it can be expected that they will be relatively comfortable with being actively engaged in their learning simply based on the demands of their academic progress. Certainly the students appear to be comfortable with the idea of dialogue. For example, it is not unusual for a discussion group of approximately 25 students to generate 150–300 messages for one two-week module. This means that for the five modules, one discussion group would likely generate 750–1,500 messages for the discussion section of the course. This does not take into account the messages for group projects. Typically, group projects, of which there are two where four to seven students collaborate, would send about 100 messages per project. This then means that any one student would be exposed to 950–1,700 messages for the course.

The levels of participation in the community college course, as stated previously, were extremely low. Part of this may be accounted for by the fact that the medium demands active participation through dialogue, while the students were used to sitting passively, listening to a lecture, and taking notes.[3] They were largely unfamiliar with dialogue and group process as a pedagogical strategy. Phipps would support this, arguing that American community college students seem less able "to think analytically, to synthesize, to creatively apply material" (1). The students lack the practice necessary to become efficient at thinking analytically, synthesizing, and applying material through group processes and dialogue with others.

In addition, Schwalm noted that different cultural groups may communicate differently in an on-line environment. Some cultures may prefer more "oral" environments (e.g., synchronous on-line communication) while other cultures depend much more on nonverbal cues. In addition, Hellreigel, Slocum, and Woodman report that "cultural context" may affect levels of comfort with group process and dialogue as a pedagogical strategy. For example, Asian cultures are considered "high context" because "interpersonal communication is characterized by, (1) the establishment of social trust before engaging in task-based discussions, (2) the value placed on personal relationship and goodwill, and (3) the importance of the surrounding circumstances during an interaction" (399). These cultures place large emphasis on nonverbal cues and close relationships, both of which are lacking in an on-line course. Lauzon ("Situating") has suggested that often the dominant culture is normalized through educational practice, and consequently this may create a "cultural" tension for students who are not from the mainstream culture. Thus the expectations of the classroom may not be congruent with the expectations of one's home culture. This, too, can have a paralyzing effect whereby the student does not know how to behave and hence does little or nothing.

All of these factors may have contributed to nonparticipation in the community college cooperative work course.

Level Five: Course Content and Design

Another factor that is related to participation is course content level of complexity and its relationship to design. Lauzon and Moore argue that the appropriateness of various technologies is contingent on the learner's knowledge of the domain. For example, learners who are introduced to a new knowledge domain need to master the language and acquire a basic understanding of the domain. It is highly unlikely that they would be able to engage in high level learning characterized by dialogue until they had mastered the language and basic concepts of the domain. For a learner entering a new knowledge domain, a medium such as CMC would not be an appropriate technology to support appropriate pedagogical strategies. Therefore, an understanding of the learner's knowledge of the domain leads to an appropriate design, which in turn leads to the selection of appropriate technologies to support the design in an on-line format.

Now recall above the high levels of participation for the communication course. Within the context of this course, students (1) are encouraged to acknowledge they have a lifetime of experience to draw upon to help them become more effective communicators, and (2) by virtue of being in this class, have demonstrated some level of "expertise" in interpersonal communication or else they would not be university students. Furthermore, they are encouraged to think of the on-line classroom as a "living laboratory" where they can observe their own interactions with the goal of becoming a more effective communicator. They are then asked to look at their strengths and weaknesses as communicators and to help others identify their strengths and weaknesses as they find new ways of looking at their communication patterns. The facilitators try to create an open and secure communicative environment, and learners are encouraged to integrate their experience with the course concepts. In this sense, it is truly a constructivist environment whereby students engage in the social process of knowledge construction. A high volume of discussion is the foundation of learning in this context.

In the community college course, it was expected that the students would reflect on and share their experiences, contrasting them with the theory. The purpose of this was to determine how theory could be helpful in understanding their work experiences.

Developmental Issues

Fundamental to our understanding of how people learn and relate to authority is cognitive development. Different stages of development may be able to participate more effectively in particular types of demands. Or, put another way, different designs may have an implicit cognitive development requirement. For example, Kegan argues that despite adult education notions of self-directed learning, few learners are actually developmentally prepared to be self-directing. Kegan captures the essence of the learner experience when they are asked to engage in activities that are developmentally inappropriate. As he states, educators are not merely asking them to take on new skills, modify their learning style, or increase their self-confidence. They are asking many of them to change the whole way they understand themselves, their world, and the relationship between the two. They are asking many of them to put at risk the loyalties and devotions that have made the foundation of their lives.(275)

In a study that examined the cognitive differences of young adults (mean age 19.8 years), middle-aged adults (mean age 34.8 years), and older adults (mean age 66.5 years), Papini's findings support the adult learning principle that middle-aged and older adults integrate personal experiences with formal logic when approaching problems. Young adults (mean age 19.8) do not seem to be able to "integrate formal logic with personal experience while reasoning about different types of problems" (5). This is congruent with Perry's cognitive development scheme, which places most young adults at the Dualistic stages when "knowledge is presumed to be absolute and known only to authorities" (Pascarella and Terenzini 29).

This could help explain why some of the young adults in the community college course did not become fully engaged in the problems and topics posed in the course. One student, in particular, tried to apply formal logic rather than personal experiences to the problems. This student may have been doing what he thought he was expected to do; he often sent e-mails to the facilitator to check that his "answer" to the assignment was correct. The most active student, on the other hand, applied her personal experiences and never applied formal logic.

While it is not known what cognitive position the students in the study held, there is evidence that many community college students may be operating at Piaget's stage of concrete operations (Humbolt 91). If this is the case, then most college students would expect the instructor to tell them what they needed to know. This would explain their "silence" in the on-line course and why they could not deal with the requirements. The structure of the conference undermined participation not only because the students could not identify with or understand it, but because of the type of participation it encouraged. Succeeding on the terms set out in the design of the course may have been beyond the developmental capacity of most of the students.

Learner Motivation

The students who chose the on-line community college course seemed to have done so with two misconceptions in mind—that it would save them time and that it would help them learn how to use the Internet. While little of the CMC research speaks to the effects of such misconceptions, McCabe did find that students who joined an on-line class with "vague expectations and little understanding about the norms of on-line classroom discussion" (182) tended to wait for the instructor to tell them to participate. In addition, if one expects something to save one time, and then finds that it actually takes more time, one may be caught off guard. As one student in the McCabe study noted, she was surprised "by the intensity of the course; she had expected a distance learning course to require much less work than her 'standard' classes" (176). Like that student, one of the students in the community cooperative course seldom responded but remained in the class as a "lurker." He too felt that the class was a lot of work and that he couldn't keep up with the requirements.

English as a second language also seems to be related to several factors that could have impacted on the students' ability or desire to participate in an on-line environment. Since approximately 75 percent of those in the community college class were ESL students, and that college found that 75 percent of the ESL population needed remedial math help, it can be presumed that approximately half of the class had low math confidence and ability. Unfortunately, for minority students, self-efficacy with computers is directly correlated with math confidence and perceived math ability (Olivier and Shapiro). Thus, half of the class may have lacked self-efficacy with computers, which impacted on their ability to progress in the course.

The structure of assignments and participation may also affect learner motivation. For example, learners in the University of Guelph communication course were graded on participation, but participation was defined in rather broad and vague terms. They were graded on contribution and the quality of their contributions. Furthermore, the facilitators in this class helped facilitate discussion by asking strategic questions. In the community college course, participation was geared to completing specific tasks. Once the task was completed there would be little reason to participate further. It is important to design for extrinsic rewards until the learner has sufficient experience to see the intrinsic rewards of participation in on-line education.

Critical Mass

The last issue we wish to examine is the idea of critical mass. It is our experience that a minimum number of students who actively participate is needed to generate adequate discussion so that it gains and maintains a momentum of its own. In the communication class we have found that the best size for an active discussion group is 20–30 students. Any less and there appears to be insufficient activity to generate the necessary momentum to sustain dialogue. People become frustrated and participation eventually dissipates. In the community college course it was decided by the college to limit the enrollment to a few students because it was a pilot project. Unfortunately, this may have undermined the whole course. Furthermore, it may have been that the feeling of anonymity or safety in a group that is normally associated with increasing participation in computer conferencing disappears when there are fewer entries. Therefore, students are less likely to participate if others are not participating; they do not want to be the first to speak out, and they do not see it as a classroom requiring their contributions. This was further complicated by the fact that the course was only six weeks long. It has been our experience at the University of Guelph that it takes a good three weeks or more before a course develops its full momentum. Unfortunately, within the context of a six-week course it is over before it ever gets going.

CONCLUSIONS

In conclusion, we believe that on-line education has great potential for differing levels and applications within higher education. However, it is also imperative, we believe, that instructors or institutions that are contemplating developing and delivering on-line education ask some fundamental questions. Based on our experience, these are the questions we would suggest:

How will the learners access the appropriate hardware and software to participate?

We often make assumptions about learners and how they will access the necessary hardware and software. For example, we assumed that the community college cooperative students would be able to access the hardware and software either from home or from the college. Consideration needs to be given to the logistics of student access. Again, we did not anticipate that it might be difficult for the community college students to get to the college to use the facilities because they were working full time on their cooperative work term. Simply stated, we ignored and did not understand the complexities of their personal lives.

The second question that educators need to ask is related to "psychological access."

How comfortable are students with the technology, and what is their skill and knowledge level?

As outsiders, we made assumptions about student abilities based on our own professional frames of reference. Being employed in an institution that supports and nurtures technological literacy within the student body, we believe we anticipated that the community college students' comfort, knowledge, and skill level would be comparable to that of the students we had dealt with in the past. For example, one oversight is the assumption that students have keyboard skills. Not all students are accurate and adequate typists. Participating in on-line education that has dialogue as its base means that students have to be fairly good typists. Even the brightest and most promising students will have a hard time communicating their ideas if they cannot type. Other issues relate to comfort with navigating the system, particularly if the students are expected to access the course from home or somewhere other than the institution. Decisions must be made about how best to provide support to most effectively meet student needs. Support needs to be as transparent as possible.

Related to the issue of comfort, knowledge, and skills is how the student views the medium. We usually encourage students to think of this medium as conversation as opposed to writing. When students approach it as conversation, they begin to feel comfort in expressing their ideas. However, our experience has shown that if they view it as "writing" they are more likely to approach it as they would an essay. This can be stifling, as students spend time crafting their response. On occasion that may be a good idea, for example, in answering an on-line assignment, but not for on-line dialogue. Instructors can help students overcome this hurdle by modeling appropriate communication strategies.

The third question that needs to be asked concerns readiness to learn.

Are learners cognitively prepared to engage in on-line learning?

On-line education presupposes that students are functionally literate in the language for the level of education that they are engaged in. In a face-to-face learning transaction those without the necessary level of literacy may be able to hide it through verbalizing their responses or by becoming invisible, deferring to those students who are more willing to be engaged. This is also related to another aspect of cognitive preparedness—being an active agent in one's own learning. Students engaged in on-line learning cannot simply sit back and take notes; they must be actively engaged in their learning by asking questions, challenging statements, and offering their own opinions.

Clearly the community college students were not as well prepared as the university level students as evidenced by the differing rates of participation. However, we should be careful not to be too harsh in rendering judgment and recall that Schwalm found that different culture groups have different communication protocols, and that may affect the way in which they participate. Lauzon ("Situating") has argued that there is an implicit bias in education technology that may negate ways of participating other than the status quo. In other words, educational technology is culturally biased and favors those cultures that are most closely aligned with the hegemonic ideals of Western education.

Related to the above issue is the issue of content and design:

Is the instructional design congruent with the developmental stage of the learner?

For example, the above discussion of dialogue presupposes that the learner view himself or herself as an active agent in the construction of knowledge. This is associated with a relatively high level of cognitive development. In the study by Bertram Gallant it is very likely that the developmental demands inherent in the instructional design exceeded the abilities of most of the community college students, whereas with the communication course it would be reasonable to expect that third and fourth year university students would view themselves as active agents in the construction of knowledge. In other words, they were developmentally prepared for the demands of an interactive and engaging instructional design.

Educators need to ask one final question:

Do institutional course requirements meet the needs of on-line education?

One thing that is clear in the Bertram Gallant study is that six weeks is far too short a time to develop the rapport and sense of community—especially in a small group—necessary to support the type of interactive and engaged learning we had hoped the community college students might participate in. At the University of Guelph we have found that it takes a minimum of two to three weeks to get the course rolling with full participation. In the case of the community college course, this constituted half the course. Clearly the time frame needs to allow for a slower start than would be encountered in most face-to-face courses.

The list of questions presented here should not be considered definitive. We simply offer them as a starting point in thinking about on-line education based on our experience. Other questions, we are sure, will arise as more educators undertake the challenge of delivering on-line education.

EPILOGUE

It is accepted that with new and complex communication technologies there will be a time lag before the technology becomes transparent and people can attend to the message it is conveying. In our earlier experiences with Communication Process, Al and Susan noted this time lag as taking several weeks to one month, and the course syllabus accordingly was built to demand little of import from the students until this phase had passed. When Tricia designed the cooperative education course, we wondered about the students' ability to adapt to the technology in time considering the short course duration (six weeks). In an attempt to accelerate this adaptation phase, Tricia went to the community college and conducted a face-to-face orientation session.

As discussed, this advance training apparently helped little to facilitate student transition through the adaptation phase to a point where they could comfortably work within the virtual classroom. We tentatively inferred from this that the time lag was developmental in nature and could not be accelerated.

Experiences the following semester, however, have caused us to revisit this assumption. While Communication Process remains unchanged in design and class size, this semester's student is more comfortable with the on-line medium and already in week two, the discussion was well under way and of high quality. We suggest two trends to explain this. First, more students now have experience with the on-line medium, thus reducing the lag time for not only themselves as sophisticated users but for others around them who benefit from the confident ambiance and leadership-by-example that they offer a virtual classroom. Second, a niche market of students may be gravitating toward on-line courses as they recognize the complementarity to busy schedules. Many of the students in the subsequent offering of Communication Process mention their jobs, their children, their commitments to nonformal learning experiences (such as Junior Farmers' courses or language exchanges) and competitive athletics in addition to carrying a full course load—any one of which could be seen as occupying them full time. It may be that exceptionally motivated students are drawn to the flexibility of on-line opportunities.

Recent experience with a second University of Guelph on-line course, Technology in Extension, validates some of the conclusions regarding motivations behind participation in on-line learning. Technology in Extension is designed in a format similar to that of the community college course, measuring credit for a noninteractive level of participation through marks for assignments posted to the course conference. This basic level of on-line participation does not require students to engage in ongoing, reflective discourse with each other but merely demands the sharing of work completed off-line and individually. Interactive dialogue is an intent of the course design but is not extrinsically rewarded with marks, and thus students, ever conscious of the time cost to mark benefit ratio, do not spend time on participation which offers only intrinsic rewards they have not yet recognized as valuable. We (and likely many faculty who have established Web pages as optional complements to courses) can testify that few students will participate in Web aspects of courses unless credit is allocated to their efforts. The ready conclusion is that in addition to appropriate on-line course design, credit for interactive participation, as evidenced by Communication Process, greatly enhances on-line dialogue.

However, this logic only carries us so far. The fact that Tricia's community college course students gained most of their marks through posting to the Web site was not sufficient motivation to participate even at the noninteractive level for her student population. We must question whether, had all the motivational issues been met and addressed, the participation of the community college students would have increased. Our experience indicates that significant weight must be given to the considerations of language and math abilities and minority status as factors hampering the on-line facility and motivation of students.

NOTES

1. For a full description and evaluation of this course, see Lauzon and George; Lauzon ("Integrating").

2. The hierarchy of access is originally premised on Abraham Maslow's concept of hierarchy of needs. However, after some thought we have decided that the concept of need is problematic within this context and that it may simply be best thought of as a hierarchy of access. This hierarchy was first published in Bertram Gallant.

3. This was revealed by students who were interviewed for the study conducted by Bertram Gallant (1999) and confirmed by a faculty member in the cooperative program. To paraphrase him, instructors do a lot of hand holding.

WORKS CITED

Becker, Henry Jay. "Equity in School Computer Use: National Data and Neglected Considerations." Paper presented at the 1986 annual meeting of the American Educational Research Association, San Francisco, 1986.

Berge, Zane. "Facilitating Computer Conferencing: Recommendations from the Field." *Educational Technology* 35.1 (1995): 22–30.

Bertram Gallant, Tricia. "Factors at Work: Why Knowledge Construction Didn't Occur in a CMC Environment for Community College Co-op Students." Master's thesis, University of Guelph, 1999.

Burge, Elizabeth. "Learning in Computer Conferenced Contexts: The Learner's Perspective." *Journal of Distance Education* 9.1 (1994): 19–43.

Cole, Michael, and Peg Giffin. *Contextual Factors in Education: Improving Science and Mathematics Education for Minorities and Women.* Madison: Wisconsin Center of Education Research, 1987.

Crook, Charles. *Computers and the Collaborative Experience of Learning.* London: Routledge, 1994.

Davie, Lynn E. "Facilitation Techniques for the On-line Tutor." *Mindweave: Communication, Computers, and Distance Education.* Ed. Robin Mason and Anthony Kaye. Oxford, U.K.: Pergamon Press, 1989. 74–85.

Davie, Lynn E., and Rosalie Wells. "Empowering the Learner Through Computer-Mediated Communication." *American Journal of Distance Education* 5.1 (1991): 15–23.

de Kerckhove, Derrek. *Connected Intelligence: The Arrival of the Web Society.* Toronto, Ont.: Somerville House Publishing, 1997.

Edwards, C. "Enhancing Minority Student Educational Opportunities Through Instructional Computing: A Report on Project Micro." Paper presented at the 1988 Council of Great City Schools National Technology Forum, San Diego, CA, 1988.

Fey, Marion Harris. "Freeing Voices: Literacy Through Computer Conferencing and Feminist Collaboration." Diss., University of Rochester, 1992.

Gaines, Brian, Douglas H. Norrie, and Mildred G. L. Shaw. "Foundations of the Learning Web." Paper presented at ED_TELECOM 96—World Conference on Educational Telecommunications, Boston, 17 June 1996.

Harasim, Linda. "On-line Education: A New Domain." In *Mindweave: Communication, Computers, and Distance Education.* Ed. Robin Mason and Anthony Kaye. Oxford, U.K.: Pergamon Press, 1989. 50–62.

———. "Teaching and Learning On-line: Issues in Computer-Mediated Graduate Courses." *Canadian Journal of Electronic Communication* 16.2 (1987): 117–35.

Hellriegel, Don, John W. Slocum, Jr., and Richard W. Woodman. *Organizational Behavior.* 7th ed. St. Paul, MN: West Publishing, 1995.

Humbolt, Clinton. "An Inquiry into the Piagetian Tradition in America as a Basis for a Philosophy of Education at the Community College Level: A Quasi-Experimental Approach." Diss., Walden University, 1973.

Kaye, Anthony. "Computer-Mediated Communication and Distance Education." In *Mindweave: Communication, Computers, and Distance Education*. Ed. Robin Mason and Anthony Kaye. Oxford, U.K.: Pergamon Press, 1989. 3–21.

———. "Learning Together Apart." In *Collaborative Learning Through Computer Conferencing: The Najaden Papers*. Ed. Anthony Kaye. Berlin: Springer-Verlag, 1992.

Kearsley, Greg. "A Guide to On-line Education." 1998. 1 Aug. 1999 <http://www.gwu.edu/~etl/online.html>.

Kegan, Robert. *In Over Our Heads: The Mental Demands of Modern Life*. Cambridge, MA: Harvard University Press, 1994.

Kinner, J., and N. Coombs. *Computer Mediated Communication and the On-line Classroom*. Ed. Zane Berge and Mauri Collins. Cresskill, NJ: Hampton Press, 1995. 53–68.

Lauzon, Allan. "Integrating Computer-Based Instructions with Computer Conferencing: An Evaluation of a Model for Designing On-line Education." *American Journal of Distance Education* 6.2 (1992): 32–46.

———. "Postmodernism, Interactive Technologies, and the Design of Distance Education." In *Distance Education Symposium 3: Course Design*. Ed. Ellen D. Wagner and Margret A. Koble. American Center for the Study of Distance Education University Park, PA: Pennsylvania State University Press, 1995. 6–21.

———. "Situating Cognition and Cross Borders: Resisting the Hegemony of Mediated Education." *British Journal of Educational Technology* 30 (1999): 261–276.

Lauzon, Allan, and A. B. Moore George. "A Fourth Generation Distance Education System: Integrating Computer-Assisted Learning and Computer-Conferencing." *American Journal of Distance Education* 3 (1989): 38–49.

Martin, Bernadette, and J. Dixon Hearne. "Computer Equity in Education." *Educational Technology* 29 (1989): 47–50.

Mason, Robin, and Anthony Kaye. "Toward a New Paradigm of Distance Education." In *Online Education: Perspectives on a New Environment*. Ed. Linda Harasim. New York: Praeger, 1990.

McCabe, Margaret Foley. "On-line Classrooms: Case Studies of Computer Conferencing in Higher Education." Diss., Columbia University, 1997.

Olivier, Terry A., and Fay Shapiro. "Self-Efficacy and Computers." *Journal of Computer-Based Instruction* 20 (1993): 81–85.

Papini, Dennis. "Higher Education and Cognitive Developmental Changes in Adulthood: An Integration of Logic and Experience." Paper presented at the Annual Convention of the Southwestern Psychological Association, New Orleans, LA, April 1987.

Pascarella, Ernest, and Patrick Terenzini. *How College Affects Students: Findings and Insights from Twenty Years of Research*. San Francisco: Jossey-Bass, 1991.

Paulsen, Morten Flate. "Moderating Educational Computer Conferences." In *Computer-mediated Communication and the On-line Classroom in Distance Education*. Ed. Zane L. Berge and Mauri Collins. Cresskill, NJ: Hampton Press, 1995.

Perry William. *Forms of Intellectual and Ethical Development in the College Years*. New York: Holt, Rinehart and Winston, 1970.

Phipps, Ronald. *Critical Thinking and Community College Students*. Seattle, WA: North Seattle Community College, 1984.

Resta, Paul. "Organizing Education for Minorities: Enhancing Minority Access and Use of the New Information Technologies in Higher Education." *Education and Computing* 8 (1992): 119–27.

Rice, Ronald, and Gail Love. "Electronic Emotion: Socio Emotional Content in a Computer-Mediated Communication Network." *Communication Research* 14 (1987): 85–108.

Robertshaw, Diane, and Lee M. Wolfle. *The Cognitive Value of Two-Year Colleges for Whites and Blacks.* Blacksburg, VA: Virginia Polytechnic Institute and State University, 1982.

Schwalm, Karen. "Providing Computer Conferencing Opportunities for Minority Students and Measuring the Results." Paper presented at the Annual National Convention of the Association for Educational Communications and Technology, Anaheim, CA, 1995.

Shedletsky, Leonard. "Minding Computer-Mediated Communication: CMC as Experiential Learning." *Educational Technology* 33.6 (1993): 5–10.

Turoff, Murry. Foreword to *On-line Education: Perspectives on a New Environment.* Ed. Linda Harasim. New York: Praeger, 1990. ix–xiii.

Chapter 23

On-line Is on Target for Motivated Learners

Michael S. Ameigh

What constitutes a motivated learner is a question for the ages. Motivation in the educational environment, after all, is a pedagogical structure tied mostly to natural anxieties about social and economic acceptance (Chou, McClintock, Moretti, and Nix). It can ebb and flow, come and go. For the typical postsecondary student it is a highly personal formulation, often beyond the control of professors or their institutions. Still, educational theorists continually cite motivation as a key pedagogical consideration in instructional design at the postsecondary level. They speculate on how to create, exploit, and measure it as if the question is simply one of finding some universally applicable set of independent variables. Perhaps this is because it is often easy for a student to articulate his or her motivation, even as the process by which it is derived is elusive.

It also stems from there having been essentially just one common knowledge-delivery system in place for centuries—the traditional classroom. Educators are always looking to validate that system in order to justify its continued application. In fact, there are countless variables that influence motivation, so many that it can be argued that the task of identifying all of them is an impossible one. Perhaps the challenge is not simply to motivate, but to learn how best to transfer knowledge and induce receptiveness to new ideas.

To me the issue is more precisely a question of perception rather than motivation. During the 1950s educational researchers began to look at the effects of perception on learning (Bills; Combs). They came up with a theory that behavior is highly influenced by individuals' perceptions of the people and objects they encounter. How people view objects, individuals, and circumstances affects their behavior toward them. This theory holds that individuals are essentially self-starters and that they constantly seek to sustain their sense of self and self-worth, while simultaneously working to enhance and refine their own sense of adequacy (Verduin and Clark).

This interests distance educators because the quest for self-improvement is not linked directly to conventional notions of either pedagogy or the transfer of knowledge. Rather, it is open to radical thinking about alternative delivery options that include on-line instruction. This is important because it helps those who use on-line courses to overcome logistical barriers to education and confront the widely held but questionable assumption that education is inherently time bound and space bound, that is, synchronous and face-to-face, instructor to student. Also significant is the fact that on-line technology is becoming ubiquitous and highly sophisticated. Futurists predict that computers and keyboards will give way to more transparent systems capable of enhancing accessibility for an even wider pool of learners. One observer notes that the on-line revolution began in the 1970s when computing was a costly and arcane science inaccessible to the general public (Ehrmann). Today the technology is much less of an issue than creativity in course design and course content.

Challenges to conventional notions about educational delivery will increase as the median age of the typical undergraduate continues to rise. The proportion of adults in that population has been increasing steadily for years, putting pressure on traditional residential campuses to become more student-centered. As recently as the early 1980s fewer than 30 percent of students in formal postsecondary education were adults (Garrison). By the end of the 1990s that proportion had almost doubled. Adults tend to be more discriminating in their perception of the way education is distributed than is the typical postadolescent college population. They often gravitate to the most convenient and efficient options relative to the value they place on the utility of those services, rejecting others that are traditionally bundled with academic offerings but which do not relate directly to their personal programs. For example, they resist paying so-called athletic fees that are typically charged to all students regardless of whether they use athletic facilities or not. Many campuses charge all students "technology" fees to support computer labs and other facilities, again without regard for how much use is made of that technology by individual students. Many adults spend as little time on campus as possible. This is yet another reason why new education providers are being drawn to the higher education marketplace. Intent upon competing for this lucrative business, they provide streamlined services that cater to adult needs and goals exclusively.

But this challenge to conventional delivery is more than simply a demand for greater convenience and efficiency. As an instructor of large groups in undergraduate courses I am familiar with pedagogical strengths and weaknesses in conventional classroom instruction. Clearly, for students of any age determined to engage one another in challenging intellectual discourse, the face-to-face dynamic of the classroom is an important element of the learning process. The serendipity of the fabled "teaching moment" often results in marvelously edifying experiences that justify using that method. For teaching faculty, professional satisfaction often emanates from just such experiences and the resulting appreciation of newly enlightened students. But there are pedagogical and logistical downsides to the classroom model as well, some of which can be overcome through the use of alternate instructional modes including asynchronous learning via computer networks.

Research shows that adult learners are often insecure in traditional classroom settings populated by mostly traditional students. They often see themselves as outsiders with different world views and are often uncomfortable with the social regimen that seems to underlie much campus-based instruction. Research has shown that under such circumstances adults tend to exhibit defensive behavior that mutes their imagination and creativity (Knox). Only by minimizing circumstances that cause this disconnect can instructors create environments for change that maximize the potential for learning. Adults are reachable only when the teaching-learning atmosphere is nonthreatening and focused on their specific needs and goals (Loewenthal, Blackwelder, and Broomall).

There is also a not-so-subtle disconnect between adults and traditional students because for many adults participation in formal education is voluntary. This heightens their desire to have their personal needs met, and to be respected and accepted as full collaborators in the learning process. Where that sense of inclusion is missing, they will drop out of the process and seek alternatives (Garrison).

Well-designed distance learning is ideal under these circumstances. Unlike the classroom, where variables related to time and space often frustrate full class participation, asynchronous computer courses demand a true one-on-one relationship between the instructor and each and every student. "Seat time," an arbitrary device contrived to put a face on highly modularized curricula, does not hinder the design of effective on-line educational methods. The student enjoys a greater degree of control, the instructor is no longer tethered to a highly arbitrary schedule, and inflexible fixed costs, logistical concerns, and social issues associated with traditional brick and mortar venues are less significant.

Asynchronous computer-based interaction is a powerful teaching tool, an ally in the campaign to develop ever more effective pedagogical techniques in higher education. The successful use of key learning processes can be induced with careful attention to course design and facilitation. Cooperative learning exercises, performance tasking, and authentic assessment techniques are easily integrated into on-line course design and delivery. The development of critical thinking skills, always the Holy Grail for designers of high-quality courses, is as achievable on-line as in the traditional classroom, and for some instructors and students, perhaps a more effective environment (Alavi).

There are three pedagogical issues that surface when courses are delivered over asynchronous computer networks. First, disparities in the levels of maturity, experience, and self-discipline among younger and older students who might interact successfully in the classroom are more pronounced and readily apparent in the on-line environment. Adult students are often accustomed to working at tasks that require they budget their time and meet deadlines on their own. Younger students accustomed to the less structured pattern of the conventional classroom often exhibit a more casual attitude toward course activities and assignments. Social, cultural, and gender-related dynamics that often interfere with teaching strategies are more easily subdued. In the on-line environment a discussion is less apt to be taken over by those who might dominate such a discussion in the conventional classroom. A person's race and ethnicity can be easily masked if doing so is desirable.

Second, the on-line classroom requires a level of student self-discipline and motivation that may not be required in the conventional classroom. As an instructor of large enrollment courses over the years I have often observed that some students will not attend classes unless forced to do so through attendance requirements or other forms of coercion that are irrelevant on-line.

Third, on-line course instructors find themselves taking different approaches to instruction from those typically employed in the classroom, an intriguing development with potential for bringing greater efficacy to pedagogy among certain populations.

On the issue of whether distance learning is appropriate for all postsecondary learners, there are caveats. Direct peer-to-peer feedback, a fundamental element and key reference point in group interaction in the classroom, is not as immediate. Also, on-line learning requires that students develop their ideas and mediate them in the word processing environment. This sometimes inhibits student-to-student interaction, a phenomenon that can be exacerbated by weak keyboarding skills. Many fear being exposed as poor writers, a deficiency that often goes unobserved or is ignored in traditional classroom instruction. Indeed, students develop personal strategies over time to mask their academic shortcomings and accentuate their strengths. And learners can be intimidated by or attracted to technology that radically changes the nature of the teacher-student relationship.

Some studies have shown that predisposed attitudes toward computers in general correlate with success in and satisfaction with on-line courses (Rice and Case; Hiltz and Johnson). Researchers at the New Jersey Institute of Technology, for example, found that class standing and scores on the math Scholastic Aptitude Test (SAT) are good predictors of student satisfaction with on-line courses. Interestingly, they also found that high scores on the verbal SAT correlate inversely with satisfaction. The researchers speculated that students with high verbal skills prefer the opportunity to use them in synchronous venues like traditional classrooms, while those with weaker verbal skills are less concerned about face-to-face interaction with peers and professors.

Equally intriguing was the discovery that the data implied a curvilinear relationship among a variety of variables such as access to professors, final grades, interaction with classmates, and personal inhibitions regarding interface technology. Students at the low end of the academic spectrum and those at the high end were more satisfied with the on-line experience than those in mid ranges. One might speculate that a high level of self-confidence among high achievers is a powerful influence on success, and that the leveling nature of asynchronous interaction afforded by on-line technology is a plus with those who struggle academically.

Students frequently reveal self-consciousness and anxiety in comments related to their perceptions of on-line learning. The instructor needs to be sensitive to these cues and make an effort to deal with them in positive ways. Classroom instructors often modulate their lectures through body language that telegraphs subtle—and sometimes not so subtle—emotions, moods, and attitudes. Students quickly learn to pick up information from this communication. Is the professor having a good day? Is she irritated? Jovial? Distracted? Lost in thought? Is he paying more attention to someone else and ignoring me? Was my response to her question what she wanted to hear? Does he think I am dumb or does she think I am bright? And, of course, body language is a two-way communication process. I have been amazed over the years at how far off the mark I can be in reading nonverbal communication from students in a classroom. Yet for many instructors, this nonverbal interaction is as important in the teacher-student relationship as the verbal give and take.

It is a relatively simple matter to establish intimate rapport with students on-line. Since the relationship is one on one between each student and the instructor, there is ample opportunity for every student to participate fully within the limits of such give and take. The monopolization of classroom discussions by a few individuals can be more easily controlled. With the appropriate course design each member of the class can be compelled to participate in discussions and group activities uninhibited by the need to think quickly on their feet during a class session. This process is more appropriate than the traditional classroom for students who benefit from self-paced learning.

Teaching has been described as a process that brings personal influence to bear in an effort to change behavior (Gage). It has also been described as reciprocal, with both the student and the teacher influencing the outcome (Rowntree). In the on-line environment the effectiveness of this mutual participation in the process is maximized because the relationship between instructor and student can be designed for highly personal interaction with or without the participation of other students and at a pace that varies from one to another.

Asynchronous on-line instruction also addresses the concerns of those who see a consistent imbalance between males and females in both the technological and cognitive processing required for effective learning in highly structured—and highly competitive—learning environments. Asynchronous learning in any guise has an advantage over synchronous course delivery where the social and intellectual behavior of one sex varies significantly from the other. This concern is particularly acute where those disparities are institutionalized and where access is restricted for one or another subpopulation. In 1989 the Radical Forum on Adult Education published a collection of research investigating the potential of distance learning to circumvent conventional barriers to education for women around the world (Faith). The conclusions were sobering. A decade ago, two-thirds of women and half of all men had never received any formal education. Social and economic impediments to access were overwhelming. Ten years later a broader awareness of the plight of women and other underserved populations as well as a growing availability of affordable on-line technology had resulted in a somewhat better environment for the acceptance of on-line education globally. The information economy had spawned a scramble to establish unprecedented international linkages among educators. The provision of educational services via the Internet will originate where educational infrastructure and resources are well established and highly respected, and where the on-line efficiencies are most compelling. Distance learning can potentially broaden access to education for individuals everywhere, inevitably mitigating the influence of social and cultural conventions that favor one population over another in the distribution of educational opportunities.

As stated previously, the on-line classroom requires a level of student self-discipline and motivation that may not be critical to success in the classroom. Clearly the logistical parameters of traditional delivery are closely associated with how a student perceives she or he must perform in a course. For many professors it is difficult to separate a student's attendance record, attitude, or contribution to classroom activities from more formal evaluative instruments when calculating a final course grade. Students are often rewarded for coming to class and maintaining cheery dispositions throughout the semester. The predictable rhythm of a course—classes that meet at the same times on the same days two or three times a week for fifteen weeks—encourages a certain type of student behavior that, while it may correlate with grading patterns, does not correlate with learning. On-line students must take the initiative to set aside sufficient time to successfully complete course assignments without the reinforcement that comes from frequent interaction with peers and instructors in the classroom.

On-line course instructors find themselves taking a different approach to instruction from that typically employed in the classroom. The course preparation process from start to finish must be done before the first student arrives at the on-line course gateway. While a great deal of work is required up front, this eliminates the need to do frequent lecture preparations and encourages the instructor to serve more as a facilitator of learning than a professor of knowledge. In the final analysis on-line teaching in the asynchronous environment more closely resembles mentoring than teaching. Students have the entire course available to work through at their own pace, and the instructor is not encumbered by the limitations of the conventional classroom.

It is also a fairly simple matter to bring new resources to the attention of students, with the flow of information very much a dynamic process. In the on-line environment clerical and logistical support is largely unnecessary. Links to other Web sites, text and graphic postings to the instructor's Web pages, streaming video and audio services as well as increasingly user-friendly archiving and presentation elements are easily incorporated in—and removed from—course presentations without sophisticated technical help. The transparency of the interface—computer terminal with course management software (CMS)—streamlines the technology to the point where the focus is on course content and learning strategy, as it should be.

Clearly, on-line instruction is not for everyone. Neither is conventional classroom instruction for everyone, and the need for alternatives is in fact becoming increasingly acute as the profile of the typical undergraduate student evolves. It appears to this veteran teacher that the pedagogical differences between traditional and nontraditional systems exist mostly in the eye of the beholder, and that advantages and disadvantages have less to do with pedagogy than with the logistics of time and space. A motivated teacher and a motivated student will succeed in any mode by developing and sustaining some form of effective engagement. On-line instruction takes advantage of the convenience afforded by information technology while shifting a good deal of control—and responsibility—to the student.

WORKS CITED

Alavi, Maryam. "Computer-Mediated Collaborative Learning: An Empirical Evaluation." *MIS Quarterly: Management Information Systems* 18 (1994): 159–74.

Bills, Robert E. "Perception and Learning." In *Learning More About Learning*. Ed. A. Frazier. Washington, DC:National Education Association/Asociation for Supervision and Curriculum Development, 1959.

Chou, Luyen, Robbi McClintock, Frank Moretti, and Don Nix. *Technology and Education: New Wine in New Bottles: Choosing Pasts and Imagining Educational Futures*. New York: Institute for Learning Technologies, Columbia University, 1993.

Combs, Arthur. *Individual Behavior: A Perceptual Approach to Behavior*. Rev. ed. New York: Harper and Row, 1959.

Ehrmann, Steven C. "Looking Backward: U.S. Efforts to Use Technology to Transform Undergraduate Education." 30 Oct. 1996. 1 Aug. 1999 <http://eee.uci.edu/programs/auctlt/LookingBack.html>.

Faith, Karlene, ed. *Toward New Horizons for Women in Distance Education: International Perspectives*. London: Routledge, 1988.

Gage, Nathaniel Lees, ed. *Handbook of Research on Teaching*. Skokie, IL: Rand McNally, 1963.

Garrison, D. Randy. *Understanding Distance Education: A Framework for the Future*. New York: Routledge, 1989.

Hiltz, Starr Roxanne, and Kenneth Johnson. "User Satisfaction with Computer-Mediated Communication Systems." *Management Science* 36 (1990): 739–65.

Knox, Allan Boyd. "Proficiency Theory of Adult Learning." *Contemporary Educational Psychology* 5 (1980): 378–404.

Loewenthal, Norman H., June Blackwelder, and James K. Broomall. "Correspondence Instruction and the Adult Student." In *Teaching Adults Effectively*. Ed. Alan Knox. San Francisco: Jossey-Bass, 1980.

Rice, Ronald E., and Donald Case. "Electronic Message Systems in the University: A Description of Use and Utility." *Journal of Communication* 33 (1983): 131–52.

Rowntree, Derek. "Two Styles of Communication and Their Implications for Learning." In *Aspects of Educational Technology*. Ed. J. Baggaly, H. Jamieson, and H. Marchant. London: Pitman, 1975.

Verduin, John R., Jr., and Thomas A. Clark. *Distance Education: The Foundations of Effective Practice*. Oxford: Jossey-Bass, 1991.

Chapter 24

Teaching Research Skills Using the Internet

Mark Gellis

INTRODUCTION

This is a nuts-and-bolts chapter. Since this collection is, among other things, a primer for people who are teaching Web-based courses, perhaps for the first time, I am going to focus on some of the most common questions and problems facing teachers who are using the Web to teach research skills. It is also intended as a primer for anyone doing Internet-based research, since this is a skill that does not change very much as long as students have at least occasional access to the Internet. In other words, think of this as the Teaching On-line Research Skills Frequently Asked Questions (commonly known on-line as FAQ) file.

Q. I'm a writing teacher. Why am I teaching research skills?

The natural response of some teachers asked to teach research papers is to question whether it is also our job to teach research skills. After all, we do not teach fact finding—we teach writing. Is not fact finding the province of librarians or faculty in specific disciplines? The reality of the situation, however, is that librarians usually do little more than help students find specific sources. They simply do not have time to teach our students research skills on a one-to-one basis. Library tours can be helpful in introducing students to the available resources in a particular library, but one should not assume that students actually learn how to do research by listening to someone else. They must do it for themselves to truly learn it. Furthermore, faculty in other disciplines frequently provide students with little or no instruction on the specifics of research in those disciplines.

It might be worth adding a "common sense" answer to this question: it is difficult to write if you lack information, and unless you are writing about yourself, you will probably have to do some research to complete any writing project. We might as well teach these two skills together. Since common sense is rarely sufficient to prove anything in academic circles, I shall continue this line of reasoning by citing from authority. Aristotle clearly identifies rhetoric—the discipline within which composition, technical writing, and similar fields are contained—as involving both artistic and nonartistic proofs (37). Nonartistic proofs are external evidence, including witness testimony and laws; in effect, rhetoric is divided between arguments generated by the rhetor and external evidence that must be discovered. Research, therefore, is part of rhetoric and within the province of the composition class.

Teaching research skills is necessary. As a rhetorician, I would argue that teaching research skills is part of the tradition and responsibility of the field of composition and rhetoric. At the same time, I believe that instruction in any discipline can be enhanced by instruction in research skills related to that discipline. For example, it is not unreasonable, I think, that accounting majors should have by the end of their first course in accounting a brief introduction to the principal scholarly and trade publications in their discipline, the main Web-based resources, and the leading professional associations. They should know how to teach themselves, how to learn more about the subject, once they have finished the course. After all, the purpose of taking these courses is not only to learn the materials covered by the professor, but to be initiated into the discipline or profession. The Internet, of course, provides a variety of opportunities for pedagogical activities that give teachers in any discipline another way to help students become effective learners and, ultimately, members of their professional communities.

So there.

Q. I am reading this book because I know I will eventually have to teach using the Web, but I have limited experience with the Internet. Any advice for getting up to speed?

Fear not. An entire branch of the publishing industry has been spawned to help people in your situation. It is impossible to cover all the available books on the Internet, Unix, and so on, but I have had very good luck with the IDG "For Dummies" series. Do not be put off by the titles; the "for dummies" part is meant as a self-deprecating joke. We all start off as dummies. These books are usually fairly detailed and answer many of the questions new users have; they are also well written, and I believe the humorous approach makes the subjects being covered easier to learn and less threatening to some people. IDG has books on many technical and Internet-related subjects, some written for beginners and others written for persons with advanced technical knowledge. They have even published *The Internet for Teachers* by Bard Williams, which combines a primer on the Internet itself with information of special interest to educators. Another good set of books, although not nearly as entertaining, is the "Unleashed" series released by SAMS publishing. Finally, there is a series of somewhat more technical titles published by O'Reilley and Associates. (This is the company that has a different animal on the cover of each of its computer books. I refuse to speculate on why they do this or whether the specific animals chosen for each cover have any symbolic relevance to the topic being covered. Doubtless, someone will write a dissertation on this.)

Even more important, however, is to learn by doing. Instead of calling colleagues or leaving Post-its in their mailboxes, send them e-mail so you can practice using the software. Research topics of personal or professional interest on-line to gain firsthand experience with the techniques and limitations of on-line research. Design some Web pages. Learn Java or Common Gateway Interface (CGI). A lot of this work can be done at home, in the early mornings or late evenings, if you have a computer with a modem.

You do not have to do it all by yourself, either. Buy beer and pizza for colleagues who know what they are doing and pick their brains. (You will be stunned by what people will do for free food; this is something smart administrators learn early in their careers.) Cultivate professional contacts. Write articles and conference papers with these people, being honest beforehand that you are a beginner and one reason you want to be involved in the project is so you can learn more. You have a lot of options.

Q. What do I need to know about teaching research skills?

There simply is not sufficient space in this chapter to provide a general examination of teaching research skills. You should, however, purchase the most recent edition of Robert Berkman's *Find It Fast*. This is probably the single best book available on doing research. *The Craft of Research*, by Booth, Colomb, and Williams, will also prove quite valuable. Finally, at the risk of seeming self-serving, I have written a chapter on teaching research skills for *The NCTE Guide to Teaching Writing*. I think I did a pretty good job, so I recommend reading that, too.

One thing to keep in mind about research, however, is that having a general plan for a project can save students a great deal of time. Berkman provides a very useful template for doing research:

1. Define your problem (i.e., identify the questions you want answered).

2. Locate your resources (i.e., identify libraries, create a working bibliography, etc.).

3. Find and read key sources to develop a basic understanding of your subject (and use these sources to help identify experts you can talk to for more detailed information).

4. Make a list of questions that still need to be answered, then contact and interview experts.

5. Evaluate progress and, if necessary, redirect focus.

6. Draft the report.

As far as I know, Berkman has no formal training in rhetoric, but it is interesting that as a professional researcher and writer, his plan of action echoes what many theorists tell us about the recursive nature of the composition process.

Q. What kind of research can one do on the Internet?

Here, it is useful to distinguish *information* from *information pointers*. Information is the information for which you are looking; information pointers are pieces of information (e.g., bibliographies, phone books, etc.) that tell you how to find the information for which you are looking.

The hidden strength of the Internet is not its wealth of information, but its wealth of information pointers. Most books and periodicals, after all, are not on-line. Most responses to questions have not been written yet, because the technical expert with the information your student needs has not yet heard that question. However, the Internet makes searching for information much easier. Here is a breakdown of how to do it.

If your students need books on subjects, the first thing for them to do is check their own library's electronic card catalogue. Often, they will find much of what they need by doing this. In addition, find out if the card catalogue (or other resources available through the campus library like the Infotrac or Firstsearch databases) can be searched via the Internet.

At large universities with millions of volumes in their library collections, this may be all students have to do much of the time. If they are still looking for printed materials, they can do the following:

• Books can be found using the on-line catalogues of various large universities. Large university libraries like the ones at Yale and the Library of Congress are among the many library systems that can be searched electronically via the Internet. The books can then be requested via interlibrary loan, assuming the student has planned ahead and given herself enough lead time. Another "library" with about 2 million volumes that can be searched for free is Amazon.com, which wants you to buy their books, of course, but effectively functions as a poor student's "Books in Print On-line."

• Students should be aware that they do not need to get the materials specifically from the libraries they are searching; the search, in this case, is to determine what material might be available for interlibrary loan. After all, it does not matter if they get the book from Yale or not as long as they get the book.

- Articles from periodicals can be searched using CARL UNCOVER. CARL is a document delivery service that wants you to purchase reprints of articles from them. They allow and encourage students and scholars to use their search engine for free, however, and even point out that people should try to find the articles at their own libraries rather than pay for them. Since their database covers approximately 18,000 periodicals from 1988 to the present, and includes more than 8 million items, it is an extremely useful tool for searching recent periodical literature. For those using CARL for research, consider using the telnet interface rather than the Web interface; while the telnet interface involves using some clunky Unix-like commands, many telnet programs (including the one bundled with Windows 95) allow you to save an entire session (in this case, a list of every source you look at on CARL) as a text log file.

- Finally, content information is available on a wide range of subjects. While the vast majority of printed material is not yet available on-line, thousands of books and articles on a wide range of subjects have been converted into on-line text or HTML. Many newspapers, magazines, government agencies, and scholarly journals now simultaneously release print and on-line electronic editions of their publications. In addition, millions of Web pages of original material have been developed; in some cases, the World Wide Web is the only place where this information is available.

- While this is not the place to give you a complete rundown on "Cool Sites for Composition Teachers," I will recommend a few basic starting points. There is no index to the entire Internet, but Yahoo is one of the best and largest indices available. A similar Web site is WebRing; Web rings are groups of sites with similar topics that are linked to form a single distributed supersite, and WebRing provides an index to several thousand of them. An enormous range of search engines is available, but AltaVista, Hotbot, Excite, Savvysearch, and Webcrawler are all quite good. There is an index of rhetoric resources at Carnegie-Mellon University. Finally, at the risk of again seeming self-serving, my own list of resources, the *Rhetoric Page at Kettering University*, is designed in part as a starting point for research for both teachers and students. It is always possible that any of these sites will move, but you can usually find them again by using a couple of search engines. For example, try typing "Gellis" and "Rhetoric" in any major search engine, and you will usually find either the *Rhetoric Page at Kettering University* or my home page (which will have a link to it) listed as one of the first ten or twenty possible sites.

Q. What about using e-mail to contact experts?

Here, the Internet serves first as a list of sources and then as a medium for communication. While many scholars now publish on-line, often the information they can provide via correspondence will be more valuable to students with specific questions. Such communication can also be used to help students clarify or amplify information already gathered from traditional sources.

- Locating experts (and their e-mail addresses) can be as simple as searching on-line directories at government, corporate, or university sites for appropriate contact persons. Other valuable resources are professional associations, which often provide directories of their members (or whose staff can be reached with a telephone call or an e-mail message). Finally, it is important to remember that if students are using a book or an article as a source, and they still have questions, they can try to contact the author of that book or article.

- A particularly good source of expert information is listserv mailing lists and news groups. Often, a student's question will have already been answered in an FAQ file. If not, students can post a question to the group, which means it may be seen by hundreds of people, allowing for multiple replies. Naturally, students must make sure that the people responding to their questions are credible sources, but often credentials are offered in the message itself (i.e., people provide not only their names but mention their institutional affiliation and title). If they are not offered, they can often be determined by using the e-mail addresses of persons posting replies to identify their institutions, whose Web pages and on-line directories will frequently identify whether the person is a student, faculty member, and so on. Of course, if students mention in their questions that their teacher requires contact information from on-line sources, including affiliation and position, the problem is usually avoided.

- Students can e-mail individual experts with their questions. If they compose polite and professional-sounding requests with clear, specific, carefully prepared questions, they will often receive detailed answers. Berkman's *Find It Fast* may prove very useful here; Berkman dedicates several chapters to finding, contacting, and interviewing subject area experts.

- An added advantage of having students contact experts is that if they are researching a topic in their intended major, they can use this opportunity to begin building a network of professional contacts. As most success gurus are happy to point out, one key to success is a fat Rolodex.

- You are likely to receive resistance about contacting experts. Many students will be terrified by the idea. After all, you are asking them to contact someone they do not know, who does not know them, and who is important, an author, and seek their help. Their fear is perfectly normal, but generally unfounded. Students should understand that it is perfectly acceptable to contact experts. Experts make their living by providing information; if they are unwilling to answer questions, they should find another job. Furthermore, most experts will try to help them out if they can. There are two major reasons for this. First, people usually like to help people. We are social creatures; we are geared by evolution to help each other, and we usually get a nice little endorphin rush as a reward when we see we have helped our fellow creatures.

- Try this out in your class. Ask your students if any of them consider themselves an expert, or at least someone with more-than-beginner knowledge, in anything. You will usually find a number of students who fit this category. Now ask one of these students how they would react if a stranger came up, politely introduced themselves, explained that they had heard that student was an expert in a certain area, and asked for help. Usually, your student would say, yes, I would try to help that person. Now ask how the student would feel if she or he saw that his advice had actually been useful or helpful to that person. Most of them will say something like, "Pretty good." Now, finally, ask them if the experts they are going to contact are likely to be any different.

- The other reason why experts will talk to people about their subject is because they are probably very interested in the subject. If they were not interested in it, they probably would not have become an expert in that subject. This means they probably enjoy talking about it. The only downside of this is that you may end up with far more information (and larger phone bills if you contact the expert by telephone rather than e-mail) than you wanted.

• The biggest reason why experts might not wish to talk to students is that they are busy. When doing interviews, one can always ask when it would be convenient to call back. E-mail often solves this problem automatically, since experts can answer at their convenience, although sometimes students may need to send a polite reminder.

• Finally, whether the expert is able to talk or not (sometimes they will be so busy that they simply do not have time to help a student), one should always ask an expert who else they think one should contact (or whose works should be read) to learn more about the subject. For the same reason, one should always look at the list of works cited in a book or article. This is a central concept in doing research—every source of information (expert, article, Web site, etc.) may also be a source of other sources.

Q. My students are interested in using the Internet not only to find sources, but to find information. How is Internet-based information different from traditional information?

There are a variety of differences. In particular, hypertext has a potential for information richness that is not possible with traditional text. Scholars such as Richard Lanham and Jay Bolter have written extensively on the promise of hypertext. For students doing research on-line, these differences create both opportunities and potential difficulties.

• *Internet-based information can be linked and nonlinear.* The Internet involves hypertext, text that embodies extensions beyond itself. These extensions can be self-referential, with glossaries, illustrations, commentary, or other reference materials kept invisible until a user invokes them. It can also involve external links, connections to texts that are entirely separate from the Internet site one is browsing. Because of this, and because Internet-based information can be nonlinear, read topically rather than sequentially, the Internet is capable of providing a level of information richness that is simply not possible with traditional text. In addition, it provides various benefits to researchers. Having direct links to the apparatus of a text can be very convenient. In addition, in some cases, the bibliography is also a set of links; one does not have to hunt down references, because they are already directly linked to the text. The only disadvantage is that such information can be overwhelming; one can miss details because one is caught up in the experience of "webbed" information.

• *Internet-based information can be dynamic.* Electronic documents can be easily updated, changed, archived, or obliterated. This creates advantages and disadvantages for students doing research on-line. With traditional text, new editions usually do not appear more frequently than once every few years. In the case of Internet-based hypertext, updates can come far more frequently. While this means that on-line information may be far more current than articles published in journals (which means the information is often a year or two old before it is disseminated), it can also create problems. Students relying on Web pages for information cannot know for certain that the information will be available indefinitely. It is wise for students to download Web pages they use for research so that they have a permanent copy of the information; it is also wise for them to keep careful track of when they visited particular Web pages for citation purposes.

• *Internet-based information can be unregulated.* I try to avoid using words like "wonderful," and I am irritated by people who use such words too frequently, but the Internet is truly wonderful in at least one respect. It is, I believe, the most American invention of the twentieth century. For the first time in human history, the freedom of the press no longer belongs only to an elite circle of people who own the press. For hundreds of years, of course, it was possible for anyone to publish a few hundred copies of anything, but reaching a large portion of the public for an extended period of time was simply beyond the resources of most people. Even relatively small publishing efforts such as local newspapers could only be accomplished by those willing to make a career out of it. Now, for one-tenth of the price of a used car, writers can reach an audience of a hundred million people. Randolph Hearst, for all his power, never had a nine-figure readership. You and I can. The downside of this is that every racist, fanatic, and well-meaning idiot on the planet can also reach a nine-figure readership. Sturgeon's Law—90 percent of everything is crap—applies to Web sites with a vengeance. *For this reason, students doing research on Web sites must be able to not only record the information but verify its accuracy. Teachers should not accept information researched from the Internet unless the student can somehow provide proof that the information is accurate.* I will discuss this issue in more detail later.

• *Internet-based information can be highly graphical.* Traditional text can involve graphics and design features, but with on-line text, dynamic graphics and multimedia features such as animations, video clips, sound clips, embodied Java applications, and the like can be built into Web pages. Once again, all this allows for a greater richness of information than is possible with printed text, but it creates a potential problem. Highly graphical information can be more persuasive than plain "vanilla" text simply because its visual richness makes it more compelling. Furthermore, inexpensive desktop publishing and Web page design software makes it easy for people with relatively little experience in design to create very attractive Web pages, Web pages with a very professional, slick look and feel that implies authority and expertise. This is another reason why students must be skeptical of on-line information. *Attractiveness indicates only that the author has prowess as a designer; it does not prove that the information contained within the design is accurate.*

Q. My students are using search engines like AltaVista to do research, but they are either getting 6 million hits or nothing at all. What should they do?

This is a common problem. With millions of Web pages available and indexed by the major search engines, it is not uncommon for even a relatively specific set of search terms to yield several thousand "hits." A related problem is that different search engines seem to employ entirely different logical processes when searching the Internet and ranking the relevance of search results, processes that are often incomprehensible to the lay person. For example, let me take on the role of a student interested in the war against Yugoslavia who wants to learn more about the weapons used to wage war. The student remembers that one of the ships involved in the conflict is the *Philippine Sea*, but does not remember anything else about it. Starting with some search engines, the student finds that the phrase "Philippine Sea" yields only two hits on Yahoo, and neither of these has anything to do with the subject. A similar search on Hotbot yields nearly five thousand hits, far more than would be practical to examine. Discouraging. Here are a few strategies for making Internet searches more effective and less time-consuming.

- *If a search yields more than a few hundred hits, add an additional search term to narrow the search.* For "Philippine Sea," I add the term "ship." This reduces the number to a little under six hundred and, unfortunately, the first hit is for another warship, a carrier, now retired, with the same name. I add a fourth term, "modern," and I reduce the number to under one hundred hits, the first of which covers cruisers. I am going to assume that most students do not know the difference between cruisers and carriers, but I decide to check the link out anyway. From here, I quickly find a Web site that leads me to the home page for the USS *Philippine Sea*, CG 58, which unfortunately had been disabled when I was writing this chapter or I would have told you more about it.

- *Do not be discouraged by dead ends.* The Internet is dynamic. Sometimes terrific sites will shut down, sometimes for a few weeks and sometimes forever.

- *Try multiple search engines.* The same search term(s) will yield different results on different search engines. There are several hundred search engines available, many of them very different from the half-dozen or so most popular ones. "Philippine Sea" yields everything from two hits on Yahoo to three hundred thousand on AltaVista. However, the AltaVista search highlights two topics before it even starts listing specific Web sites, and one of them is the CG 58 *Philippine Sea*. The second page listed under this topic is a "facts and figures" page that would answer many of my student's technical questions.

- *Limit yourself to checking out the first fifty or sixty hits.* Anything beyond that is usually irrelevant to your research project. If you scan fifty or sixty hits on a search engine, and you have reached a dead end, it is time to try different search terms or a different search engine.

- *Resist the urge to surf.* Every time you check a link that has nothing to do with your subject, you have wasted time. I would have loved to spend half an hour reliving the carrier battles of yesteryear, of which one is the namesake of the current *Philippine Sea*. (Currently, American cruisers are named for battles; destroyers and frigates are named for people. See? You learn something new every day!)

- *Take advantage of secondary links.* Sometimes the answer will not be found in a Web page identified by a search engine, but in a Web page identified in *that* Web page. Remember, also, that the nonlinear nature of the Internet means that the relationships between resources may not be readily apparent.

- *Try a variety of terms, including synonyms.* If you get stuck, brainstorm for a few minutes to create a list of related terms that might lead you to the information you are seeking. Open a browser window to the on-line version of *Roget's Thesaurus* and take advantage of it.

• *Make a list of relevant keywords and use them for later searches.* For example, while searching for information on the *Philippine Sea*, I found terms like CG, AEGIS, VLS, chaff, Harpoon, and SH-60B. Most students do not know that these are, respectively, the abbreviation for guided missile cruisers, a fire control system, a missile vertical launch system that lets American cruisers carry twice the firepower of a World War II battleship four times their size, strips of metal foil used to confuse the radar on incoming missiles so they do not sink you, an anti-ship missile not carried by the VLS system, and an anti-submarine helicopter; but now that they know these terms exist, they can use them with search engines to locate more specific and relevant information. For example, using "Philippine Sea Aegis" in Hotbot rapidly led me to a detailed technical paper that includes a discussion of the capabilities of the class of ship to which the *Philippine Sea* belongs, the VLS-capable generation of the Ticonderoga-class AEGIS cruiser.

Q. Are Internet resources reliable? How do you evaluate sources from the Internet?

I believe that, while there are a few special problems created by on-line information, the criteria that distinguish good and bad information are the same whether a source is on-line or traditional. The medium, after all, has nothing to do with the veracity of the information; it only affects the credibility of the information. There are a number of systems available for evaluating sources, but I like the CARS system developed by Robert Harris. You can find the CARS system on-line. I strongly recommend that you read his discussion in full, but briefly, what Harris says is that there are four basic criteria for researched information:

• Credibility

• Accuracy

• Reasonableness

• Support

A source is *credible* when there is reason to find it trustworthy, such as the author's credentials, the reputation of the publisher, evidence of quality control (e.g., journals with blind peer review of articles), and so on. It is here that we have one of the great dangers of using the Internet for research. It is extremely easy to create Web pages that have a slick, published look, regardless of whether or not one actually knows anything about the subject. For example, it may not always be possible to determine if the person who has created the *Locust Resource Page* is an entomologist, a pastor with a theological interest in locusts but no formal training in their biology, or a fifth grader putting his class project on grasshoppers on the Web because he thinks bugs are cool.

My recommendation for solving this problem is that Internet-based sources may not be anonymous; the authors must identify themselves and their credentials (or affiliation) in the Web page. By effectively limiting Web pages to those that can be identified as being produced by experts in industry, academia, or government, or official Web pages of corporations, research centers, universities, government agencies, and other organizations, we eliminate many of the problems with reliability created by using Internet sources.

A source is *accurate* when it is current, sufficiently detailed and accurate in its coverage of the subject, and so on. Accuracy is, of course, relative. A source that is too old or too general in its discussion of the topic may not be inaccurate, but it may not be accurate enough to be useful.

A source is *reasonable* when it examines its subject fairly, in a balanced and objective manner, sometimes by considering alternate points of view. Logical fallacies, conflict of interest, obvious bias, or an overly emotional tone can be signs that a source is not reasonable.

A source is *supported* when its information can be corroborated, often by the author listing sources or providing documentation or contact information.

A source that meets these four criteria is probably reliable; a source that cannot meet these four criteria may still be reliable, but the writer should treat it with suspicion and expect that audiences will do so, too, and should probably find other sources that corroborate its information before using it in his or her paper.

Q. How do I help my students deal with pornography and other offensive sites on the Internet?

While most of your college-age students are probably not shocked at the sight of naked bodies, and many find the barrage of on-line nudity simply laughable, some will be unsettled or disgusted by some of the images, texts, and so on that they may encounter. (They will also encounter them unexpectedly; we all have stories about people typing in the URL of what they thought was a normal Web site and suddenly finding themselves looking at images most adult magazines would not publish.) Some of our students, after all, have very strong views, and on-line nudity will be offensive to them. A related problem is that there are numerous Web sites that feature ideas that many people find profoundly offensive, such as hate speech. In some cases, this will translate into resistance to Web-based pedagogy or hostility toward instructors who are now viewed as being responsible for the trauma.

- Be supportive. Even if you do not believe there is anything wrong with on-line pornography, be sympathetic to the fact that some people will be offended by what they may see. It goes without saying, I hope, that one should be careful when developing Web-based assignments so that students are not likely to have on-line pornography or hate speech inflicted upon them. (There may be some exceptions here, but I find it difficult to imagine a pedagogy where it would be essential to view tasteless erotic images.)

- In some cases, it may be possible to use these experiences as an opportunity to discuss the nature of a free press in a free society. At the same time, be sympathetic to students whose views are more liberal or conservative than your own, and who may be uncomfortable with having to closely examine, perhaps for the first time, their own assumptions about society and morality. Even if you do not agree with these students, treat them and their ideas with respect; if not, you will make it difficult for them to learn anything from you.

Q. I believe students learn by doing. What kind of research activities do you suggest?

Here are ten activities to help students develop their research skills.

1. Students can develop a bibliography using on-line sources such as CARL and Amazon.com.

2. Students can create a subject dossier. This goes beyond the bibliography, which is simply a list of sources, and includes information gathered from Web pages. A variation on this is to set a time limit—students have to work intensely for an hour or so and gather as much information as they can about a subject. Teachers can even make it a contest, offering prizes or at least kudos for students who find the most information, the best information, the weirdest Web site discovered by accident, and so on.

3. Students can develop an information map, creating a graphical representation of how information from one Web site connects to other Web sites, and how those Web sites connect to still more Web sites. The interesting thing is that even if you are looking at the same subject, the map changes radically depending on which Web site you choose as a starting point. This can be useful for understanding the nonlinear nature of on-line information.

4. Students can evaluate one or more Web pages in terms of information quality, design, credibility, readability, and so on. If more than one Web page is examined, students can compose short comparison and contrast reports.

5. Students can explore on-line directories and develop a list of possible contacts who could provide information on a certain subject.

6. Students can compose and send e-mail messages to subject area experts, asking them specific questions about their research topics.

7. Students can critique the letters they and others have sent, or are planning to send, to experts.

8. Students can record and evaluate their research procedures. What did they do to find the information they wanted? Why did they do it that way? Would they use this plan again? What have they learned from the process?

9. Students can brainstorm collaboratively on-line, using either e-mail or one of the many synchronous communication (e.g., IRC, MOO, etc.) programs available, recording their brainstorming sessions, developing a research topic, research questions, and so on. Students can either work with fellow students in their own class or, if you can get one or more faculty members at your institution to sign on with you, engage in collaborative multiclass projects.

10. Students can collaborate on a research project with students at other universities. They will not only have to research and write the paper, but they will also gain experience in solving problems in geographically distributed teams. For this last assignment, of course, you will need the cooperation of another faculty member at another institution, but many composition teachers are interested in the learning that can take place in such distributed meta-classes.

Q. How do you cite sources from the Internet?

This is a difficult question. The format for citation appears to be in flux. Slightly different formats have appeared in different handbooks and textbooks. I have generally relied on Li and Crane's *Electronic Styles: A Handbook for Citing Electronic Information* as a final authority. It is certainly one of the most complete examinations of this issue available. With any luck, by the time you read this chapter, the newest editions of the *MLA Handbook* and the *APA Publication Manual* will have come to terms with the new electronic media and will include detailed sections explaining how to cite various on-line sources both internally and in bibliographies.

Q. You mentioned before that students can use these skills regardless of how much Internet access they have. Are there any differences between different classroom settings?

I am going to start by creating a rough classification grid for the different kinds of classrooms. These are the general categories.

- In a *traditional classroom*, we have little if any Internet access in the classroom itself. While some classrooms now have the wiring necessary to link a portable computer to the Internet for a period of time, let's assume we are almost always working with only the bare bones here—walls, desks, chairs, and a blackboard. What this means is that instruction will be separated from actual Internet experience. Explaining Internet-based concepts and skills may become more difficult and more time-consuming for this reason. Overheads illustrating screen shots can be helpful here, as students will be able to see what you are describing even as you describe it, but there are limits to how much one can do with this technique.

- In a *computer-assisted classroom*, we have at least one terminal, and usually at least one display system for presentations. This is significantly better than a traditional classroom because students will be able to see what you are describing. It has the disadvantage that students will often be learning passively, listening and watching a demonstration by the instructor or by another student, rather than learning by doing.

- In a *computer lab or computer classroom*, we have many terminals where students can work on papers, presentations, and so on. A computer lab may or may not be networked (allowing students to communicate with each other within the lab) or have Internet access (the latter usually allows for the former, since students can communicate with each other via the Internet even if there are no direct connections between terminals in the lab). Such classrooms often employ layouts that facilitate decentered teaching and group activities. This is often done using pods (four or five terminals at a table). This is an expensive option, requiring twenty or so computers, presentation equipment, software, wiring, furniture, and so on. It also involves ongoing costs in the form of upgrades and support personnel. It is, however, enormously flexible. Students can listen to presentations, work on projects individually or in groups, either writing or doing research, on their own or consulting with you or with others. It is ideal for active learning, since students can listen to an instructor explain an Internet-based or writing-based concept or skill and then try it out for themselves while the information is still fresh in their minds. In addition, if the layout of the classroom allows for it, students can not only work with assigned groups but form their own ad hoc groups. Be sure, if you are creating such a lab, to get chairs with rollers; it is a small detail, but it makes it much easier for students to engage in these flexible ad hoc groups.

There is a large body of literature available on computer classrooms that covers the advantages and difficulties of such learning spaces. Some recent volumes include *Computers and the Teaching of Writing in American Higher Education, 1979–1994: A History*, by Gail E. Hawisher, Paul LeBlanc, Charles Moran, and Cynthia L. Selfe; *Transitions: Teaching Writing in Computer-Supported and Traditional Classrooms*, by Mike Palmquist, Kate Kiefer, James Hartvigsen, and Barbara Goodlew; and *Electronic Communication Across the Curriculum*, edited by Donna Reiss, Dickie Selfe, and Art Young. Also available is a large on-line bibliography on computers and composition (Bridgeford et al.).

- Finally, we have what could be called a *distributed classroom*. In this situation, most or all of the class is not conducted in a common space. Instead, students log on from wherever they are, communicating with their instructor and with fellow students by e-mail, IRC, MOO, or some other on-line protocol. Face-to-face meetings occur infrequently, if ever, although the steadily dropping cost of videoconferencing may make virtual face-to-face meetings easier and more frequent. While I believe this kind of distance learning can be very effective, it can be very difficult to make it so. Distance learning traditionally has a very high dropout rate. Without the physical community of the classroom, and without direct in-person contact with instructors, many students become discouraged or, at the very least, are not motivated to do their best work.

Q. My students are not afraid of the Internet. In fact, they are convinced they only need to do on-line research. They want to know why they should do traditional research, too. What do I tell them?

This is a common problem. Students who are already familiar with the Internet often do not want to use anything else. It is understandable. The Internet is huge; it is hard for many students to believe that there is information that is not on the Internet. So why drag yourself down to the library when you can do all the work in your pajamas, coffee in hand, and with the newest game playing in another window?

- First, you can focus on the Internet as a conduit rather than a source. The Internet has a lot of full-text resources, but its real value is that it points to an even larger body of print sources and allows for easy access to expert sources via e-mail, listservs, and on-line conversations.

• Second, you can focus on information depth in their writing. Since on-line sources need clear support for their reliability or corroboration from other sources, it makes sense for students to look at print sources in the library. A variation on this is not to *require* traditional print sources, but to remind students that you require their examination of the topic to achieve a certain level of comprehensiveness, and if their final drafts do not do this, they will either receive a lower grade or be required to revise and resubmit the draft.

• Finally, you can simply tell students that since one of the goals of the course is to develop research skills, they must include traditional and on-line sources in a final draft in order to demonstrate competence in both areas of research. A less arbitrary approach, if such things concern you, is to design assignments like working bibliographies that require students to learn to use traditional sources while giving them the option to employ only on-line sources in the final draft, if it is appropriate for them to do so.

Q. What problems could my students face? What kind of resistance should I expect?

You are likely to face three kinds of problems. The first is that some students will lack familiarity with many on-line technologies. As a result, you will have to spend time, either in class or in conference, helping them learn the basics of navigating the Internet or on-line databases in the library. While other faculty, tutors, more experienced students in your own classes, and others may be able to help you here, teachers have to expect that students will enter their classes at different levels of skills. Some students may have limited experience with the Internet due to poor funding in their school districts. Teachers need to find out how experienced their students are and then determine how to get those who lack basic knowledge of the Internet up to speed. Instructional videos and supplementary textbooks (again, I recommend books from the IDG "For Dummies" series) may help. Setting up workshops with library staff and your college computer center is another possibility.

The second problem is that students may fear technology. It may seem surprising, but many students are fearful of computers and related technology. Fear will manifest itself in a number of ways, but two of them might be reluctance to use the Internet and resistance or even hostility toward teachers who want them to do so. Patience and flexibility are your best tools here. You must remain sympathetic to fearful students while encouraging them to become familiar with the Internet, computers, and so on. You may need to work one-on-one with such students or have them get counseling at your Student Health Center. The solutions will vary with the individual student. The important thing is to be aware that many students who resist Web-based pedagogy do so out of anxiety rather than an unwillingness to learn or to work.

The third problem is availability of technology. We cheerfully assign Internet-based writing assignments assuming that all of our students have more and better computers than we do. In some cases, this is an accurate assessment. But for many students, the only computers to which they have access are those in a college computer lab, which may have forty terminals to serve four hundred students. Not to mention it is a ten-minute walk from their dorm and in early February the temperature is zero and the wind chill is twenty below. And the printer is not working. You get the idea. The problem is often even more serious for nontraditional students, many of whom are single parents, who cannot afford their own computers and who cannot afford to hire babysitters every time they need to jaunt back to campus for a few hours to work on our e-mail assignments. It is necessary to assess the availability of technology before we build the necessity of using such technology into our pedagogy. If we do not do this, we are guilty of an unacceptable elitism.

Q. Any parting words of wisdom?

I think the ten smartest words I ever heard about teaching, told to me by my colleague Al Boysen, who teaches at the South Dakota School of Mines and Technology, are the following: "Talk less. Listen more. Involve students. Let them take charge." I believe this advice, which sums up very effectively much of what we know about active learning, is particularly important to faculty responsible for teaching composition, technical writing, oral communication, and related areas. This is because what we teach emphasizes skills rather than content knowledge. Ultimately, in our disciplines, what matters is not what our students know after they leave our classes, but what they can do. The art of research is intimately linked to the art of rhetoric, but teaching research skills is important in every discipline. For our students, the ability to find useful information quickly is a critical aspect of their ability to succeed as professionals and citizens. Web-based pedagogy provides us with many opportunities for changing passive learning into active learning—learning that will foster not only essential knowledge, but also essential skills such as research.

NOTE

A small portion of this chapter appears in *The NCTE Guide to Teaching Writing* (Urbana, IL: National Council of Teachers of English, forthcoming). Reprinted with permission.

WORKS CITED

Alta Vista. Home page. 1 Aug. 1999 <http://www.altavista.com/>.
Amazon.com. Home page. 1 Aug. 1999 <http://www.amazon.com>.
Aristotle. *On Rhetoric*. Trans. George Kennedy. New York: Oxford University Press, 1991.

Berkman, Robert I. *Find It Fast: How to Uncover Expert Information on Any Subject.* 4th ed. New York: HarperPerennial, 1997.

Bolter, Jay David. *Writing Space: The Computer, Hypertext, and the History of Writing.* Hillsdale, NJ: Lawrence Erlbaum Associates, 1991.

Booth, Wayne C., Gregory G. Colomb, and Joseph M. Williams. *The Craft of Research.* Chicago: University of Chicago Press, 1995.

Bridgeford, Tracy, Margaret L. FalerSweany, Danielle DeVoss, and Cheryl Malgay Heath. "Comprehensive Bibliography." *Computers and Composition.* 1 Aug. 1999 <http://www.hu.mtu.edu/~candc/bib/>.

CARL UNCOVER. *Carl Corporation.* Home page. 1 Aug. 1999 <http://www.carl.org/>.

Carnegie-Mellon University. *Rhetoric and Composition.* 1 Aug. 1999 <http://english-www.hss.cmu.edu/rhetoric/>.

Excite. Home page. 1 Aug. 1999 <http://www.excite.com/>.

Gellis, Mark. *Rhetoric Page at Kettering University.* Home page. 1 Aug. 1999 <http://www.kettering.edu/~mgellis/GMI_Rhet.htm>.

———. "Teaching Research Skills in the Freshman Composition Class." In *The NCTE Guide to Teaching Writing.* Ed. Duane Roen. Urbana, IL: NCTE, forthcoming.

Harris, Robert. *Evaluating Internet Research Sources.* 17 Nov. 1997. 1 Aug. 1999 <http://www.sccu.edu/faculty/R_Harris/evalu8it.htm>.

Hawisher, Gail E., Paul LeBlanc, Charles Moran, and Cynthia L. Selfe. *Computers and the Teaching of Writing in American Higher Education, 1979–1994: A History.* Norwood, NJ: Ablex, 1996.

Hotbot. Home page. 1 Aug. 1999 <http://www.hotbot.com/>.

IDG. Home page. 1 Aug. 1999 <http://www.idg.com>.

Lanham, Richard A. *The Electronic Word: Democracy, Technology, and the Arts.* Chicago: University of Chicago Press, 1993.

Li, Xia, and Nancy B. Crane. *Electronic Styles: A Handbook for Citing Electronic Information.* 2nd ed. Medford, NJ: Information Today, 1996.

Library of Congress. Home page. 1 Aug. 1999 <http://lcweb.loc.gov/homepage/lchp.html>.

O'Reilley and Associates. Home page. 1 Aug. 1999 <http://www.ora.com>.

Palmquist, Mike, Kate Kiefer, James Hartvigsen, and Barbara Goodlew. *Transitions: Teaching Writing in Computer-Supported and Traditional Classrooms.* Greenwich, CT: Ablex, 1998.

Reiss, Donna, Dickie Selfe, and Art Young, eds. *Electronic Communication Across the Curriculum.* Urbana, IL: National Council of Teachers of English, 1998.

Roget's Thesaurus. Thesaurus.com. Home page. 1 Aug. 1999 <http://thesaurus.com/>.

SAMS Publishing. Macmillan. Home page. 1 Aug. 1999 <http://www.mcp.com/publishers/sams/>.

Savvy Search. Home page. 1 Aug. 1999 <http://www.savvysearch.com/>.

Webcrawler. Home page. 1 Aug. 1999 <http://webcrawler.com/>.

WebRing. Home page. 1 Aug. 1999 <http://www.webring.net/>.

Williams, Bard. *The Internet for Teachers.* 2nd ed. Foster City, CA: IDG Books, 1996.

Yahoo. Home page. 1 Aug. 1999 <http://www.yahoo.com>.

Yale University Library. 1 Aug. 1999 <http://www.library.yale.edu>.

Chapter 25

Tearing Down Barriers and Building Communities: Pedagogical Strategies for the Web-Based Environment

Autumn Grubb and Margaret Hines

As Karen Cerulo notes, "Recent developments have touched issues at the very heart of sociological discourse—the definition of interaction, the nature of social ties, and the scope of experience and reality. Indeed, the developing technologies are creating an expanded social environment that requires amendments and alterations to ways in which we conceptualize social processes" (49).

Cerulo suggests that technologically generated communities force us to reformulate the way in which we view three key analytic concepts: social interaction, social bonding, and empirical experience. Designers and instructors of Web-based distance learning communities understand and appreciate the importance of redefining critical concepts that make up a "sense of community" among participants in a virtual learning environment. To manifest a sense of community in Web-based instruction, one must develop cyberspace interpersonal rituals that exist in effective learning environments. The use of Internet technologies for delivering instruction requires us to refashion pedagogical strategies that encourage the development of rituals that allow our students to create on-line social and academic interaction, bonding events, and knowledge creation.

Internet and Web-based technologies, which have recently emerged as the newest form of distance learning, are, like other forms of distance learning in the past, being touted as the medium that will change the face of education. However, these technologies must overcome the same barriers to learning that have plagued distance learners in the past. To achieve the success promised, barriers to learning must be recognized and appropriate pedagogical strategies must be employed. Additionally, as Cerulo cautions, we must reformulate our meanings of social interaction, social bonding, and empirical experience as they relate to the virtual instructional learning environment.

BARRIERS TO DISTANCE LEARNERS

Barriers that plague the adult distance learner's efforts in educational pursuits are well documented. These barriers range from personal feelings of insecurity and isolation to a lack of technical support. A brief description of these barriers can help us understand the kinds of struggles distance learners experience in their instructional environments.

Knapper suggests that adult distance learners experience personal and school-related insecurities while engaged in distance learning. These insecurities are often driven by time and place constraints for students bearing familial and financial responsibilities. The fear of not being able to juggle these responsibilities in addition to work demands and school demands can often seem overwhelming to the adult distance learner.

Adult distance learners experience fear related to academic discourse engagement and report difficulty building a shared understanding among students with multiple backgrounds, located in multiple cultures (Christiansen and Dirckinck-Holmfeld). Overcoming the fear of engaging the academic discourse and at the same time negotiating and developing relationships with fellow learners from diverse cultures can be daunting tasks, as well as time-consuming efforts.

Technical issues can also become barriers to learning, as can a lack of technical and content support (Galusha). If the learner cannot negotiate (or determine) required technical skills or locate appropriate technical or content support when a problem arises, learning becomes impossible.

In addition, a perceived lack of feedback or contact with the teacher creates barriers to learning for the adult distance student. This perceived lack of feedback in distance learning environments may be driven by the lack of common interpersonal rituals that exist in face-to-face experiences (Keegan). Subsequently, students often report a feeling of isolation in the distance learning environment (Meacham and Evans).

These barriers have a common thread in that they all refer in some way to communicating, engaging, and interacting with others. This chapter explores how Web-based instruction can reduce, and possibly remove, some of the many barriers facing adult distance learning students. Appropriate pedagogical strategies that help us redefine social interaction, social bonding, and empirical experience must be employed. But first, there must be an understanding of what is required to bond a diverse group of distance learners into a cohesive virtual community of learners.

Creating a Virtual Community of Learners

Dede states that for distance students to bond as a cohesive group of learners, three cultural commodities must be present: social network capital, knowledge capital, and communion. Social network capital refers to an "instant web of contacts with useful skills" (17). This web of contacts provides the collaborative goods or glue that binds the group because immediate instructional and inter-personal needs are being met. Virtual contacts can include interactions with content experts, fellow learners, the instructor, technical support personnel, peo-ple actively applying the content in a professional capacity, or mentors. These contacts might assist with content-related tasks, technology skills or support information, knowledge about how to access resources associated with the course content, or strategies to be successful in class.

Knowledge capital is defined as a "personal, distributed brain trust with just-in-time answers to immediate questions" (Dede 17). Knowledge capital provides on-line information related to the technical, collaborative, and content compe-tencies the instructor has determined necessary of the learners. Individuals who create this brain trust could include fellow students, instructors, technical support personnel, and content experts practicing in the field.

Communion involves the "psychological/spiritual support from people who share common joys and trials" (Dede 17). This support is what develops a sense of community in Web-based learning environments, helping the learners to feel they are connected to other learners experiencing the same frustrations, suc-cesses, and eurekas. Communion might take the form of on-line help groups (listservs, discussion forums, or chat rooms) as well as face-to-face meetings between students or between students and the faculty member.

The absence of well-known rituals that bond students as a cohesive group often hinders the development of these cultural commodities in the on-line en-vironment. Implementing computer-mediated communication strategies within Web-based instruction/learning can serve to address the three cultural commodities Dede suggests must be present for a group of people to develop a cohesive bond as learners. Computer conferencing (discussion forums, chat rooms, e-mail) can play a major role in successful Web-based instruction/learn-ing by encouraging and nurturing a collaborative sense of community and de-veloping components of the knowledge capital and social network capital.

Paulsen identifies four paradigms faculty members must negotiate when em-ploying computer-mediated communication in Web-based instruction/learning: one-alone, one to one, one to many, and many to many. The one-alone paradigm is realized through pedagogical strategies such as requiring students to search databases, to explore on-line journals and software libraries, or to lurk within on-line interest groups. The one-to-one paradigm is evident when strategies such as learning contracts, apprenticeships, internships, or correspondence are em-ployed. The one-to-many paradigm is made visible when faculty members present lecture content on Web pages, organize symposiums, or create skits. The many-to-many model is evident in Web-based learning environments when instructors employ debates, simulations, role plays, case studies, discussion groups, content reflection exercises, brainstorming, group projects, or forums.

However, simply integrating computer mediated communication paradigms and strategies into the Web-based learning environment is not adequate to diminish or remove the barriers distance learning students experience. Knowing how to moderate and facilitate on-line discussions or chats can be significant to the success level of the teaching/learning experience on the Web.

Mason identifies three role functions that computer conferencing moderators must possess. First, moderators must serve in an organizational role, setting the agenda and tone. Second, moderation must be crafted to convey a friendly, caring environment that welcomes participation and provides quality feedback to the learners. Third, the moderator must fulfill an intellectual role, encouraging deeper analysis or synthesis of material by asking probing questions, providing discussion summaries, or requesting further discussion.

As Web-based instructors, the authors believe that Dede, Paulsen, and Mason provide vision and a foundation for the Web-based instructor who wishes to design on-line instruction that diminishes the documented barriers to instruction for adult distance learners, and encourages group cohesion and sense of community. This chapter offers a case study focusing on two on-line teaching experiences. Autumn Grubb delivered EDIT 6225—Telecommunications and Distance Learning as a Web-based course in the fall 1998 semester to graduate education students. Margaret Hines delivered BSHE 560R—Web-Based Information Sources as a Web-based course in the spring 1999 semester to graduate public health students.

Three key questions helped the authors form the foundation for revealing how social interaction, social bonding, and empirical experiences for Web-based learning environments were created. The key questions are: (1) What pedagogical strategies were employed to create and sustain the existence of communion in a Web-based course? (2) What pedagogical strategies were employed to create dynamic knowledge capital in a Web-based course? (3) What pedagogical strategies were employed to create social network capital in a Web-based course?

METHOD

To build responses to the three key questions the authors examined several data sources. First, on-line dialogues pertaining to the courses were studied. These interactions included all discussions conducted by learners and faculty members, evaluative and module summaries from the faculty members, and chat transcripts of synchronous on-line meetings between faculty members and on-line learners. The second set of data includes all listserv messages created by the learners and instructors during the delivery of courses. The third set of data is the authors' documentation of initial design and development phases of the on-line courses. The fourth set of data includes evaluations administered by the authors to determine the students' attitudes about the course's success or failure to create community and/or reduce traditional barriers to distance learning.

Each data set was coded for instructional strategies and moderation/facilitation roles that reduced barriers to learning. The strategies and roles were then assigned to one of three categories: (1) knowledge capital, (2) social network capital, or (3) communion. All names of students have been removed from discussions and e-mail messages to maintain anonymity. No URLs are offered for the course sites because they are password protected.

Knowledge Capital

In addition to the usual instructional artifacts such as a class syllabus, schedule, and required reading material, students in Web-based courses have to be given additional pieces of information related to taking the on-line courses. For example, communication protocols and strategies, course site navigation hints, directions for downloading software to their home computers, and how to subscribe to a listserv were all critical pieces of information to the students, particularly in the first few weeks of the on-line classes. Hardware and software requirements, as well as descriptions of how the courses would be managed, had to be available within the course Web site. These new types of instructional artifacts are all components of what Dede calls knowledge capital, the "personal, distributed brain trust with just-in-time answers to immediate questions" (Dede 17). As revealed in a discussion forum posting, there was a great deal of on-line jargon within the knowledge capital, which also had to be internalized by the students. One student mentions some of the jargon by stating, "Before I took this class I didn't know anything about java, CyberCafes, how to download documents, or what a listserv was" (EDIT 6225 student).

However, all of the knowledge capital for the courses was not created before the classes began. Construction of the knowledge capital in the on-line environment is often dynamic, and "in-the-moment." In other words, based on the students' experiences with the content and assignments, requests for new information regularly occur. For example, during a chat session three months into the semester with the BSHE 560R students, Margaret Hines revealed that the students were more than welcome to create Web pages for their final project. The following request for knowledge ensued:

Student 2: I think I am going to do a web page.

Student 3: Great! Do you have a topic yet?

Student 3: Oh I know—SPC, right?

Student 2: Yes, I think I want to create a page with links to the different women and SCI resources.

Student 3: Peggy, is it hard to create a web page?

Student 3: (be honest)

Peggy: Well, making a simple web page with links is not hard at all. It can get very complicated if you want lots of other things.

Peggy: Let me ease your mind by telling you this:

Peggy: I work with instructors who have their undergraduate students create web pages every semester and they do fine—the entire class!

Student 3: Can you show us how in an app't?

Peggy: I will give you basic instructions, as well as tips and hints, and I will answer questions.

Student 3: Student 1, have you ever made a web page?

Peggy: It's really not hard, student 3 . . . give it a shot first. I teach people how to do this all the time—people who are in [another state]!

Peggy: They never see me—but they get their web pages done.

Student 1: I have not actually made a web page myself, but have overseen the development of one. I need the hands on experience.

Student 2: Me too.

Peggy: If after trying to do it you still need help, I can try to schedule the lab and hold a class on it.

Student 3: Student 2 have you done one before, or is this the first attempt?

Student 2: I have helped work on one but not done the actual creation.

Student 3: Do you have handouts, or guidelines you could give us? I don't know how to start.

Peggy: There is another, easier way . . . an HTML editor, which is like Word. It is a free application, and you simply download it from the web and install it on your machine.

Peggy: Yes, I will provide instruction, hints and tips, and places to go to get free stuff.

The instructor subsequently posted multiple Web pages with information about the Web site to download the software, and basic Web page construction guidelines. The students who decided to create Web pages for their final project had the necessary information available in the course site for their use.

In the first chat session example, the instructor agreed to provide the necessary information requested by the learners. However, in a second chat session example from EDIT 6225, we witness a student offering the critical information needed by a fellow student.

Autumn: Go into the weekly schedule with me.

Student 1: Right now?

Autumn: Yes, if you open a second Netscape Window

Autumn: Then go to the class page

Autumn: and choose weekly schedules

Autumn: you can then move between that window and the chat window

Student 2: I'm there

Student 3: Me too

Student 1: I checked out the weekly schedule but lost everything else.

Autumn: You've got to open a second window in Netscape.

Student 4: I have two open

Autumn: Anyway, Week 12 you have the listserv assignment and the final draft of your proposals are due.

Student 3: Student 1—go to File at the top left of your window—click and hold—it will say new window—release mouse—a new window will open.

The instructor failed to realize Student 1 didn't know how to open a second browser window. Fortunately, Student 3 recognized her fellow learner's need for information. These kinds of requests for information occurred regularly.

The chat room was only one of the communication mediums used by students to request new information. Another medium used to request and receive new information was the class listserv. One student tried to make sense of the listserv by stating, "The class listserv begins where more traditional references such as dictionaries end. The listserv offers 24-hour opportunity for you to ask questions of the students and instructor within the class. (Of course, it may take a day or so to get an answer since most of us are also working full-time.)" (EDIT 6225 student). Another student also comments about the listserv by saying, "I had heard of listservs, but really did not understand the concept. Needless to say, I had not ever subscribed to one. Now I check the course listserv daily for messages and post messages there, too. Using the listserv, I learn a lot from my classmates. And it provides an environment in which we can support and encourage one another" (EDIT 6225 student). The listserv played a vital role in helping EDIT 6225 students request and receive critical just-in-time information. Frequency of listerv use documents its critical role in the class: 119 listserv messages were generated by the instructor, and 264 messages were posted by students.

The CyberCafe, originally intended by the instructor to be a virtual asynchronous space for communion, ended up being a place where students posted suggestions or directions to ongoing technical issues, and posted Web sites they felt would be of particular interest and use to the rest of the class. The CyberCafe, as a virtual space, was located at the course site within the discussion and chat area. This communication medium served as a fourth location for students to find just-in-time answers to critical questions related to the class.

The instructor can play a critical role in the creation of knowledge capital by encouraging the creation and use of the on-line knowledge capital in the module summaries and evaluations. In BSHE 560R, for example, the instructor provided the following reinforcement to students after completing the first module: "It was obvious from your comments in your posts and in the chat sessions that some of you are reading other's posts—outstanding! This is a way to share information and resources, as well as a way to get to know one another." These two sentences in the instructor's summary and evaluation of the students' work for Module 1 reveal boundaries to students about participating in the generation and use of knowledge capital for the course.

The students in EDIT 6225 played an active role in adding to the knowledge capital for future students by creating a class FAQ (Frequently Asked Questions). Many of their contributions to the FAQ came from the knowledge capital they had enjoyed throughout the course.

Strategies used to encourage and enhance the development and robust growth of the knowledge capital in an on-line Web course require certain types of communication. These include (1) contributing to the course dialogue in discussion, chat, and listserv messages by pointing to specific resources that already exist or by redirecting the dialogue; (2) creating new on-line content based on specific requests; and (3) encouraging students to participate in the creation of the knowledge capital for current and future students.

Social Network Capital

The social network capital experienced in a Web-based course is the "instant web of contacts with useful skills" (Dede 17). This learning commodity refers to the ability to reach and communicate instantly with other people for the specific purpose of requesting they share their skills. It is also a critical component to creating and sustaining community on-line. Again, chat sessions, the listserv, and the CyberCafe were used to manifest social network capital. The students revealed that they understood the value and importance of social network capital in one of the discussion forums when asked to reflect on what they had learned about on-line learning communities. The first student posted, "Online communities can be a great source of support as well as an efficient tool for disseminating information" (BSHE 560R student response). A second student followed up by saying, "Members of the on-line community play a key role in the shaping of the on-line community" (BSHE 560R student response). A third student added to the discussion by stating, "An on-line community has community members. Those community members have a vested interest in the community in which they 'live' and post to many discussion boards on a variety of topics, contributing meaningful information, exchanging dialogue, opinions, and simply engaging other people" (BSHE 560R student response).

Specific examples of students and the faculty member engaging in social network capital ranged from asking for technical expertise to routine computer file management questions and answers. All of the examples below were generated in EDIT 6225:

I cannot check my mail through my new computer. It says my time has run out—login failed. I have not done anything any different. I have tried since I talked to you yesterday on the chat line. What to do? Could you please forward this to [Student 2]. It is time for me to leave and I am running out of time this morning. If anyone can help, please call me or e-mail me. (EDIT 6225 student listserv posting)

The student's problem was resolved in a private chat session with Student 2 (the university Web master), a fellow student in the class.

Please be advised that I am having trouble with my computer as it will not accept "cookies." Since it will not accept cookies, I am not able to access my yahoo mail account from home. On Thursday last week, I was able to down load Netscape into a file on my hard drive, but ran out of memory in my Prodigy Web browser, therefore, I deleted Netscape. I need to find out how to pull up Netscape from my file. Also, while at the Milledgeville Campus I was able to print off Chris Dede's article. I apologize for not replying to you sooner. I left Friday morning and returned late last night from a wedding anniversary weekend. I will be working on my computer in the next couple of days in hopes of downloading Netscape and installing Office 95 or 97, as needed for this class. (EDIT 6225 student listserv posting)

The student managed to resolve the problem with "cookies" and downloading Netscape without help.

I was trying to get the discussion article to come up. I do not understand how to download it. It seems to just sit and do nothing. Please help. (EDIT 6225 student listserv posting)

This request for assistance was handled by a listserv message initiated by the faculty member:

Hi [student's name removed],
   I sent an earlier listserv message with a Web site that has instructions on how to download Netscape Communicator. The Web site is http://www.faculty.de.gcsu.edu/~agrubb/help.html. These directions for Netscape show you the type of computer screens you get when downloading most software.
   In order to open Chris Dede's article you will have to download and install a different software, Adobe Acrobat Reader. When you go to the web site containing Chris Dede's articles, there is a link to click to download the Adobe Acrobat Reader. If you print out the instructions on how to download Netscape, you can use them as a guide to download and install the Adobe Acrobat Reader. Once you have the Adobe Reader program downloaded and installed to the computer you are using, you can go back to the web site and click on the article and it should open. If you download and install Adobe Reader then click on the article and it still does nothing, call my office and leave a message.

In the above situation, the faculty member simply pointed to an already existing resource that described the necessary processes the student needed to follow.

Can anyone tell me how to copy my messages that I will post to the assignments and discussions? I am currently using Microsoft Internet Explorer. I would like to copy it to

Word '97 in a specified file folder. Do I post it first, then copy it, or do I copy it first, then post it? (EDIT 6225 student listserv posting)

This request for assistance was handled by a private e-mail message initiated by the faculty member. Autumn Grubb replied, "Hi [student's name removed], I would compose my message in Word, then copy and paste it into the discussion forum. That way you don't ever lose your posting should you find yourself logged out once you click the 'post my message' button." Grubb then provided explicit instructions for how to create the desired folder, and how to create a Word document. She also provided instructions about how to copy and paste the document into the discussion forum.

After the first four weeks of the course, most of the technical and file management issues had been worked out and students were able to use their new computer competencies to move forward in the course. As stated earlier, the social network capital is key to developing a strong on-line sense of community. Six weeks into the course, the listserv messages had changed. The following thread is just one example:

Dr. Grubb,
   Well, in week 6 I was able to put active links in my postings (DEOS-L listserv assignment) thanks to you and especially to [Student 2] for his very simple instructions.
   I have a question about my link. After I posted my message, I went back to review my posting to see if the links were active. They were. I clicked on the links and they took me to the Web sites. But when I finished, the links changed colors as they should since I already clicked on them. My question is, now when I went back to review my message again, the links did not appear active (bright blue), but purple as if already reviewed. Will everyone that reads my message get the active blue links. I hope so. I am thinking that my computer is holding in memory that I reviewed those links previously. Am I correct on that assumption? That has been my experience in the past, but I want to be sure. Your help and your guidance will be greatly appreciated.

Before the faculty member saw the listserv message requesting help, a fellow student responded to her request:

Thought I'd put in my two cents worth. . . . The reason your screen doesn't show the link active is that it is reading your cookie file (not anything close to the kind of cookies that we have come to love, but let's pretend . . .). When I or another person read the same page you have read, the link would appear on our screen as active because the computer would read our cookie file and know that the human at the keyboard hasn't eaten that cookie yet . . . or something like that. If the human at the keyboard clicks on the link, then the link would no longer appear active on our screen either. Kind of scary isn't it!?! Your computer is watching what you are doing and recording every bit of it so to speak until you tell it to stop being so invasive and that you want to eat your cookie in peace and privacy. Of course I don't know how to put the lid on the cookie jar. Maybe [Student 2] can walk us through???

Student 2 dutifully responded with the following listserv message:

[Student 7] is almost correct and in fact gives a very good explanation of a cookie and what a cookie can do. Cookies are a way for a web site to remember that you have been there already. But the reason your link changes color is due to your browser "remembering" that you have already been to this link. This is maintained in your browser history file and in the browser cache. You can change this in your individual browser preferences area.

In Netscape 4.0*, go to "Edit" then "preferences" and click on the "navigator" section on the left side of the window that opens. Change the number in the "History" box to 1. Now click on the + sign next to the "advanced" area on the left. Click on "Cache" and then in the window on the right check the "Every time" option. Now click OK at the bottom of the window and you are all set. I would not recommend doing this as it will slow down your web surfing.

The listserv messages generated in the initial three weeks of the course had a sense of distress and urgency to them. By week 6, a sense of community had obviously begun to develop based on the references to help given by others and calling on members of the community to further assist with instructions.

Strategies to encourage and enhance the development and use of social network capital in an on-line course are best described by a student in BSHE 560R. The following excerpt is from a student's reflection about the role of an on-line manager:

A manager of an on-line community has to be a facilitator. One who provides enough stimulation, structure and encouragement to get people to interact, but does not get in the way. A good facilitator knows when to step back, and maybe even let people struggle with things. That doesn't mean not to respond appropriately. If an on-line manager always steps in right away to make someone "feel" better, it might keep others in the community from reaching out and prevent bonding from happening. A lot of this balance has to do with timing. Much like moderating a "real" discussion, it takes skill to know when to stand back and let people debate issues, experience cognitive dissonance and frustration as they sift through new ideas, and when to jump back in and provide a new direction for the discussion, structure, or even boundaries.

The key element in the student's reflection about on-line community management is timing. Managing the social network capital not only means making sure everyone is getting their requests for help met, but also encouraging everyone to take an active role in keeping the on-line community of learners moving forward and staying productive. This leads to the discussion about creating and sustaining communion.

Communion

In a face-to-face course, communion occurs before and after class, and during breaks. Communion is the act of sharing in one another's traumas, joys, and eurekas. Communion can be related specifically to the class or might involve discussing the day-to-day experiences of being a full-time working student, parent, and/or spouse.

The fear of technology failure can produce stress in the on-line learners. Communion becomes critical in keeping the on-line community of learners moving forward and can also be used to reduce the stress students experience. In both of the courses, technology failures occurred. In EDIT 6225, the server housing the course Web site went down for several days, making it impossible for students to post their work or read the assignments. The instructor initiated the following listserv message after realizing students were panicking about meeting course deadlines:

I have posted Week 12 assignments. Quick, go look at them and print them out in case WebX goes down again. There are only two . . . 1) your final project proposal, and 2) subscribing to the listserv. Should WebX fail and you are stressing to get the project proposal posted, feel free to send it to me via e-mail. Just be clear in your e-mail that you are sending me one of Week 12's assignments. For the second assignment related to the listserv, you do not need to inform me that you have posted to the listserv. I'm subscribed to DEOS-L and will see your questions as they come up on the listserv.

There are no discussion questions for week 12. [Student 2] used this area to do a test on enclosures. Please ignore the discussion area for Week 12.

I hope the technology gremlins get tired of wreaking havoc and calm down. Remember to print out next week's assignments so if you can't get into WebX later, you can continue with your work and meet deadlines. CYA. Autumn

In BSHE 560R, technology problems began with the chat room, witnessed by the listserv message sent by the instructor. She states, "To any of you who plan to use the chat room tonight—or if you are reading this on Thursday and tried to use the chat room last night—it is gone! I don't know what happened to it, and have sent a message to the info tech people, who will find it, I'm sure. In any case, use the 'Main Room' to chat until our class chat room reappears. Peggy." A student experiencing additional technology problems responded to this message, stating, "Is there something wrong with the class web site? I was unable to pull it up on my computer at home last night, and it is still not working here at work this morning. I am trying to post my reply to Module 4 that was due yesterday. I'll keep trying." Before the instructor could respond, another student sent a message, "The network was down last night."

This thread of listserv messages took care of alerting the class members to temporary technology problems, sharing some individual experiences that alerted everyone to other problems, and provided everyone with information so they could take appropriate action and understand what was happening.

Technology problems experienced personally by the faculty member in EDIT 6225 were usually shared with the group (if they impacted the class) as a way to self-reveal to the students that the faculty member also experienced minor technology gremlins from time to time. For example:

Finally! Sorry I couldn't get the weekly evaluation and summary posted sooner. I was in class all morning. When I sat down to do this in my office shortly after noon I discovered that my office computer was refusing to connect to the internet (Aaaahhhh!!) So I had to pack up everything and come home.

Also, I'm having difficulty sending you the responses to your group questions from Week 9. I began trying to post them as an attachment in WebCrossing on Friday night. This did not seem to work. After conferring with [Student 2], he suggested I save the document as a txt or html document and try attaching it to a post. I did, with no success. I would send the document as an attachment to this list, but it won't accept attachments. ☹ So, I've sent out a request to another faculty member for help. Hopefully those darn answers will get posted in WebCrossing within the next 24 hours. If I can't get a solution to this my other option is to send out an e-mail and type in everyone's e-mail address in the To: and Cc: line (yahoo.mail will only accept a max of 10 e-mail addresses in each of the TO:, Cc:, and Bcc: lines. It is an anti-spam feature of the e-mail package). Anyway, I've been trying to send them since Friday with no luck (why do I feel like the student who's dog ate their homework?) ☺ Autumn

Making sure communion takes place in an on-line learning environment is critical when the community of learners exhibits confusion or frustration about a specific instructional activity. After assigning virtual group projects during Week 9 in EDIT 6225, the listserv became very active with student questions. They needed more information about the process and each member's role, and a clearer understanding of the expected end product. The faculty member responded to the listserv in the following manner:

OK . . . for those of you feeling like you are struggling with how to make this group project thing work . . . breathe . . . close your eyes and breathe . . . ok . . .

Virtual group projects are not necessarily the easiest things to accomplish. It takes practice and requires a letting go of all the bad feelings you ever had about group projects. You all are adults, you've all read the material, and each of you knows the burning questions you've had over the semester about this course. I'm willing to bet holes in donuts that all those questions fall within the three categories of design, development, or delivery (implementation).

If chatting or e-mail just isn't cutting getting the group moving forward, the best thing to do is take the bull by the horns, go into the group area and post what your thoughts are about the assignment related to the reading and what your own questions are. Many of you have already done this. If each group member does this asynchronously, then at least the three members of each group can see what their team mates are thinking, and can respond when it is convenient to them. By looking at each other's questions you should be able to begin formulating the themes as well as the diversity across each person's thoughts.

Have you gone in and investigated what the other groups are doing? This might help you to see similarities and differences across groups. Is everyone getting ready to ask me the same questions and only about the design?

I understand I've just yanked you out of the accepted way of dealing with this course and asked you to negotiate the content and assignments in very different ways. Remember, we are a community of learners. Relax! You all have suddenly gotten very tight on me. If the group thing doesn't work our first time out nobody is going to take anybody's birthday away! Everyone has worked really hard up to this point. I know it is midterm, everything is coming down on your heads with multiple voices demanding this and that, family emergencies, and a need to take a break from it all. I'm feeling all this as well.

What I recommend at this point in the week is to make sure everyone gets their individual thoughts up in the group area quickly. Then divide out roles among your group. Someone take the responsibility of going out and looking at what the other groups have done and reporting back, another person agree to then take up the role of analyzing the group's thoughts and compiling them, and the third person taking the responsibility of webmaster/diva (editing and posting the final results with questions). Autumn

Another time during the on-line class when communion becomes critical for on-line learners is when an unforeseen personal event occurs, causing the learner to be unable to meet course deadlines.

Hi Dr. Grubb,
What I'm about to tell you is true and if you like I will fax the paperwork to you. I say all this so that you'll know that I wasn't anywhere near a computer today because I was stranded in downtown Atlanta. I did not plan to be in Atlanta today, but my daughter needed me to be there with her (she's 17) because she informed me last night that she had to be in traffic court in downtown Atlanta at 10:30 this morning. I asked her why and then she told me she had gotten a ticket for going 90 in a 55 mph zone in downtown Atlanta on 19 September. She said she was afraid to tell me about it, so she waited until the last minute because she couldn't find a way to work out of the mess she made. So, of course, I went with her and after we got through with court, having been fined $501.00 and having had her license revoked, we proceeded to where the car was parked only to find that it wasn't there. I spent the rest of the day chasing down my towed car. I was soon to learn that it was towed because the sign that said "No Parking 7–9am" said also on the bottom of the sign "Truck Loading zone 9–4." Of course my brain only processed the text on the bottom of the sign after I discovered my car was missing and read the sign again. Needless to say, it's been one of those days.

I've just arrived at work (7:00 pm) and respectfully request your full pardon in the matter of my late submission of questions for this week's reading. I'm really hoping for a full pardon since I totally blew last week's submission and just plain forgot to do it.

Thank you for believing this unbelievable tale, [Name of student removed]

Upon receiving this e-mail from a student who generally completed all required work on time, the instructor responded by e-mail: "I believe every single word of your tale. You have a full pardon. I offer sympathy for the pain of the lesson your daughter learned and I'm sorry for the stress life unfortunately deals us on sunny October days. Breathe.☺ Autumn"

Strategies to promote and encourage communion are again based in communication skills. Recognizing when students need reassurance, redirection, or just empathy to keep moving forward in their academic endeavors is the key to nurturing and sustaining communion in the Web-based environment. An EDIT 6225 student reflection discusses the importance of communion:

In this course, I have seen where we as learners are "nurtured" by Dr. Grubb. She is very flexible and wants to do what works best for us. Many of us, myself included, were very apprehensive about taking this course because of the lack of human contact and f2f instruction. To my surprise, I have found that I really enjoy this type of learning. I feel like I have ample contact with Dr. Grubb and the other students in this course. It almost seems as if I have more feedback from this course than I've had from those I've attended weekly.

Everyone in this distance learning environment seems much more willing to help one another.

Last week when the server went down, I didn't worry because we were all able to still communicate with one another and we received plenty of support and reassurance. I think Dr. Grubb has been very effective in her design of this course. I do feel like we as learners have been the center of this course. I know my nerves have subsided and I would love to take another class like this one.

A BSHE 560R student also commented on communion in a discussion forum post by stating, "Social support comes in many forms, and this form can be quite potent."

In summary, we have shown how specific strategies can be employed to create knowledge capital, social network capital, and communion. These three critical teaching and learning commodities can exist in an on-line learning environment when appropriate moderation and facilitation roles are employed. Nurturing and encouraging the development of knowledge capital, social network capital, and communion by the faculty member can reduce the impact of documented barriers to distance learning.

CONCLUSION

Knowledge is socially constructed, and people's knowledge of the world and of the society in which they live is mediated by their beliefs about the information from which they are constructing knowledge, about the people who provided it to them, and about their own needs and abilities to deal with it (Bandura; Salomon). If knowledge is constructed within a social context, then the development of "virtual communities" is crucial to the success of a distance learning environment.

As Web-based instruction proliferates across the academic landscape we must be mindful to avoid pedagogical design and delivery strategies that perpetuate well-documented barriers to on-line learning. In fact, design and delivery strategies should reduce these barriers. Along with the onset of widespread implementation of Web-based instruction and computer mediated communication there has been a great deal of academic discussion about creating virtual or cyber communities. It would seem, based on the barriers of isolation, lack of contact with the faculty member, and a fear of engaging in academic discourse, special attention must be directed toward developing robust, connected virtual learning communities. Using appropriate pedagogical strategies, these learning environments can be designed to encourage and support adult distance learners to become actively engaged in academic discourse, develop strong networks of support, and recognize the importance of skills that help them locate content experts, resources, and information on-line.

WORKS CITED

Bandura, Albert. *Social Learning Theory*. Englewood Cliffs, NJ: Prentice-Hall, 1977.

Cerulo, Karen A. "Reframing Social Concepts for a Brave New (Virtual) World." *Sociological Inquiry* 67.1 (1997): 48–58.

Christiansen, Ellen, and Lone Dirckinck-Holmfeld. "Making Distance Learning Collaborative." 1 Aug. 1999 <http://www-csc195.indiana.edu/csc195/christia.html>.

Dede, Chris. "The Evolution of Distance Education: Emerging Technologies and Distributed Learning." *American Journal of Distance Education* 10.2 (1996): 4–36.

Galusha, Jill. "Barriers to Learning in Distance Education." 1 Aug. 1999 <http://www.infrastruction.com/articles.htm>.

Keegan, Desmond. *The Foundations of Distance Education*. London: Croom Helm, 1986.

Knapper, Christopher. "Lifelong Learning and Distance Education." *American Journal of Distance Education* 2.1 (1988): 63–72.

Mason, R. "Moderating Educational Computer Conferencing." *DEOSNEWS* 1.19 (1991). (Archived as DEOSNEWS 91–00011 on LISTSERV @ LISTS.PSU.EDU)

Meacham, Dave, and Denis Evans. *Distance Education: The Design of Study Materials*. Waga Waga, NSW, Australia: Open Learning Institute, Charles Sturt University, 1989.

Paulsen, Morten F. "An Overview of CMC and the Online Classroom in Distance Education." In *Computer Mediated Communication and the Online Classroom, Volume 3: Distance Learning*. Ed. Zane L. Berge and Mauri Collins. Cresskill, NJ: Hampton Press, 1995.

Salomon, Gavriel. *Communication and Education*. Beverly Hills, CA: Sage, 1981.

Chapter 26

Facilitating On-line Discussion in an Asynchronous Format

Tisha Bender

For me, the best things often happen for the wrong reason; just as when I was a schoolgirl struggling over my mathematics, if my answer was fortunately ever correct, my reasoning was abysmally askew. So was it for me with the idea of on-line teaching. If truth be told, I only ventured into this arena because of an invitation to a wine and cheese party to learn all about the marvels of distance learning. I, however, went only for the wine and cheese.

But thereafter, despite initial feelings of bewilderment, my pursuit of teaching at a distance became deliberate. Mindful of George Bernard Shaw having once remarked that "[t]he reasonable man adapts himself to the world: the unreasonable one persists in trying to adapt the world to himself. Therefore all progress depends on the unreasonable man" (260), and feeling exhilaratingly unreasonable myself because of the thrill of the innovative, I set off in this marvelous cyber voyage.

In my mind, too, was an observation made by Edward de Bono: "Some time ago, on a journey across the Atlantic, I reflected that the spoonful of mashed potato I was about to put into my mouth was actually travelling faster than a rifle bullet" (53). How quickly we take what's new and innovative for granted; how much we come to rely upon the conveniences each new paradigm shift and technological innovation heaps upon our grateful laps. Well, I wanted to be a pioneer in this intriguing new field of education, before the snowball effect; before many, many others would jump onto the bandwagon.

This was all very well and good, but as the day drew nearer for my on-line class to begin, I found myself struggling with questions. What exactly did I think I was doing? How would I, a very convivial person, like working in the lonely isolation of my computer room, with no friendly smiles to greet me or excited voices putting forth clever ideas to the controversial questions I liked to throw out into my classroom? Also, how would it feel working asynchronously, in this twenty-four hour environment in which the classroom doors never close and responses are always welcome? If the interaction between the students and myself was not required to occur at the same time, how much of a time lag would there be in conversations, and how might this impede the flow of ideas?

What occurred, in this, my first virtual classroom, was instantly amazing to me. The first time I logged into my class, I was immediately greeted by a score of responses from students as stimulated and eager as myself. It was as exciting as waiting for the postman to arrive, to deliver letters that I had been wanting to read. And each and every time that I logged on after that, it was the same. My screen would inform me that I had three, seven, two new responses, and I couldn't wait to see what they said. Furthermore, because we were all meeting each other asynchronously on-line, space and time no longer offered the same constraints. I have had throughout the various on-line classes I have taught students scattered from Paris, to Mexico City, to London, to Nantucket Island, as well as the New York metropolitan area. In short, there is the potential for a truly global network, with participants joining the class from different time zones and at different times, yet all benefiting from having access to the same recorded responses. This flexibility is also beneficial to those who have numerous demands on their time, such as jobs, family, or other obligations. It also helped one student of mine who was pregnant and ordered complete bed rest, and it assisted two dancers on tour to still achieve their education.

The on-line environment has the potential to be excellently interactive. The pedagogical stance that works best is the Socratic method, in which students are encouraged, by a range of questions from the instructor, to enter into active dialogue. Otherwise how else would the instructor know they are there? And furthermore, if two students both turned in a brilliant final paper, yet one was actively involved throughout the semester, and the other you hardly heard from, how could you determine the authenticity of the second student's work, or feel that this student was equally worthy of obtaining an A?

This need for continuous participation, implying that all students are actively contributing to the evolving dialogue, rather than being passive recipients of information washing over them, has the added benefit of stimulating their degree of learning. As John Dewey said in *Education and Experience*, "I assume that amid all uncertainties there is one permanent frame of reference; namely the organic connection between education and personal experience" (25). Making information relevant, letting students draw on their own knowledge and experience, is extremely beneficial. At the start of my on-line classes, I ask my students to imagine that we are sitting in a circle, all contributing to the growing pool of knowledge that constitutes my class content. And even though I am sitting in the same circle as my students, I still have the prerogative to guide the discussion, introduce new concepts, steer things along, much the same as parents do residing in the family circle, yet still in charge (Dewey).

But what are the parameters that lend themselves to stimulating on-line discussion? I would say that the first is to set the stage, even before the class begins. A certain minimum level of required participation should be specified, such as three to five times a week. The level of participation could even count toward the final grade. Of course, this requirement should be accompanied by the statement that the quality of the response will equally contribute in the assessment. Generally I have found that as the semester progresses, the class gathers a momentum of its own and some topics heat up, causing participants to log on even several times a day.

Along with this, I think the instructor sets the tone, and as such even the first greeting to students is crucial. In fact, I often start my on-line class with a phone call to each student to welcome them, and have been, on a few occasions, greeted with a very surprised, yet pleased student saying, "Gosh; a real voice!"

I also believe it crucial to define the expectations for the class dynamic at the outset of the class. In one of my on-line classes, after making an initial welcoming phone call to one particular student, I was immediately impressed with how intelligent, enthusiastic, and articulate she sounded, yet for at least the next five days after our conversation, I saw nothing from her on-line. Surprised by this, I called her again, and was so pleased that I had, as she told me, "Yes, I'll be ready to put up an answer in a couple of days. I'm just developing the outline and gathering the footnotes." "Hold on!" I told her. "You don't need to do this now. For now, just consider we are having a seminar and, after reading the sections of the book that I cited, are all bouncing intelligent ideas off each other in a spontaneous stream of consciousness. The time for a polished response is for the midterm and final exams." It was such an important discovery to me that this student had different assumptions concerning the nature of her responses than I had intended, so with her permission, I wrote into my class about our telephone conversation and made my expectations more explicit. Thereafter, the class positively exploded with new responses from each student.

Generally, long lectures do not work well on-line, as the students might well feel that they could be reading a textbook. Instead, short, snappy mini-lectures, followed by a few questions, are most readily accessible in terms of student comprehension and are most effective at eliciting responses. This does not mean that the instructor has to dilute the material presented to the class, but is instead repackaging it into smaller units which can be thrown out as responses to the ongoing discussion. Sometimes it works best, at least in the early days of the course, for the instructor to enter the first response to a series of questions. This serves to give confidence to students who might be reluctant to take the first step.

And as soon as an interactive discussion begins, it is very important for the instructor to make each student feel included, by acknowledging them personally, responding to them quickly, and mentioning them by name while referring to their contributions. Furthermore, I generally tell students that I love to thrash around in a thorough, all-perspectives-covered kind of discussion, and I welcome everyone's opinion, even if it lies counter to the prevailing ideology. In fact, so much the better, as long as the ideas can be substantiated, as this leads to the stuff of good, balanced considerations. The only request I make is that everyone maintain complete civility to each other, even if opinions differ.

There are, of course, many other methods to stimulate students into responding on-line besides asking questions about course content. One such way might be to hold a debate, by choosing two students each to represent a different point of view, and then asking the rest of the class to take a vote. Later in the semester, another two students could be chosen to debate over a subsequent issue, and so on. Another idea could be role playing, in which students try to simulate character types or situations that they are studying. A third idea is to invite in a guest or expert in the field to offer a mini-lecture and respond to student questions. Just as when, in a regular classroom, a new voice can make students sit up and take extra notice, and possibly add a fresh, new perspective, so too can this occur with a guest lecturer on-line.

Game playing can offer yet another way to stimulate on-line discussion. As an example, in writing classes that I have taught, I have asked students to arrange themselves in groups of three, and for each to send the next an e-mail containing a paragraph description of a person. I then ask them to e-mail a paragraph containing a description of a place, this time going around the triangle in the opposite direction. After this, student A should have received an e-mail of a person from student B, and an e-mail of a place from student C. Student A is then asked to compose a story, to be posted in the class, about what happens to B's person in C's place. This usually leads to a lively interchange of ideas and responses.

In the cyber-classroom, just as on campus, I like to make students feel good about themselves by trying to draw on a particular strength of theirs and building on it. I would like to relate a particular experience I had once in a traditional classroom. This class was held at 8:00 A.M., so it was a major achievement, I thought, that any of us were there at all. However, one student named Scott, a young man clad in a leather jacket and dark blue baseball cap, would stare sleepily at me for a few moments, and then his head, framed by the cap, would make its inevitable descent to the desk, where it would remain for the duration of the class. I would try everything from singing the ballads we were studying (that usually elicits lively protests) to suggesting we bring in bagels, but all to no avail. But then I discovered, quite by chance, that Scott had a terrific sense of humor. Thereafter it was easy to include him in class discussions, and we all laughed—and learned—a lot. Incidentally, Scott became an A student after that.

But how does this translate to the virtual classroom, being as it is devoid of facial expressions, body language, or tone of voice? It is my contention that distance teaching can produce a true "meeting of minds," a pure and perfect forum in which one can freely concentrate on the intellect, interests, and personality of the participants. It is a democratic system, in which age, race, and sometimes even gender do not play a part, so everyone is without prejudices, even those prejudices they had no idea they held. Furthermore, messages are not mediated through a variety of stereotypical distractions, such as clothing, hairstyle, patterns of speech, and so on. Ideas and information are free to swirl in all directions, not only between student and instructor in a hierarchical arrangement, but between students as well.

But even so, is intention always conveyed, or is there scope for misinterpretation? Many instructors, myself included, like to use humor to relax the atmosphere and help students to feel comfortable to respond. Does humor always translate? Obviously subtle nuances of face-to-face conversation are missing in the on-line environment, and it is not possible to make an immediate assessment of reaction. However, I believe humor can be transmitted, if used carefully, and always with consideration of the different ways it could be understood. That is not to imply, though, that one has to think so long and hard before writing anything even vaguely amusing that one feels strangled and the humor inhibited. Similar considerations are necessary for critiques. Without facial expressions and voice inflections, criticisms of work can sound rather harsh when just laid out in text. I feel, therefore, that it is best to handle these with tact, putting forward the positive points before voicing the negatives, and even then doing so in a constructive manner.

Being devoid of visual cues makes some instructors feel they are "navigating in the dark." As such, the question of personal photographs often comes up, with as varied a range of opinions as there are instructors themselves. I have seen classes in which the instructor's photograph has appeared on every lecture given—with the premise that in a traditional class, the students would be looking at one when one is presenting information—to other instructors who prefer to be unseen and mysterious. Whereas I understand that putting up one's picture is not dissimilar to having a photo of an author on the jacket of a book, I personally prefer not to reveal what I look like, nor do I want to see photos of my students. After all, what's to stop anyone choosing a photo of a really glamorous yet little known actress or actor and claiming it as oneself? For me, part of the fun of all this is the imagination, carving out mental pictures of what each person looks like based on what they say. And what they say is very indicative of personality—in fact, each participant's personality radiates through their response—so it is easy to recognize different student "voices" even from relatively early on in the class. Besides, to maintain this pure and democratic forum for the expression of ideas, it is, I believe, much better to leave out the photos.

It is also a beneficial idea to designate one area of the on-line course to be a less formal space in which students and the instructor can discuss issues that only tangentially relate to the main topics of the course. In my course I have often called this space "In the Corridor," as I believe campus students often discuss the most scintillating things while journeying to and from class. Another colleague of mine called this "On the Subway" for similar reasons. One instructor told me she ended up with a recipe for chicken soup with matzo balls, though discussion is not usually quite as tangential as this.

It is interesting to speculate whether behavior manifestations, such as being naturally introverted or extroverted, are altered by communicating with a group on-line. By this I mean, does the way an individual interacts with others alter when not in a face-to-face situation with them? Knowing that I can behave differently when I am teaching my class than when I am with my friends or when I open the door to the man who has come to read my gas meter, I wonder whether this new method of cyber-spatial interaction will have an impact on each individual participant, thereby affecting the dynamics of the group as a whole. As Jane Eyre said (albeit in a different context): "How much I wished to reply fully to this question! How difficult it was to frame my answer! . . . Fearful, however, of losing this first and only opportunity . . . I, after a disturbed pause, contrived to frame a meager, though, as far as it went, true response" (Bronte 167). How many students feel this? How many are terrified by the indelible quality of their response (even though they can edit their response as long as they do it quickly)? How many, in short, are cyber-shy?

I would strongly argue that we can turn this around. First, as already mentioned, if the instructor can establish that this cyber-classroom is a safe environment, one in which all responses are welcomed and encouraged, then this should make the first step easier. Second, as opposed to Jane Eyre, who was operating in "real time" and was fearful of losing her opportunity to speak, the on-line asynchronous environment provides unlimited opportunity for the addition of responses. This has many advantages. In the first place, it is advantageous to the quiet or more reticent student, who, in a traditional classroom with its finite time frame, might allow others to interrupt and so lose the chance to speak. Not so on-line! Also, we might not always feel our best, our most brilliant, at the scheduled time a class runs on campus, but on-line, we log on whenever we have an inspiration. Even if this occurs at 3 A.M., a time when I typically have my best thoughts, I can join my class by a flick of the switch, and the same applies to students, too. How much better, it seems, to grab an idea when it is hot rather than having to wait a week for the next scheduled campus class, by which time the idea might have lost much of its power, and some of its excitement, too. Furthermore, if a student asks a question that really stumps me, rather than resorting to the "Good question. Anyone have an answer for this?" or "Great. Let's spend the week researching this, and discuss it next time" comments that I might need to resort to on campus, I can merely swivel from my computer to my bookshelf, look up the answer, and produce an intelligent and informative reply. Such are the benefits of asynchronous interaction. In general it seems students are more reflective, and answer more deeply than they would in a face-to-face situation, for the same set of reasons.

However, for some shy students, participation in on-line discussions might not happen immediately, as at first they might feel they are sending out responses to the "great unknown," unsure, therefore about how their remarks will be received or interpreted. But with an encouraging and welcoming tone from the instructor, students should soon feel a sense of class community and a sound comprehension of the others in the group, which should facilitate their active involvement with the class. Some students, too, might remain quiet because of a lack of confidence in their writing skills. If it can be pointed out to them that the ability to write and communicate well is so beneficial to every aspect of their lives; that this is, in fact, a welcome return to the days of letter writing; and that writing, just like any form of exercise, does become easier with more experience, this may go a long way to overcome their inhibitions. However, if some students remain quiet after about a week, an e-mail or even a personal phone call to them might be of help. And again, enthusiasm and encouragement will be more productive than nagging in eliciting their participation.

It has, in fact, often been my observation that the shy student might feel in some way protected by the anonymity of the computer screen, and thus, with self-consciousness more or less eradicated, can overcome feelings of reticence, and join in heartily with the prevailing discussion. Furthermore, I have noticed, and have been informed by my on-line colleagues as well, that students tend to go into more intimate details than they would ever dream of in a campus class. Again, I believe working in the comfort of their own sphere, enjoying the flexibility of coming to class when they want, and knowing others will not turn round and say with incredulity, "You did what?" unleashes many of their inhibitions.

Of course, the type of subject matter taught will influence the amount of discussion that a class can engage in. On-line discussions work best in seminar style classes in the social sciences and humanities. They are also particularly effective for writers' workshops, as everyone has perfect access to each other's prose or poetry, allowing great scope for feedback and review. And of course one added advantage that the on-line class has over the traditional classroom is that in the latter the spoken word evaporates into the air, and students might not hear, listen to, or remember all that is said. The on-line class, by contrast, provides a written record of all that has transpired—in short, a perfect set of lecture notes.

Because of this heightened interaction, discussion can sometimes become quite diffuse and contain a number of different threads. It is a good idea for the instructor to weave together these strands periodically, review what is being said, isolate themes, establish priorities, and move the discussion along. An instructor could also assign this task every now and then to a student, which could help him or her determine the most salient facts (Eastmond).

It is curious how you can grow to know your students really well without ever having had face-to-face contact with them. To me, starting a new on-line class seems very much like starting a new novel. At first you need to become acquainted with the cast of characters. And then, at some indeterminate time early in the semester, you suddenly realize, just as with a novel, that you are deeply immersed, are comfortable with the students, and have a fairly accurate idea about what to expect from them. Ending a class is much like ending a terrific novel, too. There is the same feeling of not wanting it to be over; a feeling of loss; a feeling that this was something really profound.

I think, in short, it is remarkable how real this "virtual" method of communication can be; how very much a feeling of a class community among all on-line participants can be established. Some years ago, emerging from a crowded lecture hall at the University of Wisconsin, in which I had just delivered a lecture on world regional geography, I happened to overhear one excited student whisper to another while pointing at me, "See! That's our teacher! She comes from Denmark!" How much better, it seems, do my students know me on-line.

WORKS CITED

Bronte, Charlotte. *Jane Eyre*. London: Penguin Classics, 1985.

de Bono, Edward. *De Bono's Thinking Course*. New York: Facts on File Publications, 1986.

Dewey, John. *Experience and Education*. New York: Collier Books, Macmillan, 1963.

Eastmond, Dan. "Effective Facilitation of Computer Conferencing." *Continuing Higher Education Review* 56 (1992): 15–20.

Shaw, George Bernard. *Man and Superman (The Revolutionist's Handbook)*. Harmondsworth, Middlesex: Penguin Books, 1983.

Chapter 27

Web-Based Instruction and People with Disabilities

Sheryl Burgstahler

Much has been written about the potential of networking technology to revolutionize all levels of education. Although an electronic tool such as the World Wide Web is unlikely to completely replace traditional classroom instruction, this powerful option for the delivery of information and the facilitation of communication should not be underestimated. How best to create and deliver instruction using this medium will be a topic of discussion for academics and practitioners for years to come. Whatever positive outcomes are derived from Web-based instruction, how can we assure that these benefits are available to everyone, including those with a wide range of abilities and disabilities?

For many people, the desire to provide access to Web-based instruction for students with disabilities grows from a sense of equity and fairness. They feel that everyone should have access to this revolutionary mode of instruction. For others, legal compliance is the motivator. The Americans with Disabilities Act (ADA) of 1990 requires that people with disabilities be provided access to the same public services that are offered to those without disabilities. The ADA requirements apply to Internet resources. As stated in a 1996 Department of Justice opinion letter, "Covered entities that use the Internet for communications regarding their programs, goods, or services must be prepared to offer those communications through accessible means as well" ("ADA Accessibility Requirements"). To comply with the law, the content of public Web pages must be made available to visitors who have disabilities (Waddell and Thomason). When Web-based instruction is offered, steps should be taken to assure that individuals with disabilities can fully participate in the learning experience. This chapter describes some of the technologies individuals with disabilities use to operate computers and then summarizes simple design features that can make Web-based materials accessible to students and instructors with disabilities.

STUDENTS AND INSTRUCTORS WITH DISABILITIES

The rapid development of adaptive technologies allows people with a wide range of disabilities to access computers and the World Wide Web ("Closing the Gap 1999 Resource Directory"). As an instructor, you may not be aware of the disabilities of students enrolled in your class. Imagine, for a moment, that Julie signs up for your class. Julie, blind since birth, uses special screen-reading software on her computer. This software works with her voice synthesizer to read material that is presented on the screen in text format. She uses a text-based WWW browser called Lynx for most of her work. She can also use multimedia browsers with the feature that loads images turned off. Screen-reading software handles text easily, but cannot "read" graphics or photos. Will Julie be able to fully participate in your Web-based class? Let's take a look at some of the challenges she may face.

Simply providing a consistent layout and simple screen presentation will help any student find the information you provide on your Web pages. Since she cannot "view" the entire screen at one time, Julie will benefit if your Web pages are consistent and simple in design. For example, placing navigational links in the same place on each page will help Julie locate course content.

Using standard HTML (hypertext markup language) will also ensure access for Julie. HTML is a code used to display Web pages on the screen. Web browsers use these tags to format and present information. A nonstandard tag such as <BLINK> will create an interesting blinking effect for some site visitors, but not all Web browsers will recognize it. Therefore, nonstandard HTML should be avoided. Be sure that students are not required to use a specific browser to access the content of your class.

Julie's screen-reading software cannot directly "read" pictures or drawings presented on your Web pages. Provide alternate text for each graphic so that she can access the critical information that the image holds. For each graphical feature on a page, include an "ALT" attribute that tells about the appearance and content of the graphic. The ALT attribute works with HTML image tags to present the alternative text on the screen. When sighted people with graphical browsers access the page, they will see the graphic; when Julie "views" the page, her voice output system will read the alternative text to her. For example, if your program, "Distance Learning University," displays a logo on its Web pages, simply include an ALT attribute "Distance Learning University logo." This description will be available to those not viewing the graphic. Similarly, provide a text transcription of any manuscript that is presented in an image format. And, for each picture on a Web page, include a caption worded in such a way that it provides relevant information about the picture for a student who cannot view the image itself.

Do you include image maps on your Web pages? Image maps are graphical images with multiple areas that, when selected with a mouse or other pointing device, link to other Web pages or sections. For example, an image map could display a map of the United States. Clicking on a city or state would bring up information about the region selected. The content of this image map could be made accessible to Julie by providing a text-only link just before the image map. From the text-only link, she could find information about the content of the image map as well as the links that are embedded in the map.

Like many blind Internet surfers, Julie often sets her software to read only the links on a page. This option speeds up her access to the content of a page. It is, therefore, important to her that the text in links provide enough information when read without surrounding material. Make your Web page links descriptive so that they can be understood out of context. For example, "Click here" does not provide adequate information for Julie to determine if this is a link she wishes to pursue. However, "Click here for the course syllabus" gives her the guidance she needs.

Julie's screen reader, like most, reads from left to right, making the information presented in complex tables confusing to her. Similarly, Applets, plug-ins, frames, databases, forms, PDF (Portable Document Format) files, and other special features and formats are often inaccessible to her. Consider using simpler, more accessible methods to present information. However, if special features are used, test the pages to see if they are adequately supported by a text-based browser. In some cases, the best access solution may be to provide an alternative text-only page with equivalent content. If some Web content cannot be made accessible to everyone, direct students who cannot access the information to your electronic mail address for help. Testing your site with a text-based browser or with the graphics loading feature of a multimedia browser turned off gives a sighted person a good idea of how accessible it is to those who cannot see.

Julie provides a good example of a student who might enroll in your Web-based class. She may not inform you of her disability because, if your Web resources are designed with access in mind, she will not require special accommodations. The Web-access challenges she faces are the same as those that would be faced by an instructor of the course who is blind. Other potential students and instructors could include people with the following characteristics:

• Erin is a graduate student with poor vision. Special software to enlarge screen images and a large monitor allow her to access Web pages, but she can only view a small portion of a page at a time. She is often confused by Web sites where page layout is cluttered and inconsistent from page to page.

• Doug is deaf. In on-site classes he requires a sign language interpreter. He enjoys taking Web-based classes because the ability to hear is usually not required. He becomes totally lost, however, at sites where audio and video clips do not include captioning or transcription.

- Cathy, a college professor, acquired multiple sclerosis as a young adult. Her disability makes it difficult for her to travel to campus every day. She prefers to teach some of her courses in a Web-based format so that she can work from home. Because her fine motor skills are limited, she has difficulty selecting buttons when they are very small.

- Ryan, a bright college student, has dyslexia, a learning disability that makes it difficult for him to comprehend printed information. His voice synthesizer, working in conjunction with his screen reader, reads to him the text on the screen. He has difficulty following Web instruction when pages are cluttered and unorganized and when the screen layout changes from page to page.

As can be seen from these examples, adaptive technologies allow people with disabilities to access computers and the Internet. Disabilities are wide ranging. Equitable access requires that individuals with any of these characteristics be able to participate in a Web-based instructional program. Unfortunately, few Web content developers consider the great diversity of potential visitors when they design their sites. Rather, they think only of the average visitor, who does not have a disability.

UNIVERSAL DESIGN OF WEB RESOURCES

When students and instructors with disabilities have not been considered in the original design process, a great deal of time and effort may be required to rework the materials to make them accessible. To maximize access and reduce development costs, principles of "universal design" should be employed from the outset of the development of Web-based courses. Universal design considers the diverse set of characteristics of potential users of a product being developed. In the case of Web-based instruction, care should be taken to assure that students and instructors with a wide range of capabilities can access the information provided via the Web. Potential users include people with limited reading skills, individuals who cannot use their hands, and people with sensory impairments.

When developing a Web-based class, one is tempted to include all of the newest "bells and whistles." However, simplicity and consistency in design assure that Web-based learning is accessible to a wider range of students and instructors. Redundancy in presentation format is another quality that enhances the accessibility of Web pages. A few design tips are summarized below (see also Burgstahler; Burgstahler, Comden, and Fraser; Dixon; Kautzman).

Redundancy in Format

People with sensory impairments have difficulty using auditory and/or visual content. If audio or video clips are included on Web pages, captions or text transcription of the audio content should be provided for those who have hearing impairments. To make Web page content accessible to those who are blind, simply provide a descriptive text alternative for information presented in graphical form so that voice output systems can read the text aloud. Captions on pictures should be worded in such a way that they are meaningful to those who cannot see the pictures. Manuscripts displayed in an image format should be accompanied by transcriptions in text format. Provide the embedded links in image maps in an alternative, text-based list. Forms, frames, tables, databases, PDF files, and other special features and formats should be used sparingly as they are often difficult or impossible for blind students to use. When special features cannot be made accessible, provide a separate, text-based version of the content. In addition, make sure that information conveyed with color is also available to those who cannot perceive color differences.

Simplicity and Consistency in Presentation

Web pages should present content that is easy to understand and navigate. Use language that is clear and simple. Position navigational links and logos in logical places on each page. A simple page is particularly beneficial to people with specific learning disabilities that make it difficult to process written information and to those with visual impairments who are using voice output or screen enlargement systems. Likewise, individuals with visual impairments benefit when there is high contrast between the background and the text on the screen and when background designs are simple. It is also important to keep in mind that using universally recognized HTML tags allows all Web browsers to accurately display the content, thereby enhancing access for individuals with disabilities.

Buttons, navigational links, and logos should be located in the same place on each of your course Web pages. Maintaining the same layout from page to page makes navigating the site easier for everyone, but particularly for people who have poor vision, blindness, and specific learning disabilities. And don't forget that, for people who have limited fine motor skills, small buttons for navigational links make difficult targets; making them larger will benefit this group of users.

Resources

The Web Accessibility Initiative of the World Wide Web Consortium (W3C) has developed comprehensive guidelines for designing Web pages that are accessible to individuals with a wide range of disabilities (Randall). Other sites on the Web that provide guidelines for developing accessible Web sites include the following:

- Center for Applied Special Technology (CAST)
- The Center for Universal Design

- Disabilities, Opportunities, Internetworking, and Technology (DO-IT)
- Equal Access to Software and Information (EASI)
- National Center for Accessible Media (NCAM)
- The Trace Research and Development Center
- Web Accessibility Initiative (WAI), World Wide Web Consortium (W3C)
- WebABLE

TESTING WEB-BASED LEARNING MATERIALS

Test your Web pages with individuals who have a variety of disabilities, if possible. They should also be tested with a variety of Web browsers and monitors. Be sure to test the pages using a text-only browser, such as Lynx, and using multimedia browsers with the loading graphics feature turned off. If your pages make sense when accessed in these ways, they will probably also make sense for an individual who is blind and using a speech synthesizer. In addition, make sure that students without the ability to hear can access the information on each page. Your site can be tested for accessibility using an HTML validator program, such as Bobby. Bobby, created at the Center for Applied Special Technology, tests for accessibility and identifies nonstandard and incorrect HTML coding.

CONCLUSION

The Internet is a powerful, flexible, and efficient tool for the delivery of instruction. It provides new ways for us to teach and learn. Properly implemented, Web-based instruction promotes the full inclusion of individuals with disabilities in education and leads to greater independence and productivity in employment. Educators should design their materials so that they are accessible not only to the average student in a class, but to all students who might enroll, including those with disabilities. Employing principles of universal design is an important step in this process. With carefully designed Web-based instruction, individuals with limited abilities to speak, hear, see, or move will not be limited in participation.

Building in access as part of the design process can take a little extra work initially, but designing products with access to individuals with disabilities in mind often leads to better products for everyone. For example, captioning videotapes for individuals who are deaf also benefits people for whom English is a second language. Text descriptions of graphic images on Web pages provide access to blind users, but also facilitate word searching for others. And everyone benefits from simple, uncluttered pages that are consistent from page to page. A teen skateboarder, a father with a baby stroller, and a delivery man with a hand-truck using sidewalk curbcuts that were installed for people who use wheelchairs remind us that we all benefit when universal design principles are employed.

ACKNOWLEDGMENT

This material is based upon work supported by the National Science Foundation under Grant No. 9800324. Any opinions, findings, and conclusions or recommendations expressed in this material are those of the author and do not necessarily reflect the views of the National Science Foundation.

WORKS CITED

"ADA Accessibility Requirements Apply to Internet Web Pages." *Law Reporter* 11 Sept. 1997: 1053–84.

Bobby. Home page. 1 Aug. 1999 <http://www.cast.org/bobby>.

Burgstahler, Sheryl. "Universal Access." *Journal of Telecommunications in Higher Education* 2.1 (1998): 18–22.

Burgstahler, Sheryl, Dan Comden, and Beth Fraser. "Universal Access: Designing and Evaluating Web Sites for Accessibility." *CHOICE: Current Reviews for Academic Libraries (Supplement)* 34 (1997): 19–22.

Center for Applied Special Technology (CAST). Home page. 1 Aug. 1999 <http://www.cast.org/>.

Center for Universal Design. Home page. 1 Aug. 1999 <http://www.design.ncsu.edu/cud/>.

"Closing the Gap 1999 Resource Directory." *Closing the Gap* 17.6 (1999): 41–185.

Disabilities, Opportunities, Internetworking, and Technology (DO-IT). Home page. 1 Aug. 1999 <http://weber.u.washington.edu/~doit/Resources/web-design.html>.

Dixon, Judith M. "Leveling the Road Ahead: Guidelines for the Creation of WWW Pages Accessible to Blind and Visually Handicapped Users." *Library Hi Tech* 14.1 (1996): 65–68.

Equal Access to Software and Information (EASI). Home page. 1 Aug. 1999 <http://www.rit.edu/~easi/access.html>.

Kautzman, Amy M. "Virtuous, Virtual Access: Making Web Pages Accessible to People with Disabilities." *SEARCHER: The Magazine for Database Professionals* 6.6 (1998): 42–49.

National Center for Accessible Media (NCAM). Home page. 1 Aug. 1999 <www.wgbh.org/ncam>.

Randall, Laura. "W3C Proposes Guidelines on Web Accessibility." *Newsbytes*, 25 Mar. 1999. 1 Aug. 1999 <http://www.newsbytes.com/>.

Trace Research and Development Center. Home page. 1 Aug. 1999 <http://www.tracecenter.org/world/>.

Waddell, Cynthia D., and Kevin Lee Thomason. "Is Your Site ADA-Compliant . . . or a Lawsuit-in-Waiting?" *Internet Lawyer.* Nov. 1998. 1 Aug. 1999 <http://www.internetlawyer.com/ada.htm>.

WebABLE. Home page. 1 Aug. 1999 <http://www.webable.com/>.

Web Accessibility Initiative (WAI). Home page. 1 Aug. 1999 <http://www.w3.org/WAI/>.

World Wide Web Consortium (W3C). Home page. 1 Aug. 1999 <http://www.w3.org/>.

Index

About the Contributors

MICHAEL S. AMEIGH is the Assistant Provost for Distance Learning and Information Resources and Associate Professor of Communication Studies, State University of New York at Oswego. He has extensive experience as an online instructor and has served as a member of the SUNY Learning Network Academic Advisory Panel and the SUNY Distance Learning Advisory Panel. He is a consultant in institutional media systems and has managed and owned commercial broadcast stations and a video production company.

TISHA BENDER has taught at NYU and the University of Wisconsin. She started teaching on DIAL (Distance Instruction for Adult Learners) at New School University in 1994, and then in 1996 became the Acting Program Coordinator at DIAL, training New School faculty to teach effectively on-line. In 1997 she became an Instructional Designer for the SUNY Learning Network. Bender continues to teach a variety of courses on DIAL at New School University. She is also a consultant for the Equal Commission at NYU and is a counselor at the Off Campus College of Cornell University.

LAURA BLASI is currently a doctoral candidate in English education at the Curry School of Education at the University of Virginia. She is also a Fellow at the university's Center for Technology and Teacher Education. In conjunction with the Center, she and Walter Heinecke have been using two-way video over

Internet II to facilitate a course on the social consequences of technology—bringing together students at Curry and at the University of Iowa. She is also developing a course on literacy and technology to be held in partnership with North Carolina State University in the fall of 1999. In Washington, DC, she directed DiversityWeb (http://www.diversityweb.org/) and contributed to other equity and race-related programs for the Association of American Colleges and Universities (AAC&U).

ROBERT J. BULIK is an Assistant Professor at the University of Texas Medical Branch in the Office of Educational Development. His research and publications focus on self-directed learning, faculty development, and distance education.

SHERYL BURGSTAHLER is an Affiliate Associate Professor at the University of Washington. She is also an Assistant Director of Information Systems, Computing & Communications. She directs project DO-IT (Disabilities, Opportunities, Internetworking, and Technology), which is primarily funded by the National Science Foundation, the U.S. Department of Education, and the state of Washington. DO-IT employs adaptive technology, computers, and the Internet to help people with disabilities succeed in academics and careers. Burgstahler has written numerous articles that spread the word about making computers and Web resources accessible to people with disabilities. She is also the primary author of the New Kids on the Net Internet training series for students and teachers.

ROBERT A. COLE is an Assistant Professor in the Department of Communication Studies at State University of New York at Oswego, and is also part of the Women's Studies faculty. He teaches a variety of courses including Communication Theories, Qualitative Research Methods, and Cultural Narratives of Film. In addition to his interest in technology and pedagogy, he researches the social construction of our identities, and in particular how it is that language and discourse constitute and sustain who we are.

MARTHA DAUGHERTY is a professor in the Psychology Department of Georgia College and State University. Her primary content focus is research methodology. She developed and taught a graduate Web-based educational research course which led to an interest in the evaluation of Web-based instruction. Her research, recently published in the *Journal of Distance Education*, examines student perceptions of Web-based instruction.

KAY S. DENNIS was the Director of Learning Resources at East Carolina University for ten years. Currently she is Assistant Professor of Adult Health Nursing at the East Carolina University School of Nursing. Her teaching responsibilities include Computer Applications in Nursing, which she has taught on-line as well as on-site. Dennis has received several grants in support of computing technology and is a member of technology committees at the university. She provides consultation on instructional design and technology integration. She also has an appointment to the School of Medicine, where she provides consultation on the evaluation of curricular and faculty development initiatives. Prior to joining East Carolina University, she was involved with technology-based continuing professional development projects at a 700-bed tertiary care center in Greenville, North Carolina.

TRICIA BERTRAM GALLANT is the Co-ordinator of Co-operative Education Services at the University of Guelph, Ontario, Canada. She teaches a course to co-op students to prepare them for the co-op employment process and the world of work and will be involved in adapting this course to the online environment as well.

MARK GELLIS teaches technical writing, speech, and humanities at Kettering University.

BIJAN B. GILLANI is Coordinator and Associate Professor of the Graduate Program in Educational Technology Leadership in California State University, Hayward's School of Education and Allied Studies.

H. L. "LEE" GILLIS is a Professor of Psychology at Georgia College and State University in Milledgeville, Georgia. He is a licensed psychologist who specializes in work with groups, families, and other healthy and unhealthy systems. Most of his published work has focused on the use of adventure experiences as therapy; he maintains a listserv and Web page on this subject as well. He teaches courses in interpersonal relations, group dynamics, group leadership, and personality theory.

DONALD L. GOFF is Program Director and adjunct associate professor of telecommunications and computer systems management in the Graduate School of Management and Technology, University of Maryland University College. He specializes in the application of advanced information technologies to business problems, particularly in telemedicine, information warfare, and distance learning. Retired from both AT&T and the Army Reserve, he has extensive experience in government, business, and academia.

AUTUMN GRUBB is a Distinguished Professor of Teaching and Learning in the Distance Education Department at Georgia College and State University. She entered into the realm of Web-based teaching and training in 1995. This endeavor has opened an opportunity for her to embrace lifelong learning in praxis, developing new skills and competencies in dealing with chaos, change, technology, teaching, and learning. Her Ph.D. in cultural/media studies with an emphasis in race, class, gender, and sexuality theories has served her well in being able to see the many perspectives of administration, teacher, and learner. Through these many lenses, she endeavors to provide instructional and training experiences that help learners and trainees flourish as human beings while interacting in a virtual environment.

R. STANTON HALES is the President of and Professor of Mathematics at the College of Wooster.

JOAN HANOR is an Assistant Professor in educational technology at California State University, San Marcos. Her research and publications focus on the aesthetics of learning with technology and the important role aesthetics play in issues of equity and diversity.

WALTER F. HEINECKE is Assistant Professor of Educational Evaluation Studies in the Department of Educational Foundations, Leadership and Policy at the Curry School of Education, University of Virginia. He teaches courses in research and evaluation methods and educational technology policy. His research is focused on educational policy and its influences on educational practice. He has conducted research and published in the areas of desegregation and school reform, educational technology policy and practice, distance education, and educational reform and assessment policy. He lectures on the social consequences of technology in elementary, secondary, and postsecondary education.

MARGARET HINES serves as Coordinator for the Web-based Career Master of Public Health at the Rollins School of Public Health of Emory University. She holds a master's degree in communications and has been working in the field of distance learning since 1995. Peggy has designed, developed, and delivered faculty training for several institutions, worked one-on-one with faculty as they rethink strategies for teaching in the virtual environment, designed courses in distance learning and technology, and taught Web-based courses.

JUDE HIRSCH is an Associate Professor of Outdoor Education and Coordinator of Outdoor Education Degree Programs in the Department of Health, Physical Education, and Recreation at Georgia College & State University. She is an experiential educator who had to be convinced that technology could not only enhance her teaching, but is a necessary condition for students to be successful in their chosen careers. Her academic background in curriculum and instruction and in program evaluation has led her to consider how technological objectives are woven throughout a program and in specific courses. Presently she is engaged in a qualitative investigation of student reactions to Web-based learning as experiential education.

JULIAN KILKER is an Assistant Professor of New Communication Technologies in the Hank Greenspun School of Communication at the University of Nevada, Las Vegas. His dissertation, "Networking Identity: A Case Study Examining Social Interactions and Identity in the Early Development of E-mail Technology," explored on-line collaboration within heterogeneous distributed social groups. He researches the intersection of social interaction, technology, and design, particularly in relation to communication resources.

GRAEME LANG is an Associate Professor in the Department of Applied Sociology at the City University of Hong Kong, Kowloon. He teaches the courses Science, Technology, and Society and Southeast Asian Societies. His current research includes studies of environmental policy issues in China, and a comparative study of China and Europe in regard to the rise of modern science. His earlier research on Chinese religion led to publication of *The Rise of a Refugee God* (1993), co-authored with Lars Ragvald.

ALLAN CRAIG LAUZON is an Associate Professor in the School of Rural Extension Studies at the University of Guelph. His current research interests are in the foundations of adult and distance education with a particular focus on the implications of critical theory and critical pedagogy for adult and distance education.

DAVID C. LEONARD is Assistant Dean at Mercer University, School of Engineering, Atlanta Campus. He developed and teaches in the Internet-based distance learning master's degree program in technical communication management at Mercer University. Leonard previously taught and developed graduate and undergraduate technical communication programs/courses at the Georgia Institute of Technology, the University of Maryland, and the University of Tennessee at Chattanooga. With his wife, Linda, he co-founded IDC, Information Design Corporation, in 1983 and has since worked with over 150 Fortune 500 and other companies consulting in on-line information, hypermedia, multimedia, and usability evaluation.

MAY LOWRY is an Assistant Professor in the Information and Learning Technologies Program at the University of Colorado at Denver. She is one of the founders of the Technology and Learning Team, which offers instructional design and development consultation to CU-Denver faculty.

MICHAEL MARGOLIS is Professor of Political Science at the University of Cincinnati, where he teaches courses on parties, elections, public opinion, democratic theory, research methods, and data analysis. His publications include *Viable Democracy* (1979), *Manipulating Public Opinion* (1989), *Machine Politics, Soundbites and Nostalgia* (1993), and numerous articles in professional and popular periodicals. He is co-author (with David Resnick) of *Politics as Usual: The Cyberspace "Revolution."*

MARVIN J. MCDONALD is an Associate Professor and coordinator of the community agency track in the master's program in Counselling Psychology at

Trinity Western University. He writes on theoretical psychology, science and religion dialogue, and professional issues. He is co-author, with D. Vaden House, of "Realist Brains and Virtual Conversations: Morals, Molecules, and Meanings in Social Constructionism," in *Toward a Psychology of Persons*, ed. W. E. Smythe (1998).

PETER NAVARRO is an Associate Professor of Economics and Public Policy at the University of California-Irvine. He is the author of four books on public policy, including *The Policy Game* and *The Dimming of America*. His articles have appeared in a wide range of publications from the *Harvard Business Review* and *Wall Street Journal* to the *Journal of Business* and the *New York Times*. Navarro is also the author of *The Power of Microeconomics* and *The Power of Macroeconomics*, a set of CD-ROM lectures which are being used in on-line courses for students throughout the world.

PATRICK B. O'SULLIVAN is an Assistant Professor in the Department of Communication at Illinois State University. His research and teaching interests center on uses and consequences of communication technologies (new and old) in social interaction and in relationships.

DAVID C. PARIS is Associate Dean of the Faculty and James S. Sherman Professor of Political Science at Hamilton College. He has published a number of books and articles on a variety of topics in political theory and education policy, including liberal political thought and moral education, the relationship of schools and skills, and national standards and charter experiments. His most recent article, "Standards and Charters: Horace Mann Meets Tinker Bell," appeared in *Educational Policy* (1998). His publications also include a book on public education, *Ideology and Educational Reform: Themes and Theories in Public Education* (1995).

SUSAN RIMKUS is an Instructional Development and Instructional Support Program Planner and an Instructor at the University of Guelph, Ontario, Canada.

PAULETTE ROBINSON has been doing research and writing on topics of education and technology for the past five years. Her dissertation, "Within the Matrix: A Hermeneutic Phenomenological Study of Student Experiences in Web-Based Computer Conferencing," is an exploration of ontological and epistemological issues confronting students as they participate in on-line learning environments. She teaches a Computers for Teachers course, required for elementary school majors, at the University of Maryland, where students are required to be on-line for a large portion of the course. Currently, she is training faculty at the University of Maryland to develop instruction in WebCT, a Web-based learning environment.

CLAUDINE SCHWEBER is currently the acting Associate Vice President, Distance Education and Lifelong Learning, at the University of Maryland University College and an Adjunct Professor of Management. She has been involved in the field of distance education for several years as an on-line instructor, as an author, and formerly as Director of Distance Education and Instructional Technology at the Graduate School of Management and Technology. SchWeber's academic field is negotiation and conflict management; she has done training, writing, and teaching in this field since the mid-1980s. In recent years, she has written about the use of technology in conflict management, especially as it impacts those at great distances or those with disabilities. She is the author of one book, *Criminal Justice Politics and Women* (1984), more than thirty-five articles, and over one hundred presentations in the United States, Western Europe, and Bulgaria conducted in English and French. She is a native of Paris, France, and a U.S. citizen.

JOHN STEEL is a researcher in the Learning and Teaching Institute at Sheffield Hallam University, London UK. His main research is focused on teaching and learning with educational technology. His particular interests are in economic, social, and cultural factors impacting the use of technology in higher education. In addition to full-time research, he is completing his doctoral thesis, which examines political philosophy and praxis surrounding the struggle for free speech in Britain during the nineteenth century.

ALEC M. TESTA is the Director of Assessment with Western Governors University. Prior to this, he held various positions at Eastern New Mexico University, including Executive Director of Planning and Analysis, Coordinator of Assessment Resource Office, and Adjunct Faculty in Psychology. He was the founding president of the New Mexico Higher Education Assessment Association, and has been professionally involved through conference planning and presenting with the American Association of Higher Education and its technology affiliate, the Teaching and Technology Group.

CHRISTINE THORNAM is an Instructional Designer with the Technology and Learning Team at the University of Colorado at Denver. She has designed and produced instructional media in health-related fields over the last twelve years, and has recently implemented programs preparing faculty and students to teach and learn nursing from a distance.

DAVID W. THRONE is a doctoral student and Instructor in Educational Technology at the University of Northern Colorado, Greeley. He also teaches on-line for Colorado Electronic Community College and has taught in the classroom at the Community College of Denver and other colleges in the Denver metro area for the past eleven years.

CASON T. WHITE is a Senior Instructional Designer with the Technology and Learning Team at the University of Colorado at Denver. He is an information architect, designing the structure and user interface of large-scale e-commerce sites for Fortune 1000 companies. His master's degree is in information and learning technologies from the University of Colorado at Denver, with a specialty in Web-based instructional programs for both educational and corporate settings.

SHERRY WULFF is a doctoral student and an Associate Professor in the Professional Communication Department of Alverno College. Her research and publications focus on assessment, media literacy, and analyses of communicative structures in pedagogy.